Stratford Library Association
2203 Main Street
Stratford, CT 06615
203-385-4160

 **W9-CAZ-285**

LIBRARY IN A BOOK

PRISONS
REVISED EDITION

Jeffrey Ferro

An imprint of Infobase Publishing

Prisons, Revised Edition

Facts On File, Inc.
An imprint of Infobase Publishing
132 West 31st Street
New York NY 10001

Library of Congress Cataloging-in-Publication Data

Ferro, Jeffrey.
  Prisons / Jeffrey Ferro. — Rev. ed.
    p. cm. — (Library in a book)
  Includes bibliographical references and index.
  ISBN 978-0-8160-8236-0
  1. Prisons—United States. 2. Prisons—Research—United States. 3. Prisons—United States—Bibliography. I. Title.
  HV9471.F465 2011
  365'.973—dc22   2010049855

Facts On File books are available at special discounts when purchased in bulk quantities for businesses, associations, institutions or sales promotions. Please call our Special Sales Department in New York at (212) 967-8800 or (800) 322-8755.

You can find Facts On File on the World Wide Web at http://www.factsonfile.com

Text design by Ron Monteleone
Composition by Hermitage Publishing Services
Cover printed by Art Print, Taylor, Pa.
Book printed and bound by Maple Press, York, Pa.
Date printed: January 2011
Printed in the United States of America

10 9 8 7 6 5 4 3 2 1

This book is printed on acid-free paper.

CONTENTS

PART III
APPENDICES

PART I

OVERVIEW OF THE TOPIC

CHAPTER 1

INTRODUCTION TO PRISONS

According to a quote attributed to the 19th-century Russian novelist and onetime prisoner Fyodor Dostoyevsky, "The degree of civilization in a society can be judged by entering its prisons." Entering state and federal correctional facilities in the United States today would reveal myriad issues of social concern. Among them are prison gangs that engage in violence and trade in contraband, an inmate population disproportionately composed of racial minorities, and overcrowding fueled by the highest rate of incarceration in the world.

As states and the federal government grapple with the worst economy since the Great Depression, legislators face hard choices in seeking to balance the costs of incarceration with the safety of society. The effort to strike that balance has opened up several areas of consideration, including reexamining tough sentencing laws, many of which were enacted in the 1980s and 1990s, that resulted in sending more people to prison for longer periods of time. Another focus is community corrections, as demonstrated by the passage of the Second Chance Act of 2007, which is federal legislation aimed at reducing the rate of recidivism by providing mentoring programs, drug treatment, job training, and educational opportunities to prisoners who are reentering society. Decriminalizing minor drug offenses and offering minor drug offenders the option of treatment in lieu of incarceration are also areas that hold promise for easing the pressures inside underfunded and overcrowded prisons.

Nonetheless, day-to-day life inside state and federal prisons nationwide continues to be dangerous for inmates and staff alike. In 2009, prison rape and other sexual abuse were widespread, according to a report by the Prison Rape Elimination Commission. Deficient medical and mental health services were a growing problem, based on the findings of the first comprehensive study of all inmates in U.S. prisons and jails conducted by Harvard Medical School. Housing a mix of criminal offenders, from drug abusers to murderers, while ensuring the safety of correctional officers and safeguarding the rights of inmates are daunting challenges undertaken each day in prisons nationwide.

HISTORICAL BACKGROUND

The use of incarceration as a form of punishment was not articulated in the earliest known codes of conduct. Instead, retaliation was the recommended redress for wrongdoing. The doctrine of "an eye for an eye, a tooth for a tooth," as articulated in the Bible (Exodus 21:24), was set forth in both the Sumerian codes, circa 1860 B.C., and in the code of King Hammurabi of Babylon, circa 1750 B.C. Punishment under both the Sumerian and Hammurabi codes of conduct was based on vengeance and included mutilation, flogging, and execution—often personally administered upon the wrong-doer by the victim.

Penal servitude, the enslavement of an individual to perform forced labor, was also used as punishment in ancient societies and served the dual purpose of helping to provide goods and services to society. Penal servitude was widely used in ancient Rome as a source of laborers to build and maintain public works. The idea of work as a form of punishment remained popular throughout history, including the modern era. For example, although penal servitude was illegal in the United States, chain gangs of prisoners shackled together to perform hard labor, often road work, was a common form of punishment in the early 20th century in state prisons in the South. Throughout the United States, offenders convicted of minor offenses are often required to perform community service, such as graffiti removal or picking up litter along public highways, sometimes as an alternative to incarceration.

In 621 B.C., Draco, ruler of Greece, implemented a harsh set of laws under which citizens and slaves received equal punishment. Under the Draconian code, any citizen could prosecute an offender in the name of the injured party for the protection of society. As the goal of punishment began to shift from personal vengeance to maintaining social order, the burden of punishment also shifted from the individual to the state. Because the line between church and state was often blurred, ancient codes of conduct included laws against both crime and sin. As such, the goal of punishment by the state was twofold: to deter crime and to inoculate the greater society from the wrath of God caused by the sins of a few. In effect, the state became an arm of God. Punishment in the name of God was often severe. For example, during the Salem witch hunts in colonial New England, beginning in 1692 in Salem, Massachusetts, those even suspected of witchcraft were tortured and sometimes burned alive by local authorities.

The concept of proportionality in punishment—that is, that the punishment should fit the crime—was established in the sixth century A.D. by the Byzantine emperor Justinian. Art from the Justinian period first depicted the scales of justice, a familiar symbol in modern-day jurisprudence. The dual concepts that punishment was to be administered by the state, as set forth in the Draconian code, and that the severity of punishment must be balanced with the gravity of the underlying crime, as established under the Justinian Code, helped to form the basis of Western law and its use of incarceration—the denial of liberty for a prescribed period of time—as a punishment for wrongdoing.

Although proportionality in punishment was established under Justinian, the practice of subjecting wrongdoers to severe physical abuse and agonizing forms of death persisted into the Middle Ages and beyond. In A.D. 1215, the church instituted the concept of trial by ordeal, in which individuals under the slightest suspicion of wrongdoing were tortured in the belief that the innocent would survive unharmed, while the guilty would suffer and die. Crimes prosecuted in this way included heresy, witchcraft, and "unnatural acts," which included what are today considered normal forms of sexual expression. Although barbaric, the medieval church's practice of punishment to determine guilt underscored the concept of free will—that individuals choose their actions and are responsible for their choices. Free will continues to be a cornerstone of modern justice systems worldwide, including that of the United States.

Throughout history, the practice of punishing offenders in public was common. Public punishment was intended as a lesson in deterrence: Behave badly and this will happen to you. Executions by hanging, crucifixion, burning, and drowning were carried out in public squares and meeting places as a way of showing the ultimate price one could pay for violating the law. Nonlethal punishments such as flogging, branding, mutilation, or simple humiliation were also carried out in public as a means of deterring others in the community from engaging in crime or other transgressions as minor as gossiping. The spectacle of public punishment fueled a sense of social revenge. Punishment was expected to be brutal so as to deter others, repay society, and redeem the wrongdoer in the eyes of God. Incarceration was used to hold the wrongdoer until the actual punishment could be meted out.

The concept that incarceration was a form of punishment evolved slowly. The earliest known prison was the Mamertine, a series of underground dungeons built circa 64 B.C. in ancient Rome. It is not known if the Mamertine prison functioned in the manner of modern-day prisons by depriving inmates of their liberty as a form of punishment or if the dungeons at Mamertine were simply holding areas for lawbreakers awaiting punishment.

During the Middle Ages, following the fall of Rome around A.D. 476, fortresses and fortified town gates were constructed throughout Europe to defend against roving bands of outlaws. As gunpowder came into wider use in Europe during the 14th century, however, such barriers became increasingly useless against invaders armed with cannons and other artillery. The structures previously built for defensive purposes were often converted to places of confinement for prisoners. These fortified structures included walled monasteries, where during the Inquisition of the 13th and 14th centuries, prisons were built to confine those believed to have violated church law. In such prisons, solitary confinement was sometimes utilized to create an atmosphere of atonement and penitence for prisoners.

In 1557, the Bridewell workhouse was established in London to house undesirables, including the homeless, the unemployed, and sometimes juveniles who were orphaned or considered incorrigible. Residents were subjected to strict discipline and forced to work long hours in harsh conditions. Bridewell was deemed a success, at least in terms of public perception, for keeping undesirables out of sight and out of mind. In 1576, the English Parliament ordered the construction of a workhouse in every county in England. Soon the workhouse concept spread throughout Europe. Conditions inside workhouses were often deplorable. There was no attempt to segregate males and females or juvenile and adults. As a result, violence and abuse among inmates and exploitation by jailers was common, as the strong freely preyed upon the weak. Poor sanitation in workhouses resulted in outbreaks of typhus, also known as jail fever. The highly contagious disease often spread to the surrounding communities.

EUROPEAN REFORMERS

By the early 18th century, workhouses were in place throughout Europe. Although designed as places of training and care for the poor, in reality workhouses functioned as penal institutions. Their squalid conditions were similar to those found in local jails, which held inmates awaiting trial or execution. Jails also held inmates who owed fines but could not afford to pay them. In some cases, inmates were held indefinitely as a means of extorting payments from them. Corruption, violence, and unsafe living conditions were pervasive in workhouses and jails throughout Europe in the early 18th century. At the same time, the idea of the importance of the individual began to take hold in Europe. Many social reformers began to focus on the abuses in the criminal justice system. The French philosopher Voltaire was an outspoken opponent of torture and other inhumane practices carried out by the state against lawbreakers. Voltaire believed that an individual's fear of shame, not corporal punishment, was a deterrent to crime. Eventually Voltaire was imprisoned in the Bastille for his ideas, and in 1726, he was ordered to leave France in exchange for his freedom. In Italy, Cesare Beccaria was perhaps the most influential reformer of the era on issues of crime and punishment. Beccaria's most widely known work, *An Essay on Crimes and Punishment*, published in 1764, established the following principles:

- Every crime is an injury to society, and the seriousness of a crime must be determined by the extent of the injury caused by the crime.
- Prevention of crime is more important to society than punishing crime. Therefore, the main justification for punishment is to prevent crime.
- A person accused of a crime should be treated humanely and afforded the right to present evidence in his or her behalf in a public trial.
- When the purpose of punishment is to deter crime, and not to exact social revenge, then the certainty and swiftness of the punishment is more important than the severity of the punishment.
- Life imprisonment is a more effective deterrent to crime than capital punishment, which is irreparable and impossible to correct if mistakes are later discovered in the criminal justice process.
- Crimes of property should be punished by fines, or by imprisonment when the offender is unable to pay the fine.
- Imprisonment should replace corporal punishment as a mode of punishment.
- The conditions of imprisonment should be humane and include the segregation of prisoners by age, sex, and their degree of criminality.

Beccaria understood that his ideas were controversial for the time, so much so that his work was originally published anonymously because he feared retribution by the government. Instead, Beccaria's ideas were embraced by reformers throughout Europe, especially in France, where in 1810 the French penal code was revised to incorporate principles promoted by Beccaria. Among them:

- An accused is innocent until proved guilty.
- An accused has the right against self-incrimination, the right to legal counsel, and the right to cross-examine the state's witnesses.
- An accused has the right to a speedy public trial and, in most cases, to a trial by jury.

An 18th-century English reformer, Jeremy Bentham, promoted Beccaria's idea that punishment could act as a deterrent to crime, but only when the punishment was appropriate to the underlying crime. John Howard, Bentham's contemporary in England, advanced the concept that the rights of the accused extended to individuals who were convicted of crimes and incarcerated by the state. In 1773, Howard was appointed sheriff of Bedfordshire and witnessed firsthand the deplorable conditions in local jails. Howard observed inmates being starved because they could not afford food sold at inflated prices by their jailers. Prisoners were not segregated by sex or age and were crowded into cage-like cells with little or no sanitation. Appalled by what he saw, Howard began to tour prison facilities throughout Europe and found similar conditions almost everywhere, with some exceptions in Belgium, France, and Italy. In 1777, Howard published the *State of Prisons*, in which he described the best of the correctional facilities he had seen during his tours and suggested reforms. Some of Howard's reforms were enacted into law in 1779, when the English Parliament passed the Penitentiary Act, which contained the following principles:

- Construct and maintain secure and sanitary correctional facilities.
- Conduct regular inspections of correctional facilities.
- Abolish all fees charged to inmates by their jailers or the correctional institution.
- Implement a reformatory model designed to deter inmates from re-offending.

Following the passage of the Penitentiary Act, the first penitentiary was built at Wyndonham in Norfolk, England. The guidelines established by the Penitentiary Act proved difficult to implement, however, due to the strain placed on correctional facilities by the rising urban crime rate and the resulting influx of inmates. By the late 18th century, English authorities sought to ease prison overcrowding by deporting more criminals. The practice of deporting lawbreakers had begun in England in 1596 when convicts were shipped to the American colonies. In 1776, however, deportation abruptly ended as a consequence of the American Revolution. English authorities used Australia as an alternative, but transportation was limited and arduous. In what was intended as a quick fix to ease overcrowding in correctional facilities, some inmates were confined in hulks, old transport ships and obsolete war vessels abandoned in harbors and waterways throughout the British Isles. The conditions in hulks were worse than those in local jails. Hulks were unventilated and infested with vermin. Disease was rampant and sometimes wiped out entire populations of inmates. Males and females, adults and juveniles, were unsegregated and forced to perform labor. Offenders, from hardened felons to misdemeanants who could not afford to pay fines, were routinely flogged and physically abused. Some, including minors, were sexually abused by jailers and other inmates. Although intended as a temporary solution to alleviate prison overcrowding, the practice of using hulks as prisons persisted in England for 80 years, until 1858. Later in the 19th century, hulks were used in California to house inmates, and New York City converted a war barge into a floating jail.

After his tours of jails, John Howard documented the deplorable conditions of confinement throughout Europe. He also documented two notable exceptions: the Maison de Force in Ghent, Belgium, and the Hospice of San Michele in Rome. The Maison de Force was built in 1773 under the direction of Belgian administrator Jean-Jacques Vilain, who followed the basic pattern of European workhouses when designing the facility. At Maison de Force, however, Vilain segregated females and juveniles from serious offenders and housed inmates in individual cells. Although considered a strict disciplinarian who required prisoners to work in silence, Vilain opposed cruelty as a means of inmate control. The Hospice of San Michele, built in 1704 by Pope Clement XI, was one of the first correctional institutions designed exclusively for juvenile offenders. Those confined at San Michele were subjected to a regimen of hard work and Bible reading. The system of separate cells for sleeping quarters and a large central hall for working, modeled after monasteries, became the structural blueprint for penal institutions in the 19th century. The use of silence and prayer at both Maison de Force and the Hospice of San Michele was also patterned on monastic life.

EARLY AMERICAN CORRECTIONS

The reforms advocated by John Howard and Cesare Beccaria, among others in Europe, and the improved treatment of prisoners at facilities such as Belgium's Maison de Force and the Hospice of San Michele in Rome, were owed in part to the influence of William Penn, who in 1681 founded the Quaker settlement at Pennsylvania in colonial America. The American colonies were then governed under English codes, including the Hampshire code of 1664 and the codes established by the duke of York in 1676, which allowed for the use of executions and harsh corporal punishment for lawbreakers. Under the English codes, offenders were routinely branded, flogged, or subjected to public humiliation in devices such as the pillory, in which an offender's hands and head were immobilized between two boards that served as a backstop while the offender was pelted, or *pilloried*, with raw eggs, rotten fruit, and the like.

As a Quaker leader, Penn advocated a more humane treatment of lawbreakers, as set forth in the Quaker code known as the Great Law. Under the Great Law, most offenses were punishable by hard labor in a house of correction, even some serious offenses punishable by execution under the English codes. The concept of confinement as a component of punishment, and not merely as the prelude to execution or corporal punishment, was unique in colonial America. Also unique under the Great Law was that punishable offenses were secular and did not include religious offenses like the English codes.

The Great Law was in force in colonial Pennsylvania from 1682 until 1718, when it was repealed one day after the death of William Penn. It was replaced by the English Anglican code, which was harsher in its treatment of lawbreakers than the earlier codes of the duke of York. The concept of punishment by confinement to a house of correction, or prison, however, remained part of the Quaker legacy.

In 1773, a state prison for felons was established in Simsbury, Connecticut, on the site of an abandoned copper mine. Inmates were confined in dank mine shafts. The facility was little more than a throwback to the underground dungeons of the Mamertine prison in ancient Rome. As a result of the poor conditions of confinement, in 1774, one year after it began operation, the prison was the site of one of America's earliest inmate riots.

THE PENNSYLVANIA SYSTEM

Not until 1790 was the prototype for the first correctional facility created in the United States, when the Pennsylvania legislature permitted the Quakers to operate a wing of the Walnut Street jail in Philadelphia as a penitentiary for convicted felons, except those sentenced to death. Reformers including Benjamin Franklin and Benjamin Rush, both signers of the U.S. Declaration of Independence, and Revolutionary War army hero William Bradford helped to develop a system of prison discipline at the Walnut Street jail that borrowed from the principles for the humane treatment of inmates advanced by Quaker William Penn and European reformers like Cesare Beccaria and John Howard. Eventually, the system developed at the Walnut Street jail became formally known as the Pennsylvania system.

Under the Pennsylvania system, inmates were isolated in solitary cells without work in order to reflect upon their crimes and repent their sins. As the prolonged effects of isolation and inactivity began to physically and psychologically debilitate inmates, work schedules of eight to 10 hours were introduced into the daily routine at the Walnut Street jail. Still, prisoners were required to work in isolation, usually on handicrafts and piecework. Eventually, the system broke down altogether due to overcrowding, which forced prison officials to house more than one felon per cell and compromised the segregation of male and female inmates.

Despite the failure of the Walnut Street jail, the Pennsylvania system continued to serve as the architectural and administrative model for other U.S. prisons in the early 19th century. The Pennsylvania system's emphasis on isolation and work was implemented to some degree at Newgate Prison in New York City, built in 1797, and state penitentiaries at Lamberton, New Jersey (1798); Frankfort, Kentucky, and Richmond, Virginia (1800); Charlestown, Massachusetts (1805); Windsor, Vermont (1809); Baltimore, Maryland, and Concord, New Hampshire (1812); Columbus, Ohio (1816); and Milledgeville, Georgia (1817). Like these prisons, the Western Penitentiary, built in 1826 in Pittsburgh, Pennsylvania, was designed with small, dark cells where prisoners were to live in near-total isolation. As at the Walnut Street jail, however, work was eventually added to the daily routine to alleviate some of the strain of solitary confinement. In 1833, the interior cells at the Western Penitentiary were demolished to alleviate the oppressive darkness in which inmates lived, and larger cells were built along the outside walls of the prison. This system of outside cells was quickly copied at the Eastern Penitentiary in Philadelphia, which was built in 1835 around a central hub from which rows of cell blocks extended like the spokes of a wheel. Still, the daily routine under the Pennsylvania system continued to be isolation, silence, and individual labor.

THE AUBURN SYSTEM

In 1816, a new prison at Auburn, New York, was built to ease overcrowding at Newgate prison. The design of the Auburn prison included communal areas where inmates could congregate for work and meals. Cells at Auburn, built vertically in tiers on five floors, were small and designed as individual sleeping quarters for inmates. Most prisoners at Auburn were allowed to work and eat in silence together during the day and separated only at night. Larger individual cells were added in 1819 to house prisoners placed in permanent solitary confinement as punishment for disobeying rules. Silence was used to foster an atmosphere of contemplation and repentance among inmates, but it also had the practical effect of minimizing escape plans. The philosophy behind the Auburn system, as it came to be known, was to give inmates the incentive to avoid permanent solitary confinement by obeying prison rules. The practice of permanent solitary confinement was eventually abandoned at Auburn in 1823 as the result of suicides, self-mutilations, and mental breakdowns that occurred because of the unrelenting isolation. In place of isolation, prisoners who breached the rules were whipped.

Under the Auburn system, inmates were effectively managed after 1823 without the use of solitary confinement and its often debilitating consequences. On the other hand, the Pennsylvania system's reliance upon solitary confinement effectively eliminated the formation of criminal associations of inmates allowed to mingle in common areas. Eventually, the Auburn system prevailed, largely because of economics. Under the Auburn system, the building of prisons with smaller cells and centralized areas was more cost-effective. In addition, prison industries operated under Auburn's congregate system were more profitable for the state than piecework performed by solitary inmates. From 1825 to 1869, the Auburn system was implemented at some 35 U.S. prisons, including Ossining (Sing Sing) prison in New York, built in 1825, and San Quentin state prison in California, built in 1852. The Auburn system's structural design of tiers of cells, also known as cell blocks, became the model for most prisons built in the United States for the next 150 years.

Prison discipline under both the Auburn and Pennsylvania systems was built upon a monastic-like silence required of all inmates. Under the Auburn system, however, there was the challenge of controlling groups of inmates in common areas that outnumbered prison guards. Elam Lynds, warden at Auburn prison and later at Sing Sing, developed methods of inmate control and discipline that, although effective and modeled on other institutions, were also brutal and degrading to inmates. Lynds's methods of discipline were based on his belief that it was necessary to break an inmate's will or spirit before it was possible to control an inmate. Lynds punished even slight infractions with immediate whippings, either with a rawhide whip or a flogging device made from strands of wire. Silence was strictly enforced at all times. During meals, inmates were required to sit face-to-back and eat all of their food. The only permissible communication was to raise one hand for more food or to raise the other for less food.

At Auburn, Lynds developed a lockstep formation that required prisoners to line up with their hands placed on the shoulders or under the arms of the inmate in front, then move forward rapidly by shuffling, without lifting their feet off the ground. Prisoners who fell out of step risked being whipped or being trampled under the swiftly moving formation.

Clothing was also used as a means of inmate control. White uniforms with black stripes, also known as prison stripes, were introduced in 1815 in New York prisons. At Auburn and Sing Sing, Elam Lynds implemented color-coded clothing that signaled whether an inmate was a first-time or a repeat offender.

THE REFORMATORY ERA

In 1870, prison administrators met in Cincinnati, Ohio, at the American Prison Congress to discuss the future of corrections in the United States. They formed the National Prison Association, renamed the American Correctional Association in 1954, and elected as their first president the governor of Ohio, Rutherford B. Hayes, who in 1877 would become the 19th president of the United States. Many of the prison administrators in attendance were concerned about prison overcrowding and how to better design correctional facilities to alleviate it. Reform-minded corrections professionals advocated a new approach to the treatment of inmates, based in part upon the work of Captain Alexander Maconochie in England and Sir Walter Frederick Crofton in Ireland.

In 1840, Maconochie had been placed in charge of a British penal colony on Norfolk Island, some 800 miles east of Australia, which housed some of the United Kingdom's worst offenders. He implemented a series of reforms, including the elimination of so-called *flat* sentences under which an inmate was required to serve the full term of his sentence before there was any possibility of release. In its place Maconochie implemented a system of early release earned by good conduct and hard work. Under this system, a convict could earn points, called *marks*. With enough marks, it was possible for an inmate to purchase the right to perform the work of his choice and to gain other liberties, in preparation for the inmate's eventual release to society.

Building upon Maconochie's idea, in 1850 Sir Walter Crofton developed a system of indeterminate sentencing, which became know as the Irish system. Crofton reasoned that if penitentiaries were designed as places of repentance and personal reform, then there must be a mechanism in place for prisoners to benefit when they demonstrate their reform. Crofton's system had several stages. Completing each stage brought an inmate closer to release and shortened the length of the initial sentence. During the first stage, prisoners were placed in solitary confinement and required to perform monotonous work. In a series of intermediate stages, prisoners were awarded better work assignments and greater degrees of liberty within the prison. In the final stage, inmates were sent to an intermediate prison and allowed to work without supervision and to move freely in and out of the local community. Upon release, each prisoner was given a ticket-of-leave that could be revoked for any violation of law. The ticket-of-leave remained in force for the full length of the prisoner's original sentence. Crofton's plan of conditional liberty later evolved into the modern system of parole, under which an inmate is granted early release from prison by a parole board but remains under the supervision of a parole officer while living in the community. As under Crofton's ticket-of-leave plan, if a parolee violates any of the conditions of parole, he or she can be returned to prison.

At their meeting in Cincinnati, Ohio, in 1870, the members of the National Prison Association endorsed the ideas of Maconochie and Crofton that prisons should be places of reform, or reformatories, and issued a broad set of principles embodying that ideal. They included establishing a three-stage system of punishment, reform, and probation in all prisons and using indeterminate sentencing as a way to reward inmates for good behavior and hard work. The administrators also established the goals of providing education to inmates, treating inmates with respect, minimizing the use of physical force against inmates, and segregating juveniles, females, and males in separate facilities.

As a result of the National Prison Association's focus on reform over punishment, the first reformatory in the United States was built in 1876 in Elmira, New York. The Elmira reformatory was originally designed to house adult felons. Under the direction of Zebulon Brockway, the first superintendent at Elmira, however, the reformatory was used for first-time male offenders between the ages of 16 and 30, in the hope that they could be more effectively rehabilitated than hardened criminals. The programs at Elmira emphasized personal change through education and vocational training. A program of indeterminate sentencing was implemented, including a grading system that allowed inmates to earn points for early release through good conduct and hard work.

From 1876 to 1913, reformatories modeled after Elmira were built in 17 U.S. states. The reformatories were designed with the goal of providing educational and vocational training to both juvenile and adult offenders. Indeterminate sentencing and early-release plans were implemented to reward hard work and obedience. The reformatories were often staffed, however, with the same underpaid and poorly qualified personnel who worked in prisons. Harsh prison discipline quickly replaced the loftier ideal of reform, and conditions in many reformatories deteriorated to the point where there was little difference between reformatories and conventional prisons.

THE INDUSTRIAL PRISON

In addition to reformatories, some 16 state prisons were built in the 29 years from 1871 to 1900 after the National Prison Association established principles encouraging the humane treatment of inmates. Apart from the addition of plumbing and running water, these prisons were little changed from penitentiaries of the past that had been modeled on the Auburn system. The growing population of inmates in U.S. prisons represented a source of cheap labor to private industry. Increasingly, prisoners were put to work manufacturing goods that were sold on the open market.

At the end of the Civil War in 1865, able-bodied male inmates began to be exploited as laborers on a national scale. In the South, where the agrarian economy relied upon cheap farm labor, prisoners were used to replace the freed slaves. Because the prison population in the southern United States included many plantation blacks, the use of prison laborers became almost an extension of slavery. In the North, state prisons were commonly paid an annual fee by companies for the use of their inmate workers. In some cases, industry officials were allowed inside prisons to supervise inmates as they worked.

As prison industries grew, so did opposition from organized labor, which was hard-pressed to compete against a labor market of inmates working for a fraction of the cost of other workers. By 1900, some states placed restrictions on the sale of prison-made products. As a result of the high unemployment caused by the Great Depression, from 1929 to 1933, labor unions and industries that did not use inmate workers pressured state and federal legislatures to further restrict the availability of prison products to promote job growth in the private sector. With the passage of the Hawes-Cooper Act in

1929, interstate prison products became subject to the law of the state to which they were shipped. The Amhurst-Sumners Act, passed in 1935 and amended in 1940, permanently stopped the transport of all prison products shipped out-of-state. Most state prison industries were effectively eliminated, except for license plate manufacturing and some small state furniture shops. As a result, prisoners had little opportunity to earn work credits or acquire vocational training, and prisons reverted to being little more than warehouses for inmates, where order was maintained by punishment.

On June 23, 1934, the U.S. Congress established Federal Prison Industries (FPI) to provide vocational training and employment to federal inmates. The FPI is commonly referred to by its trade name, UNICOR. For fiscal year 2009, UNICOR operated 98 factories in 71 federal prison facilities nationwide where nearly 19,000 federal prison inmates were employed in various manufacturing industries, including clothing and textiles, electronics, and office furniture. UNICOR products are sold to various agencies of the federal government, including the U.S. Departments of Defense, Homeland Security, and Justice. Goods produced by UNICOR are designed so as not to directly compete with products produced by private industry. UNICOR posted a net loss of nearly $36 million in fiscal year 2009, which was largely attributed to cutbacks by its customers as a result of the weak national economy.[1]

In 1979, the U.S. Congress created the Prison Industry Enhancement Certification Program (PIECP), which was designed to allow state and federal prison inmates to work for private-sector employers at prevailing wages comparable to the earnings of non-inmate workers. Since the inception of PIECP, industries participating in the program have included agricultural growers of various produce and manufacturers—of windows and screens, circuit boards for electronics, brushes for street sweepers, and corrugated boxes—and have employed some 70,000 prison inmates from 1979 to 2005, according to the census of U.S. prisons conducted every five years by the Bureau of Justice Statistics. In 2005, 6,555 offenders incarcerated in state and federal prisons participated in the PIECP program. According to the Bureau of Justice Statistics, inmates who participated in the PIECP program while in prison were somewhat more successful at finding employment upon their release from prison than were those inmates who participated in traditional prison work programs.

Many state and federal prisons offer inmate work programs in cooperation with private industry, either through PIECP or similar programs, such as the private, nonprofit Prison Rehabilitative Industries Diversified Enterprises (PRIDE), which in 1981 assumed control of prison industries in Florida. Such arrangements between prisons and the private sector fall into four general categories. The *employer model* uses inmate labor to produce goods or services under the authority of a private company, which has complete control over the supervision of the inmate workforce, including hiring and firing. Under the *investor model,* a correctional agency operates an industry that is financed by private investors who seek a return on their investment but exert no direct control over the operation of the industry. The *customer model* allows a private company to purchase most or all of the products that are generated by a prison industry that is controlled by the correctional agency. The purchased products are commonly sold for a profit by the private company. The *manager model* refers to an arrangement in which a private company manages a prison industry that is owned by a correctional agency.

MODERN CORRECTIONS

In 1934, Sanford Bates, the director of the U.S. Bureau of Prisons, introduced procedures in federal prisons for the diagnostic classification of inmates and for the use of mental health professionals in designing rehabilitation programs for prisoners. The procedures implemented under the leadership of Bates were credited with advancing the humane treatment of inmates and improving living conditions in the federal prison system. Despite these advances, however, long hours of idleness in locked and often forbidding institutions inevitably produced tensions among inmates and between inmates and staff.

As the result of rising inmate populations from 1930 to 1950, state and federal prison officials implemented restrictive measures to maintain order and security in overcrowded facilities. Women's reformatories, for instance, began to adopt a more custodial and disciplinary atmosphere, with less emphasis on education and job training.

In 1960, the modern era of corrections began during a period of social change in the United States. Prisoners demanded not only better conditions of confinement, but also the opportunity to exercise their basic rights under the U.S. Constitution. In 1969, in the case *Johnson v. Avery* the U.S. Supreme Court issued the first in a series of landmark rulings on prisoners' rights on issues including legal representation, cruel and unusual punishment, religious freedom, and medical care. In response to the Supreme Court's rulings, which are discussed in Chapter 2, corrections professionals implemented new prison policies that provided inmates with better access to medical care and legal representation, including access to legal materials in prison libraries. Also, prison officials were required to eliminate any use of force against inmates that was not necessary to maintain security and order in the institution.

As a result of the prison reform movement, women's prisons in the United States began to return to some of the principles of the women's reformatory movement. For example, in-prison maternity units were established in some prisons that permitted infants to remain with incarcerated mothers for a period of weeks or months, instead of being separated from their mothers at birth. Other parent-child services, including expanded visitation, were adopted, and female inmates began to receive the same educational and training opportunities as male inmates. However, some of these services were later curtailed as the population of female prisoners rose during the 1980s and 1990s, and many women's prisons adopted more custodial and punitive approaches to incarceration.

During the 25 years from 1970 to 1995, the rate of violent crime in the United States turned public sentiment away from prison reform toward punishment, including long periods of incarceration for the most serious offenders. According to the Bureau of Justice Statistics (BJS), between 1973 and 1995, victimizations from violent crimes for individuals 12 years of age and older occurred at a rate of between 47 and 52 victims for every 1,000 people in the U.S. population.[2] As a result, state and federal legislation was passed during the 1990s giving courts less discretion in sentencing repeat offenders. Advocates of stricter sentencing laws credited them with reducing the rate of violent crime, between 1996 and 2008, from 41.6 violent victimizations per 1,000 persons age 12 or over in the U.S. population to 19.3. The impact of such laws on the inmate populations of federal and state prisons was dramatic. The total number of inmates confined in state and federal prisons more than doubled, from 783,382 in 1990 to more than 1.6 million in 2008. The annual rate of increase in the prison population was at its highest during the 1990s, when many of the stricter sentencing laws were enacted and imposed on offenders nationwide: From 1990 to 1999, the U.S. prison population increased at a rate of 6.5 percent per year. By comparison, the annual rate of increase was 1.8 percent from 2000 to 2008, when Americans began to reexamine and modify strict sentencing laws, which had contributed to a rapid expansion of the prison population. Despite recent reductions in the annual rate of increase in the prison population, in 2008 about 500 individuals out of every 100,000 people in the U.S. population were in prison, representing the highest rate of incarceration in the world. By gender, in 2008, 952 males out of every 100,000 males in the U.S. population was in prison, while the rate of incarceration for females was 62 prisoners for every 100,000 females in the U.S. population.[3]

Modern developments in areas including prisoner classification, juvenile corrections, private prisons, and the shift in correctional philosophies from rehabilitation to punishment are discussed later in this chapter.

MODERN CORRECTIONAL PHILOSOPHIES

Historically the handling of lawbreakers evolved from simple retaliation in ancient societies to modern-day correctional approaches that include punishment, treatment, and prevention. These approaches sometimes overlap in correctional settings that must serve a variety of prisoners, from first-time offenders to habitual predators. Still, they represent distinct and competing ideologies on how society metes out the consequences of crime.

PUNISHMENT

Incarceration and execution are the most serious forms of punishment administered to criminal offenders in the United States. Probation, which places a convicted misdemeanant or felon under court supervision for a period of months or years, is imposed in combination with or in lieu of incarceration. Probation restricts an offender's liberty to an extent, such as where an offender is allowed to go or with whom an offender is allowed to associate. As such, probation constitutes a milder form of punishment than incarceration.

The three general rationales for punishment are retribution, deterrence, and incapacitation of the offender. From ancient times, the criminal was viewed as an enemy of society who purposely violated the rules of social order. Retribution satisfied the need to retaliate against those who caused such harm. From a theological perspective, retribution required wrongdoers, or sinners, to suffer for their sins. Sinners expiated their guilt through suffering and cleansed their souls through atonement. Under the Pennsylvania system, introduced in colonial America, the Quakers were among the first to promote the idea of incarceration as a form of retribution. The Quakers opposed corporal punishment and public humiliation, as was commonly practiced in the American colonies, and believed that retribution could be achieved by confining a criminal in total isolation in order to repent. Retribution also fulfilled the sociological function of restoring a sense of fairness, or justice, by holding lawbreakers accountable for their actions and imposing personal consequences upon them. Society expected criminal offenders to experience the same measure of suffering as their victims. Satisfying that social expectation helped to maintain social order.

Historically, deterrence was the lesson taught by punishment. That lesson was specific to the offender, who was discouraged by punishment from committing future offenses. Ultimately, the success of deterrence is in the hands of the offender. If an offender feels unjustly punished by society, negative behavior patterns are more likely to persist, and deterrence is ineffective. Conversely, deterrence has the best chance of success when an offender acknowledges wrongdoing and believes that the punishment was fair. In addition, successful deterrence gives the punished offender an opportunity to return to society and resume a normal life without stigma. Unfortunately, in the United States, the stigma of conviction often dogs ex-convicts for years after their release from prison, interfering with their ability to secure employment and, in many states, disqualifying them from voting and exercising other rights under felony disenfranchisement laws, as discussed later in this chapter.

By making an example of the offender, deterrence also served the general purpose of discouraging others from engaging in crime.

Incapacitation, also known as disablement, uses the punishment of incarceration as a crime-control strategy. In other words, keeping offenders locked up for many years eliminates any chance that they will reoffend, except in prison. Under incapacitation, there is little or no attempt at rehabilitation. Incapacitation is the rationale for three-strikes laws and determinate sentencing, which impose fixed prison terms on certain classes of offenders, such as violent or habitual felons. Similarly, truth-in-sentencing laws require imprisonment for no less than the stated term of the sentence. Some states, including California, have implemented a blend of determinate and indeterminate sentencing. Under California's three-strikes law, offenders convicted of any felony with two prior convictions for violent felonies receive 25 years to life in state prison, with no possibility of release until completing the full determinate period of 25 years. After 25 years, three-strikes felons are periodically eligible for parole. However, there is no guarantee that parole will be granted, and felons may remain incarcerated for the rest of their lives. As a result of such laws, which afford courts little or no discretion in sentencing, about 10 percent of U.S. prisoners in 2008 were serving life sentences. About 29 percent of those had no possibility of parole.[4] Proponents of the incapacitation theory correlate stricter sentencing laws with the reduction in the rate of violent crime in the United States since the mid-1990s, when many such sentencing provisions became law.

TREATMENT

Under the punishment model, the offender is viewed as an enemy of society. By contrast, the treatment model in corrections views criminal behavior as a symptom of an underlying pathology, such as mental illness or drug addiction. Under the treatment model, the offender is incarcerated for placement in some type of correctional program, with the goal of reintegration in the community. There is also a component of punishment, however, in removing an offender's liberty through incarceration.

Treatment in corrections consists of several stages, beginning with the diagnosis of an offender's underlying condition and needs. A program is then designed to meet the offender's needs, usually by placing the offender in an existing program where others with similar problems receive treatment. Periodic monitoring of the offender's progress and modification of the treatment plan are also essential for effective treatment. The rationale for treatment in modern-day corrections developed over time as the result of four main treatment doctrines: penitence, the educational doctrine, the medical model, and the reintegration model.

Beginning in colonial America, Quakers advocated for the use of penitence instead of the common practice of corporal punishment and public humiliation of offenders. Quakers believed that offenders were out of touch with God. Their treatment model was the isolation of an offender in solitary confinement under a strict regimen of Bible reading, reflection, and enforced silence. The goal was for the offender to reconnect with God. Quakers believed that once a reconnection with God was achieved, the offender's criminal behavior would cease, and the offender could safely return to the community.

Prison reformers in the late 19th century viewed offenders as disadvantaged and generally lacking in education and self-discipline. The first reformatory, opened in 1876 at Elmira, New York, and others that followed during the late 19th century operated according to the principles of the educational doctrine. Unlike traditional prisons at the time, where inmates were simply housed and punished, reformatories provided educational and vocational training under a regimen of strict discipline, with the goal of instilling in offenders the skills and internal behavioral controls necessary to function in society.

The medical model was developed by Sanford Bates during his tenure from 1930 to 1937 as the director of the U.S. Bureau of Prisons. Under the medical model, criminal behavior is viewed as the result of an underlying disease. Proponents of the medical model believe that, like a disease, the pathology of criminal behavior can respond to treatment, usually psychiatric, with the potential for a cure. Inmates under the medical model are viewed as patients. In theory, once the patient is made well, he or she is ready to return to the community under a system of aftercare managed by parole officers who function in a therapeutic role, in contrast to modern parole agents whose function is more closely aligned with law enforcement. Built into the medical model is the concept of early release, which occurs after successful treatment. As a result of the treatment model, by 1975, the federal courts and all state courts utilized a system of indeterminate sentencing, which allocated a minimum and maximum length of incarceration for every criminal offense. Offenders were sentenced to a span of time, instead of a fixed term, and could be released within that time frame by parole boards, which were given broad discretion in determining when an inmate was ready for release. Since 1976, the federal system and many state systems have either limited or abolished the sentencing discretion of parole boards.

The reintegration model originated in the late 1960s and remained popular for more than 20 years. Its premise was that criminality occurred as the result of factors in an offender's environment or community, such as poverty and unemployment. The goal of reintegration of the offender into society was accomplished through aftercare or alternatives to incarceration, such as diversion programs that provide rehabilitation or training opportunities.

PREVENTION

Under the prevention model, criminal behavior is viewed as a manifestation of emotional and social problems. In corrections settings, the prevention model operates with the dual objectives of reforming individual offenders and developing community-based programs designed to reduce the risk of reoffending. These programs may serve as alternatives to incarceration, or as adjuncts to incarceration, such as aftercare programs for parolees. Sometimes, the programs provide treatment to the offender. This combination of the prevention and treatment models is known as community corrections.

In community corrections, offenders are usually diverted from incarceration. For example, in 2000, by a margin of 2 to 1, California voters passed the Substance Abuse and Crime Prevention Act. Popularly known as Proposition 36, the legislation allowed first- and second-time nonviolent offenders convicted of drug possession to receive substance abuse treatment in lieu of incarceration. The goal was the prevention of reoffending through the treatment of the offender. From the first year of enforcement, ending July 31, 2002, until July 31, 2008, Proposition 36 diverted more than 280,000 drug offenders from prisons and jails into community-based treatment programs at an estimated savings to California taxpayers of $2 billion. During the same time period, California state prisons had 40 percent fewer inmates who were incarcerated for simple drug possession. Despite the success of Proposition 36, in 2009 the state reduced funding for the program for the 2010 fiscal year by 83 percent, from $108 million, due to a budgetary crisis in California.[5]

FACILITIES AND FUNCTIONS

Prisons and jails are the two main types of correctional facilities in the United States today. In general, jails house individuals whose criminal cases are proceeding through the court system, from arraignment to sentencing. Usually, jail inmates awaiting trial cannot afford to post bail for their release, although in serious cases, such as capital murder, jail inmates are often held without bail. Jails also house convicted offenders sentenced to short terms of incarceration, usually one year or less. Many convicted jail inmates are misdemeanants, although convicted felons are sometimes sentenced to jail for terms of incarceration of one year or less. Most jails are operated by local law enforcement agencies, such as a police department or the county sheriff.

Prisons house convicted felons serving sentences of one or more years and inmates awaiting execution under a sentence of death. Prisons are under the jurisdiction of state or federal governments.

CLASSIFICATION AND HOUSING

In prison systems, incoming inmates customarily enter a reception or evaluation center, which is a prison where they are confined for a period of weeks or several months. During that time, new prisoners are assessed and classified as to their security risk and special needs, such as mental illness, pending permanent placement in an appropriate correctional facility. Classification of inmates was implemented on a national scale beginning in the late 1940s, after the end of World War II. Federal legislation had severely curtailed prison industries in the 1930s, and prison administrators were concerned about the inmate idleness that resulted. The National Prison Association, renamed the American Correctional Association in 1954, promoted the idea of assessing each incoming inmate's social, intellectual, and emotional capabilities and clinically identifying each inmate's deficiencies, with the goal of designing individualized rehabilitation and training programs for prisoners. In order to ensure that arriving prisoners were appropriately assessed, it was necessary to implement a standardized classification system.

In practice, classification systems fell short of one of their intended purposes, that of directing inmates into individualized treatment, in large part because of insufficient funding to administer programs to rehabilitate, educate, and train every inmate. There were other practical barriers as well. For example, most prisons depended upon inmate labor to operate essential prison services, including food preparation, laundry facilities, and janitorial duties, as they do today. Training and rehabilitation programs, if available, were not always the first priority in the day-to-day running of prisons. Inmates looking to earn credits for good behavior to gain early release or other privileges, such as selection of work assignments, were more inclined to please prison staff by placing institutional needs above their personal needs for education or counseling.

The primary objective of the classification system is determining the level of security necessary to safely manage each prisoner. The three basic levels of security are minimum, medium, and maximum. Of the more than 1.4 million prisoners in state and federal correctional facilities on June 30, 2005 (the most recent year for which statistics were available), about one-third (33 percent) were held in maximum-security facilities, while medium-security facilities housed some 40 percent, and minimum-security facilities held about 20 percent. The remaining number of prison inmates (about 7 percent) were held in private prisons or were in community-based corrections programs.[6]

Minimum-security prisons house the least violent and most trustworthy felons. Conditions of confinement are the least restrictive and may include guards who are unarmed and cyclone fences instead of walls around the facility. Work furloughs and educational release are commonly available to inmates, allowing them to leave the facility to go to jobs or attend classes in the community. While on prison grounds, inmates move to and from activities on their own instead of being escorted by guards. Minimum-security prisons provide inmates with maximum freedom of movement and often rely on inmates' trustworthiness to maintain security. Inmates in minimum-security prisons who violate the rules may be transferred to medium- or even maximum-security correctional facilities as a sanction for their infraction.

In the federal prison system, minimum-security prisons are commonly referred to as camps. Typically, federal prisoners assigned to such facilities have less than 10 years remaining on their sentence and have earned the right to be housed in a minimum-security setting as the result of their good behavior in maximum- or medium-security federal prisons. Typically, prisoners in federal camps with less than two years remaining on their sentence are eligible for furloughs away from the prison to spend time with their families, in order to begin the process of reintegration into the community. The quarters in federal camps are generally dormitory style, with beds separated in cubicles or simply aligned in rows. As in maximum- and minimum-security facilities, there is little personal privacy. Inmates at federal camps are usually required to work, sometimes outside the prison facility in nearby towns or military bases. Inmates at federal camps that are part of a complex with higher security facilities often provide services, such as food preparation and laundry services, to the higher security facilities. Staff members at federal minimum-security facilities often enforce rules more strictly than at higher security facilities. For example, camp inmates with more than their allotted number of books or toiletry items are likely to receive sanctions, while such minor infractions might be overlooked in medium- and maximum-security institutions, where the concern of prison officials is largely focused on safety and security. Violence in minimum-security prisons is generally low or even nonexistent, much like a workplace environment.

Medium-security prisons generally house nonviolent offenders. Security is tighter than at minimum-security facilities and generally includes armed guards and a walled perimeter. While there may be some regimentation of inmates during movement to and from activities, more personal freedom is permitted, which fosters an atmosphere more conducive to treatment and educational programs, although, unlike minimum-security facilities, inmates are limited to on-site programs. In addition, visitor privileges are often fairly relaxed and may allow for personal contact. Many medium-security prisons were designed with residential areas that are more akin to dormitories than cell blocks. Apart from outside fences, which often are topped with barbed wire or razor wire to discourage escapes, security is often maintained through electronic surveillance equipment.

Beginning in the 19th century, maximum-security prisons in the United States were built as forbidding, fortresslike structures in the tradition of Gothic architecture. The intent was to overwhelm the prisoner with feelings of insignificance as a means of psychological control. By the early 20th century, the traditional Gothic design lost favor with penologists who wanted a less oppressive prison environment that was more conducive to treatment. As a result, modern maximum-security facilities have abandoned the old design standards. Still, the function of maximum-security prisons remains the same—to minimize inmate violence and the risk of escape by maximizing control over prisoners. Walls around the perimeter of maximum-security facilities are continuously patrolled by armed guards and often reinforced with barbed wire. Some facilities utilize electrified fences that carry enough voltage to kill a human being on touch. Prisoner cells usually house one or two inmates and are often equipped with a toilet and sink to reduce the need to move inmates. Prisoners are locked inside their cells for 10 or 12 hours per day, generally from early evening until the next morning. Inmates are allowed out of their cells for meals, prison work assignments, physical exercise in the prison yard, and to attend training or counseling, if available. Prisoner movement is regimented and strictly controlled by armed guards and video surveillance.

THE SUPERMAX

The super maximum-security prison, or supermax, was designed to control inmates who are violent and disruptive by confining them to single-person cells for 23 hours per day. Supermax prisons exist either as freestanding facilities or as specialized control units within maximum-security prisons. Prior to the late 1980s there were few such facilities in the United States. However, from 1989 to 1993, 15 supermax prisons or control units were opened in the United States. Another 10 such facilities went into operation from 1994 to 2000. By 2005, about two-thirds of states and the federal government used super maximum-security prisons to hold their most dangerous inmates.[7]

Since 1989, the growth of supermax facilities has been unprecedented. The concept of the super maximum-security prison, however, is not new. During the 1930s, with severe restrictions placed on prison industries, prison administrators were hard-pressed to control the increasing numbers of idled inmates in large prisons. The severe economic hardships caused by the Great Depression left the public with little appetite for spending money on rehabilitating convicted felons. J. Edgar Hoover, director of the Federal Bureau of Investigation from 1924 to 1972, declared war on crime. It was in this social climate in 1934 when a U.S. military prison built in 1909 was converted to the first federal super maximum prison on Alcatraz Island in the San Francisco Bay. Known as the Rock, Alcatraz prison was designed to house the worst offenders, particularly those who were the least controllable and the most disruptive in other prisons. In 1954, Mississippi became the first state to open a supermax prison. Alcatraz prison closed in 1963 due to high operating costs. During its 29 years of operation, Alcatraz gained a reputation as the most repressive federal prison in the United States. In 1972, Alcatraz prison became part of the Golden Gate National Recreational Area.

In 1963, the same year Alcatraz closed, the U.S. prison at Marion, Illinois, went into operation, designed to hold 500 male felons who were difficult to control. In 1972, prisoners at Marion began a work stoppage to protest the beating of an inmate by prison guards. The work stoppage lasted for over a week until guards segregated 60 inmates identified as leaders and key participants in the work stoppage The 60 inmates were placed in the prison's H-unit and required to participate in a behavior modification program called the Control and Rehabilitation Effort, or CARE. Under the CARE program, the inmates were held in solitary confinement and subjected to intense psychological sessions designed to bring them under control. In 1973, Marion Prison's H-unit became known as a control unit.

The control unit was expanded throughout the Marion prison. Like Alcatraz, Marion prison became the end of the line for federal prisoners with serious disciplinary problems. In 1978, the U.S. Bureau of Prisons added a level 6 to its inmate classification system for the most violent and disruptive federal prisoners. In 1979, Marion prison was designated the only level 6 correctional facility in the federal prison system. As such, the U.S. prison at Marion effectively became a supermax facility.

In 1989, the Security Housing Unit, or SHU, was opened at the Pelican Bay state prison in Pelican Bay, California. The SHU at Pelican Bay became the model for supermax prisons and control units in both the state and federal prison systems. Designed for 1,056 inmates, prisoners at the SHU in Pelican Bay are confined in cells measuring 8 by 10 feet for all but 90 minutes each day, when they are allowed to go alone to a concrete exercise area that is about the size of three cells, with 20-foot walls and metal screens overhead. Cell doors are constructed of solid steel and are opened and closed by remote control. In 1993, the U.S. Bureau of Prisons opened a new supermax facility in Florence, Colorado, designed to house 480 of the most dangerous and aggressive inmates in the federal prison system.

In many supermax facilities, inmates are classified according to their level of controlled confinement. For example, the Mississippi Department of Corrections operates two supermax facilities in which inmates are assigned custody ratings. Inmates with the highest rating are considered dangerous to other inmates and the prison staff. They are segregated, not allowed visitors, and are placed in restraints during any movement within the prison. By comparison, prisoners assigned the lowest custody level are essentially housed in medium security conditions, even though they are still confined in a supermax facility. Generally, inmates must earn easement of their custody restrictions through good conduct. At the supermax facility at Ionia, Michigan, after six months of good behavior, inmates may earn the right to participate in limited activities outside the cell, including work. After one year of good conduct, restrictions can be further eased to allow participation in group activities and expanded visitation privileges.

Those critical of supermax prisons and control units contend that the long periods of isolation and severe restrictions of movement imposed upon inmates constitute cruel and unusual punishment, in violation of the Eighth Amendment of the U.S. Constitution. That argument has largely failed, primarily because the conditions of confinement within supermax facilities are considered to be within the legally permissible range of deprivations that correctional institutions may impose on noncompliant inmates to maintain discipline and order. Critics of supermax facilities also argue that, for those inmates who are not under a sentence of life imprisonment, it is difficult to justify how prolonged periods of isolation will prepare them for a successful return to society. However, proponents of the supermax system counter that by segregating extremely violent inmates, the majority of prisoners are made safer, as are prison staff members.

DEATH ROW

Prisons are responsible for the housing and execution of inmates under sentences of death in the United States. Prisoners awaiting the death penalty are typically confined in special housing units, or cell blocks, within prison facilities that are designated to administer capital punishment, which is execution by the government. Each of these special units is commonly referred to as a death row. The phrase *on death row* can refer to an individual inmate under sentence of death or collectively to all prisoners awaiting execution.

In 2009, the death penalty was legal in the federal system and in 35 states. New Mexico became the 15th without capital punishment when the death penalty was abolished on March 19, 2009. After signing the legislation into law, the New Mexico governor Bill Richardson commented that the alternative sentence of life in prison without possibility of parole was "a strong punishment" and that the high costs associated with the death penalty represented "a valid reason in this era of austerity and tight budgets" to end New Mexico's use of capital punishment.

In 2009, 52 executions were performed in the United States, and 106 criminal offenders were sentenced to the death penalty nationwide. Texas performed 24 of the 52 executions—by far the most of any state—followed by six executions in Alabama; five executions in Ohio; three executions each in Virginia, Georgia, and Oklahoma; two executions each in South Carolina, Florida, and Tennessee; and one execution each in Indiana and Missouri.[8]

Historically, one of the earliest forms of the death penalty was banishment to the wilderness, where the offender usually died from starvation, dehydration, or animal attack. Over time, methods of execution have included burning alive, burying alive, boiling in oil, stoning, beheading, disemboweling, and smothering. Executions were usually administered in public, under the rationale that the spectacle of a gruesome death would deter those in attendance from committing similar crimes. Public executions are still carried out in some countries. Most modern nations, including the United States however, no longer permit the public viewing of executions. Nonetheless, limited viewing of executions is permitted in the United States, usually by selected media representatives, law enforcement officials, and family members of both the crime victim and the condemned individual. In addition, official witnesses are required in order to verify that the execution is carried out according the protocol.

The first execution by electrocution was carried out on William Kemmler for the crime of murder on August 6, 1890, at the Auburn penitentiary in New York. Thomas Edison, among others, opposed electrocution because it was extremely painful. As an alternative, opponents of electrocution proposed the use of lethal gas. On February 8, 1924, in Nevada, Gee Jon became the first person in the United States to be executed with cyanide gas in a gas chamber.

In 1972, executions were halted in the United States when the U.S. Supreme Court ruled in *Furman v. Georgia* that Georgia's death penalty law violated the Eighth Amendment's ban against cruel and unusual punishment. However, in 1976, the Court held in *Gregg v. Georgia* that Georgia's newly revised guidelines for the application of the death penalty were constitutional, and executions resumed throughout the United States. A total of 1,188 executions were carried out in the United States from the resumption of the death penalty in 1976 through 2009. During that period Texas performed 447 executions, followed by Virginia, with 105 executions, and Oklahoma, with 91 executions.

In 1977, Oklahoma became the first state to legalize execution by lethal injection, a method viewed as more humane, or at least less cruel. On December 6, 1982, in Texas, convicted murderer Charles Brooks became the first person in the United States to be executed by lethal injection. Lethal injection became the primary mode of execution in the United States in both the federal and state correctional systems.

In the federal prison system, on June 11, 2001, Timothy McVeigh became the first person executed by lethal injection for his part in killing 168 people in the 1995 bombing of the Alfred P. Murrah Federal Building in Oklahoma City, Oklahoma. Other federal executions by lethal injection included Juan Raul Garza, on June 19, 2001, for three murders in the continuance of a criminal enterprise (drug trafficking), and Louis Jones, Jr., on March 18, 2003, for kidnapping resulting in death.

Beginning with McVeigh, all federal executions were carried out at the federal prison in Terre Haute, Indiana, where the lethal injection facility, built in 1995 at a cost of $300,000, consists of an execution chamber surrounded by five viewing rooms. During federal executions, all procedures are monitored by the Justice Department in Washington, D.C., through an open telephone line with prison officials. Only the president of the United States has the power to grant clemency after the condemned has exhausted all legal appeals.

Although execution procedures in federal and state correctional systems vary in their specifics, all executions in the United States follow a general protocol. In the hours preceding the execution, the condemned inmate is served a meal of his or her choice, with certain restrictions, including no alcoholic beverages. In some states, inmates are allowed to shower and put on freshly laundered prison clothing before the execution. In other states, the inmate is required to remove all outer clothing prior to entering the death chamber. Generally, the prison's warden or chaplain visits the inmate and often remains with the inmate through the execution process.

Inside the chamber, the condemned is placed in restraints on a gurney and connected to an electrocardiogram (EKG) machine to determine when the inmate's heart stops and the time of death. Two intravenous tubes extending from an adjacent executioner's room are then inserted with catheters into the inmate's arms or legs. Once the tubes are in place, witnesses are allowed to observe through viewing windows. Individuals permitted to witness executions generally include relatives of the crime victim and the inmate, official witnesses selected by the state, representatives of the media, a spiritual adviser, prison guards, the prison's warden, and a prison employee designated as the executioner. Some jurisdictions use execution teams composed of two or three individuals. Each of the members simultaneously delivers liquid into the intravenous lines, but none of them knows which one is actually delivering the lethal drugs. The inmate may choose to make a final statement. The statement may be verbal or written and read aloud by the inmate or a prison representative, such as the warden or chaplain. The final statement is generally tape-recorded and later released to the media. The lethal drugs are then administered, in order. In a standard three-drug protocol used by most states and the federal government, an anesthetic is first administered to induce sleep, following by a muscle relaxant administered in a dosage high enough to paralyze the lungs and stop breathing. Finally, a third drug is used to stop the heart.

In 2003, some U.S. medical experts, including the anesthesiologist Edward Brunner, raised concerns that the use of the second drug—the paralyzing agent to induce suffocation—potentially caused serious pain that could not be communicated by the condemned prisoner. Although the three-drug protocol for lethal injection continued to be used nationwide, questions persisted as to whether its use constituted cruel and unusual punishment, in violation of the Eighth Amendment to the U.S. Constitution.

In 2006, in the case of *Hill v. McDonough*, the issue came before the U.S. Supreme Court, which ruled that death row inmates had the right to challenge the method of their execution, including the protocol for the administration of lethal injection. The Court again addressed the issue in 2008, in *Baze v. Rees*, and ruled that lethal injection, as administered in Kentucky, did not violate the Eighth Amendment's ban on cruel and unusual punishment. Nonetheless, the Court's ruling in *Baze v. Rees* did not settle the controversy surrounding the use of lethal injection. In 2009, after halting executions by lethal injection for some two months due to difficulties with the lethal injection procedure, Ohio became the first state to switch from a three-drug protocol to the use of a single-drug sedative. In 2009, executions by lethal injection were effectively put on hold in California, Maryland, Kentucky, and the federal system pending court challenges to the use of the three-drug protocol.

The death penalty continues to be a source of controversy in other aspects, as well. High costs are associated with administering the death penalty, including expensive and time-consuming legal challenges in state and federal courts brought by every death row inmate, often because the challenges are mandated by law. In 2009, the estimated cost to California of maintaining the death penalty was $137 million per year. Florida spent approximately $51 million per year on its death penalty system, or about $24 million for every executed inmate. A study in Maryland reported some $186 million in costs associated with the administration of the death penalty over a 23-year period—or about $37 million per execution. As states grapple with budget cutbacks produced by difficult economic conditions, there is increasing talk of abolishing the death penalty to save money.

Support for the death penalty as a deterrent to crime is progressively waning. For example, in a nationwide poll of police chiefs in 2009, the death penalty ranked last as an effective means of crime reduction. Some 72 percent of respondents ranked expanded resources for police as the most efficient use of taxpayer's money, followed by community policing (65 percent), hiring more police officers (64 percent), longer prison sentences (52 percent), diversionary drug and alcohol treatment programs (43 percent), neighborhood watch programs (35 percent), and antigang efforts (27 percent).

There is also the moral issue surrounding the possible execution of an innocent person. In 2009, nine individuals who had been sentenced to death were exonerated of their alleged crimes. Prior to being freed the men had collectively spent 121 years on death row. Since 1973, 139 individuals have been exonerated of crimes for which they had been convicted and sentenced to death.[9]

CORRECTIONAL SYSTEMS

In the United States, there are two main prison systems: state and federal. State prison systems include correctional facilities for males, females, and juvenile offenders. Every state and the District of Columbia operates a correctional system, and each functions in an autonomous manner under the authority of its particular jurisdiction. In the federal prison system, the Bureau of Prisons in the U.S. Department of Justice operates correctional institutions for males and females, and the U.S. Department of Defense operates military prisons for criminal offenders in the armed services. Private prisons are correctional facilities operated by companies in the private sector that are under contract with state or federal correctional agencies. As such, private prisons function under the umbrella of state and federal correctional systems.

STATE PRISON SYSTEMS

As a general rule, an individual who commits a felony in violation of state law is subject to imprisonment in the state where the crime occurred. Consequently, most prison inmates in the United States are confined in state prisons, because most felonies committed each year in the United States violate state laws.

All 50 states operate prisons, usually through state departments of correction. Most state departments of correction are administered by a director appointed by the state's governor and have cabinet-level status. Directors are able to exercise a high degree of autonomy in the allocation of fiscal resources and personnel within their departments. There is no central authority governing the state prison systems in the United States. Although there are similarities among state systems of corrections, each state system is essentially autonomous. The American Correction Association (ACA), founded in 1870 as the National Prison Association and renamed in 1954, serves as an umbrella organization for correctional agencies and professionals nationwide. In 1968, the ACA established an accreditation process for correctional institutions and created a standards committee composed of criminal justice professionals to administer the accreditation process. Through accreditation, the ACA established minimum standards on issues such as inmate health, institutional safety, and staff training. The ACA also publishes *Corrections Today* magazine and the peer-reviewed research journal *Corrections Compendium.*

In 2008, some 1.4 million inmates were incarcerated in state prisons nationwide. From 2007 to 2008, the population of state prisoners increased by 10,539 inmates. As of December 30, 2005, 1,719 correctional facilities were operated by states nationwide, according to the Bureau of Justice Statistics, which conducts a census of U.S. correctional facilities every five years. At the time of the previous census of correctional facilities, in 2000, there were 1,584 state correctional facilities, representing a 9 percent increase in state prisons from 2000 to 2005.

Despite the overall increase in the number of state correctional facilities, state prisons in 2005 operated at 12 percent above rated capacity, compared to 3 percent above rated capacity in 2000. In other words, from 2000 to 2005, overcrowding in state prisons grew worse nationwide. The number of correctional staff in state prisons did not keep pace with the increase in the inmate population. (Correctional staff includes all administrative employees as well as correctional officers.) In 2005 there were 3.3 state prison inmates for each correctional staff member, compared with 3.0 in 2000. There were 10.3 state prison inmates per correctional officer in 2005, compared to an inmate-to-correctional officer ratio of 9 to 1 in 2000.

The overall cost of state corrections also increased—from $35.1 billion in 2000 to nearly $40.7 billion in 2005. The overall costs of state corrections include expenses related to operating correctional institutions, community-based programs, and parole functions.[10]

Treatment in State Prison Systems

A wide range of prison programs operate under the umbrella of treatment in state prisons nationwide. They include counseling and educational programs, vocational training, and inmate self-help through organizations such as Alcoholics Anonymous.

Counseling is generally offered in group sessions, although individual psychological counseling is sometimes available. The general goals of both group and individual counseling in a correctional setting include:

- Coping with the frustrations of life in an institution and in society
- Recognizing the emotional roots of criminal behavior
- Understanding and accepting the consequences of inappropriate conduct

- Improving the overall emotional climate of the institution through interpersonal communication

Because correctional facilities are often underfunded, the hiring of clinically trained mental health professionals is not always possible. As an alternative, many institutions utilize group leaders, often correctional staff with some type of training in counseling. Fundamental personality changes are not the goal of group counseling. Rather, group meetings may help inmates to better understand how others perceive them and, in turn, stimulate a higher sense of self-awareness to more effectively deal with common problems.

State correctional institutions commonly offer educational programs that allow inmates to earn a high school diploma or an equivalent, usually the general educational development (GED) certificate. The GED program was developed as part of the GI Bill at the end of World War II to allow armed services personnel who were returning from the war to pursue educational opportunities. Some correctional institutions offer courses for college credits toward an associate or bachelor's degree. When available, educational programs beyond a high school diploma or its equivalency are often subject to limited enrollment due to lack of funding. In states such as Connecticut, Illinois, and Texas, statewide school districts were formed to meet the educational needs of inmates.

Participation in vocational training or a prison industry is often a key consideration for parole boards in determining when an inmate is suitable for release. A stable work record while incarcerated is often an inmate's only calling card when seeking employment after release. The following are among typical prison industries:

- Food services. Inmates prepare food for inmates and correctional staff. Duties include baking bread, cooking, cleaning, and the maintenance of kitchen facilities.
- Maintenance. Inmates tend to the buildings and grounds of the prison complex. Duties include skilled labor, including electrical work, masonry, plumbing, and painting, as well as unskilled work, such as cleaning and garbage collection.
- Laundry services. Inmates operate prison laundries that serve their institution and other smaller institutions that lack laundry facilities.
- Agriculture. Inmates work on prison farms that supply produce, dairy products, and poultry for use in their institution and other prisons.

Besides prison industry, vocational training is offered at many prisons. At many prisons, enrollment in vocational training classes is limited due to budgetary constraints, and equipment for training purposes is sometimes obsolete.

Work release or furlough programs allow inmates to leave the prison grounds during the day for a job in the community and return to the prison at night. Furlough programs are available to inmates who have demonstrated their trustworthiness over a period of time, often years. Work release programs allow inmates to gain valuable on-the-job experience. However, they also present a security risk, particularly with respect to contraband smuggled into the institution. In addition, because of the remote locations of many prisons, it is sometimes impractical for inmates to travel the distances required for a job in the community.

Inmate self-help groups are also available in many prisons, although they generally are not run by the correctional facility, but are offered by outside organizations. Such programs are called self-help in the sense that they are available to inmates with the initiative to join and attend meetings. Self-help groups are sometimes organized as chapters of national organizations, such as Alcoholics Anonymous, and are designed to address the emotional issues related to alcoholism or drug addiction. Other self-help groups are organized along racial or ethnic lines, such as the Afro-American Coalition and the Native American Brotherhood. These groups may be local, regional, or national in scope. Their goal is to establish a sense of community as a means of working for individual improvement in areas including literacy and legal education. Other types of self-help groups include national organizations such as the Fortune Society and Seventh Step, which attempt to raise the self-esteem of inmates to better prepare them for success after release from prison.

State Corrections for Juveniles

Juvenile correctional systems are administered by the 50 states and the District of Columbia. The federal prison system does not house juvenile offenders. Like state adult correctional systems, there is no central controlling authority for the administration of correctional institutions for juveniles. With the enactment of the Juvenile Justice and Delinquency Prevention Act in 1974, however, the U.S. Congress established federal core requirements for the treatment and handling of juvenile offenders. The act established the Coordinating Council on Juvenile Justice and Delinquency Prevention, an independent body within the executive branch of the federal government charged with monitoring juveniles in detention.

Historically, juvenile offenders were often mixed with male and female adults in correctional settings. By the early 19th century in the United States, shelters were developed for juvenile runaways and vagrants. In 1825, the House of Refuge was established in New York City and began accepting minors who were referred by the courts, usually for vagrancy or because they were victims of neglect or abuse. Within the House of Refuge, juveniles were segregated by sex. In 1826, the House of Reformation was established in Boston as a facility for juvenile offenders. More reformatories for juveniles were subsequently established in Maine, Massachusetts, Michigan, New York, and Ohio. These facilities housed both juvenile criminal offenders and minors known as status offenders, who had not violated any criminal laws but were deemed incorrigible as the result of truancy from school or running away from home. Still, many juvenile offenders continued to be incarcerated in adult prisons and jail in the United States.

In 1899, the Illinois Juvenile Court Act created a new judicial jurisdiction for juvenile delinquents that was separate from the adult criminal justice system. Among the most important provisions of the act was the strict segregation of juvenile and adult offenders in correctional settings. Using the Illinois Juvenile Court Act as a model, juvenile courts were established in 1901 in New York and Wisconsin and in 1902 in Maryland and Ohio. By 1912, some 22 states had established juvenile jurisdictions, and by 1928, only Maine and Wyoming did not have a juvenile court system in place. In 1945, Wyoming was the last state to establish a juvenile court system. Still, juvenile court systems were not uniform from state to state. For example, the segregation of juveniles and adults in correctional facilities was not mandated by North Dakota until 1969, and Maine did not do so until 1977.

Jurisdictions differ in their administration and management of juveniles in correctional settings. As of 2006, state delinquency institutions were administered under the authority of a social or human services agency in 15 states and the District of Columbia. In 16 states such facilities were under the authority of a state department of youth services, or youth authority. Juvenile detention facilities in 10 states were administered under the umbrella of the adult corrections agency, and in eight states they were administered by children and youth agencies that provide both child protection and juvenile corrections services.[11]

The Office of Juvenile Justice and Delinquency Prevention (OJJDP) was created under the Juvenile Justice and Delinquency Prevention Act of 1974 to monitor and study all facets of juvenile justice in the United States and to disseminate that information to the public. In October 2000, the OJJDP conducted its first census of residential facilities for juvenile offenders in the United States. The census counts as juveniles all offenders in residential placement who are under 21 years of age, which is over the age of juvenile jurisdiction in all states and the District of Columbia. In most states, however, offenders who are committed to residential placement when they were juveniles may be kept in that placement until they are 21 years old.

In 2006, 92,093 offenders under 20 years of age were housed in some 2,658 juvenile facilities in the United States. Most of them—63,502—were confined in publicly operated facilities, and the remainder were in privately run facilities, which are operated under state oversight. Although nationally the number of juveniles in custody in all types of facilities declined by around 3 percent from 2004 to 2006, some 18 states reported an average increase of 11 percent from 2004 to 2006 in the number of juveniles in residential placement. Nationwide, in 2006, some 11 percent of juvenile offenders were housed in facilities that were above rated capacity.[12]

While the number of juvenile offenders in residential placement nationwide declined, the number of inmates under 18 years of age confined in state prisons in the United States rose. In other words, nationally, more juvenile offenders were tried and sentenced as adult offenders in criminal court. In 2008, some 3,650 inmates under the age of 18 were confined in state prisons nationwide—an increase from the 2,283 inmates under 18 years of age who were held in state prisons in 2007.[13]

The increase in juvenile offenders in state prison who were sentenced as adults results from changes in state sentencing laws. Beginning in 1980, gun violence and homicides by juvenile offenders began to increase in the United States. The rising trend of criminal violence by juveniles peaked in 1993, but the public perception that juvenile crime was out of control caused many states to enact tougher laws for juvenile offenders. Those measures sometimes included the lowering of the age of majority for certain crimes of violence to allow the most serious juvenile offenders to be tried as adults and, in some states, to be committed to adult correctional facilities, although under federal law juveniles must be housed separately from adults until they are 18 years of age.

Laws that sanction under certain circumstances the trial and sentencing of juvenile offenders as adults in criminal court are generally referred to as *transfer laws*. Such measures fall into three categories: *judicial waiver laws*, *statutory exclusion laws*, and *prosecutorial discretion laws*.

In 2008, 45 states had some version of judicial waiver laws, which permit juvenile court judges, under certain statutorily defined circumstances, to waive the jurisdiction of the juvenile court, thereby allowing the prosecution of a juvenile offender in criminal court. A formal hearing is required in each case to permit such a waiver.

Statutory exclusion laws essentially circumvent the juvenile court and give jurisdiction to the criminal court for certain crimes. In other words, when a juvenile offender is charged with a crime that is statutorily excluded from the juvenile court's jurisdiction, the case must be filed in criminal court, where the juvenile offender will be tried and, if convicted, sentenced as an adult. In 2008 there were 15 states with statutory exclusion laws.

Prosecutorial discretion laws—or concurrent jurisdiction laws as they are sometimes called—allow prosecutors to determine if charges against a juvenile offender should be filed in juvenile or criminal court. This is permissible only for certain crimes defined by state law, which grants concurrent jurisdiction to prosecute those crimes to both the juvenile and criminal courts. No formal hearing is required to prosecute a juvenile offender in criminal court under prosecutorial discretion laws, which in 2008 were available to prosecutors in 15 states.

Nationally, in 2008, 44 states had one or more transfer laws that permitted the prosecution of juvenile offenders as adults. In addition, 34 states had other provisions governing the prosecution of juvenile offenders as adults. Under *once an adult, always an adult* laws, a juvenile offender who was previously prosecuted in criminal court as an adult must be prosecuted in criminal court for any future offenses. *Reverse waiver laws* permit juvenile offenders who are facing pending charges as an adult to petition the court to transfer their case to juvenile court. *Blended sentencing laws* permit juvenile courts to impose harsher criminal court sentences and, conversely, allow criminal courts to impose juvenile court dispositions in certain cases.[14] Because juvenile courts are charged with rehabilitating the offender whenever possible, the term *disposition* is used instead of the term *sentence*.

According to research findings reported by the Bureau of Justice Statistics, juvenile offenders transferred to criminal court and prosecuted as adults tended to have a higher rate of re-offending than juveniles who were processed in juvenile court. In addition, juveniles prosecuted as adults in criminal court tended to re-offend sooner and more often than their counterparts in juvenile court.[15]

In 2009, some 2,600 juveniles in the United States were serving sentences of life without possibility of parole, commonly referred to as juvenile LWOP. On November 9, 2009, the U.S. Supreme Court heard oral arguments in two cases that challenge the constitutionality of imposing an LWOP sentence on juvenile offenders for crimes other than murder. In the case *Graham v. Florida*, 17-year-old Terrance Graham was sentenced to life without parole in 2004 for his participation in an armed home invasion while he was on probation for another violent crime. In *Sullivan v. Florida*, Joe Harris Sullivan was 13 years of age when, in 1989, he raped an elderly woman, for which he was later convicted and sentenced to life in prison without parole. On May 17, 2009, the U.S. Supreme Court ruled that, under the Eighth Amendment's Cruel and Unusual Punishment Clause, juvenile offenders cannot be sentenced to life in prison without parole for criminal offenses other than homicide. In 2005, the U.S. Supreme Court established a distinction between juveniles and adults in *Roper v. Simmons* by ruling as unconstitutional the imposition of the death penalty on defendants who were younger than 18 years of age at the time of their crime.[16]

THE FEDERAL PRISON SYSTEM

Unlike state correctional systems, the federal prison system is centrally administered by the federal Bureau of Prisons (BOP), an agency within the U.S. Department of Justice. The central office of the BOP is located in

Washington, D.C. The federal prison system is divided into six regional offices, each administered by a regional director. The regional offices are located in Atlanta, Georgia; Dallas, Texas; Philadelphia, Pennsylvania; Burlingame, California; Annapolis, Maryland; and Kansas City, Kansas.

Federal correctional facilities include prisons for men and women, military prisons, and privately operated correctional facilities that operate under federal oversight. Federal prisons house felons convicted in federal courts of criminal offenses against the United States. Some crimes are uniquely federal, such as treason or airline hijacking. Other crimes may overlap with state laws. For example, murder is a state crime. However, the killing of a federal employee during the course of his or her job is a federal crime, which is why Timothy McVeigh was charged and tried in federal court for his part in the 1995 bombing of the Alfred P. Murrah Federal Building that killed 168 people. Similarly, all states have drug laws, and most drug offenders are prosecuted in state courts. When individuals transport those same illegal drugs across state lines for sale, however, they commit the federal crime of interstate drug trafficking.

Historically, federal prisoners were housed in state and local institutions in the United States. In 1870, the Justice Department was established and placed in charge of the growing number of federal prisoners in state and local correctional facilities. As state prisons became increasingly overcrowded, some states only accepted federal prisoners who were residents of that state. From 1885 to 1895, the number of federal prisoners in state facilities more than doubled, from 1,027 to 2,516, and the number of federal prisoners in local jails increased from 10,000 to 15,000 during the same 10-year period.[17]

Under pressure from the states to establish federal correctional facilities to ease prison overcrowding, in 1891 the U.S. Congress authorized the construction of three penitentiaries. Until then the only federal penitentiary, at Fort Leavenworth, Kansas, was used to house military prisoners who were not confined in state or local facilities. In 1895, the U.S. War Department decided to transfer the military prisoners at Fort Leavenworth to alternate facilities at installations in the United States. As a result, space became available at the Leavenworth prison. For the first time in U.S. history, nonmilitary federal prisoners were transferred from state and local facilities for confinement in a federal prison.

On July 10, 1896, Congress appropriated funds for the construction of a federal prison for 1,200 inmates at a site approximately three miles from the Leavenworth prison. Built by convict labor, the prison was not completed until 1928. Meanwhile, a second federal penitentiary was completed in 1875 at McNeil Island, Washington, and a third in 1899 at Atlanta, Georgia. All three prisons were built in the Auburn style, with multitiered cell blocks in a fortresslike structure.

Prisons

Between 1900 and 1935, federal criminal jurisdiction expanded significantly, in large measure due to the passage of the following legislation:

- The White Slave Act of 1910, outlawing interstate commerce in prostitution.
- The Harrison Narcotic Act of 1914, establishing controlled substances that were subject to taxation and strict government monitoring.
- The Volstead Act of 1918, prohibiting the sale and consumption of alcoholic beverages.
- The Dyer Act of 1919, criminalizing the interstate transportation of stolen vehicles.

The population of federal prisons swelled as the result of the increasing number of convictions in federal courts. In 1927, a 500-bed correctional facility for women was opened at Alderson, West Virginia, in response to the rising number of females in the federal correctional population. By 1929, overcrowding was so serious in New York City correctional facilities that a newly built three-story garage was converted to the Federal Detention Headquarters. Later that year, the U.S. House of Representatives Special Committee on Federal Penal Reformatory Institutions recommended the establishment of a centralized administration for federal prisons. On May 14, 1930, President Herbert Hoover signed into law the legislation that created the Federal Bureau of Prisons (BOP) and appointed Sanford Bates, then president of the American Correctional Association, as the first director of the BOP.

As constituted in 1930, the Bureau of Prisons operated three penitentiaries, as well as the U.S. Industrial Reformatory, the Alderson correctional facility for women, the Federal Detention Headquarters jail, and eight former army camps converted to makeshift correctional facilities to house the overflow of inmates entering the federal prison system. Still, the system was overtaxed, and the lack of space in federal facilities necessitated the housing of some prisoners in local jails. In response, the BOP moved quickly to establish new correctional facilities. In 1930, control of the U.S. Mint at New Orleans, Louisiana, was transferred from the U.S. Department of the Treasury to the Department of Justice for use as a jail. New regional jails went into operation in 1932 at La Tuna, Texas, and at Lewisburg, Pennsylvania, and in 1933 at Milan, Michigan. Also opened in 1933 was a men's reformatory at El Reno, Oklahoma, and a hospital for mentally ill inmates at Springfield, Missouri. In 1934, the military prison at Alcatraz Island, California, was converted to a maximum security facility for federal inmates. As the result of prison expansion, in 1940 the BOP was able to relocate narcotics violators confined at the military barracks at Fort Leavenworth and return the prison to the War Department. For the first time in U.S. history, all federal inmates were housed in federal correctional facilities.

Overcrowding in federal correctional facilities continued to be a problem. In 1954, at the request of the Bureau of Prisons, the U.S. Navy's military prison at Terminal Island, California, was converted to a federal prison. By 1955, the BOP operated some 28 correctional institutions. Still, there was insufficient space to house the nearly 21,000 federal inmates at that time. Forty years later, in 1995, there were 77 federal correctional facilities housing nearly 81,000 inmates. Ten years later, in 2005, the Bureau of Prisons had added 25 additional facilities, for a total of 102 federal prisons. Despite the expansion in facilities, there were not enough federal prisons to keep up with the influx of inmates. In 2005, federal prisons were collectively operating at 37 percent above their rated capacity and housed some 145,780 inmates. As the result of systemwide overcrowded conditions, in 2004 the Bureau of Prisons held 22,800 inmates in privately operated correctional facilities under federal oversight.[18]

Housing more inmates resulted in significantly higher operating costs for the federal prison system. From 1980 to 2006, federal expenditures for corrections increased from $408 million to nearly $7 billion per year. In 2006, federal corrections expenditures composed about one-sixth of total justice system costs for the federal government.[19]

REHABILITATION IN THE FEDERAL PRISON SYSTEM

In 1934, under the direction of Sanford Bates, the Bureau of Prisons implemented a classification system that was unique in U.S. penology and did not exist in any of the state correctional systems at that time. Under the system, each federal correctional facility was classified as a penitentiary, reformatory, prison camp, or hospital. Also included were drug addiction treatment facilities operated by the U.S. Public Health Service. Within each facility, inmates were classified according to factors including age, sex, and type of offense, with the goal of developing individualized programs for rehabilitation. To meet that goal, the federal prison system expanded educational and vocational training departments and prison libraries. Specialists, including social workers, instructors, and chaplains, were recruited to run prison counseling and training programs. To encourage professional development, the BOP established five regional training centers for correctional staff, including corrections officers and other employees, and by 1937 all federal correctional personnel were placed under the jurisdiction of the Civil Service Commission. Federal parole was reorganized, and the supervision of parolees was transferred from the U.S. Marshall's Office to the probation offices of the federal courts in order to develop an aftercare system that was more treatment-oriented and less punitive in its approach to ex-convicts.

Prisons

Over the next 40 years, inmate rehabilitation programs in the federal correctional system were expanded and refined. For example, the caseworker method of placing a large number of inmates housed throughout a prison under the supervision of one caseworker was replaced by the unit management concept in many federal institutions. Under the unit management system, inmates were housed in contained units and worked directly with caseworkers, correctional counselors, or educational professionals assigned to their unit. Both the caseworker and unit manager systems were built around the medical model of treatment developed by Sanford Bates during his tenure from 1930 to 1937 as the director of the Bureau of Prisons. Sanford and other proponents of the medical model believed that criminal behavior was the result of an underlying disorder that could be treated through medical or psychological methods.

The medical model eventually fell out of favor among correctional professionals. The demise of the medical model occurred at a time of increasing tensions in U.S. prisons. Beginning in the late 1960s, the U.S. Supreme Court issued a series of rulings expanding the rights of inmates in areas including legal representation, humane treatment, and medical care. The lawful exercise of constitutional rights by prisoners was often at odds with the increasingly punitive style of prison management and inmate control in U.S. corrections. The result was sometimes violent. In 1971, at the Attica prison in Attica, New York, a four-day protest over prison conditions turned violent, resulting in the deaths of 32 prisoners and 11 guards who were held hostage by the rioting inmates. In 1975 the BOP officially began to phase out the use of the medical model in favor of the correctional philosophies of deterrence and incapacitation, which were more in line with the aim of maintaining control over what was viewed as an increasingly vocal and sometimes violent prisoner population. Still, prison violence continued. In 1980, 33 people were killed as the result of an inmate riot at the New Mexico state prison. In the federal system, the prisons at Oakdale, Louisiana, and at Atlanta, Georgia, were held siege for 11 days in 1987 during an inmate uprising. Some 89 hostages were released unharmed. The Department of Justice ultimately chose to hold no one accountable for the uprising.

Military Prisons

Most federal prisoners in the United States are housed in facilities operated by the federal Bureau of Prisons, a branch of the U.S. Department of Justice. However, the federal government also operates military prisons for inmates who are under the jurisdiction of the U.S. armed services, including members of the army, air force, navy, marine corps, and coast guard. Military prisons are administered by the U.S. Department of Defense.

The oldest military prison in the United States is the U.S. Disciplinary Barracks at Fort Leavenworth, Kansas. Originally called the United States Military Prison, the facility has been in continuous operation since May 15, 1875. In 2002, a new 521-bed unit was opened at the facility. Beginning in 1897, military prisoners confined at the U.S. Disciplinary Barracks assisted in the construction of the U.S. Federal Penitentiary at Leavenworth, Kansas, which was not completed until 1928. In effect, this created two prisons that are commonly referred to by the same name—Leavenworth. They are distinct facilities, however, operated by different branches of the federal government. The U.S. Disciplinary Barracks is a maximum security facility for both commissioned officers and enlistees convicted by U.S. court martial. Besides the correctional facility at Leavenworth, other military prisons in the United States are operated by various branches of the U.S. military services, including the army, navy, marine corps, and air force. In 2008, 1,658 inmates were incarcerated in military prisons in the United States.[20]

PRISONERS OF WAR

During wartime, the U.S. military operates detainment facilities for prisoners of war. Commonly, these facilities are located abroad, in or around the area of conflict. In retaliation for the domestic terrorist attacks against the United States on September 11, 2001, military forces led by the United States, with assistance from Great Britain and other countries, invaded Afghanistan, commencing with air attacks on October 7, 2001. On March 20, 2003, U.S. forces invaded Iraq, again with assistance from Great Britain and other countries. In early 2004, about one year after the invasion of Iraq, photographs were made public depicting the alleged abuse of prisoners of war by U.S. soldiers at the Abu Ghraib prison in Iraq. The photographs contained disturbing images of U.S. prisoners of war being subjected to alleged acts of physical brutality and sexual abuse. In the aftermath of the release of the photographs, the U.S. Congress and the Defense Department began investigations into alleged abuses of U.S. prisoners of war in Iraq and Afghanistan, including the deaths of some 40 prisoners of war. Chapter 2 includes a discussion of the standards of international law governing the humane treatment of prisoners of war, as established under the Geneva Conventions.

Beginning in 2002, military prisoners detained abroad—primarily in Iraq and Afghanistan—were transported to the U.S. Naval Base at Guantánamo Bay, Cuba, where they were detained as enemy combatants with limited legal rights. Many of the detainees at the Guantánamo Bay prison camp filed suit in U.S. federal court to contest the legality of their detention. In 2004, the U.S. Supreme Court ruled in the cases of *Hamdi v. Rumsfeld* and

Rasul v. Bush that detainees had limited constitutional rights to contest their detention under the writ of habeas corpus. In subsequent rulings the Court expanded upon the rights of detainees to challenge their detention: *Hamdan v. Rumsfeld* (2006), *Boumediene v. Bush* (2008), and *Munaf v. Geren* (2008). A discussion of the Supreme Court's rulings in each of the cases is presented in chapter 2.

On January 22, 2009, President Barack Obama signed an executive order for the closing of the Guantánamo Bay prison camp. Under the terms of the executive order, Attorney General Eric Holder was assigned to lead a review of what to do with the remaining detainees at the Guantánamo Bay prison camp. President Obama also appointed another task force, cochaired by Attorney General Holder, Secretary of Defense Robert Gates, and Director of National Intelligence Dennis C. Blair, to determine if standards should be expanded beyond those in the army field manual for interrogations of prisoners of war and for the practice of extraordinary rendition, in which detainees captured abroad are transferred to other countries for interrogation.

On December 15, 2009, the Obama administration announced the transfer of a limited number of detainees held at the Guantánamo Bay prison camp to the Thompson Correctional Center in rural Illinois, approximately 150 miles west of Chicago. The Thompson facility was built in 2001 as a state prison for maximum security inmates. However, due to Illinois budget deficits, the prison was never fully operational due to a lack of state funding. According to the terms of the Obama administration's announcement, the Thompson facility will be purchased by the U.S. government, upgraded to enhance security features, and operated as a federal maximum security prison.

PRIVATE PRISONS

Prior to 1870, some states leased out prisoners to private companies to work as laborers. In exchange the companies paid the costs of feeding, clothing, and housing the prisoners, usually for a flat fee per year for each prisoner. In essence, prisoners were a source of revenue for states that participated in such arrangements with private companies. Inmates under this system were used much like slaves on a plantation to farm or harvest crops. Beginning in about 1870, with the growth of industrialization, private companies leased prisoners to build roads and railroads and to manufacture goods. To keep costs low, inmates were sometimes transported in rolling cages, where they were forced to live in unsanitary conditions, often without medical care or adequate food. When working outside of the cages, prisoners were shackled with ball and chain restraints, and groups of prisoners came to be known as chain gangs. Prisoners who attempted to escape from these brutal conditions were beaten and sometimes killed by heavily armed guards, or overseers. By 1930, many of these work programs were forced out of existence due to federal legislation that placed restrictions on prison labor. In the 1970s, a series of rulings by the U.S. Supreme Court on prisoners' rights, including medical care and basic standards for conditions of confinement, essentially eliminated any type of forced labor by prison inmates.

With the loss of prisoners' labor as a source of revenue, correctional agencies shouldered all of the costs of housing prisoners. Rising inmate populations placed more financial pressure on the states. Increasingly, to save money, states turned to subcontractors in the private sector to deliver prison services, including educational and vocational training and transportation services. Prior to 1984, however, an entire correctional facility operated by a private company did not exist anywhere in the United States.

In 1984, the first privately operated correctional facility was created when the Corrections Corporation of America (CCA) was awarded a contract to run a secure county correctional facility in Hamilton County, Tennessee. In 1985, CCA offered to take over the entire state prison system in Tennessee for $200 million. The bid by CCA was eventually rejected due to opposition from state employee unions and skepticism by state legislators; however, the era of private prisons had begun in the United States. In 1984, the U.S. government awarded a contract to CCA to run a federal detention center for illegal immigrants. The Texas Department of Corrections awarded contracts to run four 500-bed correctional facilities, two to CCA and two to the Wackenhut Corrections Corporation (WCC). By 1988, prisons and jails in 39 states and the District of Columbia were under court order to improve conditions of confinement and reduce prison overcrowding. As a result, the trend toward prison privatization gained momentum.

During the next decade, the contractual capacity of secure adult correctional facilities for state and federal prisoners increased by nearly 700 percent, from 15,300 in 1990 to 121,482 in 1999. By 2005, some 105,451 inmates in U.S. prisons were incarcerated in privately operated correctional facilities. From 2000 to 2005, the number of private prisons in the United States grew from 264 to 415 facilities, accounting for nearly all of the increase in adult correctional facilities that became operational during that time period. Most private prisons that became operational from 2000 to 2005 were under contract to the federal Bureau of Prisons.

Nationwide, in 2005, approximately 66 percent of all private prisons were under contract to the Bureau of Prisons, accounting for some 22,801 federal inmates. The remaining private prisons were used by 18 states and the District of Columbia, which increased the number of private correctional facilities under contract to them. The use of private prisons increased by 30 percent in Connecticut, and 25 percent in Ohio—representing the largest increase among states in the use of private facilities. The use of privately operated prisons decreased by 27 percent in California and 16 percent in Texas between 2000 and 2005. However, among states, Texas held the largest number of inmates in private prisons (15,131), followed by Oklahoma (7,802), Colorado (6,195), Florida (5,739), Mississippi (5,683), and Tennessee (5,087).[21]

Proponents of private correctional facilities tend to make the following claims:

- Private firms are less bureaucratic and more efficient in their delivery of goods and services.

- Private firms are less restricted than governmental agencies in the hiring and firing of employees and can better manage their workforce.

- Private firms must compete in the marketplace; they are more attentive than government agencies to controlling costs and delivering high-quality service.

- Marketplace competition, which is absent in public agencies, promotes a higher level of overall effectiveness.

- Government agencies spend their allocated budgets in order to receive more funding, while private firms strive to control costs.

Conversely, some of the arguments against prison privatization include:

- Private firms are more likely to hire low-paid and inexperienced employees in an effort to save money.

- Private firms are more susceptible to corruption in the form of kickbacks and collusive bidding for government contracts, thereby driving up the costs for providing services.

- Private contractors may go out of business.

Perhaps of foremost concern is the ability of private prisons to manage serious crises. For example, on June 18, 1995, detainees at a privately operated facility for illegal immigrants rioted after making repeated allegations of inappropriate conditions of confinement. The contractor, ESMOR Inc., lost control of the 300-bed facility located in Elizabeth, New Jersey, and law enforcement officials were summoned to bring the situation in hand. The facility was closed but later reopened under new management by the Corrections Corporation of America. In 1997, violence at the Northeast Ohio Correctional Facility in Youngstown, Ohio, operated under contract with CCA, resulted in the deaths of two inmates and the escape of six dangerous offenders. The Ohio Department of Rehabilitation and Corrections was prevented from assisting CCA in restoring order at the facility because the state of .

Ohio lacked regulatory authority over private prisons. Legislation was passed in March 1998 that established state authority over private prisons in Ohio. A subsequent investigation by the U.S. Department of Justice cited a variety of reasons for the breakdown at the CCA facility, including a high rate of staff turnover and inadequate safety procedures. In August 1999, four inmates were murdered by prisoners at two private prisons in New Mexico operated by the Wackenhut Corrections Corporation. At one of the facilities, near Santa Rosa, New Mexico, prisoners rioted for three hours, during which they took control of two housing units and stabbed a guard to death. In response, over 100 of the most troublesome inmates at the Santa Rosa facility were transferred to a state prison in Virginia, raising concerns about the competence of private prisons in controlling violent inmates.

A decade later, concerns about security persisted at private correctional facilities, as exemplified by two incidents little more than a month apart at the Reeves County Detention Center in Pecos, Texas, a facility operated by Geo Group, Inc. At the time, the detention center, a low-security facility designed for 2,400 inmates, housed both federal and state prison inmates. On December 12, 2008, inmates at the facility took two staff members hostage and set fire to the recreation center. On January 31, 2009, over 2,000 inmates housed in two of the facility's three buildings engaged in fighting, resulting in the hospitalization of three inmates. The situation was not brought under control until the following day. Two prison workers taken hostage by inmates were released late on the day of the riot.

The incidents at the Reeves County Detention Center—a minimum-security prison—illustrate a broader issue. Increasing numbers of inmates require housing in maximum-security prisons, particularly violent offenders sentenced to long prison terms. But maximum-security prisons are increasingly overcrowded, often as the result of budget shortages that prevent or curtail necessary expansions in correctional capacity. In order to make room for high-risk inmates, medium-security prisoners who are housed in maximum-security facilities are sometimes moved to lower-level facilities. Private correctional companies are more likely to operate lower-security prisons, especially in states such as Texas that house large numbers of inmates in private facilities. As a result, low-security facilities are overtaxed with increasing numbers of inmates who may actually be housed at a security level that is below their classification, sometimes resulting in violence.

THE IMPACT OF PRISON EXPANSION ON COMMUNITIES

The building of a new prison brings with it inherent challenges for the community where the facility is located. Concerns over safety and the influx of criminal offenders are sometimes seen as disincentives by communities that discourage the building of new correctional facilities. For some localities, however, especially small communities with high rates of poverty and unemployment, the addition of a state prison may be welcomed as a source of new jobs and a boost to the local economy. For example, on December 15, 2009, when the Obama administration announced a plan to move some of the detainees held at Guantánamo Bay to a largely empty state prison in the village of Thomson, Illinois, the village president Jerry Hebeler reacted positively to the news: "It'll be good for the village and the surrounding area, especially with all the jobs that have been lost here."[22]

Whether economic benefits actually materialize from a new prison is another matter. A report by the Joint Center for Environmental and Urban Problems in Florida cast a positive light on the building of new prisons in communities, citing the creation of new jobs and little negative impact, such as an increase in crime or the lowering of property values. A study of the economic impact of a new prison in Potosi, Missouri, found that the prison eased unemployment somewhat by creating new jobs, despite the fact that many of the jobs went to individuals who resided outside of town. In a Colorado study, there was no difference in the rates of unemployment or per capita income in counties with prisons compared with those without prisons.[23] Another study conducted by Iowa State University concluded that the economic benefits of new prisons did not offset the investments, including free land, that were made by communities to attract and build new correctional facilities.[24]

A report by the Sentencing Project concluded that the 38 prisons built in nonmetropolitan communities in New York had little impact on the unemployment rates or per capita income of residents when compared with residents in counties without prisons. For example, from 1982 to 1988, unemployment rates declined by 42 percent in rural counties in New York with prisons, compared with a decline of 44 percent in counties without prisons. From 1988 to 1992, unemployment increased by 64 percent in counties with prisons, compared with an increase of only 55 percent in counties without prisons. Another decline in unemployment rates occurred from 1992 to 2001 in counties with and without prisons, but only by a difference of 3 percent. By comparison, from 1976 to 2000, per capita income rose by 141 percent in counties without a prison, and by 132 percent in counties with prisons. Overall in New York State, per capita income increased by 160 percent during that period.[25]

According to the report, the limited impact of new prisons on economic development in rural counties in New York may have been linked to the following factors:

- Prison employees, including correctional officers, do not always reside in the counties with prisons. Instead, they may live in nearby communities, and those communities would realize the economic benefit of new jobs created by the prison.

• Local residents of counties with prisons may not be qualified for construction jobs while the prison is being built or for other skilled work needed to run the prison. Apart from lack of skills, restrictions on union membership may also be a factor in disqualifying some local residents from benefiting from job creation as a result of the new prison.

• Local businesses may not stock the necessary materials for the construction or operation of the new prison, and contracts to purchase those supplies may be in place between the correctional agency and vendors outside the communities with prisons.

• Inmates often fill low-wage, unskilled jobs within the prison, such as custodial work. Because inmates are commonly paid wages below the legal minimum wage, residents from communities with prisons would be prevented from competing for those jobs.

Consistent with those findings, a prison built in 2002 in Stanley, Wisconsin, was expected to add 400 corrections-related jobs and, indirectly, another 319 jobs throughout the county of Chippewa, resulting in population gains in both the city and county. By 2007, when the prison was fully operational, the population of Stanley had increased by some 78 percent to 3,389 individuals; however, some 1,500 of those were inmates. As a result, the anticipated rate of growth in the population did not materialize in the city of Stanley or Chippewa County as a result of prison-related jobs, many of which were held by people who commuted from other counties.

Similarly, a 2004 study of seven counties in New York where 14 prisons had opened since 1982 showed no significant difference in employment rates when compared with seven other counties of similar size with no prisons. In other words, prison-related jobs did not reduce the unemployment rate in the seven counties with prisons.

In Texas, the low wages paid to corrections staff at rural prisons failed to attract and retain employees, resulting in significant staff shortages and, in some cases, the closure of correctional facilities. For example, in 2007, a wing housing some 300 prisoners was closed at the prison at Dalhart, Texas. As of November 2007, Texas attributed staffing shortages at eight rural prisons to low wages.[26]

THE FISCAL CRISIS IN U.S. CORRECTIONS

In 2009, corrections was nearly the fastest growing expenditure in states nationwide, second only to expenditures for Medicaid. At the same time, most states were facing serious shortfalls in revenue as a result of a national economic recession. Rising costs and shrinking budgets forced many states to implement cost-saving measures to curtail corrections expenditures. In 2009, many states reduced funding in their budgets for 2010 corrections expenditures, including double-digit reductions in Georgia, Idaho, Illinois, Kansas, Montana, Nebraska, and Washington.

The type of cuts made to corrections budgets in 2009 varied somewhat from state to state. For example, in Maine, contracts with prison health care providers were renegotiated; Georgia decreased the number of meals provided to prisoners while maintaining the same daily caloric intake; improvements in technological services were postponed in New York and Kansas. In general, when budgeting for fiscal year 2010, states cut corrections costs in three main areas—staffing, programs, and facilities.

To achieve savings in corrections staffing expenditures, states implemented hiring freezes, reduced salaries and benefits, and eliminated or postponed scheduled salary increases. For example, the Idaho Department of Corrections cut 38 jobs and required all staff members to take unpaid furlough days during fiscal year 2010. In Nevada and New Mexico, annual increases in health insurance costs were passed directly to corrections staff, effectively cutting salaries and the level of benefits provided to workers.

Some 20 states cut or eliminated prison programs, including inmate treatment programs and parole supervision services. Nationwide, for fiscal year 2010, states eliminated about 80 percent of openings available to inmates and parolees in substance abuse programs and cut by half the number of openings in sex offender programs.

Correctional facilities were closed in some states, despite opposition to the closures by corrections unions, businesses that relied on income generated by a prison slated for closing, and public safety advocates. In Michigan, eight state correctional facilities—three prisons and five minimum security camps—were closed, resulting in layoffs of some 500 corrections employees in order to achieve a savings of $118 million for fiscal year 2010. In New York, three prison camps and portions of seven prisons were slated for closure in 2010 to provide an anticipated savings of $25 million annually. Alaska and Colorado delayed opening or expanding new correctional facilities. Nationwide, 22 states closed prisons, reduced the number of beds available for inmates, and delayed expansions and openings of new prisons in order to maintain fiscal solvency in 2010.

In addition to measures to achieve short-term reductions in corrections expenditures, some states implemented new programs aimed at long-term cost savings. Such programs are commonly designed to reduce rates of recidivism by improving the supervision of recently released prison inmates. Their goals are to enhance former prisoners' odds of successful reintegration into society, thereby saving money and increasing public safety by having fewer individuals re-offend and return to prison.

In 2009, such programs were implemented in states despite budget shortfalls and cuts in overall corrections expenditures. In California, some $47 million was budgeted for 2010 to fund the Northern California Reentry Facility, a former women's prison that was converted to a reentry facility that will house up to 500 male inmates during the 12 months prior to their scheduled date of parole. Services provided to inmates in the reentry program include intensive substance abuse treatment, employment training and placement, and anger management and family counseling. For fiscal year 2010, Michigan increased funding for the Michigan Prisoner Reentry Initiative by $23 million to $56.6 million, doubling funds for reentry services in a state that cut overall corrections expenditures. Connecticut reinstated a furlough reentry program in which inmates are released 45 days early with the requirement that they participate in enhanced community supervision programs to reduce recidivism. Estimates project that the program will save the state $5 million annually beginning in 2010.

States nationwide also attempted to reduce overall inmate populations by revising formulas for good time and earned time credits. Inmates earn good time credits for good behavior. The credits are calculated in days that are subtracted from an inmate's original sentence, thereby reducing his or her time in prison. Similarly, earned time credits are awarded to inmates for productive behavior, such as participating in counseling or work programs. State statutes generally restrict participation in good time and earned time credit programs according to the degree of seriousness of an inmate's offense, with the most serious offenders barred from participation. In 2009, Colorado increased from 10 to 12 days per month the maximum earned time credits for eligible inmates. In Oregon, the total amount of earned time credit available to eligible inmates was increased from 20 percent to 30 percent of their original sentence. For example, an eligible inmate sentenced to 10 years in state prison could potentially earn enough credits to reduce the sentence by three years (30 percent of 10 years) and be released after seven years in prison.

Parole is another area that states nationwide have examined to achieve savings by reducing in their prison populations. For example, in 2009, parole boards in Michigan were expanded from 10 to 15 members in order to more efficiently review some 12,000 inmates who were eligible for parole. Aging and chronically ill inmates incur high costs for medical treatment, so some states are expanding the use of so-called medical parole for inmates deemed unlikely to re-offend due to old age or serious illness. For example, in 2009, New York projected $2 million in annual savings from the expansion of eligibility for medical parole. Similarly, Washington implemented a revised geriatric and medical parole policy that was expected to save some $1.5 million annually by releasing prison inmates aged 55 and older who are chronically or terminally ill.

In 2009, long-term policies designed to reduce the prison population were under consideration in states nationwide. The Crime Reduction Act enacted in Illinois is an example of the framework of such policies. The Crime Reduction Act calls for the use of improved assessment tools to more effectively assign parolees to appropriate supervision levels; a graduated response system for parole violators that uses enhanced treatment programs instead of automatic re-incarceration; and improved training for staff in community corrections.[27]

CHARACTERISTICS OF PRISONERS IN THE UNITED STATES

At the end of 2008, there were more than 1.6 million prisoners in the United States. Of those, some 1.4 million inmates were confined in state prisons in 2008 and approximately 201,000 inmates were incarcerated in federal prisons. From 2007 to 2008, the total number of state and federal prison inmates increased by eight-tenths of 1 percent, representing the lowest annual increase since 2000 to 2001, when the inmate population rose one-tenth of 1 percent. Between 2000 and 2008, the total number of inmates in U.S. prisons increased at an average annual rate of 1.8 percent, significantly less than the average annual increase of 6.5 percent between 1990 and 1999. Nonetheless, when compared to similar statistics from other countries, the United States remains the world leader in the incarceration of its citizens.[28]

THE PRISON EXPERIENCE

Prisons in the United States are total institutions where inmates are locked behind walls, separated from the outside world, and required to abide by strict rules. Personal possessions are limited or forbidden, institutional attire is required, and normal human interactions are severely curtailed, including heterosexual relationships and contact with family and children.

Typically, when inmates arrive at prisons they are stripped, searched, and assigned living quarters, usually at a classification or reception center, where they are evaluated on the basis of their background and criminal history. Sometimes, psychological and educational testing is performed on incoming inmates. After completing the process, each inmate receives a classification and is assigned to a permanent correctional facility. For example, violent or repeat criminal offenders are likely to be assigned to a maximum security prison. Similarly, mentally ill inmates are commonly placed in facilities with psychiatric services.

Introduction to Prisons

Upon arrival at a permanent correctional facility, inmates are assigned to a cell, usually in the prison's general population. Inmates assigned to special population units are usually those who are at high risk of violence in prison, such as child molesters, or those with special needs, such as handicapped or mentally ill inmates. As the result of prison overcrowding, inmates in the general population are commonly required to share cells that were designed to hold fewer inmates. For example, two inmates may share a one-person cell, or three inmates may share a cell designed for two individuals. Inmates experience a loss of personal privacy and autonomy.

During the initial phase of imprisonment, inmates are commonly depressed at the prospect of the amount of time they must serve in prison. Inmates must learn who they can befriend, who they must avoid, and who will grant them favors, and for what price. Inmates must quickly learn to protect themselves from predatory inmates, including gang members who may attempt to sell them to other inmates as sex slaves in exchange for drugs and other favors. Prisoners develop various methods of coping with the stress of the prison environment, including keeping to themselves or becoming involved in prison activities, such as educational or counseling programs. New inmates soon become aware of the underground prison economy, sometimes call the *hustle* or *hustling*, in contraband such as drugs, alcohol, weapons, and other commodities that are sold among inmates. Racial conflict also becomes a fact of life, and incoming inmates commonly segregate themselves along racial and ethnic lines to avoid conflicts. The process of adapting to the unique culture of prisons is commonly referred to as *prisonization*.

Women in Prison

Between 1930 and 1950 in the United States, only four correctional institutions for women were built in the United States. By comparison, from 1980 to 1990, some 34 women's prisons were built in the United States, and the number of imprisoned women increased proportionately. From 2000 to 2008, the total population of women in U.S. prisons increased from 93,234 to 114,852, representing an average annual increase of 3 percent. However, from 2007 to 2008, the number of female inmates in state and federal prisons increased by only 0.3 percent. By comparison, from 2000 to 2008, the number of male prisoners in the United States increased from some 1.3 million to nearly 1.5 million, representing an average annual increase of 1.9 percent. From 2000 to 2008, the population of female inmates in U.S. prisons grew at a faster annual rate than did the male inmate population during the same time period.

In 2008, women from 35 to 39 years of age composed nearly 20 percent of all female inmates, representing the largest segment of female prisoners in state and federal custody. In addition, in 2008, women between the ages of 35 and 39 accounted for the highest rate of incarceration among all female inmates—at 201 for every 100,000 women in the U.S. population—followed by women between 30 and 34 years of age, at a rate of 190 per 100,000 women in the U.S. population. By race, the highest rate of incarceration was among African-American female inmates in state and federal custody, at 149 per 100,000 women in the U.S. population. Hispanic females in U.S. prisons had the next highest rate of incarceration, 75 per 100,000 women in the U.S. population. The rates of incarceration for African-American and Hispanic female inmates exceeded the average rate of incarceration of 68 per 100,000 women in the U.S. population, while the incarceration rate for white female inmates of 50 per 100,000 women in the U.S. population was below the average rate of incarceration for women.[29]

The enactment of harsher sentencing laws beginning in the mid-1980s, which limited the discretion of judges when sentencing offenders, had an impact on the increase in female prisoners in U.S. prisons, just as with male prisoners. However, the underlying reasons for the increase in female criminality are more complex and cannot be attributed to a single cause. For example, in 2004, among the nearly two-thirds of female inmates who were mothers of minor children, 64.4 percent of state female inmates and 53.6 percent of federal female inmates were themselves victims of physical or sexual abuse. Among the same group, 63.2 percent of state female inmates and 52.6 of federal female inmates had symptoms of mental illness. In addition, 70.1 percent of state female inmates and 51.3 percent of federal female inmates who were mothers of minor children had histories of alcohol and drug abuse.[30]

The daily life of women in U.S. prisons differs from that of incarcerated males. For example, women's prisons tend be less violent, and inmates tend to pose less of a threat to each other and to correctional staff. Instead of directing their anger outward, like male inmates, female prisoners are more likely to engage in self-destructive acts, such as self-mutilation or attempted suicide. Also, the social code for female inmates tends to be less rigid than for male prisoners. So-called *make-believe families* are sometimes formed by female inmates to compensate for the separation from family and loved ones. In such make-believe families, females assume the masculine and feminine roles of mother and father, and some inmates take on the role of the child in the family.

THE CHILDREN AND FAMILIES
OF PRISONERS

In 2007, some 809,800 state and federal prisoners were parents of minor children under 18 years of age. Of those, 52 percent of state prison inmates and 63 percent of federal prison inmates were parents of minor children. Approximately 1.7 million children, representing 2.3 percent of the U.S. population, had one or both parents in prison in 2007. Of those, approximately 767,400 African-American children had one or both parents in prison, compared with about 484,100 white children and 362,800 Hispanic children with one or both parents in prison. African-American children were more likely to have a father in prison, as African-American males composed approximately 40 percent of all fathers in state and federal prisons, compared with 28 percent of African-American female inmates with minor children. The male versus female incarceration rates were reversed for white children with one or both parents in prison. Among white prison inmates with children in 2007, 30 percent were fathers and 48 percent were mothers. Some 10 percent of prison inmates with minor children were Hispanic fathers and about 19 percent were Hispanic mothers.

Between 1991 and 2007, the number of parents of minor children in state and federal prisons increased by 79 percent and the number of minor children with parents in prison rose by 80 percent. From 1991 to 2007, the number of minor children with a mother in prison increased by 131 percent, while the number with fathers in state or federal prisons increased by 77 percent.

In 2007, inmates in U.S. prisons for drug offenses were most likely to have minor children. Among state prison male inmates, 59 percent of drug offenders were fathers, compared with 47 percent of violent offenders who were fathers of minor children. Among federal prison male inmates, about 69 percent of drug offenders were fathers, compared with 50 percent of violent offenders and 54 percent who were incarcerated for property crimes. By comparison, among women in state prisons nationwide, some 63 percent of drug offenders were mothers of minor children. About 57 percent of violent female offenders and 65 percent of females incarcerated in state prison for property crimes were mothers. Among federal female inmates who were mothers of minor children in 2007 there was little differentiation between types of offense.

The physical separation between parents and child caused by incarceration can raise serious issues for children of inmates, especially young children, including a sense of abandonment and loss and weakened emotional attachment. In 2007, about 16 percent of children with one or both parents in state or federal prison were four years of age or younger. The immediate effects of imprisonment on children of incarcerated parents include feelings of shame, social stigma, loss of financial support, and a decline in school performance. In addition, if the incarcerated parent was the primary caregiver prior to imprisonment, children are at increased risk of suffering abuse and neglect in their new custodial setting. In 2007, approximately 42 percent of mothers and fathers in state prison were single parents prior to their arrest and incarceration. Among federal prison inmates, approximately 52 percent of mothers and 19 percent of fathers were single parents prior to imprisonment.

Imprisonment has a significant impact on families in which the incarcerated parent of minor children was in a two-parent household. The forced separation of spouses and intimate partners places a strain on those relationships. Conjugal visits are often banned in prisons or are made available on an extremely limited basis, further straining relationships between spouses and intimate partners. As a result, divorce, relocation, and other changes in the family structure during an inmate's absence make it difficult or impossible for some inmates to return to the life they left prior to their incarceration. For example, when an inmate's spouse remarries, the introduction of a new parental figure in the lives of the inmate's children can alter their relationship with the incarcerated parent. Also, the social stigma of incarceration may alienate family members and cause estrangement. The financial impact of incarceration can damage family relationships. In 2007, among state and federal prison inmates with minor children, about 52 percent of mothers and 54 percent of fathers were the primary providers of financial support prior to incarceration.

Among state prison inmates with minor children, about 9 percent of all parents reported being homeless in the year prior to their arrest and some 20 percent reported a history of physical or sexual abuse. In addition, among state prisoners who were parents of minor children, some 57 percent had verifiable mental health issues, and 67 percent engaged in substance abuse prior to imprisonment. Among federal prisoners who were parents of minor children, about 4 percent reported being homeless in the year prior to their arrest and incarceration. Some 11 percent of parents in federal prison had histories of physical or sexual abuse, about 43 percent had mental health issues, and some 56 percent of parents in federal prison engaged in substance abuse prior to their incarceration.[31]

DISPROPORTIONATE IMPRISONMENT OF MINORITIES

In 2008, the rates of incarceration for African-American males and females exceeded those for Hispanic and white males in state and federal prisons. Among African-American males, the rate of incarceration was 3,161 per 100,000 African-American males in the U.S. population, compared with 1,200 per 100,000 Hispanic males in the U.S. population and 487 per 100,000 white males in the U.S. population. Among African-American females, 149 per 100,000 in the U.S. population were in state or federal prison in 2008, compared with 75 Hispanic female inmates per

100,000 in the U.S. population and 50 white females per 100,000 in the U.S. population.

Clearly, in 2008, a disproportionate number of minorities—in particular, African Americans—were incarcerated in state and federal prisons. Nonetheless, from 2000 to 2008, the trend in imprisonment and rates of incarceration showed a modest decline among African Americans. In 2000, around 610,300 African Americans were confined in state and federal prisons nationwide, compared with around 591,900 in 2008, representing a decline of 18,400 during that time period. By contrast, from 2000 to 2008, the number of white prison inmates in state and federal prisons increased, from 471,000 to 528,200, as did the number of Hispanic inmates, from 216,900 to 313,100. Rates of incarceration were similarly lower among African Americans from 2000 to 2008, dropping from 3,457 to 3,161 African-American male inmates per 100,000 in the U.S. population and 205 to 149 African-American female inmates per 100,000 in the U.S. population. For whites, the rate of incarceration increased from 449 to 487 per 100,000 white males in the U.S. population and from 34 to 50 per 100,000 white females in the U.S. population. Among Hispanic male prison inmates, the rate of incarceration declined slightly between 2000 and 2008, from 1,220 to 1,200 per 100,000 Hispanic males in the U.S. population. However, the incarceration rate increased more significantly for Hispanic females, from 60 to 75 per 100,000 Hispanic females in the U.S. population.

One explanation for the declining incarceration trends among African-American inmates in state prisons—which house most inmates in the United States—was that fewer African Americans were incarcerated in state prisons for drug offenses. Approximately 56 percent of the decline in African Americans in state prisons from 2000 and 2006 was the result of some 29,600 fewer African Americans being imprisoned for drug offenses. By contrast, the number of white drug offenders (13,800 inmates) and Hispanic drug offenders (14,700 inmates) incarcerated in state prison increased over the same period.[32]

AGING PRISONERS

In 2008, 140,610 inmates in state and federal prisons nationwide were under a sentence of life imprisonment. Of those, more than 41,000 inmates were serving life sentences without possibility of parole. From 2003 to 2008, the number of such prisoners increased by about 22 percent.[33] As a result, those inmates will grow old in prison. Some aging inmates will die in prison. For example, from 2001 to 2004, inmates who were 65 years of age or older composed only about 1 percent of all state prisoners, yet they accounted for 15 percent of prisoner deaths.

Aging prisoners present special challenges in correctional setting. Among the challenges are vulnerability to abuse and predation as they grow older; difficulty establishing social relationships with younger inmates; and the need for special accommodations in correctional settings that are often rigid and inflexible. However, in an era of fiscal crisis in U.S. corrections, perhaps the most pressing challenge presented by aging inmates is their disproportionate use of costly resources, primarily health care services.

The mortality rates of older prisoners highlight many of the health problems that arise in the incarcerated population as a whole, because most deaths among inmates 65 and older were the result of chronic illnesses, including heart disease, cancer, and liver disease. Moreover, the death rate from illness rose with the length of time served in prison. For example, from 2001 to 2004, the mortality rate from heart disease among inmates who were imprisoned for 120 months or longer was 160 per 100,000 in the U.S. population, almost double the mortality rate of 84 per 100,000 for inmates who served 60 to 119 months in prison, and more than three times the mortality rate of 47 per 100,000 for inmates who served 60 months or less in prison. Similarly, the mortality rate from cancer in inmates who served 120 months or longer in prison was 160 per 100,000 in the U.S. population. This is nearly double the mortality rate from cancer of 84 per 100,000 for inmates who served 60 to 119 months in prison and more than three times higher than the mortality rate from cancer of 47 per 100,000 for inmates who served less than 60 months in state prison. In other words, the longer an inmate was incarcerated in prison, the greater the likelihood of developing chronic diseases such as cancer and heart disease, which require costly medical treatment.[34]

The problem of aging inmates with chronic illnesses is compounded when those conditions go untreated at a younger age and eventually become worse—which is the case in many prisons nationwide, according to "The Health and Health Care of U.S. Prisoners: A Nationwide Survey" (2009), the first comprehensive study of health care for prison and jail inmates nationwide. Among the study's findings was that, nationwide, some 20 percent of sick inmates in state prisons and nearly 14 percent of federal inmates who were ill had not been seen by a physician or a nurse since they entered prison. As a result, when compared to their counterparts in the U.S. population, state prison inmates were 31 percent more likely to suffer from asthma, 55 percent more likely to have diabetes, and 90 percent more likely to suffer a heart attack. In addition, in about 25 percent of cases of prison inmates with chronic diseases, such as diabetes, medication to treat the illness was stopped at the time of incarceration.

The denial of medical care to inmates is of consequence to communities nationwide when those inmates are released from prison or jail. According to Andrew P. Wilper, M.D., one of the authors of the report on the study's findings, "Twelve million Americans are released from prisons and jails each year.

These individuals and the communities to which they return suffer as many carry with them the costs of untreated illness and preventable disability."[35]

MENTALLY ILL PRISONERS

Historically, the mentally ill received institutional care in the United States, primarily in mental hospitals or asylums. Beginning in the early 1960s, many states began to downsize their mental institutions. This occurred for several reasons, including the development of antipsychotic medication that made the severely mentally ill more manageable and allowed them to be treated in outpatient facilities at significantly lower costs to government agencies. In addition, changes to state and federal laws gave the mentally ill due process rights that included safeguards against involuntary commitments to mental institutions and reduced the length of time that patients could be involuntarily committed to mental hospitals.

With deinstitutionalization came the promise of increased community services for the mentally ill. Many of those programs, however, never materialized due to lack of funding by the states and the federal government. The result was that mentally ill individuals were often cut off from publicly funded programs for treatment, either because the programs were limited or unavailable or because mentally ill patients did not have the ability or the support to avail themselves of the services. Without treatment, mentally ill persons sometimes resorted to self-medication through alcohol or drugs. Some became homeless, putting them at a higher risk of criminal victimization or arrest. In addition, the difficulty of obtaining court orders for involuntary commitments for the severely disturbed created a public safety issue. The consequence was that an increasing number of mentally ill individuals entered the U.S. criminal justice system, which was ill-equipped to care for them.

According to data from the Bureau of Justice Statistics' five-year census of U.S. correctional facilities, as of June 30, 2005, some 56 percent of state prison inmates and 45 percent of federal prison inmates had mental health problems, as defined by a recent history or manifestation of symptoms of a mental illness. Among state prison inmates, 73 percent of females and 55 percent of males had mental health problems. In federal prisons, about 61 percent of female inmates and 43 percent of male inmates had mental health issues.

Both state and federal inmates exhibited a broad spectrum of symptoms of mental illness. Among the most serious were psychotic disorder symptoms, and nearly 12 percent of state prisoners and almost 8 percent of federal prisoners were delusional, while nearly 8 percent of state prison inmates and almost 5 percent of federal prisoners experienced hallucinations.

Symptoms of major depressive disorders were reported five or more times in about 24 percent of state prison inmates and about 16 percent of federal prisoners.

Some 13 percent of state prison inmates suffering from mental illness reported being homeless during the year prior to their incarceration, compared with only 6.3 percent of state prisoners who did not have mental health issues. Among federal prisoners, these figures were 6.6 percent homeless for those with mental health issues and 2.6 percent for those without. Inmates with mental health disorders also reported a higher incidence of physical or sexual abuse prior to incarceration: 27 percent of state inmates and 17 percent of federal inmates with mental health disorders reported being physically abused, compared with 10.5 percent of state inmates and 6.4 percent of federal inmates without mental illness. While 12.5 percent of state prison inmates and 7.3 percent of federal inmates with mental health problems reported being sexually abused in the past, this was true of only 3.8 percent of state inmates and 1.7 percent of federal inmates without mental health disorders.

Because the mentally ill sometimes abuse alcohol and drugs as a means of self-medicating—as an effort to alleviate the symptoms of their mental illness—it is not surprising that prison inmates with mental illness reported higher rates of substance abuse prior to incarceration than inmates without mental health issues. Nearly three-quarters (74.1 percent) of state prisoners and nearly two-thirds (63.6 percent) of federal prisoners with a mental health problem reported substance abuse or dependence prior to incarceration. In comparison, about 55 percent of state prison inmates and about 50 percent of federal inmates without mental health problems reported substance abuse or dependence prior to imprisonment. In addition, inmates with mental health problems were more likely to have been using alcohol or drugs at the time they committed the offense for which they were arrested and sentenced to prison. About 53.2 percent of state prison inmates and 41.1 percent of federal prisoners were using alcohol or drugs at the time of their offense, compared with 42.5 percent of state inmates and 30.6 percent of federal inmates without mental health issues. Failure to take prescribed psychiatric medications also contributes to the incarceration of mentally ill offenders. Of all mentally ill state and federal prison inmates who were being treated with psychiatric medications prior to their arrest, about two-thirds of them were not using the medication at the time of their arrest.[36]

PRISONERS ON DEATH ROW

The number of prisoners under sentence of death in the United States increased from about 150 in 1953 to just over 500 in 1970. In 1972, the U.S.

Supreme Court in *Furman v. Georgia* ruled that the death penalty violated the Eighth Amendment's ban against cruel and unusual punishment. However, in its 1976 ruling in *Gregg v. Georgia*, the U.S. Supreme Court effectively lifted the ban on the death penalty in the United States, and executions resumed nationwide.

In 2009 there were 52 executions in the United States, an increase from 37 executions in 2008. One hundred six individuals received sentences of death in 2009, for a total of 3,279 individuals under sentence of death in the United States. In 2009, nine men under sentences of death were exonerated and released from prison, representing the second highest number of exonerations in one year since 2003, when 12 individuals facing the death penalty were exonerated and set free.[37]

As of 2008, 56.1 percent of death row inmates were white or of Hispanic origin, while 41.7 percent were African American. Since African Americans composed about 12 percent of the U.S. population, they were disproportionately represented on death row. On average, death row inmates were 43 years of age in 2008. Of those, one-half were 27 years old or younger at the time they committed the offense for which they received the death penalty.[38]

On March 1, 2005, the U.S. Supreme Court ruled in the case of *Roper v. Simmons* that the imposition of the death penalty for juveniles who were under 18 years of age at the time they committed a capital offense was a violation of the Eight Amendment's ban on cruel and unusual punishment and the Fourteenth Amendment's guarantee of due process. The Court's 5 to 4 decision in *Roper* abolished the death penalty for juvenile offenders in all state and federal jurisdictions.

The Supreme Court's decision in *Roper v. Simmons* is discussed in detail in Chapter 2, in the *Cruel and Unusual Punishment* section of *U.S. Supreme Court Cases.*

PRISON VIOLENCE

The regimented daily routine of prison life gives inmates little individual responsibility. By not conforming to the order of prison life, inmates run the risk of being ostracized and becoming victims of violence. Even those who conform sometimes find it difficult to avoid conflict and violence in an oppressive and intolerant prison environment.

Prison violence is generally inflicted by one inmate against another inmate, although violence may also be directed against corrections staff. Inmate-on-inmate violence is most common in male prisons. Female prisoners are more likely to be victimized by staff members or to engage in self-inflicted violence, such as self-mutilation or attempted suicide.

There are myriad causes of prison violence, and the incidence of violence is usually a factor of the particular conditions and inmate population at a given institution. However, in general, one of the main causes of prison violence is overcrowding, which can make inmates more prone to commit acts of violence by creating elevated rates of depression, anxiety, and stress among inmates. Also, the shift from rehabilitation to punishment has exacerbated conditions that may lead to prison violence, such as harsh disciplinary action for even minor infractions.

From 2001 to 2006, 299 state prison inmates were victims of homicide. Of those, 55 state prisoners died in custody in 2006, compared with 56 in 2005.[39] In 2005, inmate assaults were twice as likely to occur between inmates than between inmates and correctional staff. However, inmate-on-inmate and staff-on-inmate assaults are sometimes not reported due to fear of retaliation against the inmate reporting such an assault.

PRISON GANGS

Prison gangs operate in state and federal prisons nationwide as highly structured criminal enterprises that engage in the trafficking of various types of contraband, including illicit drugs and cellular telephones. Like street gangs, prison gangs often operate by means of intimidation and violence in order to advance their criminal enterprises. As a result, affiliation with a prison gang is a significant indicator of an inmate's potential for misconduct in prison, including acts of physical and sexual violence.

Increasingly, prison gangs have extended their reach into communities. Members of prison gangs who are released from custody commonly return to their local communities and resume gang activity on behalf of the prison gang. This often includes the recruitment of new gang members who, although they are technically street gang members, operate under the direction of prison gang leaders. Because prison gangs have extended their reach—and their potential for intimidation and violence—into communities, inmates affiliated with gangs in prison often have difficulty leaving the prison gang after their release from prison.

In general, there are three levels of prison gangs in active operation inside U.S. correctional facilities. National-level prison gangs pose the most serious threat to institutional safety, as they are highly organized and maintain rigid rules of conduct that are strictly enforced by gang leaders in prison, who are sometimes referred to as shot-callers. Regional-level prison gangs are organized like their national-level counterparts but generally operate in a limited number of state prison systems. Local-level prison gangs, also referred to as state-level prison gangs, are typically confined to operation within one state.[40]

Introduction to Prisons

The National Gang Intelligence Center (NGIC), part of the U.S. Department of Justice, is a centralized resource for information on prison gangs and other types of gangs operating in the United States. In 2009, seven prison gangs of significance were operating in U.S. state and federal correctional facilities, according to NGIC, which provided the following profiles.

The **Aryan Brotherhood** (AB) was originally ruled by consensus but is now highly structured with two factions—one in the California Department of Corrections and Rehabilitation and the other in the Federal Bureau of Prisons (BOP). The majority of members are Caucasian males, and the gang is active primarily in the southwestern and Pacific regions of the United States. The Aryan Brotherhood's main source of income is the distribution of cocaine, heroin, marijuana, and methamphetamine within prison systems and on the streets. Some AB members have business relationships with Mexican drug trafficking operations that smuggle illegal drugs into California for distribution by the Aryan Brotherhood. The Aryan Brotherhood is historically linked to the Mexican Mafia, also known as La Eme, which is a California-based Hispanic prison gang. However, there is increasing tension between the two gangs.

Barrio Azteca is a violent, highly structured prison gang that had some 2,000 members in 2009. Most members were Mexican nationals or Mexican-American males. Barrio Azteca is most active in the Southwest, primarily in federal, state, and local corrections facilities in Texas. The gang's main source of income is smuggling heroin, powder cocaine, and marijuana from Mexico into the United States for distribution both inside and outside prisons. Gang members operating outside of prison often transport illicit drugs across the U.S.-Mexico border. Barrio Azteca members have also been involved in arson, auto theft, burglary, extortion, kidnapping, robbery, and weapons violations.

The **Black Guerrilla Family** (BGF), originally called Black Family or Black Vanguard, was founded in 1966 at the state prison at San Quentin, California. The gang is organized along paramilitary lines, with a supreme leader and a central committee. The BGF has a national charter, code of ethics, and oath of allegiance, with members operating primarily in California and Maryland. In 2009 the gang had up to 300 members, most of whom were African-American males. A primary source of income for the gang was cocaine and marijuana distribution. Members of the gang were also involved in other criminal activities, including auto theft, burglary, and homicide.

The **Hermanos de Pistoleros Latinos** (HPL) is a Hispanic prison gang formed in the late 1980s within the Texas Department of Criminal Justice. In 2009, the HPL operated in most Texas state prisons in communities throughout Texas, particularly Laredo, Texas. In addition, the HPL is active in several cities in Mexico, primarily in Nuevo Laredo. Estimated at

1,000 members in 2009, the HPL was involved in the trafficking of cocaine and marijuana from Mexico into the United States.

The **Mexikanemi** prison gang (also known as the Texas Mexican Mafia, or Emi) was formed in the early 1980s within the Texas Department of Criminal Justice. The gang is highly structured and is estimated to have 2,000 members, most of whom are Mexican nationals or Mexican-American males who were living in Texas at the time of their incarceration. Mexikanemi engages in drug trafficking in the southwestern United States, particularly Texas. In addition, the Mexikanemi gang maintains a relationship with Los Zetas, a Mexican paramilitary organization suspected of engaging in criminal activity.

The **Mexican Mafia** prison gang, also known as La Eme (the Spanish pronunciation for the letter *M*) was formed in the late 1950s within the California Department of Corrections and Rehabilitation. The gang is loosely structured but imposes strict rules on its approximately 200 members. Most members of the Mexican Mafia are Mexican-American males who previously belonged to southern California street gangs. The Mexican Mafia is primarily active in the southwestern and Pacific regions of the United States, but its power base is in California. The gang's main source of income is extorting drug distributors outside prison and distributing methamphetamine, cocaine, heroin, and marijuana within prison systems and in communities. The Mexican Mafia also is involved in other criminal activities, including gambling.

Ñeta is a prison gang that began in Puerto Rico and gained a foothold in the continental United States. In 2009, Ñeta was one of the largest and most violent prison gangs, with about 7,000 members in Puerto Rico and 5,000 in the United States. Ñeta chapters in Puerto Rico exist exclusively inside prisons. Once members are released from prison they are no longer considered part of the gang. In the United States, Ñeta chapters exist inside and outside prisons in 36 cities in nine states, primarily in the Northeast. The gang's main income is derived from the distribution of powder and crack cocaine, heroin, and marijuana. Ñeta has also been associated with auto theft, burglary, extortion, money laundering, and trafficking in weapons and explosives.[41]

PRISONER RAPE
AND SEXUAL ASSAULT

Under the Prison Rape Elimination Act of 2003, the U.S. Bureau of Justice Statistics (BJS) is authorized to monitor and collect data on the incidence of rape and sexual victimization in state and federal prisons nationwide. (A discussion of the Prison Rape Elimination Act of 2003 is presented in chapter 2, and the Executive Summary of the Prison Rape Elimination Act Commission's 2009 report is presented as Appendix B.) According to BJS data, in 2007, there were some 27,500 reported occurrences of sexual assault in prisons nationwide. Of those, approximately 16,800 were nonconsensual sexual acts, while about 10,600 were reported as "abusive sexual contacts" that involved unwanted touching of a victim's body in a sexually suggestive manner. In addition, there were approximately 38,600 reported occurrences of sexual misconduct by correctional staff in 2007. Of those, some 22,700 involved an unwilling inmate, while in 15,900, inmates reported that they were willing to engage in the sexual acts.[42]

Most perpetrators of rape on male prisoners were heterosexual males. Their victims tended to be inmates who were incarcerated for less serious offenses than those of their rapists. Most inmate-on-inmate sexual abuse in prison was between individuals who knew each other. Generally, the sexual attack was preceded by a period of sexually aggressive comments and threats.

The most serious concern of victims after being raped was the risk of contracting the human immunodeficiency virus (HIV), which in 2008 infected about 1.5 percent of inmates held in state and federal prisons. In 2008, there were some 21,987 reported cases of HIV/AIDS (acquired immunodeficiency syndrome) in state and federal prisons, representing a slight increase from 2007, when there were some 21,644 reported cases of HIV/AIDS in prisons nationwide. State prisons accounted for most of the reported cases of HIV/AIDS—20,499—while federal prisons accounted for the remaining 1,538 reported cases. In 2008, cases of HIV/AIDS were reported in about 1.5 percent of male prison inmates, accounting for 20,075 of such cases, while cases of HIV/AIDS were reported among 1.9 percent of female inmates, for a total of 1,912 such cases.[43]

CORRECTIONAL STAFF

Prisons are 24-hour institutions. As such, there must be correctional staff members in place at all times for prisons to function. Among prison staff members, correctional officers are responsible for the control, security, and movement of inmates within correctional institutions. Correctional officers regularly interact with inmates, and individual officers often must control entire groups of prisoners in common areas of an institution, such as hallways and work areas.

Correctional officers perform a variety of duties in prisons, including the following:

- Block Officers are responsible for supervising as many as 300 to 400 prisoners confined in a cell block. Their duties include watching for signs of self-destructive behavior, checking cells for fires or other hazards, and managing any behavioral or medical problem that may arise.

- Work Detail Supervisors oversee groups of inmates assigned to various work details within a prison, including the laundry room, kitchen, and industrial shop. They control access to supplies, including cutlery and work tools that can be used as weapons by prisoners against other inmates or correctional officers.

- Industrial Shop and School Officers are generally assigned in groups of two or three to supervise groups of inmates in vocational or educational settings. Generally, these officers work with civilian employees, such as teachers, and are therefore responsible for their security and safety, as well as that of inmates.

- Administrative Building Assignment Officers are responsible for the overall functioning of the correctional facility. Their duties include opening and closing security doors and staffing checkpoints where visitors enter and exit the prison. Generally, these officers have little direct contact with inmates.

- Wall Posts are correctional officers who are stationed on the wall towers located on the outer perimeter of most prisons. These officers generally work in small guard towers, where they are confined for most of their work shift.

- Relief Officers substitute for other correctional officers on their days off. Because relief officers are required to perform a variety of duties, their jobs offer some variety but are also stressful.

Job-related stress was widely reported by correctional officers, according to a 2000 report by the National Institute of Corrections. Sources of correctional officer stress include the need to work overtime and rotating shifts as the result of understaffing, threats and actual incidents of inmate violence against staff, poor public image, low pay, and the risk of job burnout. Another source of stress that was widely reported by correctional officers was inmates who attempt to manipulate correctional staff. For example, officers reported that some inmates repeatedly made demands for items such as cigarettes and extra food in exchange for their implicit promise to keep other inmates in line. In addition, about 22 percent of correctional officers reported that problems with coworkers created the most stressful aspect of their job. These problems included burned-out coworkers venting their frustrations on their colleagues, fear that certain coworkers would not assist in confrontations with inmates, and inappropriate behavior of coworkers toward inmates, such as helping prisoners smuggle contraband into the prison or using unnecessary force against inmates. Female correctional officers reported sexist attitudes by their colleagues and sexual harassment by their supervisors as a common source of stress on the job.[44]

According to data from the Bureau of Justice Statistics' five-year census of U.S. correctional facilities, in 2005, about 445,000 correctional staff members were working in state and federal correctional facilities nationwide. Of those, 295,261 were employed as correctional officers, of whom 85 percent of were male. Nationally, the ratio of inmates to corrections officers in state and federal prisons increased from 4.8 to 1 in 2000 to 5.1 to 1 in 2005.

Additional occupational categories in correctional facilities in 2005 included administrators, who accounted for about 2 percent of all correctional staff; clerical and maintenance employees, who composed about 12 percent of correctional staff; and educational instructors and staff, who accounted for about 3 percent of correctional staff nationwide. Professional and technical correctional staff—composed of physicians, dentists, nurses, counselors, chaplains, mental health professionals, and classification officers—accounted for 10 percent of U.S. prison corrections staff in 2005.[45]

PAROLE AND RECIDIVISM

There are three legal ways out of prison: death, pardon, and parole. Pardons are rare. Although state governors and the president of the United States have the power to pardon anyone, pardons are generally granted only in cases of false imprisonment due to egregious miscarriages of justice. Parole is the most common way that prisoners are released from prison. Parole is administered by federal and state correctional agencies. Parole is sometimes confused with probation, which is a period of court supervision imposed on a criminal offender at the time of sentencing. Probation is imposed as an alternative to incarceration or as an adjunct to incarceration of one year or less in county jail. By contrast, parole occurs only after a period of imprisonment. Prisoners become eligible for parole after they have served the portion of their sentence required by law. For example, in California, individuals sentenced to prison for violent crimes, such as robbery, must serve 85 percent of their total sentence before becoming eligible for parole. If parole is granted, the term of parole is the amount of time remaining on the original sentence. For example, for an individual who is paroled after serving eight years of a 10-year sentence, the maximum term of parole is two years. Parole expires after that period of time, absent any violations of the law or of the conditions of parole.

The term *parole* originated in 1846, when it was first used by Boston philanthropist S. G. Howe in a letter to the Prison Association of New York. States began to adopt parole selection procedures, which were usually administered by a commissioner of parole appointed by the governor. As the result of abuses of power, however, many states replaced parole commissioners with parole boards, beginning around 1945. In some states, parole boards are part of the department of corrections, while in others they function independently. In both cases, members of a state's parole boards are usually appointed by the governor.

Federal parole began in 1910, when parole boards were established at each of the three federal prisons. In 1930, the U.S. Congress created the Board of Parole, which consisted of three members appointed by the U.S. attorney general. In 1950, membership was increased to eight. The Board of Parole was reorganized in 1972 into five regions, with one board member and five hearing examiners assigned to each region. The Comprehensive Crime Control Act of 1984 established the U.S. Sentencing Commission, which in 1987 promulgated determinate sentencing guidelines that significantly limited the power of the Board of Parole. The Comprehensive Crime Control Act of 1984 also contained a provision to phase out the Board of Parole by 1992 and to establish the U.S. Parole Commission to oversee defendants who committed offenses prior to adoption of federal sentencing guidelines on November 1, 1987. As a result, the responsibility of the Parole Commission shifted from overseeing all federal parolees to primarily overseeing federal parolees in Washington, D.C. The Parole Commission Phaseout Act of 1996 required the attorney general to report annually to Congress whether it was more cost-effective to maintain the Parole Commission as a separate agency or to incorporate its functions into another government agency. By 2006, more than two-thirds of the approximately 15,000 individuals under the supervision of the Parole Commission were convicted of criminal offenses in Washington, D.C.

In both the state and federal parole systems, when an inmate is eligible for parole, he or she appears before the parole board at a hearing. Often, representatives of the prisoner's crime victims also have the right to be present if they wish to advocate against parole. If parole is granted based on an inmate's favorable behavior while incarcerated and the belief that the inmate is not likely to reoffend the parolee is required to report to a parole officer or agent in the community where the parolee plans to reside or is allowed to reside by the parole board. Often, paroled sex offenders are ordered to reside in localities other than their home communities in order to protect the sex offender from possible harassment or violence and to avoid inflaming the sex offender's home community. Parole is granted under certain conditions established by law and set forth by the parole board. Those conditions often include not associating with convicted felons, not owning or carrying a firearm, and reporting to a parole agent on a regular basis. Failure to comply with any of these conditions constitutes a technical violation of parole and may necessitate a parole revocation hearing. An arrest for a new felony also is grounds for revocation of parole. As a result of the 1971 ruling by the U.S. Supreme Court in *Morrissey v. Brewer* (408 U.S. 271), parolees are guaranteed certain rights at parole revocation hearings, including written notification of the pending charges or reasons for parole revocation and the right to hear evidence against them, refute testimony, and cross-examine witnesses.

In 2002, there were more than 750,000 individuals on parole in the United States, an increase of almost 3 percent from 2001 and almost twice the average increase of 1.5 percent since 1995. Mandatory releases accounted for 52 percent of those entering parole, compared with 45 percent in 1995. In other words, more prisoners were released on parole because it was required by law and not as the result of their good behavior or successful rehabilitation while in prison. Such mandatory releases are commonly part of the stricter sentencing laws implemented by many states and the federal government.

In 2008, 828,869 individuals were on parole in the United States, representing almost a 1 percent increase from the number of parolees in 2007. However, the growth in parolees from 2007 to 2008 was less than the 1.7 percent average annual increase of individuals on parole from 2000 to 2008. In 2008, approximately 574,000 individuals exited parole. The exit rate for parolees in 2008 was 70 per 100 parolees—meaning that 70 percent of all individuals on parole were discharged at some time during 2008. Of those, about 49 percent were discharged as the result of successful completion of parole, while 36 percent were discharged as the result of being re-incarcerated in state prison. Among all parolees in 2008, about 9 percent were returned to prison for committing a new offense, and another 36 percent were re-incarcerated as the result of parole revocation, usually for failing to comply with the terms and conditions of their parole.[46]

FELONY DISENFRANCHISEMENT

In most states in 2008, convicted felons were not allowed to exercise certain rights, including the right to vote in elections. Laws prohibiting felons from voting and exercising other rights are known as felony disenfranchisement laws. Only in Vermont and Maine are convicted felons in prison allowed to vote in elections, according to a report by the Sentencing Project. All other states and the District of Columbia prohibit voting by prisoners. In addition, 35 states do not allow convicted felons on parole to vote. Two states, Louisiana and Virginia, deny the right to vote to all individuals who have completed their sentence in state prison.

An estimated 5.3 million people in the United States in 2008 have lost their right to vote, either temporarily or permanently, as the result of a felony conviction or imprisonment. Of those, in 2008, some 1.4 million African-American men were disenfranchised. This represents 13 percent of all African-American males in the United States, or approximately seven times the national average for felony disenfranchisement. Among women, nearly 677,000 females in the United States in 2008 were ineligible to vote as the result of felony convictions or incarceration in prison.

A number of states have begun to reconsider their disenfranchisement laws. Most recently, in 2007, the Office of Executive Clemency in Florida voted to reinstate voting rights for most individuals convicted of nonviolent offenses. That same year the Maryland legislature repealed the state's lifetime voting ban for prisoners and instituted a policy to restore voting rights to individuals upon successful completion of their sentences. In 2006, voters in Rhode Island approved a referendum to restore voting rights to individuals on probation and parole, and Tennessee simplified its voting restoration procedures to allow for all convicted felons to restore their voting rights.[47]

[1] *Fiscal Year 2009 Annual Report*, Federal Prison Industries, Federal Bureau of Prisons, U.S. Department of Justice, p. 14.

[2] *National Crime Victimization Survey Violent Crime Trends, 1973–2002*. Bureau of Justice Statistics, Office of Justice Programs, U.S. Department of Justice, 2003, p. 1.

[3] William J. Sabol, et al. *Prisoners in 2008*. Bureau of Justice Statistics, Office of Justice Programs, U.S. Department of Justice, December 2009, p. 2.

[4] Ashley Nellis and Ryan S. King. "No Exit: The Expanding Use of Life Sentences in America." The Sentencing Project, July 2009, p. 3.

[5] Press Release, Drug Policy News, Drug Policy Alliance Network, July 27, 2009, p. 1.

[6] James J. Stephan. *Census of State and Federal Correctional Facilities, 2005*. National Prisoner Statistics Program, Office of Justice Programs, U.S. Department of Justice, October 2008, p. 4.

[7] Daniel P. Mears. *Evaluating the Effectiveness of Supermax Prisons*. Justice Police Center, Urban Institute, June 2005, p. 3.

[8] "The Death Penalty in 2009: Year End Report." Death Penalty Information Center, January 2010, pp. 1–4.

[9] "The Death Penalty in 2009: Year End Report." Death Penalty Information Center, January 2010, pp. 4–8.

[10] James J. Stephan. *Census of State and Federal Correctional Facilities, 2005*. National Prisoner Statistics Program, Office of Justice Programs, U.S. Department of Justice, October 2008, pp. 1–5.

[11] Patrick Griffin and Melanie King. *State Juvenile Justice Profiles*, National Center for Juvenile Justice, May 2006, p. 1.

[12] Sarah Hockenberry, et al. *Juvenile Residential Facility Census, 2006: Selected Findings*. National Report Series, Office of Juvenile Justice and Delinquency Preven-

tion, Office of Justice Programs, U.S. Department of Justice, December 2009, pp. 2–7.

[13] Heather C. West and William J. Sabol. *Prison Inmates at Midyear 2008—Statistical Tables*, Bureau of Justice Statistics, Office of Justice Programs, U.S. Department of Justice, March 2009, p. 20.

[14] *Different from Adults: An Updated Analysis of Juvenile Transfer and Blended Sentencing Laws, with Recommendations for Reform*, National Center for Juvenile Justice, November 2008, pp. 1–4.

[15] R. Redding. *Juvenile Transfer Laws: An Effective Deterrent to Delinquency?* Office of Juvenile Justice and Delinquency Prevention, Office of Justice Programs, U.S. Department of Justice, August 2008, pp. 1–3.

[16] Kristin Henning. *The Case Against Juvenile Life Without Parole: Good Policy and Good Law.* FindLaw.com, October 2009, pp. 1–2.

[17] Henry E. Allen and Clifford E. Simonsen. *Corrections in America: An Introduction*, Ninth Edition. Upper Saddle River, N.J.: Prentice Hall, 2000, p. 295.

[18] James J. Stephan. *Census of State and Federal Correctional Facilities, 2005.* National Prisoner Statistics Program, Office of Justice Programs, U.S. Department of Justice, October 2008, pp. 2–4.

[19] *Sourcebook of Criminal Justice Statistics*, Bureau of Justice Statistics, Office of Justice Programs, U.S. Department of Justice, August 2007, Table 1.2.2006.

[20] William J. Sabol et al. *Prisoners in 2008.* Bureau of Justice Statistics, Office of Justice Programs, U.S. Department of Justice, December 2009, p. 8.

[21] James J. Stephan. *Census of State and Federal Correctional Facilities, 2005.* National Prisoner Statistics Program, Office of Justice Programs, U.S. Department of Justice, October 2008, pp. 1–3.

[22] News report, National Public Radio, December 15, 2009.

[23] Ryan S. King et al. "Big Prisons, Small Towns: Prison Economics in Rural America." Report, The Sentencing Project, February 2003, p. 13.

[24] Terry Besser. "The Development of Last Resort." Paper, presented at the Rural Sociological Society, August 2003, p. 2.

[25] Ryan S. King et al. "Big Prisons, Small Towns: Prison Economics in Rural America." Report, The Sentencing Project, February 2003, pp. 8–11.

[26] Dexter Whitfield. *Economic Impact of Prisons in Rural Areas, a Review of the Issues.* European Services Strategy Unit, September 2008, pp. 8–11.

[27] Christine S. Scott-Hayward. *The Fiscal Crisis in Corrections: Rethinking Policies and Practice.* Vera Institute of Justice, July 2009, pp. 1–12.

[28] William J. Sabol et al. *Prisoners in 2008.* Bureau of Justice Statistics, Office of Justice Programs, U.S. Department of Justice, December 2009, p. 1.

[29] ———. *Prisoners in 2008.* Bureau of Justice Statistics, Office of Justice Programs, U.S. Department of Justice, December 2009, pp. 8–21.

[30] Lauren E. Glaze and Laura M. Maruschak. *Parents in Prison and Their Minor Children.* Special Report, Bureau of Justice Statistics, Office of Justice Programs, U.S. Department of Justice, revised January 2009, p. 19.

[31] ———. *Parents in Prison and Their Minor Children.* Special Report, Bureau of Justice Statistics, Office of Justice Programs, U.S. Department of Justice, revised January 2009, pp. 1–7.

[32] William J. Sabol et al. *Prisoners in 2008.* Bureau of Justice Statistics, Office of Justice Programs, U.S. Department of Justice, December 2009, pp. 4–6.

[33] Ashley Nellis and Ryan S. King. *No Exit: The Expanding Use of Life Sentences in America.* The Sentencing Project, July 2009, p. 3.

[34] Christopher J. Mumola. *Medical Causes of Death in State Prisons, 2001–2004.* Data Brief, Bureau of Justice Statistics, Office of Justice Programs, U.S. Department of Justice, January 2007, pp. 2–3.

[35] Andrew P. Wilper, M.D., et al. "The Health and Health Care of U.S. Prisoners: A Nationwide Survey." *American Journal of Public Health*, vol. 99, no. 4 (January 2009): 1–2.

[36] Doris J. James and Lauren E. Glaze. *Mental Health Problems of Prison and Jail Inmates.* Special Report, Bureau of Justice Statistics, Office of Justice Programs, U.S. Department of Justice, revised December 2006, pp. 1–6.

[37] "The Death Penalty in 2009: Year End Report." Death Penalty Information Center, January 2010, pp. 1–2.

[38] Tracy L. Snell. *Capital Punishment, 2008—Statistical Tables.* Bureau of Justice Statistics, Office of Justice Programs, U.S. Department of Justice, December 2009, Tables 5, 7.

[39] Christopher J. Mumola and Margaret E. Noonan. *Deaths in Custody Statistical Tables,* Bureau of Justice Statistics, Office of Justice Programs, U.S. Department of Justice, 2009, Table 1.

[40] *The National Gang Threat Assessment 2009,* National Gang Intelligence Center, January 2009, pp. 7–8.

[41] *The National Gang Threat Assessment 2009,* National Gang Intelligence Center, January 2009, Appendix C.

[42] Allen J. Beck and Paige M. Harrison. *Sexual Victimization in State and Federal Prisons Reported by Inmates, 2007.* Special Report, Bureau of Justice Statistics, Office of Justice Programs, U.S. Department of Justice, Revised April 2008, pp. 1–2.

[43] Laura M. Marushak. *HIV in Prisons, 2007–08.* Bulletin, Bureau of Justice Statistics, Office of Justice Programs, U.S. Department of Justice, revised January 2010, pp. 1–2.

[44] Peter Finn. "Addressing Correctional Officer Stress: Programs and Strategies." *Issues and Practices in Criminal Justice,* National Institute of Justice, December 2000, pp. 11–14.

[45] James J. Stephan. *Census of State and Federal Correctional Facilities, 2005.* National Prisoner Statistics Program, Office of Justice Programs, U.S. Department of Justice, October 2008, pp. 4–5.

[46] Lauren E. Glaze and Thomas P. Bonczar. *Probation and Parole in the United States, 2008.* Bulletin, Bureau of Justice Statistics, Office of Justice Programs, U.S. Department of Justice, December 2009, pp. 1–7.

[47] "Felony Disenfranchisement Laws in the United States," The Sentencing Project, September 2008, pp. 1–3.

CHAPTER 2

THE LAW OF PRISONS

The U.S. Constitution is the cornerstone of the legal system in the United States. The first 10 amendments to the Constitution compose the Bill of Rights, which articulate the basic individual rights afforded to all Americans, including prisoners. They include the right of freedom of speech and religion under the First Amendment, the right of privacy and freedom from unreasonable searches under the Fourth Amendment, and the ban against cruel or unusual punishment under the Eighth Amendment. As originally articulated, the Bill of Rights applied only to actions by the federal government. However, under the due process clause of the Fourteenth Amendment, state and local governments are now held to the same standard. As a result, state and federal laws governing the administration of prisons and the treatment of prisoners in the United States must comply with constitutional protections. Otherwise, the laws may be challenged in state and federal courts, including the U.S. Supreme Court. A large body of rulings by the U.S. Supreme Court on the issues of prisons and prisoners' rights is presented later in this chapter, following a discussion of significant legislation on prisoners' rights and sentencing.

FEDERAL LEGISLATION

Section 1983 of Title 42 of the U.S. Code gives individuals the right to seek legal remedy in federal court if their constitutional rights are violated by state or local laws. Originally passed by the U.S. Congress as the Ku Klux Klan Act of 1871, section 1983 was enacted as a way to protect the newly acquired constitutional rights of African Americans after the end of the Civil War in 1865. Those rights included the prohibition of slavery under the Thirteenth Amendment, the right to due process of law and equal protection under the Fourteenth Amendment, and the right of every male citizen to vote under the Fifteenth Amendment. Because those rights were sometimes violated by state and local authorities, section 1983 gave victims the opportunity to bypass state courts and seek redress in the federal courts. The effect of section 1983 was largely muted, however, because of a tendency by federal judges to send cases back to the same state courts that had originally violated the victims' constitutional rights. Eventually, that practice helped to fuel the civil rights movement of the 1960s. As the cause of civil rights became national in scope, section 1983 began to be more effectively utilized by African Americans and others claiming violations of their civil rights, including prisoners.

Historically in the United States, prisoners were considered civilly dead. As such, state and federal courts adopted a *hands-off doctrine* toward prisoners who filed lawsuits, severely limiting the ability of prisoners to use the court system to seek redress for violations of their constitutional rights. The courts used the following rationales for their hands-off approach to prisoner litigation:

- Conditions of confinement in correctional facilities were an administrative matter that was best left to prison officials.
- Because society was largely unconcerned with conditions in prison, the courts had no public duty to interfere in the administration of prisons.
- Prisoners had fewer constitutional rights than other members of society. Therefore, prisoners' complaints were largely about their lack of privileges in prison and did not constitute a violation of their rights.

Beginning in the early 1960s, federal district courts began to move away from the hands-off doctrine, in part due to the efforts to advance prisoner litigation by organizations including the NAACP Legal Defense Fund and the American Civil Liberties Union's National Prison Project. In addition, the Black Muslims filed lawsuits on behalf of prisoners who were denied racial and religious equality. The legal avenue most widely used for prisoner litigation in federal courts was U.S. Code section 1983:

> *Every person who, under color of any statute, ordinance, regulation, custom, or usage of any State or Territory . . . subjects, or causes to be subjected, any citizen of the United States or other person within the jurisdiction thereof to the deprivation of any rights, privileges, or immunities secured by the Constitution and laws, shall be liable to the party innured in an action at law, suit in equity, or other proper proceeding for redress.*

Prisoners began to organize around the idea of equal rights and to protest the conditions of their confinement. Such protests sometimes erupted into inmate uprisings in prisons nationwide, including the riot at the state prison at Attica in New York in 1971, which resulted in 39 deaths. Many prisoners, however, sought remedy through the court system, especially in federal courts under section 1983. As a result of such court actions, prisoners won court victories on a number of issues, including the following:

- Equal Protection. Prison officials were not allowed to discriminate against inmates on the basis of race, religion, nationality, sex, political beliefs, or for any other arbitrary reason.
- Due Process. Prison officials were not allowed to restrict inmates' access to attorneys or the courts and were required to implement fair administrative procedures governing the punishment of prisoners for infractions in prison.
- Free Speech. The right of prisoners to freedom of speech and expression was extended to access to certain reading materials, limits on the censorship of certain mail, telephone access, and freedom of religious activity.
- Conditions of Confinement. The Eighth Amendment's prohibition of cruel and unusual punishment was broadened in scope to include decent living conditions, medical care, and the opportunity for physical exercise.

Under section 1983, remedy is available in the form of monetary damages paid to the injured party by those responsible for the injury. Monetary damages may include compensatory damages to repay the costs suffered by the injured party and additional punitive damages that are intended to punish the party responsible for the injury and deter that behavior in the future. Remedy under section 1983 is also possible through injunctions and declaratory judgments. An injunction is a court order requiring a defendant to do or not to do something. For example, under an injunction, prison officials can be ordered to make changes in the prison conditions that caused injury to the victims who won the lawsuit. A declaratory judgment is a legal finding by a court that the defendant has certain legal obligations or duties that must be met. If those obligations are not met, then at a later date the court may issue an injunction ordering the changes necessary to meet the legal obligation.

THE PRISON LITIGATION REFORM ACT

As prisoners achieved court victories on issues of prisoners' rights, more lawsuits were filed, particularly by state prison inmates seeking redress in the federal court system. For example, in 1966, some 218 cases were filed in federal courts by state prisoners. In 1992, there were 26,824 such filings by state inmates, and in 1996, there were more than 42,000 petitions filed in U.S. district courts by both federal and state inmates.[1]

Prisons

As early as 1980, the U.S. Congress attempted to reduce the rising number of federal court actions brought by prison inmates by passing the Civil Rights of Institutionalized Persons Act (CRIPA). One provision of CRIPA required state prisoners to exhaust their state prison grievance procedures before filing any action in federal court under section 1983. Because state participation in CRIPA was voluntary, however, the act had minimal effect on the increasing number of federal actions brought by prisoners. Federal courts exercised judicial discretion as another means of eliminating claims without merit that were brought by prisoners. For example, courts may dismiss actions that lack any arguable basis in fact or law. In some cases, federal courts dismissed claims by prisoners attempting to re-litigate previous actions. However, these efforts also failed to abate the rising number of federal lawsuits by prisoners. In part, the limited impact of CRIPA and judicial discretion was due to the rising number of prisoners in the United States as the result of sentencing reforms. For example, between 1980 and 1996, the rate at which prisoners filed actions in federal courts actually declined by some 17 percent.[2] In other words, decrease in the rate of filings was offset by the increase in prisoners nationwide, resulting in a net increase in filings in federal courts. In addition, news reports of frivolous filings by prisoners over issues such as being deprived of shampoo or deodorant helped to fuel the public's impression that lawsuits brought by prisoners were often without merit.

On April 26, 1996, the U.S. Congress passed the Prison Litigation Reform Act of 1995 (PLRA), which placed significant restrictions on the ability of prisoners to file civil rights claims in federal court under U.S. Code section 1983. The controlling authority for the PLRA is contained in U.S. Code, Title VIII, sections 801 and 802.

The PLRA was divided into two parts. The first part contained provisions originally included in the Stop Turning Out Prisoners Act of 1995, which was incorporated into the PLRA. Those provisions limited the ability of federal courts to enter injunctions against certain types of prison conditions, including overcrowding, in order to discourage courts from attempting to manage prisons. In that sense, the provisions in part one of the PLRA were a throwback to the *hands-off doctrine* of courts prior to 1960. The second part of the PLRA established a procedural framework for the filing of civil suits in federal court by prisoners. The procedures, which attempted to limit the number of actions in federal courts by making it more difficult to file lawsuits, included the following:

- Indigent litigants must pay a filing fee, although the fee may be paid in installments.
- Courts may dismiss lawsuits brought by prisoners if the action is "frivolous, malicious, or fails to state a claim" or if the named defendant is immune from such litigation.

- Prisoners are disqualified from filing lawsuits if they have three prior lawsuits that were dismissed as frivolous, malicious, or failing to state a claim. The only exception is if the prisoner is in imminent danger of serious harm.

- Prisoners must exhaust all administrative remedies before filing a lawsuit over prison conditions.

- Courts must dismiss all lawsuits by prisoners for "mental or emotional injury suffered while in custody" unless there is also a showing that there was physical injury.

- Attorneys are limited in the amount of fees they may collect for representing prisoner litigants.

By limiting federal actions available to prisoners, proponents of the PLRA hoped to reduce the caseload in federal courts and to encourage state and local correctional agencies to develop alternatives to litigation in the federal courts. Four common alternatives to litigation are the grievance board, the inmate grievance committee, the ombudsman, and mediation.

The grievance board is typically composed of correctional staff and may include lay members from the jurisdiction of the correctional facility. Grievance boards are charged with hearing and investigating complaints from inmates. After such an investigation, the board may issue recommendations, although the recommendations are not usually binding on staff members. If the recommendations are ignored by correctional staff, however, additional grievances may be filed with the grievance board. On the other hand, if the inmate's complaint is investigated but shown to have no merit, the grievance board has a record of the investigation, which may be used to demonstrate their good-faith effort to resolve the issue if it is pursued in court.

Inmate grievance committees operate much like grievance boards. The main difference is that inmate grievance committees include inmates among their members. Allowing inmates to sit on such committees is an attempt to bring some legitimacy to the process of investigating grievances, both to the inmates who filed complaints and to officials who oversee the board's actions. The use of inmates on grievance committees can be problematic, however. For example, inmates who sit on such committees might attempt to use their influence to control or intimidate other prisoners. Conversely, inmate committee members could be subjected to intimidation by inmates with grievances before the committee.

Ombudsman programs use an individual to represent the interests of the inmate filing a grievance. The ombudsman may be a correctional employee or someone from outside the correctional facility who is appointed or hired to fulfill that role. The role of the ombudsman is to ensure that the inmate has a fair hearing. To that end, the ombudsman is commonly allowed access to all parts of the correctional institution, including its records. An ombudsman is often free to expand an investigation if there is evidence of a more widespread problem than the inmate's initial complaint.

In most mediations, a professional mediator with no connections to the correctional institution or its controlling agency intervenes to reach a resolution that is binding on the parties to a dispute. Both parties enter into mediation with the understanding that the decision by the mediator is binding. In some jurisdictions, however, the prison's warden is given final authority over the mediator's decision. If the mediator's decision is overruled, the warden is generally required to do so in writing, and the warden's decision is commonly reviewed by officials within the correctional agency.

THE PRISON RAPE ELIMINATION ACT

In 2001, the report *No Escape: Male Rape in U.S. Prisons* by Human Rights Watch reported what many prison inmates and penologists already knew: Despite widespread anecdotal evidence of prison rape and sexual assault, there was no conclusive national data on the prevalence of inmate-on-inmate rape and sexual abuse in U.S. prisons. The paucity of data was due to a number of factors, including:

- Widespread underreporting of rapes and sexual abuse by inmate victims due to shame and fear of retaliation from predatory inmates.
- A failure among prison administrators to recognize the serious nature of sexual victimization in correctional settings and to implement meaningful prevention programs.
- A lack of specialized training for correctional staff charged with investigating reported incidents of prison rape and sexual abuse, resulting in a failure to preserve crime scene evidence and inadequate forensic interviewing of victims and perpetrators.

In response to reports of widespread prison rape and sexual assault by former inmates, activist organizations such as Human Rights Watch, and others, the Prison Rape Elimination Act (PREA) was passed by the 108th Congress of the United States and enacted into law on January 7, 2003.

The PREA established a zero-tolerance for prison rape in state and federal prisons nationwide, with the goal of implementing national standards for the reporting, punishment, and prevention of prison rape. Under the PREA, the Bureau of Justice Statistics (BJS) was mandated to conduct an annual statistic review of the incidence and effects of prison rape in correctional institutions nationwide. The PREA appropriated $15 million annually from fiscal years 2004 to 2010 to conduct the mandated research.

In 2009 the commission formed under PREA issued a report on prison rape and sexual assault in prisons and other detention facilities nationwide. The report contained nine findings:

1. Protecting prisoners from sexual abuse remains a challenge in correctional facilities across the country. Too often, in what should be secure environments, men, women, and children are raped or abused by other incarcerated individuals and corrections staff.
2. Sexual abuse is not an inevitable feature of incarceration. Leadership matters because corrections administrators can create a culture within facilities that promotes safety instead of one that tolerates abuse.
3. Certain individuals are more at risk of sexual abuse than others. Corrections administrators must routinely do more to identify those who are vulnerable and protect them in ways that do not leave them isolated and without access to rehabilitative programming.
4. Few correctional facilities are subject to the kind of rigorous internal monitoring and external oversight that would reveal why abuse occurs and how to prevent it. Dramatic reductions in sexual abuse depend on both.
5. Many victims cannot safely and easily report sexual abuse, and those who speak out often do so to no avail. Reporting procedures must be improved to instill confidence and protect individuals from retaliation without relying on isolation. Investigations must be thorough and competent. Perpetrators must be held accountable through administrative sanctions and criminal prosecution.
6. Victims are unlikely to receive the treatment and support known to minimize the trauma of abuse. Correctional facilities need to ensure immediate and ongoing access to medical and mental health care and supportive services.
7. Juveniles in confinement are much more likely than incarcerated adults to be sexually abused, and they are particularly at risk when confined with adults. To be effective, sexual abuse prevention, investigation, and treatment must be tailored to the developmental capacities and needs of youth.
8. Individuals under correctional supervision in the community, who outnumber prisoners by more than two to one, are at risk of sexual abuse. The nature and consequences of the abuse are no less severe, and it jeopardizes the likelihood of their successful reentry.
9. A large and growing number of detained immigrants are at risk of sexual abuse. Their heightened vulnerability and unusual circumstances require special interventions.

The findings are supported by statistical data and anecdotal accounts of prison rape and sexual assault by inmates and correctional staff in the Executive Summary of the National Prison Rape Elimination Commission Report, which is reprinted in Appendix B.

FEDERAL SENTENCING GUIDELINES

In 1984, amid public concern over prison unrest and rising crime rates nationwide, Congress established the U.S. Sentencing Commission as an independent agency within the judicial branch of the federal government. In 1985, the commission called for strict federal sentencing guidelines and issued the following recommendations for federal courts:

- Reducing the use of probation, especially for crimes against persons and serious drug offenses.
- Eliminating straight probation without incarceration in favor of probation with conditions of confinement, which requires imprisonment for a fixed period of time for any violation of probation or new offense.
- Increasing the length of prison terms for violent crimes.

The Comprehensive Crime Control Act of 1984 included provisions for lengthy sentences for repeat offenders. The Anti-Drug Abuse Act of 1986 contained similar provisions for serious drug offenders. Those laws combined with the implementation of the guidelines recommended by the U.S. Sentencing Commission effectively eliminated the use in federal courts of indeterminate sentencing, which was an outgrowth of the medical model in corrections and gave broad discretion to parole boards in granting early release to inmates. As a result, many more criminal offenders in federal courts received fixed and often lengthy determinate sentences for their offenses. For federal prisons, that meant housing more prisoners for longer periods of incarceration and a shift in correctional philosophy from rehabilitation to incapacitation.

THE SECOND CHANCE ACT OF 2007

The Second Chance Act of 2007 was signed into law on April 9, 2008, by President George W. Bush. Because 95 percent of all prison and jail inmates who are currently incarcerated will eventually be released, the Act is intended to provide resources to help states and communities achieve a more successful reintegration of inmates into the community and reduce the rate of recidivism.

Key provisions of the Second Chance Act of 2007 include:

- **Demonstration Grants** to states and local governments to provide employment services, substance abuse treatment, and housing for returning inmates.

- **Mentoring Grants** to nonprofit organizations for the mentoring of adult offenders and to provide other transitional services for reintegration into the community.

- **Offender Reentry Substance Abuse Treatment Grants** to qualified agencies and programs to improve the availability of drug treatment to returning offenders.

- **Family Drug Treatment Programs** providing grants to states, local governments, and Indian tribes to develop and implement family-based treatment programs for incarcerated parents who have minor children.

- **Federal Reentry Initiative** to provide guidance to the U.S. Bureau of Prisons for improved reentry planning procedures for federal prison inmates.

- **Reentry Research** authorizing the U.S. Justice Department's National Institute of Justice and the Bureau of Justice Statistics to conduct research on prisoner reentry.

- **National Adult and Juvenile Offender Reentry Resource Center** to establish a national resource center to collect and disseminate research findings and other information on prisoner reentry, and to provide training and support for reentry programs.

At the time of the enactment of the legislation, nearly two-thirds of prison and jail inmates were rearrested within three years of being released, and more than half of all inmates were re-incarcerated.

STATE LEGISLATION

State prisons house nearly 90 percent of all prisoners nationwide. During the 1980s, in reaction to rising rates of violent crimes, many states passed legislation aimed at keeping criminal offenders in prison for longer periods of time. As a direct result of sentencing reforms, state prison populations increased significantly, as did expenditures for state correctional agencies nationwide. Sentencing reform at the state level included three general types of legislation: habitual offenders statutes, determinate sentencing, and sentencing enhancements.

Habitual offender statutes provide for the mandatory long-term sentences for repeat criminal offenders and commonly do not give courts any discretion in sentencing. In other words, under habitual offender statutes, judges are forced to ignore any mitigating factors that may be associated with a crime and, instead, must focus solely on the prior criminal history of repeat offenders. For example, under California's habitual offender statute, commonly known as the three-strikes law, any criminal offender with two prior convictions for violent felonies who commits a third felony must be sentenced to a term of 25 years to life in prison. The third felony need not be violent under California's three-strikes law. In addition, there is no possibility for parole until after serving 25 years of the sentence.

Under determinate sentencing laws, also known as truth-in-sentencing laws, a crime is assigned a fixed term of imprisonment that must be served by an offender convicted of that crime. As with habitual offender statutes, courts are commonly afforded no discretion at sentencing. Determinate sentences take a one-size-fits-all approach to crime and ignore both mitigating and aggravating factors of a criminal offense.

Sentencing enhancement laws are used to increase the penalties for crimes under certain circumstances. For example, in each state, the crime of robbery is assigned a term or range of imprisonment. With sentencing enhancements, however, the use of a gun during the commission of a robbery will add prison time. In other words, the use of a firearm enhances the sentence for robbery, which is the underlying crime. Such enhancements are usually prescribed by law and do not give discretion to courts as to whether or not to add the sentencing enhancement.

State sentencing reforms using habitual offender statutes, determinate sentencing, and sentencing enhancements have significantly increased the number of state and federal prisoners serving life sentences. For example, in 1992, nearly 70,000 prisoners in the United States were serving life sentences. By 2008, the number of "lifers" had more than doubled, with some 140,600 individuals under life sentences in state and federal prisons. Of those, nearly 42,000 inmates nationwide were serving life without possibility of parole.

Stricter sentencing laws had the most negative impact on African Americans. In 2008 African Americans composed about 48 percent of U.S. prison inmates serving life sentences. The issue of racial disparity among inmates sentenced to life without possibility of parole was more pronounced among African Americans, who in 2008 made up 56 percent of inmates with no hope of being released from prison.[3]

The fiscal impact of rising incarceration rates and longer sentences as the result of stricter sentencing laws placed serious budgetary pressures on states nationwide. Those pressures were exacerbated during the economic recession that began in 2008. In the 2009 fiscal year, 43 states reported budget deficits totaling approximately $100 billion, with more shortfalls projected for fiscal year 2010, forcing states to implement cutbacks in health care, education, and corrections.

When faced with cutting costs for corrections, states grapple with a difficult trade-off between public safety and fiscal solvency. In the short term, state governors and legislators have focused on cost savings in state corrections by measures that include reducing operating expenses of correctional facilities, implementing early-release programs for certain nonviolent offenders, and adjusting formulas for the amount of "good time" credit inmates may earn in order to reduce their time served in prison. However, many states have undertaken long-term systemic measures to reduce costs in corrections by focusing on sentencing reforms. In particular, a number of states have established or expanded the use of state sentencing commissions to develop guidelines and suggest policies, both to reduce the rate of incarceration among nonviolent and low-risk individuals and to expand the use of lower-cost community corrections programs in order to reduce recidivism. For example, in 2007, Colorado, Nevada, New York, and Vermont legislatures created sentencing commissions charged with reforming sentencing guidelines. In 2008, the Illinois legislature established a Sentencing Policy Advisory Council, and Connecticut established a Sentencing Task Force. In 2009, the Colorado legislature passed a bill mandating the state's sentencing commission to focus on sentencing reform.

The use of Risk-Reduction Sentences, adopted by Pennsylvania in 2008 and Wisconsin in 2009, allows courts to impose on low-level offenders a two-tiered sentence that consists of a standard minimum sentence and a shorter risk-reduction sentence that allows the inmate to be released earlier by completing certain programs while in state prison. The goal of risk-reduction sentencing is to reduce corrections costs in two ways: first, by lowering an inmate's period of incarceration and, second, by reducing the rate of recidivism for inmates who successfully complete the mandated programs while in prison.[4]

Among the most common measures by states to reduce the number of individuals sentenced to prison, thereby eliminating the costs of incarcerating them, was to relax laws on nonviolent drug possession, particularly possession of marijuana. For example, in 2008, Louisiana enacted legislation that expanded the use of drug court diversion programs; voters in Massachusetts passed by a two-to-one margin a state initiative decriminalizing the possession of marijuana of one ounce or less; New Jersey passed legislation creating a special type of probation for persons convicted of certain drug offenses who previously would have been ineligible for probation; and the Vermont general assembly passed a bill that permits a court, at the request of the Department of Corrections, to reduce an inmate's sentence to probation if the individual has successfully completed alcohol and substance abuse programs.[5]

INTERNATIONAL LAW AND PRISONERS' RIGHTS

When U.S. armed forces are engaged in conflict with a foreign enemy, it is often necessary to detain prisoners of war for interrogation or pending further legal action, including criminal prosecution. The standards of confinement and treatment of prisoners of war detained by U.S. military personnel is controlled under international law, primarily by the Geneva Conventions.

There are four Geneva Conventions, signed on August 12, 1949, by the United States and other countries that are parties to the conventions. Convention I establishes the protections for members of the armed forces who become wounded or sick. Convention II expands those protections to wounded, sick, and shipwrecked members of naval forces. Convention III lists the rights of prisoners of war. Convention IV outlines the protections afforded to civilians during times of war. On June 8, 1977, two protocols were added to the Geneva Conventions that deal with the protections given to victims of international armed conflict, including victims of wars against racist regimes, wars of self-determination, and wars against invading forces.

The Geneva Conventions include the following key provisions:

- Prisoners of war must be humanely treated at all times. Any unlawful act which causes death or seriously endangers the health of a prisoner of war is a grave breach of the Geneva Conventions. In particular, prisoners must not be subject to physical mutilation, biological experiments, violence, intimidation, insults, and public curiosity. *Convention III, Article 13.*

- Prisoners of war must be interred on land and only in clean and healthy areas. *Convention III, Article 22.*

- Prisoners of war are entitled to the same treatment given to a country's own forces, including total surface and cubic space of dormitories, fire protection, adequate heating and lighting, and separate dormitories for women. *Convention III, Article 25.*

- Prisoners of war must receive enough food to maintain weight and to prevent nutritional deficiencies. Food must be similar to the prisoners regular diet, if possible. Food must not be used for disciplinary purposes. *Convention III, Article 26.*

- Prisoners of war must receive adequate clothing, including underwear and footwear. The clothing must be kept in good repair and prisoners who work must receive clothing appropriate to their tasks. *Convention III, Article 27.*

- Prisoners of war must have adequate sanitary facilities, with separate facilities for women prisoners. *Convention III, Article 29.*

- Prisoners of war must receive adequate medical attention. *Convention III, Article 30.*

- Collective punishment for individual acts, corporal punishment, imprisonment without daylight, and all forms of torture and cruelty are forbidden. *Convention III, Article 87.*

- Imprisonment in premises without daylight is forbidden. *Convention III, Article 87.*

- Immediately upon capture or within a week after arrival at a prisoner-of-war camp, transit camp, or hospital, prisoners have the right to write directly to their families. *Convention III, Article 70.*

- Prisoners of war must receive adequate medical attention. Each camp must have an adequate infirmary, with isolation wards if needed for cases of contagious or mental disease. *Convention III, Article 30.*

- Those seriously ill or requiring special treatment must be admitted to any military or civilian medical unit where such treatment can be given. *Convention III, Article 30.*

- Prisoners may not be prevented from seeing medical personnel. Any costs of treatment, including dentures, eyeglasses, and other artificial appliances, will be borne by the detaining power. *Convention III, Article 30.*

- Medical inspections, which must include the recording of the weight of each prisoner, must be held at least once a month for the purpose of supervising the general state of health, nutrition and cleanliness and to detect contagious diseases. *Convention III, Article 31.*

In addition, the Geneva Conventions stipulate that prisoners of war must receive due process and fair trials, that any time spent in confinement waiting for trial will count toward time served, and that all prisoners have the right of appeal and must be informed of these rights and of any time limits on them. *(Convention III, Article 106.)*

THE RIGHTS OF DETAINEES IN U.S. CUSTODY AT GUANTÁNAMO BAY, CUBA

Beginning in 2002, in the aftermath of the terrorist attacks on the United States that occurred on September 11, 2001, individuals suspected of possible involvement in terrorist activities against the United States were taken as prisoners and held in the custody of U.S. military forces abroad. Of the individuals captured, many were taken as prisoners of war in Afghanistan and Iraq, although their citizenship was sometimes from other countries, including the United States. Many of the prisoners, the so-called enemy combatants, were subsequently transferred to the U.S. Naval Station in Guantánamo Bay, Cuba, where they were detained without the benefit of traditional constitutional protections, including the right under habeas corpus to legally challenge their detention in U.S. courts. As a result, attorneys for some of the detainees at the Guantánamo Bay facility sought legal remedy for what they argued was a violation of the detainees' constitutional rights as prisoners held in U.S. custody.

On June 28, 2004, the U.S. Supreme Court simultaneously issued two key rulings on the legal rights of detainees held as enemy combatants in U.S. custody. In *Hamdi v. Rumsfeld* (542 U.S. 507), which concerned the arrest in Afghanistan by U.S. military forces of American citizen Yaser Hamdi for fighting for the Taliban against the United States, the Court held that a U.S. citizen has the right to contest his or her detention under the due process clause of the Fifth Amendment. In *Rasul v. Bush* (542 U.S. 466), the Court expanded the right to contest one's detention to noncitizens held as "enemy combatants" under the federal habeas corpus statute codified in 28 U.S.C.—section 2241. The Court's rulings in *Hamdi* and *Rasul* essentially granted access to federal courts to all of the enemy combatants detained at the U.S. Naval Station in Guantánamo Bay, Cuba.

As a result of the Court's rulings in *Hamdi* and *Rasul*, the U.S. Department of Defense established Combatant Status Review Tribunals as an administrative process to determine if a detainee held at Guantánamo Bay should be classified as an "enemy combatant." Meanwhile, attorneys filed petitions in the U.S. District Court for the District of Columbia on behalf of dozens of detainees held at Guantánamo Bay, which resulted in conflicting rulings by various judges on the issue of whether the detainees had any enforceable rights to challenge their detention.

In 2005, the U.S. Supreme Court agreed to hear the case of *Hamdan v. Rumsfeld* (548 U.S. 557), which challenged the legality of conducting trials of detainees by military tribunals. This manner of trying detainees was established in a 2001 order by President George W. Bush, after the U.S. Congress had passed legislation authorizing the president to use military force in response to the "war on terror." Dismayed that the Supreme Court had decided to hear the challenge to the legality of military tribunals, the U.S. Congress passed the Detainee Treatment Act of 2005 (DTA). Among other things, this legislation divested U.S. courts of their jurisdiction over challenges to detention brought under habeas corpus by detainees who were not U.S. citizens. Instead, the DTA permitted detainees to present limited appeals before Combatant Status Review Tribunals and military commissions.

On June 29, 2006, the U.S. Supreme Court ruled in *Hamdan v. Rumsfeld* that the military tribunals established by President Bush failed to comply with the Uniform Code of Military Justice or the 1949 Geneva Conventions and, therefore, were not legally acceptable for conducting trials of detainees. The Court also held that the provision in the Detainee Treatment Act of 2005 that divested U.S. courts of jurisdiction over detainees' challenges to their detention under habeas corpus was not applicable to habeas cases that were pending before the DTA became law.

In response to the Court's ruling in *Hamdan,* the U.S. Congress passed the Military Commissions Act of 2006 (MCA). It authorized trials of "unlawful alien combatants" by military commissions convened by the president. Significantly, the MCA also eliminated the jurisdiction of federal courts over all pending and future cases brought by detainees to challenge their detention under habeas corpus. As a result, federal courts were compelled to address the question of whether the constitutional writ of habeas corpus extended to all detainees held at Guantánamo Bay who were not U.S. citizens, regardless of whether the filing of their habeas challenges occurred after the passage of the Detainee Treatment Act of 2005 or the superseding Military Commissions Act of 2006.

On June 12, 2008, the Supreme Court settled the question by ruling in *Boumediene v. Bush* (553 U.S. 723) in favor of the right of detainees at Guantánamo Bay prison camp to challenge their detention under the writ of habeas corpus. The Court held that the procedures set forth in the Detainee Treatment Act of 2005 were not adequate substitutes for the habeas writ. Further, the Court ruled that the Military Commissions Act of 2006 was unconstitutional due to its reliance on the DTA's inadequate procedures for addressing habeas challenges brought by detainees at Guantánamo Bay.

On January 22, 2009, President Barack Obama issued an executive order for the closing of the Guantánamo Bay detention facility as soon as practicable. The executive order also ordered the review of all detainees at Guantánamo Bay to determine if they should continue to be held in military custody, transferred to another country, or prosecuted in U.S. courts for criminal offenses. On March 13, 2009, the Obama administration announced new standards for the government's authority to detain terrorist suspects. The standards eliminated the use of the term *enemy combatant.*[6]

Summaries of all these cases are presented later in this chapter, in the section *Access to the Courts* on page 86. A more in-depth review of habeas corpus challenges brought by detainees in federal court is presented in Appendix C.

U.S. SUPREME COURT CASES

Beginning in 1964, with its decision in *Cooper v. Pate* (378 U.S. 546), the U.S. Supreme Court departed from the *hands-off doctrine* historically used by U.S. courts to dismiss actions brought by prison inmates. The court ruled that prisoners had the same right as other U.S. citizens to seek remedy for grievances brought under the Civil Rights Act of 1871. In the wake of *Cooper v. Pate*, the U.S. Supreme Court ruled in dozens of cases brought by prisoners nationwide, including the landmark cases presented in this chapter that addressed the rights of inmates in the following areas:

- **Access to the Courts** *Cooper v. Pate* (1964), *Johnson v. Avery* (1969), *Bounds v. Smith* (1977), *Lewis v. Casey* (1996), *Rasul v. Bush* (2004), *Rompilla v. Beard* (2005), *Hamdan v. Rumsfeld* (2006), *Boumediene v. Bush* (2008)
- **Free Speech and Discrimination** *Procunier v. Martinez* (1974), *Pell v. Procunier* (1974), *Jones v. North Carolina Prisoners' Labor Union, Inc.* (1977), *Turner v. Safley* (1987), *O'Lone v. Estate of Shabazz* (1987), *Thornburgh v. Abbott* (1989), *Johnson v. California* (2005)
- **Due Process** *Wolff v. McDonnell* (1974), *Superintendant v. Hill* (1985), *Sandin v. Conner* (1995), *District Attorney's Office v. Osborne* (2009)
- **Cruel and Unusual Punishment** *Rhodes v. Chapman* (1981), *Whitley v. Albers* (1986), *Wilson v. Seiter* (1991), *Hudson v. McMillian* (1992), *Roper v. Simmons* (2005), *Hill v. McDonough* (2006), *Base v. Rees* (2008), *Kennedy v. Louisiana* (2008)
- **Medical Care** *Estelle v. Gamble* (1976), *Washington v. Harper* (1990)
- **Parole** *Morrissey v. Brewer* (1972), *Johnson v. United States* (2000)
- **Sentencing** *Apprendi v. New Jersey* (2000), *Blakely v. Washington* (2004)
- **Capital Sentencing** *Ring v. Arizona* (2002)

Access to the Courts

COOPER V. PATE, 378 U.S. 546 (1964)

Background

In 1963, Thomas Cooper was an inmate at the Illinois State Penitentiary. Cooper requested copies of the Koran (Qur'an) and other books dealing with Islam and the Muslim faith but was denied access to books. The prison's warden, Frank J. Pate, forbade the dissemination of any materials associated with the Black Muslims, which prison officials considered to be a revolutionary movement that advocated black supremacy and had the potential of disrupting security in the prison. Cooper denied that he was an organizer for the Black Muslims or that he had any other ulterior motive for requesting the reading materials. Cooper's insistence on receiving the books he requested resulted in Cooper being placed in solitary confinement as a disciplinary measure.

Legal Issues

Cooper claimed that by being placed in solitary confinement he was segregated as the result of his religious beliefs and deprived of his right to worship under the First Amendment. Cooper also claimed that he was the victim of discrimination because inmates of other faiths were allowed to receive religious reading materials, including the Bible. Cooper brought action in federal court under Title 42 of the U.S. Code, section 1983, and other statutes for a violation of his civil rights. The U.S. District Court dismissed the action. On appeal, the U.S. Court of Appeal, Second District, affirmed the ruling. The circuit court noted that, while prisoners had an absolute right to their religious beliefs, the expression of "inflammatory doctrines" by certain religious groups, including the Black Muslims, constituted a "threat to maintaining order in a crowded prison environment."

Decision

The U.S. Supreme Court reversed the decision on the grounds that Cooper's complaint contained a legitimate cause of action—that Cooper was the victim of discrimination when he was denied access to Muslim publications while other prisoners were allowed to have reading materials from other religious faiths. The Court held that the lower courts were in error to dismiss the cause of action stated in Cooper's complaint without a hearing as to its merits, regardless of Cooper's status as an inmate in a state prison.

Impact

The *Cooper* ruling did not address the issue of Cooper's civil rights. Rather, the Supreme Court simply held that Cooper had a legitimate cause of action and therefore had legitimate standing to be heard. Still, with its ruling, the Supreme Court moved away from the *hands-off doctrine* that previous courts had used to deny prisoners the right to litigate their grievances. The *hands-off doctrine* was articulated in 1866 by the U.S. Supreme Court in the case of *Pervear v. Massachusetts* (72 U.S. 678), in which the plaintiff, a state prisoner in Massachusetts, argued that poor prison conditions constituted a violation of the Eighth Amendment's ban on cruel or unusual punishment. In its ruling the *Pervear* court declared that because the federal government lacked a legitimate interest in the administration of state institutions, state prison inmates could not invoke the protections afforded under the Eighth Amendment. Similarly, in 1871, the Virginia Supreme Court in *Ruffin v. Commonwealth* (62 Va. 790) ruled that inmates were effectively "slaves of the state" who lacked standing in a court of law to seek remedy for violations of their civil rights because they forfeited those rights when sentenced to prison.

In 1941, in the case *Ex parte Hull* (312 U.S. 546), the U.S. Supreme Court acknowledged that prisoners had a right to judicial review. However, the Court's finding that relief was not merited based on the facts of the *Hull* case effectively reinforced the use of the *hands-off doctrine*. As late as 1958, in the case of *Gore v. United States* (357 U.S. 386), the U.S. Supreme Court maintained its noninterventionist policy with regard to prisoners seeking redress for violations of their civil rights. The *Cooper* case effectively opened the courthouse doors to thousands of U.S. prisoners to be heard in federal courts.

JOHNSON V. AVERY, 393 U.S. 483 (1969)

Background

In 1965, while serving a life sentence at the Tennessee state penitentiary, William Joe Johnson was moved to a maximum security prison as a disciplinary action for assisting other prisoners in preparing legal documents, which was a violation of the prison's regulations. Johnson sought remedy in federal district court, claiming that he had been unfairly disciplined and asking the court for access to law books and a typewriter in order to continue preparing legal documents for other inmates.

Legal Issues

The district court ruled in Johnson's favor, holding that the prison regulation preventing Johnson from assisting other inmates was in conflict with federal law because the rule effectively barred illiterate prisoners from access to the courts. The circuit court reversed the ruling, however, on the grounds that maintaining prison discipline by limiting the practice of law to attorneys justified the potential burden on illiterate prisoners in filing court documents without the assistance of legal counsel.

Decision

In reversing the circuit court the Supreme Court ruled that, absent "reasonable alternatives" by the state of Tennessee to assist illiterate or poorly educated inmates in preparing post-conviction petitions, the state's regulation against allowing prisoners to help other inmates prepare court documents was unconstitutional. The Court recognized that inmates who provided legal assistance were placed in a position of power that could be used to exploit disadvantaged prisoners and potentially disrupt prison order. The Court ruled, however, that the right of legal assistance in a correctional setting was more important.

Impact

The *Johnson* ruling went a step further in giving prisoners access to relief in federal court by allowing them to assist each other in the preparation of post-conviction petitions, as well as other court documents. However, the Court left open the possibility of closing that opportunity for inmates in the interest of institutional security if the state provided "reasonable alternatives" for disadvantaged inmates to obtain legal assistance in prison. The precise meaning of "reasonable alternatives" was not articulated by the Court until its later ruling in *Lewis v. Casey* (presented later in this section).

BOUNDS V. SMITH, 430 U.S. 817 (1977)

Background

In 1976, three lawsuits against the Division of Prisons of the North Carolina Department of Corrections were brought by several inmates. Their cases were consolidated by the U.S. Supreme Court. The inmates initially sought relief in district court under Title 42 of the U.S. Code, section 1983, for the failure of the state of North Carolina to provide them with access to legal research materials, in violation of their due process rights under the Fourteenth Amendment.

Legal Issues

The district court ruled in favor of the inmates, declaring that North Carolina's sole prison library was inadequate to meet the needs of state inmates with no other legal assistance available to them. The state proposed to open seven libraries in correctional institutions throughout North Carolina. Under the state's plan, inmates were required to make appointments to use the prison library. Inmates in institutions without a library would be provided with transportation and housing. Still, given North Carolina's inmate population at the time, there was a waiting time of three or four weeks to use a library. The parties to the lawsuit returned to district court and claimed that the state's plan was inadequate. The district court rejected their claim and ruled that the state's plan afforded the inmates reasonable access to legal research materials in order to effectively pursue actions in court. On appeal, the Court of Appeals for the Fourth Circuit affirmed the district court's ruling and approved the state's plan for new libraries, with one exception. The circuit court held that North Carolina's library plan failed to provide female prisoners with the same library access as male prisoners. Absent any legal justification by the state for this oversight, the court held that female prisoners were unconstitutionally discriminated against under the state's plan.

Decision

The U.S. Supreme Court ruled in favor of the inmates who objected to the state's library plan. The Court held that prisoners were entitled to the fundamental constitutional right of access to the courts. As such, correctional authorities were required to provide inmates with access to legal resources, including assistance from persons trained in matters of law. In other words, by denying inmates the ability to prepare and file documents with the courts, the state was effectively denying them access to the courts, which was an unconstitutional violation of their Fourteenth Amendment rights.

Impact

The ruling in *Bounds* built upon the 1971 decision by the U.S. Supreme Court in *Young v. Gilmore* (404 U.S. 15) that the rights of access to the courts and equal protection under the law were violated when prisoners did not have access to assistance in the initial preparation of post-conviction petitions filed in federal court. In *Bounds*, the Court broadened the scope of its ruling in *Young* by declaring that inmates must have *meaningful* access to the courts and, therefore, to legal research materials and other supplies in order to competently prepare petitions and other court documents. As such, correctional agencies were obligated to afford such access to prisoners under their authority.

LEWIS V. CASEY, 518 U.S. 343 (1996)

Background

Twenty-three inmates from several state prisons in Arizona filed a class action lawsuit in district court claiming the Arizona Department of Corrections (ADOC) failed to provide them with adequate legal research facilities, thereby depriving them of their constitutional right of access to the courts as established in the 1977 ruling by the U.S. Supreme Court in *Bounds v. Smith*.

Legal Issues

The district court ruled in favor of the prisoners and issued an injunction against the ADOC to make sweeping improvements in its system of law libraries and legal assistance programs for inmates. On appeal by the ADOC, the U.S. Court of Appeals, Ninth Circuit, affirmed the district court's ruling and agreed in large part with the terms of the injunction against the ADOC, which included detailed instructions, including the hours of operation of prison libraries.

Decision

The U.S. Supreme Court reversed both the district and circuit courts, citing the failure of the prisoners to show a systemic failure by the ADOC to provide inmates with access to legal research facilities and legal assistance. Instead, the Court found that the prisoners had only identified isolated instances of the ADOC's failure to provide such access and services. Citing the decision in *Bounds*, the Court held, in part, that *"Bounds* did not create an abstract, free-standing right to a law library or legal assistance; rather, the right that *Bounds* acknowledged was the right of access to the courts . . . Moreover, *Bounds* does not guarantee inmates the wherewithal to file any and every type of legal claim, but requires only that they be provided with the tools to attack their sentences . . . and to challenge the conditions of their confinement." The Court held that any remedy provided by a court must be limited to the actual injury to the plaintiff and, therefore, the injunction against the ADOC issued by the district court and upheld by the circuit court was "inordinately intrusive" and improper.

Impact

The Court clarified the right of access to the courts by inmates and limited the remedy imposed by a court upon a correctional agency to address only the actual injury to the plaintiff. The Court held that the widespread systemic failure of a correctional agency to provide inmates with access to the courts requires proof by the plaintiffs showing a widespread pattern of injury. The ruling decried the use of courts to micromanage correctional institutions and in that respect was somewhat reminiscent of the *hand-off doctrine* of the Court prior to its 1964 decision in *Cooper v. Pate*. Further, the Court made clear that while *Bounds* held that correctional institutions bear a duty to provide inmates with legal resources to assist them in post-conviction actions, that duty does not extend to assisting inmates in discovering new grievances.

RASUL V. BUSH, 542 U.S. 466 (2004)

Background

In 2002, during hostilities between the United States and the Taliban as a result of the terrorist attack on the United States on September 11, 2001, two Australian citizens and 12 Kuwaiti; citizens were captured in Afghanistan by U.S. forces. The detainees were subsequently transported to the U.S. Naval Base at Guantánamo Bay, Cuba, where they were held along with some 640 other enemy combatants captured abroad by U.S. forces during the war on terrorism.

Prisons

Legal Issues

The two Australians, Mamdouh Habib and David Hicks, each filed petitions in the U.S. Court for the District of Columbia challenging the legality of their detention and seeking release from custody, access to legal counsel, and freedom from interrogations. Shafiq Rasul and the other 11 detainees from Kuwait filed a complaint in federal court seeking to be informed of the charges against them, access to legal counsel, and the right to be heard in a U.S. court of law or some other impartial tribunal. The district court dismissed all of the actions on the grounds that the court lacked jurisdiction because the U.S. Naval Base at Guantánamo Bay, Cuba, was not within the jurisdiction of any federal court. The court held, in part, that "the privilege of litigation does not extend to aliens in military custody who have no presence in any territory over which the United States is sovereign." As such, the detainees at Guantánamo Bay, Cuba, lacked standing to bring an action in federal court. In affirming the ruling, the Court of Appeals agreed that the district court correctly interpreted the 1973 U.S. Supreme Court's decision in *Johnson v. Eisentrager* (339 U.S. 763) to mean that aliens detained outside the sovereign territory of the United States did not have the right to bring actions in federal court.

Decision

On June 28, 2004, the U.S. Supreme Court reversed the decision and ruled that U.S. courts had at least limited jurisdiction to consider challenges to the legality of the detention of foreign nationals captured abroad and held at Guantánamo Bay, Cuba. The court based its ruling, in part, on Title 28 of the U.S. Code, section 2241, which authorized federal district courts to consider actions brought by individuals claiming to be held "in custody in violation of the laws of the United States." The Court interpreted the language of the statute to include "aliens held in a territory over which the United States exercises . . . jurisdiction, but not sovereignty." Because the United States exercised jurisdiction over the Naval Base at Guantánamo Bay, Cuba, detainees there had standing to at least challenge their detention in federal district courts under the writ of habeas corpus.

The Court rejected the district court's interpretation of the *Eisentrager* case on the grounds that the detainees at Guantánamo Bay, Cuba, were not nationals of countries at war with the United States, as the German prisoners were in *Eisentrager*. The court noted that the detainees at Guantánamo Bay, Cuba, denied that they engaged in terrorist plots against the United States and were never charged or convicted of any wrongdoing, yet they were detained for over two years without access to any court or impartial tribunal.

Impact

The Court's ruling clarified that detainees held by authorities have at least the limited right of access to courts to challenge their detention, whether they are held in the sovereign United States or in territorial areas over which the United States exercised some jurisdiction. In its ruling in *Rasul*, the Court expanded upon its ruling in *Hamdi v. Rumsfeld* (542 U.S. 507), which, like *Rasul*, was decided on June 28, 2004. In the *Hamdi* case, the Court addressed the narrower issue of the right of an American citizen who was arrested and detained abroad as a so-called enemy combatant to challenge his detention in federal court under the writ of habeas corpus. Yaser Esam Hamdi was born an American citizen in Louisiana in 1980 and later moved with his family to Saudi Arabia. In 2002, Hamdi was captured in Afghanistan by coalition forces and turned over to the custody of the United States, in part because of his status as a U.S. citizen. Hamdi was interrogated and detained by the United States and classified as an enemy combatant for allegedly taking up arms with the Taliban in Afghanistan. Hamdi was transferred to the U.S. Naval Base at Guantánamo Bay, Cuba, and later to the naval brig at Norfolk, Virginia, and held without formal charges or court proceedings. Hamdi's capture and detention was challenged on the basis of his rights to due process under the Fifth and Fourteenth Amendments to the U.S. Constitution. In *Hamdi*, the U.S. Supreme Court ruled that Hamdi had the right to "a limited judicial inquiry into his detention's legality . . . but not a search reviewing of the factual determinations underlying his seizure." In both *Hamdi* and *Rasul*, the Court made clear that detainees have an absolute right to challenge their detentions and be heard in a court of law, even if that hearing is limited to the narrow issue of the legality of their detention.

ROMPILLA V. BEARD, 545 U.S. 374 (JUNE 20, 2005)

Background

On January 14, 1998, the stabbed and badly burned body of James Scanlon was discovered by police in a bar in Allentown, Pennsylvania. Ronald Rompilla was arrested for killing Scanlon and charged with capital murder. After the jury found Rompilla guilty of the crime, the trial moved into the penalty phase for the jury to determine if Rompilla should be sentenced to death. Arguing for the imposition of the death penalty, the prosecution presented factors in aggravation that included Rompilla's significant criminal history, including prior convictions for rape and assault. The defense, in an effort to spare Rompilla from the death penalty, offered the testimony of Rompilla's family members who begged jurors for mercy. However, neither Rompilla nor his family members suggested that there were any mitigating factors in

Rompilla's background. The defense did not conduct an investigation for mitigating factors in Rompilla's background, even knowing that the prosecution would use factors in Rompilla's background in aggravation, including Rompilla's prior criminal history. Finding that the factors in aggravation outweighed the pleas for mercy by Rompilla's family, the jury sentenced Rompilla to death.

Legal Issues

On appeal, Rompilla's new lawyers argued that the failure of Rompilla's trial lawyer to investigate Rompilla's background, which included a history of mental illness and an extremely abusive childhood, constituted ineffective assistance of counsel. A state appellate court ruled that Rompilla's trial counsel was sufficient and affirmed the verdict. However, on appeal in federal court, the U.S. Circuit Court for the Third District reversed the state appellate court and ruled that Rompilla's trial counsel was ineffective for failing to investigate Rompilla's personal history of abuse as a child and mental illness.

Decision

The U.S. Supreme Court reviewed the case on the question of whether Rompilla's trial counsel had a duty to investigate aggravating factors introduced by the prosecution, including Rompilla's prior criminal history, in order to discover potentially mitigating factors, which in Rompilla's case included abuse as a child and mental illness. In a 5 to 4 ruling, the U.S. Supreme Court agreed with the U.S. Third Circuit Court that Rompilla's trial lawyer provided ineffective assistance of counsel. The Supreme Court held that the Sixth Amendment's right to effective counsel required a defense attorney in a capital murder case to investigate information presented at trial by the prosecution in order to develop potentially mitigating evidence.

Impact

The U.S. Supreme Court's ruling in *Rompilla* expanded upon the Court's 2003 decision in *Wiggins v. Smith* (539 U.S. 510), in which the Court held that the failure by trial defense counsel in a death penalty case to investigate the defendant's childhood and personal background before deciding not to present mitigating evidence was a violation of the Sixth Amendment's right to effective counsel. The Court's ruling in *Rompilla* underscores the duty of defense counsel in a death penalty case to fully investigate the client's personal background, and it establishes an absolute requirement to do so when the prosecution presents aggravating factors in the defendant's background.

The Law of Prisons

HAMDAN V. RUMSFELD, 548 U.S. 557 (JUNE 29, 2006)

Background

Salim Ahmed Hamdan was the former chauffeur for al-Qaeda leader Osama bin Laden, who claimed responsibility for the terrorist attacks of September 11, 2001, against the United States. After the United States-led invasion of Afghanistan in 2002, Hamdan was captured, charged with fighting against U.S. forces, and subsequently imprisoned by the U.S. military at the detention facility at Guantánamo Bay, Cuba. Hamdan filed petition for a writ of habeas corpus in federal court to challenge the legality of his detention.

Legal Issues

Prior to a ruling on his habeas petition, Hamdan appeared before a military tribunal and was declared an enemy combatant. Several months later, the federal court granted Hamdan's habeas petition, ruling that the military tribunal did not have authority to declare Hamdan an enemy combatant until a federal court determined whether Hamdan was, in fact, a prisoner of war under the terms of the Geneva Conventions. On appeal, the Circuit Court of Appeals for the District of Columbia reversed the lower court's ruling and held that the Geneva Conventions were not enforceable in federal court. The Circuit Court further held that Hamdan's hearing before a military tribunal was constitutional because military tribunals were authorized by the U.S. Congress.

Decision

In a 5 to 3 decision (Chief Justice Roberts did not participate because he had previously ruled on the case while serving on the Circuit Court), the U.S. Supreme Court ruled that the U.S. Constitution did not authorize, either by an act of Congress or by executive order, the use of military tribunals used in the *Hamdan* case. The Court also held that any military tribunal was required to comply with the laws of the United States and the laws of war, including those set forth in the Geneva Conventions. Therefore, in finding that both the U.S. Uniform Code of Military Justice and the Geneva Conventions were enforceable in federal court, the U.S. Supreme Court reversed the decision of the U.S. Circuit Court of Appeals for the District of Columbia and affirmed the lower court's granting of Hamdan's habeas petition.

Impact

In *Hamdan*, the U.S. Supreme Court further expanded the rights of detainees held in U.S. military custody to challenge the legality of their detention under the writ of habeas corpus, as established in the Court's 2004 rulings in *Rasul v. Bush* and *Hamdi v. Rumsfeld*. In *Hamdan*, the Court specifically addressed the use of military tribunals, or military commissions, as established by Congress. It held that the jurisdiction of such tribunals did not supersede the jurisdiction of federal courts on the right of military detainees to challenge their detention.

BOUMEDIENE V. BUSH, 553 U.S. 723 (JUNE 12, 2008)

Background

In 2002, police in Bosnia arrested six Algerians, including Lakhdar Boumediene, because U.S. intelligence officers suspected them of plotting an attack on the U.S. embassy in Bosnia. Classified by the U.S. government as "enemy combatants" in the war on terror, Boumediene and the other five arrestees were transported and detained at the U.S. Naval Base at Guantánamo Bay, Cuba. Boumediene challenged his detention and filed a writ of habeas corpus, alleging various violations of his rights under the due process clause of the U.S. Constitution, common law, international law, and other statutes and treaties.

Legal Issues

The federal district court granted a motion brought by the U.S. government to dismiss all of Boumediene's claims on the ground that Boumediene was an alien detained at an overseas military base and, as such, had no right to challenge his detention under habeas corpus. The U.S. Circuit Court of Appeals for the District of Columbia affirmed the district court's dismissal of Boumediene's claims for relief. This ruling ran counter to the U.S. Supreme Court's decision in 2004 in *Rasul v. Bush*, which had extended the right to file habeas petitions in federal court to detainees held at the Guantánamo Bay prison camp who were not U.S. citizens. Instead, the Circuit Court relied upon provisions in the U.S. Military Commissions Act (MCA) of 2006. Enacted after the Supreme Court's ruling in *Rasul v. Bush*, MCA eliminated the jurisdiction of federal courts to hear habeas petitions brought by detainees who were formally designated "enemy combatants."

Decision

In a 5 to 4 decision, the U.S. Supreme Court reversed the lower courts. In stripping federal courts of jurisdiction in habeas claims brought by "enemy combatants," the Military Commissions Act of 2006 relied on the earlier Detainee Treatment Act, which did not provide adequate judicial substitutions for the writ of habeas corpus. Therefore, the majority of the Court reasoned, the Military Commissions Act of 2006 was unconstitutional and so-called enemy combatants held at the Guantánamo Bay prison camp were entitled to challenge their detention under habeas corpus in federal court.

In a related case, *Munaf v. Geren* (553 U.S. ____), that was decided on the same date as *Boumediene*, the Supreme Court ruled unanimously that the habeas corpus statute extended to U.S. citizens detained abroad by U.S. military forces, even if the American forces were operating under a larger multinational force. In 2005, U.S. military forces operating as part of a larger multinational force in Iraq arrested Mohammad Munaf, a U.S. citizen, for kidnapping. Munaf stood trial in an Iraqi court, where he was convicted and sentenced to death. A U.S. district court dismissed the conviction. However, both the district court and the U.S. circuit court later ruled that they did not have jurisdiction in the habeas petition filed on Munaf's behalf. The U.S. Supreme Court disagreed and held that when U.S. citizens are held in custody "under the color of the authority of the United States," the federal courts have sufficient jurisdiction.

Free Speech and Discrimination

PROCUNIER V. MARTINEZ, 416 U.S. 396 (APRIL 29, 1974)

Background

In 1973, the California Department of Corrections authorized the censorship of prisoner's mail. Prison regulations prohibited inmates from mailing correspondence in which they "unduly complained, magnified grievances, or expressed inflammatory political, racial, religious, or other views or beliefs," or in which inmates expressed any views deemed by prison officials to be "defamatory" or "otherwise inappropriate." Under the same rationale, California prison regulations permitted inmates to meet with their attorneys but not with their attorney's law clerks or paralegals, who were sometimes dispatched to conduct interviews with inmates or to provide legal information or assistance under the direction of the inmates' attorneys.

Legal Issues

California state prison inmates brought a class action lawsuit against the California Department of Corrections in which they challenged the prison regulations. The central justification for the challenge was that by censoring the inmates' mail, prison officials violated the prisoners' right of free speech, as guaranteed under the First Amendment to the U.S. Constitution. The district court agreed with the prisoners, holding that the prison regulations violated their right of free speech under the First Amendment and that the regulations were vague, in violation of the due process clause of the Fourteenth Amendment. The district court also held that banning inmates from meeting with law clerks and paralegals violated the inmates' right of access to the courts.

Decision

The U.S. Supreme Court affirmed the lower court's ruling on the issue of the First Amendment. The Court held that "censorship of direct personal correspondence involves incidental restrictions on the right to free speech of both prisoners and their correspondents." However, the Court held that censorship of mail by prison officials was justifiable under certain conditions. First, the censorship "must further one or more of the important and substantial governmental interests of security, order, and the rehabilitation of inmates." Secondly, the censorship "must be no greater than is necessary to further the legitimate governmental interest involved." Using this two-pronged standard, known as the "strict scrutiny" standard, the Court held that the regulations concerning prisoners' mail by the California Department of Corrections were "far broader than any legitimate interest of penal administration demands. . . ."

The Court also agreed with the district court on the issue of prohibiting inmates from meeting with law clerks and paralegals. The Court held that such a ban constituted an unjustifiable restriction on inmates' access to the courts because the ban "created an arbitrary distinction between law students employed by attorneys and those associated with law school programs," who were not banned from meeting with inmates under the same California prison regulations.

Impact

The *Procunier v. Martinez* ruling was significant in two ways. First, the Court clearly upheld the right of free speech for prisoners. Second, the Court established a two-pronged standard to guide penal institutions in the regulation of inmates' mail. As such, the Court attempted to strike a balance between the constitutional rights of prisoners as citizens and the duty of correctional institutions to maintain order and control for the safety of their prisoners and the protection of society. Significantly, the Court's ruling only addressed the censorship of mail between prisoners and individuals outside the prison. The court did not take up the issue of inmate-to-inmate mail until 1987 in its ruling in *Turner v. Safley*, which is presented later in this section.

The Law of Prisons

PELL V. PROCUNIER, 417 U.S. 817 (JUNE 24, 1974)

Background

In 1973, a regulation contained in the California Department of Corrections Manual prohibited "press and other media interviews with specific inmates." Under the regulation, the press was generally allowed to interview inmates but prohibited from conducting individual face-to-face interviews or giving special media coverage to a particular inmate. The California Department of Corrections instituted the regulation after certain inmates gained notoriety as a result of such interviews with the press. Because of their notoriety, the department claimed, those inmates gained influence over other prisoners and threatened to undermine the control and discipline of the institution.

Legal Issues

Four California state prison inmates and three journalists challenged the regulation in a federal district court. With regard to the inmates, the court declared that the regulation was an unconstitutional violation of free speech under the First Amendment. The court also held that the regulation was vague and, therefore, violated the Fourteenth Amendment's due process clause. However, the court dismissed the claims brought by the journalists that the regulation was unfair to them by limiting their access to prisoners. The court held that the regulation did not infringe upon the rights of the journalists because they were allowed to enter correctional institutions for the purpose of conducting general interviews with inmates.

Decision

On an appeal brought by the journalists and prison officials, the U.S. Supreme Court affirmed the lower court's ruling with regard to the journalists and reversed it with regard to the prisoners' rights, ruling that the regulations by the California Department of Corrections violated neither the journalists' nor the prisoners' free speech. According to the Court, the ban on face-to-face media interviews with inmates was reasonable because it did not prevent the press communicating with inmates by other means, including the mail. The Court held that "the First Amendment does not guarantee the press a constitutional right of special access to information not available to the public generally." As for the inmates, the Court ruled that they had many avenues of communication, including the mail and visits from family members, attorneys, and clergy. As such, the ban against face-to-face media interviews did not constitute an unconstitutional restriction on prisoners' free speech. The Court reasoned that constitutional rights, including freedom of speech, must be balanced against the needs of a correctional institution to maintain order and discipline for the protection of inmates and the public. As the Court stated, "such considerations are peculiarly within the province and professional expertise of corrections officials, and . . . courts should ordinarily defer to their expert judgment in such matters."

Impact

Following its ruling in *Procunier v. Martinez*, the Court declared that prisoners do not have an unlimited right of free speech and that communication between inmates and others outside of prison, including the press, must be balanced against institutional needs for security and safety. In combination, the *Martinez* and *Pell* decisions gave prison officials the authority to limit prisoners' expression of certain constitutional rights and provided a two-pronged standard by which to formulate prison regulations limiting free speech and other rights.

JONES V. NORTH CAROLINA PRISONERS' LABOR UNION, INC., 433 U.S. 119 (1977)

Background

In 1974, a group of prisoners under the authority of the North Carolina Department of Corrections formed the North Carolina Prisoners' Labor Union. The union was incorporated with the stated goal of installing a chapter of the union at every prison and jail in North Carolina and of working through collective bargaining to improve prison conditions. By early 1975, some 2,000 inmates in 40 different prisons throughout the state had joined the union. The North Carolina Department of Corrections was unhappy with this development and, on March 26, 1975, passed a regulation prohibiting inmates from soliciting other prisoners to join the union. The regulation also banned union meetings and mass mailings concerning union activities.

Legal Issues

Under Title 42 of the U.S. Code, section 1983, the union filed action in federal court claiming that the regulation violated their rights of free speech and association guaranteed by the First Amendment. The union members also claimed that their rights were violated under the equal protection clause of the Fourteenth Amendment because other organizations, including the Jaycees and Alcoholics Anonymous, were permitted to conduct meetings, recruit members, and distribute bulk mailing materials within prisons in North Carolina. The district court ruled that if inmates were allowed to join the union, then the North Carolina Department of Corrections could not prohibit them from soliciting new members or holding meetings. The district court also agreed with the union on the issue of bulk mailings, holding that the North Carolina Department of Corrections could not "pick and choose" which groups could engage in such mailings and which groups could not utilize bulk mailings to promote their activities.

Decision

The U.S. Supreme Court reversed the lower court and ruled that the regulation by the North Carolina Department of Corrections did not violate the rights of the prisoners under either the First or Fourteenth Amendments to the U.S. Constitution. Citing its previous decision in *Martinez* and *Pell,* the Court criticized the district court for not deferring to the needs of prison officials to maintain order and security in correctional settings. The Court held that the North Carolina Department of Corrections' regulation limiting union activity "was no broader than necessary to meet the perceived threat of group meetings and organizational activity to [prison] order and security." The Court faulted the district court's reasoning that mass mailings must be permitted for the prisoners' union if they are permitted for other groups, including the Jaycees and Alcoholics Anonymous. The court reasoned that a prison was not a public forum and, as such, prison officials were only obligated to demonstrate a "rational basis" for distinguishing between various organizations. As such, organizations like the Jaycees and Alcoholics Anonymous conducted rehabilitative work in accord with the goals of the prison, whereas the prisoners' union constituted "an adversarial organization at odds with institutional goals."

Impact

Unionization by prisoners reached its peak during the 1970s, and union activities by prisoners have significantly diminished since that time. Nonetheless, while the *Jones* case placed limits on the rights of prisoners to conduct union activities in correctional settings, the Court did not establish clear guidelines for correctional officials in formulating rules governing prisoners' unions. In the 1987 case of *Turner v. Safley,* however, the Court established guidelines regarding inmate-to-inmate communications that may be applicable in other cases involving prisoners' unions.

TURNER V. SAFLEY, 482 U.S. 78 (JUNE 1, 1987)

Background

In 1986, the Missouri Division of Corrections allowed written correspondence between two prisoners if they were immediate family members housed at different institutions in Missouri or if the correspondence dealt with legal matters. Otherwise, Missouri state prisoners were allowed to write to each other only if prison officials deemed that the correspondence was in the best interest of both parties. Another prison regulation permitted a Missouri state prisoner to marry only with the prison superintendent's permission, which was usually granted only in cases of pregnancy where there was an impending birth of an illegitimate child. Missouri state inmates filed a class action lawsuit in district court challenging the constitutionality of both regulations.

Legal Issues

The federal district court ruled that both regulations were unconstitutional, and the court of appeals affirmed the ruling. Both courts found that the Missouri Division of Correction's regulations on inmate-to-inmate correspondence restricted the free speech of prisoners. The courts also agreed that prisoners had a constitutional right to marry.

Decision

The U.S. Supreme Court then reversed on the issue of intra-institutional correspondence between inmates, holding that the prison's regulation was reasonable based on the following four relevant factors:

- The regulation was reasonably related to a legitimate or neutral government interest. In other words, banning most inmate-to-inmate communications reduced the risk of a breach in control or security. Allowing such communication increased that risk. Therefore, the regulation was reasonably related to the correctional agency's interest of maintaining security and control in prisons under its authority.

- The regulation did not preclude all alternative means of expressing the same constitutional right. For example, Missouri inmates could still communicate by mail with relatives or friends outside prison to convey information to immediate family members at other institutions.

- The potential impact of modifying or abolishing the regulation placed an unreasonable burden on Missouri prison officials, whose primary responsibility was for the security and control of correctional institutions.

- There was no valid alternative to the regulation that did not compromise the safety and security of the institution.

On the issue of a prisoner's right to marry, the Court agreed with the lower courts, holding that "prisoners have a constitutionally protected right to marry [even if] such a marriage is subject to substantial restrictions as a result of incarceration. . . ."

Impact

The Court established a new precedent for balancing the constitutional rights of prisoners with the duty of prison officials to maintain institutional order and security. The Court held that the district and circuit courts incorrectly applied the previous standard of "strict scrutiny" that was established in *Procunier v. Martinez*. Under the two-pronged "strict scrutiny" standard, prison officials were required to make a showing that any violation of a prisoner's constitutional rights was justified by "the important and substantial governmental interests of security, order, and the rehabilitation of inmates" and that the infringement upon a prisoner's constitutional rights "must be no greater than is necessary to further the legitimate governmental interest involved." In *Turner*, the Court introduced a less rigorous "rational basis" test to determine if a prison regulation violated prisoners' constitutional rights. According to the Court, the "rational basis" for determining the constitutionality of prison regulations and policy was determining the reasonableness of those polices, based upon a four-pronged test devised by the Court.

O'LONE V. ESTATE OF SHABAZZ, 482 U.S. 342 (JUNE 9, 1987)

Background

In 1983, New Jersey state prisoners confined at the Leesburg prison were placed in one of three security classifications. The highest security classification was "maximum status," followed by "gang minimum status." The lowest security classification was "full minimum status." Under a new prison regulation, prisoners classified as gang minimum status or full minimum status were assigned to work crews outside of the main building. The new regulation, known as Standard 853, was implemented gradually. During the initial phase, some Muslim inmates assigned to outside work crews were allowed to remain in the main building on Fridays in order to attend Jumu'ah, a weekly Islamic religious service. In March 1984, however, inmates on minimum gang status or full minimum status were no longer allowed in the main building while assigned to outside work crews, except in cases of emergency. As a result, some Muslim inmates were prevented from attending Jumu'ah on Fridays.

Legal Issues

Muslim inmates filed suit in federal court alleging a violation of the First Amendment right of freedom of religious expression. The district court ruled that work detail procedure at Leesburg State Prison did not violate the rights of the Muslim inmates and that prison officials had authority to regulate work details in order to maintain a secure and orderly prison environment. However, the U.S. Court of Appeals for the Third Circuit reversed the ruling and held that New Jersey prison officials failed to demonstrate that they explored every reasonable method to accommodate the Muslim inmates. Absent that showing, the court of appeals ruled that the Muslim inmates were correct in claiming their rights were violated under the First Amendment.

Decision

In a 5 to 4 opinion written by Chief Justice William Rehnquist, the U.S. Supreme Court reversed the Third Circuit and rejected the idea that prison administrators must explore every possible means of avoiding infringements on prisoners' constitutional rights. Deferring to the authority of prison administrators, Chief Justice Rehnquist wrote, "This court will not substitute its judgment on difficult and sensitive matters of institutional administration for the determinations of those charged with the formidable task of running a prison." Although the Court recognized that the prison's policies prevented some Muslim inmates from attending Jumu'ah, the Court held that the "reasonableness [of the prison policies] is supported by the fact that they do not deprive respondents of all forms of religious exercise, but instead allow participation in a number of Muslim religious ceremonies." The Court also noted that prison officials accommodated Muslim inmates in other ways. For example, Muslim inmates were offered different meals whenever pork was served at the prison. In addition, Muslim inmates were allowed to have early breakfasts and late dinners to accommodate the observance of Ramadan, a monthlong period of fasting and prayer during daylight hours.

Impact

This was the first case in which the Supreme Court applied the *Turner v. Safley* test for the impact of prison regulations on inmates' First Amendment right of freedom of religious expression. In applying the "rational basis" test, the Court moved away from the previous "strict scrutiny" test that required courts to more rigorously examine the impact of prison regulations on the exercise of constitutional rights.

THORNBURGH V. ABBOTT, 490 U.S. 401 (1989)

Background

In 1989, the Federal Bureau of Prisons permitted federal prisoners to subscribe to or receive periodicals or other publications without prior approval by their prison's warden. However, each warden was authorized to reject any publication considered to be "detrimental to the security, good order, or discipline of the institution, or if [the publication] might facilitate criminal activity." Publications could not be rejected solely because a publication's content was "religious, philosophical, political, or sexual, or because its content [was] unpopular or repugnant."

Legal Issues

Certain inmates and some of the publishers of the 46 publications rejected in federal prisons filed suit in federal district court claiming that their First Amendment right of free speech was violated according to the "strict scrutiny" standards established in *Procunier v. Martinez*. The district court analyzed the plaintiff's claim by applying the "rational basis" test set forth in *Turner v. Safely* and upheld the federal prison regulations. The Court of Appeals, however, followed *Martinez* and reversed the district court, holding that the federal prison regulations on publications were unconstitutional and invalid.

Decision

The U.S. Supreme Court reversed the Court of Appeals and upheld the district court's ruling using the "rational basis" test articulated in *Turner v. Safley*. The Court found that, under the standard of reasonableness articulated in *Turner*, the Bureau of Prison's regulations concerning publications were constitutionally valid. However, the Court agreed in part with the appellate court that the plaintiffs were entitled to a case-by-case review of all 46 publications.

Impact

The court reestablished its reliance on the *Turner v. Safley* test of reasonableness and not the *Martinez* test of "strict scrutiny" in balancing the civil right of prisoners with the duty of prison officials to maintain order and control in institutions. This effectively shifted the burden to plaintiffs to demonstrate not only that their constitutional rights were violated, but also that the prison's regulation or policy abridging that right was unreasonable in its intent to maintain order and control.

JOHNSON V. CALIFORNIA, 543 U.S. 499 (FEBRUARY 23, 2005)

Background

Garrison Johnson, an African-American inmate, was racially segregated when he entered the state prison system in California. Johnson's segregation was the result of an unwritten policy by the California Department of

Corrections (CDC) to racially segregate incoming prisoners confined to two-person cells during the first 60 days of their incarceration in order to prevent fighting among cellmates of different races who belonged to racial gangs. Johnson filed suit in federal district court claiming that the CDC's policy of segregating new prisoners violated his right to equal protection under the Fourteenth Amendment to the U.S. Constitution.

Legal Issues

The CDC claimed that the policy of racially segregating new inmates was consistent with the U.S. Supreme Court's ruling in 1987 in *Turner v. Safely* in which the Court held that prison regulations that are at odds with inmates' constitutional rights are valid if the regulations are "reasonably related to a legitimate penological interest." Both the federal district and appellate courts agreed with the CDC's contention that the racial segregation of incoming inmates in order to prevent fighting was "reasonably related to a legitimate penological interest," and they applied that standard in ruling against Johnson.

Decision

The U.S. Supreme Court reversed the rulings and held that the standard applied by the lower courts was incorrect. Instead, the Court ruled, the lower courts should have applied the standard of "strict scrutiny," as established in the Supreme Court's 1968 ruling in *Lee v. Washington.* Writing for the majority in the Court's 5 to 3 ruling (with Chief Justice Rehnquist abstaining), Justice Sandra Day O'Connor stated, ". . . In the prison context, when the government's power is at its apex, we think that searching judicial review of racial classification is necessary to guard against invidious discrimination. Granting the CDC an exemption from the rule that strict scrutiny applies to all racial classifications would undermine our 'unceasing efforts to eradicate racial prejudice from our criminal justice system.'"

Impact

The Court's ruling established that, although inmates have diminished constitutional rights due to the fact of their incarceration, the racial segregation of prisoners must be strictly scrutinized by the courts and cannot be justified absent "a compelling state interest." In other words, according to the Court, on the issue of racial segregation inmates enjoy the same constitutional protections as every other American.

It is important to note that the Court's ruling did not preclude prison authorities from ever imposing racial segregation. However, in order to do so, prison authorities were required to meet a stricter two-pronged test of presenting proof that a compelling state interest justifies racial segregation and requiring any policy of racial segregation to be narrowly tailored to satisfy the compelling state interest. The broader justification that a prison policy that imposes racial segregation is "reasonably related to a legitimate penological interest" was no longer sufficient, according to the Court.

Due Process

WOLFF V. MCDONNELL, 418 U.S. 539 (1974)

Background

In 1974, Nebraska state prisoners were subjected to disciplinary procedures, including confinement in a disciplinary cell and forfeiture or withholding of good-time credits, which inmates could accumulate in order to move up their date of release. Nebraska state prisons used the following procedure in cases of alleged misconduct: (1) the inmate was orally informed of the charges, and the merits of the allegations were discussed in a preliminary conference with the chief corrections supervisor and the charging party; (2) a conduct report was prepared; (3) a hearing was held before the prison's disciplinary board at which the accused inmate was able to question the charging party.

Legal Issues

Inmate Robert O. McDonnell, on behalf of himself and other Nebraska state prisoners, filed an action in federal district court alleging that his due process rights were violated and seeking damages and injunctive relief under Title 42 of the U.S. Code, section 1983. The district court rejected McDonnell's claim. However, the Court of Appeals reversed and held that McDonnell's due process claim should be evaluated under the U.S. Supreme Court 1972 decision in *Morrissey v. Brewer* (408 U.S. 471) and the Court's 1973 decision in *Gagnon v. Scarpelli* (411 U.S. 778), which set forth a series of procedures for parole and probation revocation hearings.

Decision

The U.S. Supreme Court affirmed the appellate court and held that inmates have constitutionally guaranteed due process rights in prison disciplinary proceedings. According to the Court, while prisoners did not enjoy the full range of due process rights, those rights must be accommodated in disciplinary proceedings to the extent that institutional needs allowed. The Court held that inmates were entitled to advance written notice of disciplinary actions no less than 24 hours prior to their appearance before the disciplinary board and that the disciplinary board must be impartial. In addition, the inmate must be provided with a written statement by the fact finders stating what evidence they relied upon and their reasons for recommending disciplinary action. In balancing the due process rights of inmates with institutional safety, the Court held that inmates have the right to call witnesses and present evidence in their defense, as long as doing so does not endanger other inmates or otherwise jeopardize institutional control. The Court concluded that inmates' constitutional rights in disciplinary hearings do not include the right to confront and cross-examine witnesses or the right to an attorney.

Impact

In its ruling, the Court was specific in defining the minimal due process rights for inmates at disciplinary hearings. The effect of the ruling, however, was to discourage the use of arbitrary decision making in such hearings, which remain tightly controlled by prison officials. The Court still allowed prison officials significant leeway in leveraging the due process rights of inmates against the interests of institutional security and control.

SUPERINTENDANT V. HILL, 472 U.S. 445 (1985)

Background

In 1982, at the state prison in Walpole, Massachusetts, a correctional officer heard commotion in a prison corridor. When the officer went to the location to investigate the source of the noise, he observed an injured inmate and three other inmates fleeing down the corridor, including Gerald Hill and Joseph Crawford. Hill, Crawford, and the third inmate observed fleeing the scene of the assault received disciplinary reports alleging that they had assaulted the injured inmate discovered by the correctional officer. At a hearing, the prison's disciplinary board heard testimony from the correctional officer and received the officer's written report. Based on the officer's testimony and written report, the board held the inmates responsible for the assault and revoked their good-time credits. Hill and Crawford unsuccessfully appealed the board's decision to the prison superintendent.

Legal Issues

Hill and Crawford filed suit in the Massachusetts Superior Court claiming that their due process rights were violated because there was no evidence, other than the correctional officer's testimony and report, that supported the prison board's ruling. The Superior Court ruled in favor of the inmates and held that the evidence supporting the board's finding of guilt was constitutionally inadequate. On appeal by the prison administration, the Massachusetts Supreme Judicial Court affirmed the superior court's ruling in favor of the inmates Hill and Crawford.

Decision

The U.S. Supreme Court reversed the decisions of the Massachusetts courts. The Court held that good-time credits constituted a protected liberty interest and, as such, the minimum requirements of due process were required in order to revoke them. The Court ruled that the minimum requirement of due process in prison disciplinary hearings was necessary in order to prevent "arbitrary deprivation" of the constitutional rights of inmates. However, in balancing the due process requirements against the imposition of "undue administrative burdens" on the prison, the Court held that, as long as there is "some evidence" of guilt, the standard of due process is satisfied in prison disciplinary hearings. The Court noted that prison officials were not required to weigh the entire record of evidence or to conduct independent assessments of the credibility of witnesses. Rather, "the relevant question is whether there is any evidence in the record to support the disciplinary board's conclusion." The Court found that there was enough evidence to support a finding of guilt against Hill and Crawford based on the correctional officer's testimony and written statement presented before the prison disciplinary board at the Walpole State Prison. As such, Hill and Crawford were afforded a minimal standard of due process sufficient to protect their constitutional rights.

Impact

The Court acknowledged the rights of due process in prison disciplinary hearings but only insofar as the standard of due process does not interfere with the administration of the prison. As in its rulings on First Amendment issues, the Court stressed the need for a balance between protecting inmates' rights and managing a prison. The Court articulated a minimal standard for prison officials to use in disciplinary hearings, without intruding on the ability of prison officials to maintain institutional safety and control.

SANDIN V. CONNER, 515 U.S. 472 (1995)

Background

DeMont Conner was serving a sentence of 30 years to life for the crimes of murder, kidnapping, robbery, and burglary. In August 1987, while a prisoner at the Halawa Correctional Facility, a maximum security prison at

Oahu, Hawaii, Conner was strip-searched by a correctional officer. Conner was angered by the search and uttered profanities at the correctional officer. Conner was later notified that he was being charged with disciplinary infractions, including the use of physical interference to impair a correctional function and harassment of a correctional officer with abusive language. Conner appeared before the prison disciplinary committee, which denied Conner's request to present witnesses at his hearing because the witnesses were unavailable. The board found Conner guilty of misconduct and placed him in disciplinary segregation for 30 days. Conner requested an administrative review. Nine months later, Conner was advised by the prison's deputy administrator that the disciplinary charges against him were unsupported. By that time, however, Conner had filed a lawsuit against prison officials in federal district court.

Legal Issues

Conner alleged that he was deprived of his due process rights at the prison disciplinary hearing when he was not permitted to present witnesses. The district court disagreed and ruled in favor of the prison officials. The Court of Appeals for the Ninth Circuit reversed the judgment, however, and held that Conner had a liberty interest in remaining free from disciplinary segregation. The Ninth Circuit questioned whether Conner received all of the due process protections articulated in the 1974 Supreme Court case *Wolff v. McDonnell* (418 U.S. 539), in light of a Hawaii state prison regulation that a finding of misconduct in disciplinary hearings must be supported by "substantial evidence."

Decision

The U.S. Supreme Court reversed the Ninth Circuit. The Court held that Conner did not have a protected liberty interest under the due process clause of the Fourteenth Amendment or the Hawaii prison regulation. As such, the Court ruled that Conner was not entitled to the procedural due process protections set forth in *Wolff*, in which the Court held that Nebraska state law, not the U.S. Constitution, created a liberty interest in good-time credits. Because the liberty interest was created under state law in *Wolff*, state prisoners were entitled to due process protections before their good-time credits were taken away as a form of disciplinary punishment. The Court held that while states may create such liberty interests for prisoners, they generally apply only when significant deprivations are placed on inmates, such as a longer term of imprisonment by losing good-time credits. The Court found that Conner's 30-day segregation in a disciplinary housing unit did not constitute a significant hardship or deprivation because Conner was already serving a sentence of 30 years to life. As the Court noted, "Conner's situation . . . does not present a case where the State's action will inevitably affect the duration of his sentence." Therefore, Conner's procedural due process rights were not violated under Constitution nor under Hawaii state law.

Impact

In the 1983 case *Hewitt v. Helmes* (459 U.S. 460), the Supreme Court expanded the ability of prisoners to claim a violation of due process rights under a state-created liberty interest. In *Hewitt*, the Court held that the language of state laws and prison regulations was critical and that the words "shall" or "will" in reference to a particular action automatically triggered the due process clause. In *Sandin*, however, the Court backed away from its strict interpretation of language as set forth in *Hewitt*, saying that mandatory language in a law or regulation was not the test for triggering a liberty interest. The Court held that liberty interests are limited, regardless of statutory language, and that the due process clause is only triggered when the disciplinary action imposed upon a prisoner creates a significant hardship.

DISTRICT ATTORNEY'S OFFICE V. OSBORNE, 557 U.S. ____ (JUNE 18, 2009)

Background

In 1994, William Osborne was convicted in an Alaska state court of multiple crimes, including kidnapping and sexual assault. Osborne later sought to use DNA testing that was not available at the time of his conviction in the hope of exonerating himself and requested samples of the biological evidence that was used to convict him. After his request was denied by the district attorney's office (DAO) in Anchorage, Osborne filed suit against the DAO in federal district court on the grounds that his due process rights under the Fourteenth Amendment were violated because he was denied post-conviction access to potentially exculpatory evidence.

Legal Issues

A motion to dismiss the case by the DAO was granted by the district court. Osborne filed an appeal in the U.S. Court of Appeals for the Ninth Circuit, which reversed the lower court's ruling and remanded the case to the district court. In turn, the district court granted summary judgment for Osborne. The DAO appealed to the circuit court, claiming that Osborne should be required to show that the disclosure of evidence would "affirmatively prove that he is probably innocent." The DAO also argued that Osborne was precluded from post-conviction relief because of Osborne's confession to the crimes prior to his trial. The circuit court sided with Osborne and affirmed the district court's ruling, holding that Osborne had due process rights to perform DNA testing on the biological evidence used against him at trial. Further, the circuit court held that Osborne's prior confession did not preclude him from seeking post-conviction relief because scientifically based exculpatory evidence would undermine the validity of Osborne's confession.

Decision

The U.S. Supreme Court reversed the circuit court and, in a 5 to 4 decision, ruled that Osborne did not possess a constitutional right of access to biological evidence used to convict him at trial. The Court held that Alaska's post-conviction relief process—which did not include specific provisions for DNA testing of evidence—provided an adequate protection of Osborne's rights under due process. In a strong dissent, Justice John Paul Stevens—joined by Justices Ruth Bader Ginsburg, Stephen G. Breyer, and David H. Souter—argued that in order to ensure that justice is achieved, Osborne should be allowed to conclusively prove his guilt or innocence by using DNA testing that was not available to him at trial.

Impact

At the time of the Court's ruling in *Osborne*, 47 states had laws that allowed inmates access to biological evidence used against them at trial in order to perform DNA testing, although the laws lacked a uniform standard of access. For example, Alabama limited post-conviction access to DNA testing to inmates under sentence of death, while Ohio permitted much broader access to potentially exculpatory evidence. Only Alaska, Massachusetts, and Oklahoma did not have laws specifically addressing post-conviction access to DNA testing at the time of the decision in *Osborne*. By deferring to post-conviction relief procedures in place at the state level, the Court deemed as sufficient a patchwork of state laws that did not uniformly provide for post-conviction access to DNA testing for all inmates. The Court also left in place state-by-state variations in the threshold of proof required of inmates to show the likelihood that post-conviction DNA testing will result in their exoneration.

Cruel and Unusual Punishment

RHODES V. CHAPMAN, 452 U.S. 337 (1981)

Background

In 1975, the Southern Ohio Correctional Facility, a maximum security state prison in Lucasville, Ohio, began assigning two inmates to cells that were designed for single inmate occupancy. This practice, called double-celling, was deemed necessary due to overcrowding in prisons throughout Ohio. Inmates Kelly Chapman and Richard Jaworski were among the prisoners at the Southern Ohio Correctional Facility who were required to share a single-occupancy cell.

Legal Issues

Chapman and Jaworski filed suit in federal district court on behalf of themselves and all inmates who were double-celled at the Southern Ohio Correctional Facility. Under Title 42 of the U.S. Code, section 1983, Chapman and Jaworski claimed that the practice of double-celling was an unconstitutional violation of the ban against cruel and unusual punishment in the Eighth Amendment, made applicable to states under the due process clause of the Fourteenth Amendment. The district court agreed with Chapman and Jaworski that their conditions of confinement constituted cruel and unusual punishment. The court based its ruling on the following five criteria: (1) double-celled inmates at the prison were serving long sentences; (2) the prison was seriously overcrowded and operating at 138 percent of design capacity; (3) double-celled inmates were forced to share a space of 63 square feet, despite several studies that recommended at least 55 square feet of living space for each inmate; (4) double-celled inmates were forced to spend most of their day confined to their cells; (5) double-celling was not a temporary measure but a permanent condition of confinement at the prison. The court granted the injunction sought by Chapman and Jaworski that barred officials at the Southern Ohio Correctional Facility from housing more than one inmate in a cell, except as a temporary measure. The Court of Appeals for the Sixth Circuit affirmed the district court's ruling.

Decision

The U.S. Supreme Court reversed the lower courts and held that the practice of double-celling at the Southern Ohio Correctional Facility did not rise to the level of cruel and unusual punishment prohibited by the Eighth Amendment. According to the Court, conditions of confinement could be deemed cruel and unusual only if they involved "the wanton and unnecessary infliction of pain [or were] grossly disproportionate to the severity of the crime warranting imprisonment." The Court ruled that simply because conditions of confinement are restrictive, or even harsh, "they are part of the penalty that criminals pay for their offenses against society." As such, they do not rise to the level of cruel and unusual punishment. The Court noted that the five criteria used by the district court to support a finding of cruel and unusual punishment at the prison were "insufficient to support its constitutional conclusion." As such, the Court found no violation of the constitutional rights of Chapman or Jaworski absent evidence that double-celling "either inflicts unnecessary or wanton pain, or is grossly disproportionate to the severity of the crime warranting imprisonment." The Court deferred to the judgment of prison officials regarding conditions of confinement, stating that "courts cannot assume that state legislatures and prison officials are insensitive to the requirements of the Constitution or to the sociological problems of how best to achieve the goals of the penal function in the criminal justice system."

Impact

As with issues concerning first amendment rights and due process, the Court allowed leeway for prison officials in doing the best they can to safely operate penal institutions. Furthermore, the Court made clear that, in its view, criminals must pay a penalty for their crimes, and that penalty may include confinement in unpleasant and even harsh conditions. The Court clarified that the standard of cruel and unusual punishment is not that prisoners suffer, but that they suffer the wanton infliction of pain or equally severe measures that are grossly disproportionate to their crime.

WHITLEY V. ALBERS, 475 U.S. 312 (1986)

Background

On June 27, 1980, Gerald Albers was a prisoner at the Oregon state penitentiary. Prison guards attempted to move several intoxicated prisoners from an annex. The intoxicated prisoners resisted the guards, in full view of Albers and some 200 other inmates confined in Albers's cellblock. Some of the onlookers became agitated, thinking the guards were using unnecessary force on the drunken inmates. Correctional officers ordered Albers and the other prisoners in the cellblock to return to their cells, but some inmates refused to obey the order. A fight erupted between the guards and some of the inmates, and one of the correctional officers was taken hostage. The uprising escalated, and Harold Whitley, the prison security manager, organized an assault squad. Whitley ordered the members of the squad to arm themselves with shotguns and to take control of the cellblock by force. Shooting erupted, and Albers was wounded in his left knee as he was running up a flight of stairs during the confusion. As a result, Albers sustained a severe leg injury and mental and emotional distress.

Legal Issues

Albers filed suit in federal district court under Title 42 of the U.S. Code, section 1983, alleging that his shooting constituted cruel and unusual punishment and, as such, his constitutional rights were violated under the Eighth Amendment. The district court ruled against Albers. The Court of Appeals for the Ninth Circuit however, reversed on the issue of Albers's claims that he was subjected to cruel and unusual punishment in violation of his constitutional rights. The Ninth Circuit held that an Eighth Amendment violation would be established if Albers was deliberately shot by a prison official who knew or should have known that shooting Albers was unnecessary or if the retaking of the cellblock by prison guards was carried out with deliberate indifference to the right of Albers to be free of cruel unusual punishment. In its ruling, the Ninth Circuit noted that there was evidence that the uprising in the cellblock was subsiding when Albers was shot and that the use of deadly force by the prison guard was excessive and should have been preceded by a verbal warning to Albers to stop running.

Decision

The U.S. Supreme Court reversed the appellate court and ruled that the shooting of Albers by a prison guard during an inmate uprising did not constitute cruel and unusual punishment under the Eighth Amendment. The Court held that in a correctional setting neither inadvertence nor an error made in good faith by corrections officials "characterizes the conduct prohibited by the cruel and unusual punishments clause, whether that conduct occurs in connection with establishing conditions of confinement, supplying medical needs, or restoring control over a tumultuous cellblock." As to the appellate court's finding that the deadly force used against Albers by the prison guard was excessive and should have been preceded by a warning, The court noted that "the infliction of pain in the course of a prison security measure . . . does not amount to cruel and unusual punishment simply because it may appear in retrospect that the degree of force authorized or applied for security purposes was unreasonable and . . . unnecessary in the strict sense." The Court held that, in evaluating the totality of circumstances at the time of Albers's injury, the shooting must be viewed as "part and parcel of a good-faith effort to restore prison security."

Impact

In ruling that prison officials could not be held liable for the use of deadly force without showing that they acted in a wanton manner, the Court set a high standard for inmates to meet on constitutional claims of cruel and unusual punishment as the result of deadly force. However, the Court's ruling left unclear if that standard applied only in situations involving deadly force or in all situations involving any degree of force. That issue was later addressed by the Court in its 1992 ruling in *Hudson v. McMillian* (503 U.S. 1), which is presented later in this section.

Prisons

WILSON V. SEITER, 501 U.S. 294 (1991)

Background

In 1990, Pearly L. Wilson was a state prisoner incarcerated at the Hocking Correctional Facility in Nelsonville, Ohio. Wilson objected to numerous conditions of his confinement, including overcrowding, excessive noise, insufficient locker storage space, inadequate heating and cooling, improper ventilation, unclean restrooms, unsanitary dining facilities and food preparation, and being housed with mentally and physically ill inmates. Wilson had complained to prison officials about the conditions but claimed that no action was taken to improve them.

Legal Issues

Wilson filed suit in federal district court seeking declaratory and injunctive relief and $900,000 in compensatory and punitive damages under Title 42 of the U.S. Code, section 1983. In his action, brought against Carl Humphreys, the prison's warden, and Richard P. Seiter, director of the Ohio Department of Corrections, Wilson alleged that the conditions of his confinement constituted cruel and unusual punishment in violation of the Eighth Amendment. The district court ruled in favor of prison officials. The court of appeals affirmed, ruling that Wilson failed to establish a culpable state of mind on the part of prison officials who had taken no action to improve the conditions in the prison. The appellate court held that it was necessary to establish the standard of "behavior marked by persistent malicious cruelty" in order to make a showing of a culpable state of mind.

Decision

The U.S. Supreme Court held that the appellate court applied the incorrect standard in establishing that a culpable state of mind by prison officials was necessary to establish that the prison's conditions of confinement constituted cruel and unusual punishment in violation of the Eighth Amendment. The Court ruled that the appropriate standard was the "deliberate indifference" standard applied in *Estelle v. Gamble* (429 U.S. 97), a case involving the medical care of prisoners, which is presented later in this chapter. The Court held that the application of the wrong standard to establish a culpable state of mind may have constituted harmless error. Nonetheless, the Court remanded the case to the lower courts.

Impact

The significance of *Wilson v. Seiter* is that courts must use the standard of deliberate indifference to prove a culpable state of mind by prison officials when considering whether conditions of confinement rise to the level of cruel and unusual punishment. The Court cited the case of *Estelle v. Gamble* as establishing the deliberate indifference standard. The standard, however, was not clearly defined in either *Estelle* or *Seiter*. The Court provided some clarification on the issue in its 1994 ruling in *Farmer v. Brennan* (511 U.S. 825), in which a subjective standard was applied to determine deliberate indifference by prison officials to a substantial risk of serious harm to an inmate, in violation of the Eighth Amendment. Under the subjective standard, "prison officials may not be held liable if they prove that they were unaware of even an obvious risk, or if they responded reasonably to a known risk, even if the harm ultimately was not averted." As such, the Court set a very high bar for plaintiffs claiming a violation of their rights under the Eighth Amendment as the result of inaction by third parties, such as prison administrators, to inmates whose conditions of confinement place them at substantial risk of harm or injury.

HUDSON V. MCMILLIAN, 503 U.S. 1 (1992)

Background

On October 30, 1983, Keith Hudson was an inmate at the state penitentiary in Angola, Louisiana. Hudson had an argument with Jack McMillian, a corrections officer at the prison. With the assistance of another officer, McMillian placed Hudson in handcuffs and shackles and escorted him to the lockdown area of the prison. En route, Hudson claimed he was punched by McMillian "in the mouth, eyes, chest, and stomach," while the other corrections officer held Hudson from behind while kicking and punching Hudson. A supervisor witnessed the beating. Instead of intervening, the supervisor told the officers "not to have too much fun." As a result of this incident, Hudson suffered loose teeth, minor bruises, and swelling of his face, mouth, and lip. Hudson's partial dental plate was cracked, and Hudson was unable to use it for several months.

Legal Issues

Hudson filed suit against the two corrections officer and the supervisor in federal district court under Title 42 of the U.S. Code, section 1983, alleging a violation of the Eighth Amendment's ban on cruel and unusual punishments. The parties consented to disposition of the case before a magistrate, who found in favor of Hudson and awarded him $800 in compensatory damages. The Court of Appeals for the Fifth Circuit reversed on the grounds that inmates who allege the use of excessive force in violation of the Eighth Amendment must prove significant injury resulting directly from the use of excessive force that was objectively unreasonable and constituted

117

an "unnecessary and wanton infliction of pain." However, the appellate court held that the use of force against Hudson was objectively unreasonable because no force was required, since Hudson was in handcuffs and shackles. The court also found that the conduct of the correctional officers constituted excessive force through "an unnecessary and wanton infliction of pain." However, the appellate court ruled Hudson fell short of his claim that his mistreatment constituted cruel and unusual punishment under the Eighth Amendment because Hudson's injuries were "minor" and required no medical attention.

Decision

The U.S. Supreme Court reversed the appellate court and ruled that the use of excessive physical force against a prisoner may constitute cruel and unusual punishment under the Eighth Amendment regardless of the degree of the injury to the prisoner. The Court began by applying the standard set forth in *Whitley v. Albers* (475 U.S. 312) to determine "whether force was applied in a good faith effort to maintain or restore discipline, or maliciously and sadistically to cause harm." The Court found that the force against Hudson was applied maliciously and sadistically to cause harm and, by extension, constituted an "unnecessary and wanton infliction of pain" that rises to the level of cruel and unusual punishment. The Court ruled that the absence of serious injury is relevant to an Eighth Amendment inquiry but not essential to establish a constitutional violation.

Impact

The Court reiterated the standard set forth in *Whitley* that force applied "maliciously and sadistically to cause harm" violates the Eighth Amendment. The Court reasoned that once that standard is met, the use of force passes the test for the "unnecessary and wanton infliction of pain," regardless of the extent of injury to the prisoner. In 2002, in the case *Hope v. Pelzer* (536 U.S. 730), the Court returned to the issue of the unnecessary and wanton infliction of pain as a benchmark for a violation of a prisoner's rights under the Eighth Amendment. In *Hope* the Court found clear evidence that an Alabama state prison's disciplinary procedure of handcuffing an inmate to a hitching post and subjecting him to exposure from the elements, thirst, and injury violated the Eighth Amendment's prohibition of cruel and unusual punishment. The question in *Hope* was whether correctional officers who subjected the inmate to such disciplinary action were shielded from liability because their conduct did not violate "clearly established statutory or constitutional rights of which a reasonable person would have known." In other words, did the correctional officers know that their conduct was unlawful before they engaged in the conduct at question. The Court ruled in favor of Hope, the Alabama inmate who brought suit, holding that correctional officers who "reasonably" should have known that their conduct was unlawful are not shielded from liability.

ROPER, SUPERINTENDENT, POTOSI CORRECTIONAL CENTER, V. SIMMONS, 543 U.S. 551 (2005)

Background

On September 8, 1993, Christopher Simmons was 17 years of age and still in junior high school when he and his 15-year-old friend, Charles Benjamin, entered the home of Shirley Crook at approximately 2 A.M. by reaching through an open window and unlocking the back door. Simmons and Benjamin bound Crook with duct tape, drove her to a Missouri state park, and threw her from a railroad trestle into the Meramec River, where her body was recovered the next afternoon by fishermen. The day after Crook's body was found, Simmons was arrested at school on suspicion of murder. After nearly two hours of interrogation, Simmons not only confessed to Crook's murder but admitted that he had proposed the crime to Benjamin because Simmons thought they could get away with it because they were minors. Simmons told police that he resolved to kill Crook after entering her home and recognizing her from a previous auto accident that had involved both of them. In addition, Simmons allowed police to videotape him as he performed a reenactment of the crime.

Legal Issues

Although Simmons was 17 at the time of Crook's murder, he was tried as an adult and eligible for the death penalty under Missouri state law, which permitted the imposition of the death penalty for capital crimes committed at the age of 16 or older. At trial, Simmons's videotaped reenactment of the crime was played to the jury, who also heard testimony from Simmons's friends that he bragged to them about the killing. Simmons was convicted and the trial proceeded to the penalty phase, at which the defense argued for leniency based on Simmons's age and his lack of a criminal history. However, the jury returned with a recommendation for the death penalty.

Simmons obtained a new attorney, who moved to set aside the conviction based on ineffective assistance of counsel, contending in part that Simmons's former attorney failed to present testimony that Simmons had a difficult home life which contributed to his poor grades and his abuse of alcohol and drugs. After reviewing the case, the court denied Simmons's motion for a new trial based on ineffective assistance of counsel. The decision was ultimately affirmed by the Missouri Supreme Court.

Simmons then filed a new appeal in state court based on the U.S. Supreme Court's ruling in 2002 in *Atkins v. Virginia* (536 U.S. 304) that the execution of mentally retarded persons was unconstitutional. Using the Court's reasoning in *Atkins*, Simmons argued that the execution of juveniles who were under 18 years of age at the time of their crimes violated the Eighth Amendment's ban against cruel and unusual punishment and the Fourteenth Amendment's right of due process. The Missouri Supreme Court agreed and set aside Simmons's death sentence in favor of life imprisonment without the possibility of parole.

Decision

In a 5 to 4 decision, the U.S. Supreme Court affirmed the ruling of the state court. In the majority opinion for the Court, Justice Anthony M. Kennedy wrote that "from a moral standpoint, it would be misguided to equate the failings of a minor with those of an adult, for a greater possibility exists that a minor's character deficiencies will be reformed." The Court noted three general differences between juveniles under 18 years of age and adult offenders. First, because juveniles are susceptible to immature behavior, "their irresponsible conduct is not as morally reprehensible as an adult." Second, when compared to adults, juveniles lack control over their immediate surroundings and, therefore, "have a greater claim than adults to be forgiven for failing to escape negative influences in their whole environment." Finally, the fact that juveniles are struggling to define their identity "means it is less supportable to conclude that even a heinous crime committed by a juvenile is evidence of irretrievably depraved character."

In rejecting the imposition of the death penalty on juveniles as a violation of the Eighth Amendment's ban against cruel and unusual punishment, the Court held that capital punishment must be limited to those offenders who commit "a narrow category of the most serious crimes," and whose "extreme culpability makes them the most deserving of execution." Justice Kennedy, who was joined by Justices John Paul Stevens, David H. Souter, Ruth Bader Ginsburg, and Stephen G. Breyer, noted that the United States was the only country in the world that continued to sanction the juvenile death penalty. Representatives of the European Union and attorneys from the United Kingdom were among those in the international community who filed briefs as friends of the court urging the Supreme Court to strike down the death penalty for juveniles in the United States.

In a show of strong disagreement, Justice Antonin Scalia read the dissenting opinion from the bench and criticized the majority for concluding "that juries cannot be trusted with the delicate task of weighing a defendant's youth along with other mitigating and aggravating factors of his crime. This startling conclusion undermines the very foundations of our capital sentencing system, which entrusts juries with making the difficult and uniquely human judgments that defy codification and that build discretion, equity, and flexibility into a legal system." Justice Scalia was joined in the dissent by Chief Justice William H. Rehnquist and Justices Sandra Day O'Connor and Clarence Thomas.

Impact

In its ruling of *Atkins* in 2002, the Court reasoned that current standards of decency—not the standards in place at the time the Eighth Amendment was adopted—must be considered in determining when punishment is cruel and excessive. The Court recognized state and federal legislation as the best objective evidence of evolving standards of decency. It noted that in 1989, when the U.S. Supreme Court ruled in *Penry v. Lynaugh* (492 U.S. 302) that the Eighth Amendment did not bar the execution of mentally retarded individuals, only Georgia and Maryland prohibited executing mentally retarded capital offenders. In the intervening years from the Court's decision in *Penry* in 1989 until the *Atkins* decision in 2002, an additional 15 states and the federal government enacted legislation barring the execution of mentally retarded individuals. The Court reasoned that the increasing number of jurisdictions since 1989 that banned such executions was evidence of a trend in evolving standards of decency that viewed the death penalty as cruel and excessive when applied to persons with mental retardation. In response, the Court ruled in *Atkins* that the execution of mentally retarded individuals was unconstitutional under the Eighth Amendment's ban against cruel and unusual punishment, as measured by modern standards of decency.

Applying similar reasoning in *Roper*, the Court held that evolving standards of decency in the United States and among the international community did not support the idea of holding juvenile offenders to the same degree of culpability as adults, even in the most repugnant cases of violent crimes. As such, the Court determined that executing juvenile offenders was morally and socially unacceptable by modern standards of decency. As in *Atkins*, the Court's decision in *Roper* was far-reaching by saying that the right of a jury to recommend capital punishment in the most egregious cases was trumped by an evolving sense of social justice that placed juveniles, like the mentally retarded, beyond the reach of the executioner.

HILL V. MCDONOUGH, 547 U.S. 573 (JUNE 12, 2006)

Background

Clarence Hill was convicted and sentenced to death in 1987 in a Florida state court for first-degree murder. Hill's conviction and death sentence became legally final in 1992, when electrocution was the method of execution under Florida law. However, in 2000, when Hill was still on death row, the law was amended and lethal injection was designated as the primary method of execution. On November 29, 2005, Hill's death warrant was signed by the governor of Florida and the state began preparation to execute Hill by lethal injection.

Legal Issues

Hill challenged Florida's procedure for lethal injection, arguing that sodium pentothal, as the first of three drugs to be administered, would not provide sufficient anesthesia to eliminate potential suffering caused by the other two drugs—pancuronium bromide, a muscle relaxant used to paralyze the lungs, and potassium chloride, which stops the heart. After he was procedurally barred from relief in state court, Hill filed a petition under habeas corpus in federal district court challenging the method of lethal injection used in Florida as a violation of the ban on cruel and unusual punishment contained in the Eighth Amendment of the U.S. Constitution. The district court rejected Hill's petition because Hill had previously filed a writ of habeas corpus challenging his conviction, which the district court found to be "the practical equivalent" of Hill's habeas petition challenging the method of lethal injection. The U.S. Court of Appeals for the Eleventh Circuit affirmed the district court's holding that successive habeas corpus appeals were not permitted under federal law.

Decision

In a unanimous decision, the U.S. Supreme Court ruled that Hill's challenge under habeas corpus of the form of execution was fundamentally different than his previous habeas challenge of the lawfulness of his conviction. Writing for the Court, Justice Anthony Kennedy stated, ". . . Hill's action, if successful, would not necessarily prevent the State from executing [Hill] by lethal injection. The complaint does not challenge the lethal injection sentence as a general matter but seeks instead only to enjoin the respondents from executing [Hill] in the manner they currently intend. . . . Hill concedes that other methods of lethal injection the Department could choose to use would be constitutional. . . . Although the injection of lethal chemicals is an obvious necessity for the execution, Hill alleges that the challenged procedure presents a risk of pain the State can avoid while still being able to enforce the sentence ordering a lethal injection." In other words, had Hill sought to avoid execution altogether, his habeas petition may have been viewed by the court as fundamentally equivalent to his previous petition seeking to overturn his conviction and thereby escape a death sentence. Rather than seeking to prevent his execution, however, Hill was challenging Florida's three-drug protocol for lethal injection and was willing to accept another more humane protocol that was available to the state of Florida for his execution.

Impact

As a result of *Hill*, habeas corpus petitions filed in federal court by death row inmates who are challenging the method of their execution are permissible, regardless of a prior filing of a habeas petition challenging the constitutionality of a sentence of death. Since the court's decision in *Hill*, the three-drug protocol for the administration of lethal injection has come under increasing scrutiny. In 2009, moratoriums on executions occurred in California, Maryland, Kentucky, and the federal system as the result of court challenges that the three-drug protocol constituted cruel and unusual punishment, in violation of the Eighth Amendment. In addition, in 2009, Ohio became the first state to change from the three-drug protocol to a single-drug method of lethal injection deemed more humane.

BAZE V. REES, 553 U.S. 35 (APRIL 14, 2008)

Background

Ralph Baze and Thomas Bowling were under sentences of death by lethal injection in Kentucky. Like many other states, Kentucky administered lethal injection by using a three-drug protocol: first, a drug to induce unconsciousness; second, a drug to stop respiration; and, third, a drug to cause cardiac arrest. Kentucky's protocol required the drugs to be administered in succession. In addition, under the protocol, if the first drug administered did not induce unconsciousness within 60 seconds then another dose of the first drug was required until the person being executed was unconscious. Finally, Kentucky required that the insertion of an intravenous catheter to deliver the drugs was to be performed by a qualified medical technician with at least one year of professional experience.

Legal Issues

Baze and Rees challenged Kentucky's method of execution as a violation of the Eighth Amendment's ban of cruel and unusual punishment. However, the issue was not Kentucky's use of a three-drug protocol to administer execution by lethal injection. Baze and Rees conceded that the use of the three-drug protocol was not cruel. Instead, they argued that there was a significant risk that individuals would err in the proper administration of the three-drug protocol and, as a result, cause undue pain and suffering to the person who was being put to death. The Kentucky Supreme Court disagreed and ruled that the state's system of administering lethal injection contained appropriate safeguards and was not a violation of the Eighth Amendment's ban of cruel and unusual punishment.

Decision

In a 7 to 2 decision, with dissents by Justices Ruth Bader Ginsburg and David Souter, the U.S. Supreme Court affirmed the Kentucky Supreme Court's decision. Writing for the majority, Chief Justice John G. Roberts, Jr., stated, "A State's refusal to adopt proffered alternative procedures may violate the Eighth Amendment only where the alternative procedure is feasible, readily implemented, and in fact significantly reduces substantial risk of severe pain. If a State refuses to adopt such an alternative in the face of these documented advantages, without a legitimate penological justification for adhering to its current method of execution, then a State's refusal to change its method can be viewed as 'cruel and unusual' under the Eighth Amendment."

Impact

At the time of the Court's decision some 30 states and the Federal Bureau of Prisons used the same three-drug protocol for lethal injection as Kentucky. The Court's ruling enabled those states and the federal system to continue to use the same protocol in performing executions by lethal injection. The Court established a standard to determine when procedures to implement the death penalty rise to the level of cruel and unusual punishment. According to the Court, "To constitute cruel and unusual punishment, an execution method must present a 'substantial' or 'objectively intolerable' risk of serious harm." Therefore, the fact that more humane methods of execution are available is not enough to satisfy a claim that the current method of execution constitutes a violation of the Eight Amendment. As the Court held, "allowing a condemned prisoner to challenge a State's execution method merely by showing a slightly or marginally safer alternative finds no support in this Court's cases, would embroil the courts in ongoing scientific controversies beyond their expertise, and would substantially intrude on the role of state legislatures in implementing execution procedures." On May 6, 2008, three weeks after the Court's decision, the first post-*Baze* execution by lethal injection was carried out in Georgia.

KENNEDY V. LOUISIANA, 554 U.S. _____ (JUNE 25, 2008)

Background

In March 1998, Patrick Kennedy raped his eight-year-old stepdaughter, who was so brutalized by the attack that she required emergency surgery. The stepdaughter ultimately named Kennedy as her attacker, and in 2003 Kennedy was convicted of the crime in a Louisiana court.

The Law of Prisons

Legal Issues

At the time of Kennedy's conviction, Louisiana law permitted the imposition of the death penalty in cases of rape when the victim was under 12 years of age. After he was sentenced to death, Kennedy filed an appeal with the Supreme Court of Louisiana claiming that, under the Eighth Amendment's ban of excessive punishments, imposition of the death penalty for the crime of rape violated his constitutional rights. The Louisiana Supreme Court disagreed and upheld Kennedy's death sentence.

Decision

In a 5 to 4 decision, the U.S. Supreme Court reversed the Louisiana court. It held as unconstitutional under the Eighth and Fourteenth Amendments the imposition of the death penalty for the rape of a child if the crime did not result, and was not intended to result, in the death of the child. Delivering the majority's opinion, Justice Anthony Kennedy wrote, "Rape has a permanent psychological, emotional, and sometimes physical impact on the child. . . . It does not follow, though, that capital punishment is a proportionate penalty for the crime. The constitutional prohibition against excessive or cruel and unusual punishments mandates that the State's power to punish 'be exercised within the limits of civilized standards.' The goal of retribution, which reflects society's and the victim's interests in seeing that the offender is repaid for the hurt he caused, does not justify the harshness of the death penalty." In his written dissent, joined by Justices John Roberts, Antonin Scalia, and Clarence Thomas, Justice Samuel Alito argued that evolving standards of decency should permit the punishment of child rapists to the fullest extent of the law because sexual offenders who victimize children were of growing concern to society.

Impact

In the 1972 case of *Coker v. Georgia* the U.S. Supreme Court had ruled that the imposition of the death penalty for the rape of an adult was excessive and, therefore, unconstitutional under the Eighth Amendment. The Court's ruling in *Kennedy* likewise barred states from imposing the death penalty in cases involving the rape of a child unless the rapist kills or intends to kill the child at the time of the crime. However, even in cases of the murder and rape (or attempted murder and rape) of a child, offenders who are juveniles or mentally retarded at the time of the crime cannot be sentenced to death, pursuant to the Court's previous rulings in *Roper v. Simmons* (2005) and *Atkins v. Virginia* (2002), respectively.

Medical Care

ESTELLE V. GAMBLE, 429 U.S. 97 (1976)

Background

On November 9, 1973, J. W. Gamble, an inmate of the Texas Department of Corrections, was injured when a bale of cotton fell on him while he was unloading a truck. When Gamble complained of stiffness, he was sent to the prison's hospital, where he was checked for a hernia by a medical assistant and sent back to his cell. Later that day, Gamble's pain became so intense that he returned to the hospital, where he received pain pills from an inmate nurse and was subsequently examined by a physician. Gamble was diagnosed with a lower back strain and was prescribed medication. Over the next several weeks, Gamble was reexamined and received refills of his medication. In early December, Gamble was certified for light work by the prison's physician, despite Gamble's complaint that his back pain had not abated since the date of his injury. Two days later, Gamble was taken before the prison disciplinary committee for refusing to work. When the committee heard Gamble's complaint of continuing back pain and that he suffered from hypertension, Gamble was referred to another doctor, who prescribed new medication for Gamble's back pain and hypertension. On January 31, 1974, Gamble again was brought before the prison disciplinary committee for refusing to work, and he once again advised the committee that he was unable to work due to severe back pain and hypertension. The disciplinary committee placed Gamble in solitary confinement as punishment for refusing to work. Four days later, Gamble complained of chest pains and blackouts and asked to see a doctor. Gamble was hospitalized and medicated for irregular cardiac rhythm, then placed in administrative segregation. Three days later, Gamble complained of pain in his chest, back, and left arm. Gamble's ongoing requests to see a doctor were refused by prison guards. Finally, after two days, Gamble was allowed to see the prison physician.

Legal Issues

Gamble brought action in federal district court under Title 42 of the U.S. Code, section 1983, alleging that his mistreatment and poor medical care in prison constituted cruel and unusual punishment in violation of his constitutional rights under the Eighth Amendment. Gamble's complaint was dismissed by the district court for failure to state a cause of action for which relief could be granted. The ruling was reversed on appeal on the grounds that the insufficiency of Gamble's medical treatment in prison constituted a legitimate complaint.

Decision

The U.S. Supreme Court reversed the appellate court. The Court held that, while "deliberate indifference by prison personnel to a prisoner's serious illness or injury constitutes cruel and unusual punishment contravening the Eighth Amendment," the medical care received by Gamble in prison "did not suggest such indifference." The Court noted that Gamble was allowed to see medical staff, including physicians, on 17 occasions during a three-month period and that Gamble received treatment by medical staff for his injury and other medical problems. According to the Court, the failure to perform an X-ray or other diagnostic tests constituted medical malpractice, at worst, but did not rise to the level of cruel and unusual punishment.

Impact

In *Estelle v. Gamble*, the Court established "deliberate indifference" as the standard in evaluating the medical care of prisoners in the context of the Eighth Amendment's prohibition of cruel and unusual punishment. Under the deliberate indifference standard, inmates have the burden of showing that proper medical treatment was not provided because of deliberate indifference by prison officials to inmates' medical needs. In this context, behavior that constitutes deliberate indifference may include poor medical treatment, a refusal to treat, or interference with proper treatment. The action or inaction by prison officials must be intentional, however, in order to rise to the level of a violation of constitutional rights. For example, as demonstrated in *Estelle*, medical malpractice, in and of itself, does not qualify as deliberate indifference. Similarly, simple negligence by prison officials does not rise to the level of deliberate indifference. Following *Estelle v. Gamble*, more prisons privatized their medical services, primarily to reduce costs. Because privatized medical services, even within correctional settings, are not directly provided by correctional officials, however, they also at least partially insulate prisons from liability. Privatized services commonly follow well-defined medical protocols and practices, which further reduce the risk of legal exposure.

WASHINGTON V. HARPER, 494 U.S. 210 (1990)

Background

Walter Harper was sentenced to prison in 1976 for robbery and was incarcerated at the Washington state penitentiary. Harper was housed primarily in the prison's mental health unit, where he consented to psychiatric treatment and received antipsychotic medication. In 1980 Harper was paroled on the condition that he continue receiving psychiatric treatment. Harper complied, but in December 1981, his parole was revoked after he assaulted two nurses at a mental hospital where he was confined by civil commitment. Harper was returned to prison and housed in the Special Offender Center, a correctional facility for the diagnosis and treatment of convicted felons with serious mental disorders. Harper was diagnosed with a manic-depressive disorder and gave voluntary consent to mental health treatment at the center, including the administration of antipsychotic medications. However, in November 1982, Harper refused to continue taking the medications. His treating psychiatrist decided to medicate Harper over Harper's objections. Under the terms of a policy at the center, psychiatrists were permitted to subject inmates to involuntary treatment with medication if the inmate suffered from a mental disorder and was gravely disabled or posed a "likelihood of serious harm" to self, others, or their property. According to the policy, an inmate subjected to involuntary medication was entitled to an administrative hearing by a special committee composed of a psychiatrist, a psychologist, and a prison official, none of whom could be involved in the inmate's treatment. If the committee's psychiatrist and at least one other committee member determined that the inmate suffered from a mental disorder and was gravely disabled or dangerous, the inmate could be medicated involuntarily.

Legal Issues

In February 1985, Harper filed suit under Title 42 of the U.S. Code, section 1983. Harper claimed that a judicial hearing, and not merely an administrative hearing, was required to involuntarily administer medication to a mentally ill inmate. Harper alleged that the failure to provide him with a judicial hearing before being involuntarily medicated was a violation of his due process rights guaranteed under the Fourteenth Amendment of the U.S. Constitution. The trial court ruled against Harper. The Washington Supreme Court reversed, however, holding that under the due process clause of the Fourteenth Amendment, the state could administer medication to a competent, non-consenting inmate only if the inmate was afforded the full protections of a judicial hearing, which included the requirement for the state to prove by "clear, cogent, and convincing evidence" that the medication was necessary to further a compelling interest of the state.

Decision

The U.S. Supreme Court reversed the state supreme court, ruling that the involuntary administration of antipsychotic medication does not violate an inmate's due process rights if the state has first established that the inmate is dangerous to self or others or is "seriously disruptive to the environment, and that such treatment is in his 'medical interest.'" The Court held that although Harper had a liberty interest under the due process clause in being free from the arbitrary administration of medication, the prison's policy comported with substantive due process requirements in furtherance of the state's legitimate interest in averting the danger posed by a violent, mentally ill inmate. The Court found that the prison's policy was rational because it applied only to mentally ill inmates who were gravely disabled or were a significant danger to themselves or others and because of the requirement that a licensed psychiatrist administer the medication. The Court rejected Harper's contention that prior to the involuntary administration of medication the state was first required to find him incompetent and then obtain court approval. The Court held that such a requirement would impede the state's legitimate interest in treating Harper for the purpose of reducing the danger that he posed to himself and others.

Impact

In its ruling the Court gave the state authority to administer medication against an inmate's will without first being required to put the matter before a judicial hearing. The Court made clear, however, that such forced medication was permitted only when certain procedural safeguards were in place, as they were in the center where Harper received medication without his consent. In *Estelle v. Gamble*, the Court insulated prison officials from liability absent their deliberate indifference. In *Harper*, the Court further protected the state's interest in controlling inmates who present a danger to self or others.

Parole

MORRISSEY V. BREWER, 408 U.S. 471 (1972)

Background

In 1967, John J. Morrissey pleaded guilty and was convicted of false drawing or uttering of checks and was sentenced to not more than seven years in prison. After his parole from the Iowa state penitentiary in June 1968, Morrissey purchased a car under an assumed name and gave false statements about his address and insurance after a minor auto accident. Morrissey also obtained a credit card using a false name, and he failed to report his place of residence to his parole officer. As a result of his violations of state law and the conditions of his parole, Morrissey was arrested at the direction of his parole officer and incarcerated in county jail. After reviewing the parole officer's written report in the matter, the Iowa Board of Parole revoked Morrissey's parole, and he was returned to prison.

Another individual, G. Donald Booher, was convicted of forgery in 1966 and sentenced to a maximum term of 10 years in an Iowa state prison. Booher was paroled November 14, 1968. In August 1969, at his parole officer's direction, Booher was arrested for a violation of his parole and confined in county jail. A report prepared by Booher's parole officer cited numerous violations of law and parole, including that Booher obtained a driver's license under an assumed name, operated a motor vehicle without permission, and failed to remain gainfully employed, as required under his conditions of parole. The report included admissions to the parole officer by Booher to many of the violations. On September 13, 1969, based on the parole officer's written report, the Iowa Board of Parole revoked Booher's parole, and Booher was returned to state prison.

Legal Issues

After Morrissey and Booher exhausted remedies in state court, both filed petitions in federal district court alleging violations of their due process rights under the Fourteenth Amendment because each was denied a parole revocation hearing prior to the revocation of parole. The district court, ruling separately on each matter, held that the due process rights of Morrissey and Booher were not violated for lack of a parole revocation hearing. Morrissey and Booher filed appeals in federal circuit court, where their cases were consolidated. In a divided ruling of 4 to 3, the court of appeals agreed with the district court that due process does not require a hearing. The majority expressed the traditional view of parole as a privilege, not a right, and held that prison officials should have broad discretion in revoking parole. As such, the court expressed reluctance to interfere in matters that were properly under the control of state prison officials.

Decision

The U.S. Supreme Court reversed the lower courts. The Court recognized that parole revocation does not afford a defendant the same full range of rights as a criminal proceeding. However, "because a parolee's liberty involves significant values within the protection of the due process clause of the Fourteenth Amendment," an informal hearing is required in order to terminate a parolee's liberty. The Court held that "verified facts to support the revocation" of parole must be presented at the informal hearing. The Court also held that, in order to satisfy due process requirements, parolees should receive prior notice of the hearing containing the alleged violation of parole and the purpose of the hearing. At the hearing, a parolee should be allowed to present information relevant to the allegations and to question adverse informants. On the other hand, the Court held that any revocation of parole must be based on probable cause, a far less rigorous standard than beyond reasonable doubt, which is the standard in criminal trials.

Impact

Morrissey v. Brewer was a landmark case because the U.S. Supreme Court established that certain due process requirements apply to the parole process and that those minimal requirements cannot be abrogated by prison officials. Prior to *Morrissey*, states were free to revoke parole according to their own standards. While some states provided for some type of parole revocation hearing prior to *Morrissey*, the rights afforded to alleged parole violators at these hearings varied from state to state. In some states, including California, parole revocation hearings were confidential, without a written record of the proceedings. While *Morrissey* addressed due process rights in parole revocation, the issue of probation revocation itself was not addressed until 1973 in *Gagnon v. Scarpelli* (411 U.S. 778), when the U.S. Supreme Court held that the same due process standards established in *Morrissey* applied in preliminary and final probation revocation hearings.

JOHNSON V. UNITED STATES, 529 U.S. 694 (2000)

Background

Under the Sentencing Reform Act of 1984, most forms of federal parole were replaced with supervised release overseen by the sentencing court. If the conditions of supervised release were violated, the court could revoke the release and require the person to serve a prison term for all or part of the term of supervised release that was originally determined by the court, without credit for any time previously served on supervised release.

In March 1994, the United States District Court for the Eastern District of Tennessee sentenced Cornell Johnson to 25 months in federal prison, to be followed by three years of supervised release, which was the maximum term available under federal law at that time. Johnson received good-conduct credits while incarcerated that allowed him to be released on August 14, 1995, at which time he began serving his three-year term of supervised release. Seven months after his release from prison, Johnson was arrested, and he was later convicted of four state forgery offenses in Virginia. As a result, Johnson was found to be in violation of two of the conditions of his supervised release; namely, that he not commit another crime during his term of supervised release and that he remain in the judicial district where he was sentenced unless given permission to leave. The federal district court revoked Johnson's supervised release and imposed a prison term of 18 months. In addition, the court ordered Johnson placed on supervised release for 12 months following imprisonment, although the court failed to cite the source of its authority to do so.

Legal Issues

Johnson filed an appeal claiming that the district court had no authority to impose the additional term of 12 months of supervised release and that by doing so the court violated the ex post facto clause of the Constitution, which forbids punishment to be applied retroactively. The Court of Appeals for the Sixth Circuit affirmed the ruling of the district court, reasoning that the addition of 12 months of supervised release was not retroactive punishment for a previous offense but, rather, constituted punishment for Johnson's current offense of violating the conditions of his supervised release. Thus, because the punishment was not retroactive, there was no violation of the ex post facto clause.

Decision

The U.S. Supreme Court affirmed the ruling. The Court held that to prevail on an ex post facto claim, Johnson must show that the penalties are attributable to the original conviction, not to the defendant's new offenses for violating his conditions of supervised release. The Court held that the district court had statutory authority to impose a new term of supervised release.

Impact

The Court's ruling strengthened the power of the Court under the Sentencing Reform Act of 1984. As a result of the act, many more criminal offenders in federal courts received fixed and often lengthy determinate sentences for their offenses. The Court added to that the possibility for offenders to be compelled to serve additional terms of supervised release for a violation of a previously imposed term of supervised release.

Sentencing

APPRENDI V. NEW JERSEY, 530 U.S. 466 (2000)

Background

In the predawn hours of December 22, 1994, in Vineland, New Jersey, Charles C. Apprendi, Jr., fired several gunshots into the home of a family of African Americans who had recently moved into the previously all-white neighborhood. Apprendi was arrested and admitted that he was the shooter.

Apprendi made a statement to police, which he later recanted, that he did not personally know the occupants of the house but he did not want them in the neighborhood because they were "black in color." Apprendi was charged in a 23-count indictment with various shooting offenses and the unlawful possession of weapons. None of the counts referred to New Jersey's hate-crime statute or alleged that Apprendi acted with a racially biased purpose. Apprendi pleaded guilty to two counts of second-degree possession of a firearm for an unlawful purpose and one count of unlawful possession of an antipersonnel bomb. The state dismissed the other 20 counts. As part of the plea agreement, the state reserved the right to ask the court to impose a higher "enhanced" sentence for one of the counts on the grounds that the offense was committed with a biased purpose. After the plea hearing, which established evidence of Apprendi's guilt, the trial judge accepted three guilty pleas from Apprendi and held an evidentiary hearing to determine if Apprendi's sentence was subject to enhancement under New Jersey's hate-crime statute. The trial judge held that the hate-crime enhancement applied to one of the counts and sentenced Apprendi to 12 years in state prison on that count and to shorter concurrent sentences on the remaining two counts.

Legal Issues

Apprendi appealed the enhancement of his sentence under New Jersey's hate-crime law as a violation of his due process rights under the Fourteenth Amendment to the U.S. Constitution. Following the 1970 ruling by the U.S. Supreme Court in *In re Winship* (397 U.S. 358), Apprendi argued that the hate-crime sentence enhancement was based on a finding of bias, which must be proved to a jury beyond a reasonable doubt. The appeals court relied, however, on the U.S. Supreme Court's 1986 decision in *McMillan v. Pennsylvania* and held that the intent of the New Jersey state legislature was to make the state's hate-crime enhancement a "sentencing factor," not an element of an underlying offense. As such, the trial court had judicial authority to impose the enhancement based on Apprendi's "motive" in the commission of the offense and not the underlying elements of the offense. The New Jersey Supreme Court affirmed.

Decision

In reversing the lower courts, the U.S. Supreme Court held that, in order to satisfy the due process clause under the Fourteenth Amendment, "any fact that increases the penalty for a crime beyond the prescribed statutory maximum, other than the fact of a prior conviction, must be submitted to a jury and proved beyond a reasonable doubt." The Court's ruling was foreshadowed by its 1999 ruling in *Jones v. United States* (526 U.S. 227).

According to this ruling, the due process guarantee of a jury trial under the Fifth and Sixth Amendments requires that any fact that increases the maximum penalty for a crime must be charged in an indictment or complaint, submitted to a jury, and proved beyond a reasonable doubt. Thus, the Court held that the same protections must apply to due process rights under the Fourteenth Amendment. As such, a state cannot circumvent those protections by substituting the elements of crimes with factors that only increase the punishment for those crimes. In other words, the New Jersey legislature could not disguise an element of the offense by simply placing it in the state's sentencing laws and calling it an enhancement provision. The Court distinguished its ruling in *Apprendi* from its 1986 holding in *McMillan v. Pennsylvania* (477 U.S. 79), in which the Court introduced the term "sentencing factor" to mean a fact that was not part of a jury's finding but could nonetheless affect the sentence imposed by a judge. In *McMillan*, the Court upheld as constitutional the Pennsylvania Mandatory Minimum Sentencing Act. Under that law, Pennsylvania judges were permitted to impose a mandatory minimum sentence of five years in prison for certain felonies in which the offender used a firearm, as determined by the judge using the stand of a preponderance of evidence. In contrast to the situation in *Apprendi*, under the set of facts in *McMillan*, judges were prohibited from imposing any sentence greater than the statutory maximum for the crime of which the defendant was convicted.

Impact

In the Supreme Court's 2002 ruling in *Ring v. Arizona* (536 US 584), the Court overturned its 1990 ruling in *Walton v. Arizona* (530 US. 466) and held that any finding of aggravated circumstances to impose the death penalty must be made by a jury, not a judge, in order to satisfy the Sixth Amendment. The Court explained that it was required to overturn *Walton* in light of *Apprendi* because the two decisions were irreconcilable. The Supreme Court addressed the impact of *Apprendi* on U.S. Sentencing Guidelines in its 2002 ruling in *Harris v. United States* (538 U.S. 1052). In *Harris*, the Court examined Title 18 of the U.S. Code, section 924(c)(1)(A), which provides that a person who uses or carries a firearm in relation to a drug-trafficking crime "shall, in addition to the punishment for the crime" receive a sentencing enhancement of five, seven, or 10 years, depending upon circumstances defined in the statute. In a 5 to 4 decision, the Court held that the statute defines sentencing factors as elements to be determined by a judge, not elements of a crime to be found by a jury. The ruling was significant because the brandishing and firing of a weapon are factors that have an impact on sentencing in many crimes under the U.S. Sentencing Guidelines.

The Law of Prisons

BLAKELY V. WASHINGTON, 542 U.S. 296 (2004)

Background

Yolanda and Ralph Howard Blakely, Jr., were married in 1973. During their marriage, Ralph Blakely was diagnosed at various times with psychological and personality disorders, including paranoid schizophrenia. Yolanda Blakely eventually filed for divorce. In 1998, Ralph Blakely abducted Yolanda from their home in Grant County, Washington. He bound her with duct tape and forced her at knifepoint into a wooden box in the bed of his pickup truck. Blakely implored her to dismiss the divorce suit. When Ralphy Blakely, the couple's 13-year-old son, returned home from school, Blakely ordered him to follow in another car, threatening to harm Yolanda if he did not comply. Ralphy followed the couple, then escaped and sought help when they stopped at a gas station. Blakely continued to hold Yolanda captive and drove to a friend's house in Montana, where Blakely was arrested. Blakely was charged by the state with first-degree kidnapping. In a plea agreement, the charge was reduced to second-degree kidnapping involving domestic violence and the use of a firearm. When entering his plea of guilty, Blakely admitted the elements of second-degree kidnapping and the allegations of domestic violence and use of a firearm.

Legal Issues

At Blakely's sentencing hearing, the state recommended imprisonment within the statutory range of 49 to 53 months. After hearing Yolanda's description of the kidnapping, however, the trial judge imposed a sentence of 90 months in prison, which was 37 months beyond the standard maximum. The judge justified the sentence on the grounds that Blakely had acted with "deliberate cruelty," as defined in a Washington statute that allowed courts to depart from standard sentences in domestic violence cases. Blakely objected to the increase in his sentence, and the judge conducted a bench hearing, at which additional testimony was provided by Yolanda Blakely, Ralphy Blakely, a police officer, and medical experts. After the hearing, the judge justified the extended sentence of 90 months with 32 findings of fact, including that Blakely "used stealth and surprise, and took advantage of the victim's isolation ... employed physical violence ... threatened [Yolanda] with injury and death ... and violated a restraining order [that prohibited him from having contact with Yolanda]." Blakely filed an appeal, arguing that he had a federal constitutional right to have a jury determine beyond a reasonable doubt all facts that were legally essential to impose the 90-month sentence. The Washington Court of Appeals affirmed the trial court's sentence.

Decision

The U.S. Supreme Court reversed the lower courts. The Court held that Blakely's sentencing constituted a violation of his constitutional right under the Sixth Amendment to a jury trial "because the facts supporting Blakely's exceptional sentence were neither admitted by him nor found by a jury." The Court applied the rule in its decision in *Apprendi v. New Jersey* (530 U.S. 466), that "other than the fact of a prior conviction, any fact that increases the penalty for a crime beyond the prescribed statutory maximum must be submitted to a jury, and proved beyond a reasonable doubt." Under *Apprendi* the maximum sentence imposed by a judge must be based "solely on the facts reflected in the jury verdict or admitted by the defendant." The Court held that the Washington state sentencing statute that the trial judge followed was unconstitutional because the enhanced sentencing allowed by the statute was not based on the facts admitted in Blakely's guilty plea or on facts determined by a jury. The Court noted that *Blakely* was not analogous to its ruling in *McMillan v. Pennsylvania* (477 U. S. 79). In *McMillan*, the length of the enhanced sentence was not greater than the maximum term allowable based on the verdict alone. Importantly, as the Court also noted, *Blakely* "is not about the constitutionality of determinate sentencing, but only about how it can be implemented in a way that respects the Sixth Amendment. The Framers' paradigm for criminal justice is the common-law ideal of limited state power accomplished by strict division of authority between judge and jury."

Impact

The significance of *Blakely* is its potential impact on state sentencing statutes, particularly sentencing enhancement statutes that allow courts to increase maximum terms of imprisonment on facts not admitted by a defendant or elements not found by a jury. Under *Blakely* such sentencing schemes appear to be unconstitutional. The Court was clear, however, that its ruling in *Blakely* did not constitutionally undermine determinate sentencing laws but only those sentencing laws that depart from the guarantees of the Sixth Amendment.

Capital Sentencing

RING V. ARIZONA, 536 U.S. 584 (2002)

Background

Timothy Stuart Ring was placed on trial in Arizona for murder, armed robbery, and other charges. During the guilt phase of the trial, the trial judge gave the jury instructions that it could convict Ring of premeditated murder or felony murder, which is a murder that occurs during the commission of another felony. The jury deadlocked on premeditated murder but convicted Ring of felony murder occurring during the commission of an armed robbery.

Legal Issues

Based on the jury's conviction on felony murder, Ring could not be sentenced to death under Arizona law unless the judge found at least one aggravating circumstance and no mitigating circumstance compelling enough for the court to grant leniency. At Ring's sentencing hearing, the judge found two aggravating factors among those enumerated in the Arizona death penalty statute that qualified Ring to receive the death penalty. The two aggravating factors were that Ring committed the offense for monetary gain and that the offense was heinous, cruel, or depraved. The judge found Ring's minimal criminal history to be a mitigating factor, but not sufficiently compelling to call for leniency. Ring was sentenced to death. On appeal to the Arizona Supreme Court, Ring argued that the state's death penalty statute was unconstitutional under the Sixth Amendment because it permitted a judge to impose the death penalty after a jury verdict that did not qualify for the death penalty under Arizona law. However, the Arizona Supreme Court upheld Ring's death sentence.

Decision

The U.S. Supreme Court reversed the ruling. The Court held that the Sixth Amendment requires a jury to determine all of the facts, including aggravating circumstances, in order to impose the death penalty. In 1990, the U.S. Supreme Court had ruled in *Walton v. Arizona* (497 U.S. 639) that the Sixth Amendment did not require a jury to specify the aggravating factors that trigger the death penalty. Those aggravating factors were not elements of the offense that were decided by the *Ring* jury. Rather, the aggravating factors were among the sentencing considerations enumerated under the Arizona law that allowed the trial judges to decide if the death penalty was merited in certain cases. In 2000, the U.S. Supreme Court had appeared to contradict its ruling in *Walton*, however, by holding in *Apprendi v. New Jersey* (530 U.S. 466) that if a defendant's punishment is increased based on a finding of fact, that fact must be established by a jury or by a defendant's free and voluntary admission of the fact. As such, in *Apprendi* the Court held that the defendant's rights under the Sixth Amendment were violated when a New Jersey trial judge increased the defendant's maximum sentence absent any finding by a jury or any such admission by the defendant. In *Apprendi*, the Court attempted to reconcile its decision with the *Walton* ruling and held that both rulings remained valid. In *Ring*, however, the Court concluded that *Walton* was irreconcilable with *Apprendi*, and *Walton* was overruled by the Court. *Ring* established that the same constitutional protections under the Sixth Amendment must be afforded to all defendants, regardless of whether their crimes qualify for the death penalty.

Impact

Historically, challenges to the death penalty had focused on the constitutionality of the method of execution until the U.S. Supreme Court's 1972 ruling in *Furman v. Georgia* (408 U.S. 238), in which the Court considered the constitutionality of the death penalty itself. In *Furman*, the Court struck down Georgia's death penalty law because it did not give juries proper standards and guidelines for imposing the death penalty, thereby allowing the death penalty to be applied in an arbitrary manner, in violation of the Eighth Amendment's ban on cruel and unusual punishment. In 1976, just four years after *Furman*, the Court in *Gregg v. Georgia* (428 U.S. 153) upheld Georgia's rewritten death penalty law because the law provided the guidelines and standards that were lacking under *Furman*. *Gregg* established that the death penalty itself was not unconstitutional, effectively ending *Furman's* moratorium on the death penalty in the United States. Like *Furman* and *Gregg*, *Ring* addressed state laws on the death penalty. *Ring* dealt specifically with sentencing laws and guidelines, however, some of which had been enacted during the 1980s and 1990s in an attempt to get tough on crime. Under *Ring*, the Court held that a state's sentencing guidelines cannot undermine the Sixth Amendment and that a sentence in criminal court cannot be increased to death based solely on the determination of a judge, without a finding of fact by a jury.

In 2004, the U.S. Supreme Court held in *Schriro v. Summerlin* (124 S. Ct. 2519) that the *Ring* ruling did not apply retroactively to death penalty cases that were under review by appellate courts before the *Ring* decision in 2002. *Schriro* concerned the 1981 case of Warren Wesley Summerlin, who was convicted of first-degree murder and sexual assault. As in the *Ring* case, under Arizona law, the crimes of which Summerlin was convicted were not punishable by death without a finding of aggravating factors by the trial judge, not a jury. The trial judge in the case identified two aggravating factors enumerated in Arizona's death penalty law. The factors in aggravation were a prior felony conviction involving the use or threatened use of violence and commission of the offense in an especially heinous, cruel, or depraved manner. The trial judge found no mitigating factors for leniency and sentenced Summerlin to death. A series of state and federal appeals worked their way through the courts over the next 20 years. From 2000 to 2003, Summerlin's federal appeal was pending in the

U.S. Court of Appeals, Ninth Circuit. During that time period, the U.S. Supreme Court issued rulings in *Apprendi v. New Jersey* in 2000, and *Ring v. Arizona* in 2002. The Ninth Circuit, relying on *Ring*, invalidated Summerlin's death sentence, and rejected the argument that *Ring* did not apply because Summerlin's conviction and sentencing were on review before *Ring* was decided. In *Schriro v. Summerlin*, the U.S. Supreme Court reversed the Ninth Circuit. The Court held that, although new substantive rules established under rulings by the U.S. Supreme Court "generally apply retroactively . . . new procedural rules generally do not." The one exception cited by the Court was "watershed rules of criminal procedure implicating the fundamental fairness and accuracy of the criminal proceeding, [which] are given retroactive effect." The Court defined such a rule as "one without which the likelihood of an accurate conviction is seriously diminished." Technically, the *Ring* ruling did not apply to Summerlin's conviction but only to his sentencing. On that point, as stated in *Schriro*, "this Court cannot confidently say that judicial fact-finding seriously diminishes [the] accuracy [of Summerlin's death sentence]." The Court held that its ruling in *Ring* was procedural because the ruling "did not alter the range of conduct or the class of persons subject to the death penalty in Arizona but only the method of determining whether the defendant engaged in that conduct."

Writing for the majority in the Court's 5 to 4 ruling in *Schriro v. Summerlin*, Justice Antonin Scalia cited the Court's 1968 decision in *DeStefano v. Woods* (392 U. S. 631). In *DeStefano*, the Court refused to give retroactive effect to its ruling earlier in 1968 in *Duncan v. Louisiana* (391 U. S. 145), "which applied the Sixth Amendment's jury-trial guarantee to the States." As Justice Scalia wrote, joined by Justices Sandra Day O'Connor, Clarence Thomas, Anthony Kennedy, and Chief Justice William H. Rehnquist, "We noted that, although the right to jury trial generally tends to prevent arbitrariness and repression . . . we would not assert . . . that every criminal trial—or any particular trial—held before a judge alone is unfair, or that a defendant may never be as fairly treated by a judge as he would be by a jury. We concluded that 'the values implemented by the right to jury trial would not measurably be served by requiring retrial of all persons convicted in the past by procedures not consistent with the Sixth Amendment right to jury trial.' If, under *DeStefano*, a trial held entirely without a jury was not impermissibly inaccurate, it is hard to see how a trial in which a judge finds only aggravating factors could be."

In dissenting, Justice Steven Breyer, joined by Justices John Paul Stevens III, David Souter, and Justice Ruth Bader Ginsburg, wrote, "In my view, [the *Ring*] holding amounts to a 'watershed' procedural ruling that a federal habeas court must apply when considering a constitutional challenge to a 'final' death sentence—i.e., a sentence that was already final on direct review when *Ring* was decided . . . *Ring's* requirement that a jury, and not a judge, must apply the death sentence aggravators announces a watershed rule of criminal procedure that should be applied retroactively in habeas proceedings."

[1] Ann H. Matthews. "The Inapplicability of the Prison Litigation Reform Act to Prisoner Claims of Excessive Force." *New York University Law Review* 77:536 (May 2002): 542.

[2] Ann H. Matthews. "The Inapplicability of the Prison Litigation Reform Act to Prisoner Claims of Excessive Force." *New York University Law Review* 77:536 (May 2002): 551.

[3] Ashley, Nellis and Ryan S. King. "No Exit: The Expanding Use of Life Sentences in America." The Sentencing Project, July 2009, pp. 5–11.

[4] Christine S. Scott-Hayward. "The Fiscal Crisis in Corrections: Rethinking Policies and Practices." Vera Institute of Justice, Center on Sentencing and Corrections, July 2009, pp. 9–11.

[5] Ryan S. King. "The State of Sentencing 2008: Developments in Policy and Practice." The Sentencing Project, February 2009, pp. 6–7.

[6] Jennifer K. Elsea et al. "Enemy Combatant Detainees: Habeas Corpus Challenges in Federal Court." Congressional Research Service Report to Congress, April 7, 2009, pp. 1–4.

CHAPTER 3

CHRONOLOGY

This chapter presents a chronology of significant developments in the history of prisons, with emphasis on developments in corrections in the United States.

circa 1750 B.C.

- The Code of Hammurabi is established by King Hammurabi of Babylon. Like the earlier Sumerian codes, established circa 1860 B.C., punishment for wrongdoing is based on vengeance and includes mutilation, flogging, and execution, sometimes personally administered by the victim. Both the Sumerian and the Hammurabi codes predate the concept of imprisonment as a form of punishment.

621 B.C.

- Draco, ruler of Greece, implements a harsh set of laws under which citizens and slaves receive equal punishment. Under the Draconian code, any citizen can prosecute an offender in the name of the injured party for the protection of society, thus shifting the goal of punishment from personal vengeance to maintaining social order. Under the Draconian code, the burden of punishment shifts from the individual to the state.

circa 64 B.C.

- The Mamertine prison, the earliest known prison, is built in ancient Rome. It is unclear if the Mamertine prison, consisting of a series of underground dungeons, functioned in the manner of modern-day prisons by using incarceration as a form of punishment or if the dungeons at Mamertine were simply holding areas for lawbreakers awaiting other punishments.

Prisons

A.D. 529–535

- The legal code *Corpus Juris Civilis* is compiled under Byzantine emperor Justinian I. The concept of proportionality, that the punishment should fit the crime, is established, and the scales of justice are first depicted in art from the Justinian period. The administration of punishment by the state, as set forth in the Draconian code, and proportionality in punishment established under Justinian form the basis of Western law and laid the foundation for the use of incarceration as a form of punishment.

1233

- The Inquisition is created by Pope Gregory IX to abolish heresy. As a result, prisons are built within monasteries to confine those accused of heresy against the church, and solitary confinement is sometimes utilized to create an atmosphere of atonement and penitence for prisoners.

1300s

- As gunpowder comes into wider use in Europe, fortresses previously built for defensive purposes become increasingly obsolete and are sometimes converted to places of confinement for prisoners. Fortress architecture later becomes a model for prison design.

1557

- The Bridewell workhouse is established in London to house undesirables, including the homeless, the unemployed, and some orphans. Residents are subjected to strict discipline and long work hours in harsh conditions. According to public perception, Bridewell is a success for keeping undesirables out of sight.

1576

- The English Parliament orders the construction of a workhouse in every county in England, and the workhouse concept begins to spread throughout Europe. Conditions inside workhouses are often deplorable, with no segregation of males and females or juveniles and adults. Violence and abuse among inmates and exploitation by jailers is common, and poor sanitation results in outbreaks of typhus that sometimes infect the surrounding communities.

1681

- William Penn founds a Quaker settlement in Pennsylvania in colonial America. A Quaker himself, Penn advocates for more humane treatment of lawbreakers, according to the Quakers' Great Law, which calls for the punishment of most offenses with hard labor in a house of correction. The Quakers' concept of confinement as a component of punishment, instead of a prelude to execution or corporal punishment, is unique in colonial America. Also unique under the Quaker code is that punishable offenses are secular in nature and do not include religious offenses as the English codes do.

1704

- The Hospice of San Michele is built in Rome by Pope Clement XI and is one of the first correctional institutions designed exclusively for juvenile offenders. The design of separate cells for sleeping quarters and a large central hall for working is modeled after monasteries and becomes a model for U.S. penal institutions in the 19th century under the Auburn system. In *State of Prisons*, published in 1777, John Howard uses the Hospice of San Michele as an example of a model facility.

1764

- Cesare Beccaria, one of the most influential thinkers on issues of crime and punishment, publishes his most widely known work, *An Essay on Crimes and Punishment*. The book (originally published anonymously) promotes then-radical ideas, such as that the purpose of punishment is to deter crime and not to exact social revenge. For the most serious crimes, Beccaria advocates life imprisonment over the death penalty.

1773

- The Maison de Force is built in Ghent, Belgium, under the direction of Belgian administrator Jean-Jacques Vilain, who follows the basic pattern of European workhouses in designing the facility. At the Maison de Force, Vilain segregates females and juveniles from serious offenders and utilizes a system of individual cells to house inmates. Although Vilain requires prisoners to work in silence, he opposes cruelty as a means of inmate control. In *State of Prisons*, published in 1777, John Howard uses Maison de Force as an example of a model facility.
- A state prison for felons is established in Simsbury, Connecticut, on the site of an abandoned copper mine. One year later, in 1774, inmates at the prison riot over poor conditions of confinement.

1776

- The deportation of English prisoners to the American colonies abruptly ends due to the American Revolution. English authorities begin using

Australia as an alternative, but transportation is limited. To ease over-crowding in prisons, inmates are confined in old transport ships and obsolete war vessels, known as hulks. Conditions in the unventilated, ver-min-infested hulks are worse than in jails and prisons. Although English officials view the use of hulks as temporary, their use persists until 1858.

1777

■ In England, John Howard publishes *State of Prisons*, in which he describes the best of the correctional facilities he visited during his tours of cor-rectional facilities throughout Europe. Howard publishes the book in an effort to reform the deplorable conditions that he witnessed in prisons and jails. Among Howard's recommendations are regular inspections of correctional facilities to ensure compliance with basic standards of sani-tation and living conditions and the implementation of work and educa-tional programs designed to deter criminals from reoffending.

1779

■ The British Parliament passes the Penitentiary Act, which implements some of the reforms suggested by John Howard in *State of Prisons*. Due to rising urban crime rates, however, many prisons in the United Kingdom experience serious overcrowding, making it difficult to implement the reforms and muting the impact of the Penitentiary Act.

1790

■ The Pennsylvania legislature permits the Quakers to operate a wing of the Walnut Street jail in Philadelphia as a penitentiary for convicted felons, except those sentenced to death. The basic design consists of solitary cells. Reformers, including Benjamin Franklin and Benjamin Rush, both sign-ers of the U.S. Declaration of Independence, and Revolutionary Army war hero William Bradford, help to develop a system of prison discipline at the Walnut Street Jail that borrows from the principles for the humane treatment of inmates advanced by Quaker William Penn and European reformers like Cesare Beccaria and John Howard. The system developed at the Walnut Street Jail becomes known as the Pennsylvania system.

1791

■ The Bill of Rights, comprising the first 10 Amendments to the U.S. Constitution, is ratified, establishing freedom of speech and religious ex-pression under the First Amendment, the right to trial by jury under the Sixth Amendment, and the prohibition of cruel and unusual punishment under the Eighth Amendment.

Chronology

1816

- A new prison is built at Auburn, New York. Unlike the system of single cells designed for solitary confinement under the Pennsylvania system, Auburn prison's design includes communal areas where inmates congregate for work and meals. Smaller cells designed as sleeping quarters are built vertically in tiers on five floors. Prisoners work and eat in silence together during the day and are separated only at night. Under the Auburn system, as it comes to be known, solitary confinement is used as a punishment for disobeying prison rules. The use of long-term solitary confinement is abandoned at Auburn in 1823, however, because of mental breakdowns suffered by inmates as a result of the unrelenting isolation.

1825

- Sing Sing prison is built in New York. It uses the Auburn system. By 1869, the Auburn system is implemented at some 35 U.S. prisons nationwide, including San Quentin state prison in California, built in 1852. The Auburn system's structural design of tiers of cells, also known as cell blocks, becomes the model for most prisons built in the United States for the next 150 years.

1840

- In the United Kingdom, Captain Alexander Maconochie is placed in charge of a British penal colony on Norfolk Island that houses some of the country's worst offenders. Maconochie implements a series of reforms and a system of early release earned by good conduct and hard work. In 1870, the reform-minded principles advanced by the American Prison Congress are based, in part, on Maconochie's work.

1850

- In Ireland, Sir Walter Frederick Crofton develops a system of indeterminate sentencing, which becomes know as the Irish system. Crofton reasons that if penitentiaries are designed as places of repentance and personal reform, then there must be a mechanism in place for prisoners to benefit when they demonstrate their reform. In 1870, Crofton's work influences the members of the newly formed American Prison Congress, which advances principles that are based, in part, on Crofton's sentencing scheme.

1865

- With the end of the Civil War and slavery, able-bodied male inmates begin to be exploited as laborers on a national scale. In the South, prisoners are used to replace the freed slaves. In the North, state prisons are commonly paid an annual fee by companies for the use of their inmates as workers.

1868

■ The Fourteenth Amendment to the U.S. Constitution is ratified, establishing due process guarantees and equal protection under the law.

1870

■ Prison administrators and reformers meet in Cincinnati, Ohio, at the American Prison Congress to discuss the future of corrections in the United States. They form the National Prison Association (renamed the American Correctional Association in 1954) and elect as their first president the governor of Ohio, Rutherford B. Hayes, who in 1877 becomes the 19th president of the United States. Principles advanced by the National Prison Association include establishing a three-stage system of punishment, reform, and probation in all prisons and using indeterminate sentencing as a way to reward inmates for good behavior and hard work. Other principles include educational and treatment programs for prisoners, minimizing the use of physical force against inmates, and segregating juveniles, females, and males in separate facilities.
■ The Justice Department is established and, in 1871, placed in charge of the growing number of federal prisoners in state and local correctional facilities. Due to prison overcrowding, some states only accept federal prisoners who are residents of that state.

1871

■ The U.S. Congress passes the Ku Klux Klan Act of 1871, codified in part in Title 42 of the U.S. Code, section 1983, which gives individuals the right to seek legal remedy in federal court if their constitutional rights are violated by state or local laws. Originally designed to protect the newly acquired constitutional rights of African Americans after the Civil War, section 1983 is widely used by prisoners, beginning in the 1960s, to bring causes of action in federal courts for alleged violations of their constitutional rights.

1876

■ The first reformatory in the United States is built in Elmira, New York, to house adult felons. Under the direction of Zebulon Brockway, the first superintendent at Elmira, however, the reformatory is used for first-time male offenders between the ages of 16 and 30, in the hope that they are more amenable to rehabilitation than hardened criminals. The programs at Elmira include educational and vocational training. A system of indeterminate sentencing is implemented, including a grading system that allows inmates to earn points for early release through good conduct and hard work. These reforms reflect the principles advanced in 1870 by the National Prison Association. By 1913, reformatories modeled after Elmira are built in 17 U.S. states.

1890

- *August 6:* Convicted murderer William Kemmler is executed by electrocution at the Auburn penitentiary in New York. Kemmler becomes the first prisoner to be put to death in the electric chair.

1895

- The U.S. War Department transfers prisoners at the military prison in Fort Leavenworth, Kansas, to alternative facilities in the United States. As a result, space becomes available at Leavenworth for federal prisoners. For the first time in U.S. history, some nonmilitary federal prisoners are housed in a federal penitentiary instead of state or local correctional facilities.

1896

- Congress appropriates funds for the construction of a federal prison for 1,200 inmates at a site approximately three miles from the Leavenworth prison. Built by convict labor, the prison is not completed until 1928.

1899

- The Illinois Juvenile Court Act creates a new judicial jurisdiction for juvenile delinquents that is separate from the adult criminal justice system. Among the most important provisions of the act is the strict segregation of juvenile and adult offenders in correctional settings. Using the Illinois Juvenile Court Act as a model, juvenile courts are established in 1901 in New York and Wisconsin, and in 1902 in Maryland and Ohio. By 1928, only Maine and Wyoming do not have juvenile court systems in place.

1919

- The Dyer Act criminalizing the interstate transportation of stolen vehicles becomes federal law. As a result of the Dyer Act, the White Slave Act of 1910, outlawing interstate commerce in prostitution, the Harrison Narcotic Act of 1914, establishing controlled substances, and the Volstead Act of 1918, prohibiting the sale and consumption of alcoholic beverages, more Americans are arrested for violations of federal law, creating a significant increase in the number of federal prisoners nationwide.

1924

- *February 8:* Gee Jon is executed in Nevada and becomes the first U.S. prisoner to be put to death in the gas chamber.

1929

- The Hawes-Cooper Act is passed by the U.S. Congress and becomes law. Under the act, interstate prison products become subject to the law of the state to which they are shipped, allowing states to limit market competition of out-of-state prison products with goods manufactured in-state.

1930

- President Herbert Hoover signs into law the legislation that creates the Federal Bureau of Prisons (BOP) and appoints as its first director Sanford Bates, then president of the National Prison Association (renamed the American Correctional Association in 1954).

1934

- Under its director Sanford Bates, the Bureau of Prisons (BOP) implements a classification system unique in U.S. penology. Under the system, each federal correctional facility is classified as a penitentiary, reformatory, prison camp, hospital, or drug addiction treatment facility. Federal prisoners are classified according to such factors as age, sex, and type of offense, with the goal of developing individualized programs for rehabilitation. The BOP also establishes five regional training centers for correctional staff, and by 1937, all federal correctional personnel are under the jurisdiction of the Civil Service Commission. In addition, federal parole is reorganized, and the supervision of parolees is transferred from the U.S. Marshall's Office to the probation offices of the federal courts in order to develop an after-care system that is more treatment-oriented and less punitive in its approach to ex-convicts.
- The U.S. Congress establishes Federal Prison Industries (FPI) to provide vocational training and employment to federal inmates. The FPI is commonly referred to by its trade name, UNICOR, which is not an acronym. UNICOR manufactures products that are generally not available in the private sector, including signs. By fiscal year 2002, UNICOR generates $679 million in sales from operations at 111 factories nationwide and employs nearly 22,000 federal inmates, who earn from 23 cents to $1.15 per hour.

Chronology

- The U.S. military prison at Alcatraz Island in the San Francisco Bay is converted to the first federal super maximum prison in the United States. Known as the Rock, Alcatraz is designed to house the worst offenders and those who are the least controllable and the most disruptive in other federal prisons. The prison at Alcatraz closes in 1963 due to high operating costs. During its 29 years of operation, Alcatraz gains a reputation as the most repressive federal prison in the United States. In 1972, the Alcatraz prison becomes part of the Golden Gate National Recreational Area.

1935

- The Amhurst-Sumners Act is passed by the U.S. Congress and becomes law. As later amended in 1940, the act permanently stops the transport of prison products shipped out-of-state. As a result, many state prison industries are either closed or downsized, severely restricting opportunities for vocational training for many state prisoners.

1949

- The United States signs the four Geneva Conventions, which establish the rights and protections afforded to prisoners of war, including members of armed forces and civilians. On June 8, 1977, two protocols are added to the Geneva Conventions that give similar protections to other types of victims of war, including victims of wars against racist regimes.

1954

- The first state super maximum security prison is opened in Mississippi.

1963

- The federal prison at Marion, Illinois, goes into operation. The prison is designed to hold 500 male felons who are difficult to control. In 1973, a section of the Marion prison is designated as a control unit to house the most violent and disruptive inmates. The control unit model is adopted by other prisons.

1964

- In *Cooper v. Pate* (378 U.S. 546), the U.S. Supreme Court holds that prisoners have a legitimate right to be heard in federal courts. By so ruling, the Court departs from the *hands-off doctrine* used by previous courts to deny prisoners the right to litigate prison-related grievances. The *hands-off doctrine* is first articulated in 1866 by the U.S. Supreme Court

Prisons

in the case of *Pervear v. Massachusetts* (72 U.S. 678). As late as 1958, in the case of *Gore v. United States* (357 U.S. 386), the U.S. Supreme Court maintains its hands-off policy with regard to prisoners seeking redress for violations of their civil rights.

1968

- The American Correctional Association (ACA) establishes an accreditation process for correctional institutions and creates a standards committee composed of criminal justice professionals to administer the accreditation process. Through accreditation, the ACA establishes minimum standards on issues such as inmate health, institutional safety, and staff training.

1969

- In *Johnson v. Avery* (393 U.S. 483), the U.S. Supreme Court issues the first in a series of landmark rulings on prisoners' rights on issues including legal representation, cruel and unusual punishment, religious freedom, and medical care.

1970

- Three prisoners and a corrections officer are killed in a riot at the Soledad prison in Salinas, California. Inmate uprisings occur at other prisons nationwide, including the Holmesburg prison in Philadelphia, Pennsylvania, where 84 prisoners and 24 guards are injured, and at the Tombs prison in New York City, where prisoners take 26 hostages to protest overcrowded conditions of confinement.

1971

- *September:* Inmate rioting at the state prison at Attica, New York, results in 39 deaths. In reaction to this and other inmate uprisings and to the prisoners' rights movement, in 1975 the Bureau of Prisons begins to phase out the use of the rehabilitative medical model in favor of the correctional philosophies of deterrence and incapacitation, which are more in line with maintaining control over what is viewed as an increasingly vocal and sometimes violent prisoner population.

1972

- In *Morrissey v. Brewer* (408 U.S. 271), the U.S. Supreme Court rules that parolees have certain constitutional rights at parole revocation hearings, including written notification of the hearing and the alleged violations and the right to present and hear evidence against them.

Chronology

- Executions are halted in the United States when the U.S. Supreme Court, in the case of *Furman v. Georgia,* rules that Georgia's death penalty law violates the Eighth Amendment's ban against cruel and unusual punishment. In 1976, however, the Court holds in *Gregg v. Georgia* that Georgia's revised guidelines for the application of the death penalty are constitutional, and executions resume throughout the United States.

1974

- The Office of Juvenile Justice and Delinquency Prevention (OJJDP) is created under the Juvenile Justice and Delinquency Prevention Act of 1974 to monitor and study all facets of juvenile justice in the United States. In 2000, the OJJDP conducts its first census of residential facilities for juvenile offenders in the United States.

1976

- In *Estelle v. Gamble* (429 U.S. 97), the U.S. Supreme Court establishes the "deliberate indifference" standard for lawsuits brought by prisoners alleging cruel and unusual punishment, in violation of the Eighth Amendment. Under this standard, inmates are required to prove that their rights are violated because of deliberate indifference by prison officials and not mere negligence or oversight.

1977

- Oklahoma becomes the first state to legalize execution by lethal injection, which is viewed as more humane than hanging, electrocution, or other legal methods of execution. On December 6, 1982, in Texas, convicted murderer Charles Brooks is the first person in the United States executed by lethal injection, which becomes the primary mode of execution in both the federal and state correctional systems.

1978

- The U.S. Bureau of Prisons adds a level 6 to its inmate classification system for the most violent and disruptive federal prisoners. The federal prison at Marion, Illinois, is designated as the only level 6 correctional facility in the federal prison system. As such, the U.S. prison at Marion becomes a supermax facility.

1984

- The first privately operated correctional facility is created when the Corrections Corporation of America (CCA) is awarded a contract to operate

Prisons

---

a correctional facility in Hamilton County, Tennessee. In 1985, CCA offers to take over the entire state prison system in Tennessee for $200 million, but the bid is rejected due to opposition from state employee unions and skepticism by state legislators. By 1988, however, with prisons and jails in 39 states and the District of Columbia under court order to improve conditions of confinement and reduce prison overcrowding, the trend toward prison privatization gains momentum. By 2002, some 94,000 prisoners in 31 states and the federal system are confined in private correctional facilities.

1985

- The U.S. Sentencing Commission, established in 1984 by Congress as an independent agency within the judicial branch of the federal government, calls for strict federal sentencing guidelines and issues recommendations for federal courts that include increasing the length of prison terms for violent crimes and reducing the use of probation for crimes against persons and serious drug offenses.

1989

- The Security Housing Unit, or SHU, for the most violent and disruptive prisoners is opened at the state prison in Pelican Bay, California. The SHU at Pelican Bay becomes the model for supermax prisons and control units in both the state and federal prison systems. Prisoners in the SHU in Pelican Bay are confined in cells measuring 8 by 10 feet for all but 90 minutes each day, when they are allowed to go alone to an enclosed concrete exercise area. Cell doors are constructed of solid steel and are opened and closed by remote control.

1992

- In *Hudson v. McMillian* the U.S. Supreme Court rules that the use of physical force against a prisoner may constitute cruel and unusual punishment even when the prisoner does not suffer serious injury. The Court holds that the force must be administered maliciously or sadistically with intent to cause harm in order to trigger a violation of the Eighth Amendment and that force applied in a good-faith effort to maintain or restore discipline does not rise to that level.

1993

- The U.S. Bureau of Prisons opens a new supermax facility in Florence, Colorado, designed to house 480 of the most dangerous and aggressive inmates in the federal prison system.

Chronology

1995

- At the federal prison in Terre Haute, Indiana, a lethal injection facility is built at a cost of $300,000 and consists of an execution chamber surrounded by five viewing rooms. During federal executions, all procedures are monitored by the Justice Department in Washington, D.C., through an open telephone line with prison officials.

1996

- The U.S. Congress passes the Prison Litigation Reform Act of 1995 (PLRA), which places significant restrictions on the ability of prisoners to file civil rights claims in federal court. Under the PLRA, indigent prisoner litigants must post a filing fee, courts have broader discretion to dismiss prisoners' lawsuits as frivolous or malicious, and prisoners with three prior lawsuits dismissed as frivolous or malicious are disqualified from filing additional lawsuits unless they are in imminent danger of serious harm. Also, under the PLRA, prisoners must exhaust all administrative remedies before filing a lawsuit in federal court over prison conditions, and prisoners must show physical injury in order to claim mental or emotional injury. The aim of the PLRA is to reduce the caseload in federal courts and to encourage state and local correctional agencies to develop alternatives to litigation in the federal courts.

2000

- *December 13:* Seven inmates escape from the Connally Unit Prison, a maximum security facility in Karnes City, Texas. Known as the Texas Seven, prisoners George Rivas, Michael Anthony Rodriguez, Larry Harper, Joseph Garcia, Patrick Murphy, Jr., Donald Keith Newbury, and Randy Halprin remain at large for several weeks as they travel from Texas to Colorado. On January 22, four of the seven are captured at a trailer park in Woodland Park, Colorado. A fifth convict, Larry Harper, commits suicide rather than surrender to police. On January 24, the remaining two, Donald Keith Newbury and Patrick Murphy, Jr., are apprehended by federal agents at a Holiday Inn near Colorado Springs, Colorado. The six surviving members are charged with the murder of police officer Aubrey Hawkins during a robbery in Irving, Texas, on Christmas Eve. By 2004, George Rivas, Donald Newbury, Michael Rodriguez, and Joseph Garcia are convicted of the crime and sentenced to death.

2001

- *June 11:* Timothy McVeigh becomes the first federal prisoner executed by lethal injection. McVeigh is executed for his part in killing 168 people and injuring some 850 others in the 1995 bombing of the Alfred P. Murrah Federal Building in Oklahoma City, Oklahoma.

- *June 28:* Human Rights Watch issues a report stating that inmate-on-inmate rape is the most pervasive yet underreported form of violence in prisons nationwide. The underreporting of prison rape may occur for several reasons, including the reluctance of correctional officials to recognize the extent of the problem, according to the report.

2002

- *June 24:* In *Ring v. Arizona,* the U.S. Supreme Court rules that the Sixth Amendment requires a jury, not a judge, to determine all of the facts, including aggravating circumstances, in order to impose the death penalty. In *Ring,* the Court overrules its 1990 ruling in *Walton v. Arizona* that a jury is not required to determine such facts in order to satisfy the Sixth Amendment. *Ring* establishes that the same constitutional protections under the Sixth Amendment must be afforded to all defendants, regardless of whether their crimes qualify for the death penalty.
- *August 7:* A report by the National Commission on Correctional Health Care, submitted to the U.S. Congress, estimates that 2–4 percent of state prisoners are schizophrenic or psychotic. In addition, according to the report, some 13–18 percent of prisoners suffer from major depression, and between 22 and 30 percent of prison inmates have an anxiety disorder.

2003

- The Bureau of Justice Statistics announces that some 1.2 million inmates are incarcerated in state prisons nationwide, and nearly 160,000 inmates are confined in U.S. federal prisons. As a result, 429 out of every 100,000 people in the United States were in prison or jail, the highest rate of incarceration in the world.

2004

- *January 22:* A report commissioned by the California Attorney General's Office in response to a lawsuit filed by the Prison Law Office is issued. It determines that nine juvenile facilities in the California Youth Authority (CYA) are run more like adult prisons, with emphasis placed on incapacitation instead of rehabilitation. According to the report, CYA facilities are deficient in 21 out of 22 minimal standards established by experts in juvenile corrections. Violations documented in the report include the use of locked cages to confine some wards during school classes. Other violations include excessive use of psychotropic medications for behavior control and the overuse of chemical restraints, including pepper spray, by staff members with insufficient training in behavior management.

- *February 1:* Ending a 15-day standoff, corrections officer Lois Fraley is released after she and another officer were held hostage by two prisoners in an observation tower at the Lewis state prison in Buckeye, Arizona. The other hostage, corrections officer Jason Auch, was released and hospitalized on January 24, 2004.
- *February 5:* According to a report by the Sentencing Project, one out of every 21 African-American men in the United States is incarcerated on any given day. For African-American males in their late 20s, one out of eight is incarcerated on any given day in the United States.
- *March 20:* Photographs are made public that show the alleged physical and sexual abuse of prisoners of war by U.S. soldiers at the Abu Ghraib prison in Iraq, in possible violation of the standards of international law governing the humane treatment of prisoners of war, as established under the Geneva Conventions. The U.S. Congress and the Defense Department later announce investigations into the alleged abuse of U.S. prisoners of war in Iraq and Afghanistan, including the deaths of some 40 prisoners of war.
- *June 24:* In *Hamdi v. Rumsfeld* and *Rasul v. Bush*, the U.S. Supreme Court rules that prisoners detained at the U.S. Naval Base at Guantánamo Bay, Cuba, as the result of the U.S. war on terrorism have limited rights to contest their detention in courts of law.
- *June 24:* In *Blakely v. Washington* (124 S. Ct. 2531) the U.S. Supreme Court applies the rule in its holding in *Apprendi v. New Jersey* (530 U. S. 466) that "other than the fact of a prior conviction, any fact that increases the penalty for a crime beyond the prescribed statutory maximum must be submitted to a jury and proved beyond a reasonable doubt." The significance of *Blakely* is its potential impact on the constitutionality of state sentencing statutes, particularly sentencing enhancement statutes that allow courts to increase maximum terms of imprisonment on elements not found by a jury or facts not admitted by a defendant.
- *August 5:* The California Youth Authority bans the use of isolation as punishment for misbehavior by juvenile wards. The decision comes under mounting pressure from critics, including legislators and parents of incarcerated youths, who claim that the California Youth Authority fails to rehabilitate youths, provide them with basic medical care, or protect them from violence.
- *September 21:* A report by Earl Devaney, inspector general of the U.S. Interior Department, calls conditions at some 70 American Indian jails and detention centers a "national disgrace." The report documents 11 fatalities, 236 attempted suicides, and 632 escapes that occurred since 2001 at Indian detention facilities. Other serious problems reported in-

clude the failure to segregate juvenile and adult offenders, poorly trained correctional staff, and substandard facilities.

- *December 3:* A report by the U.S. Department of Defense discloses findings that military detention centers in Afghanistan and Iraq used interrogation techniques that included placing detainees in stress positions for extended periods of time and depriving them of sleep and light. The interrogation techniques fall outside the guidelines approved by Defense Secretary Donald H. Rumsfeld.
- *December 7:* New York state legislators vote to reform mandatory prison sentences for drug offenders. Under the so-called Rockefeller Drug Laws, implemented in the 1970s, some first-time drug offenders were sentenced to as much as 15 years to life in prison. Under the revised guidelines, similar drug offenses carry a sentence of eight to 20 years in prison. In addition, the law includes a provision allowing offenders sentenced under the old law to apply for early release.

2005

- *January 15:* Correctional Officer Manuel A. Gonzalez becomes the first prison guard in 20 years to be killed while on active duty in a California state prison. Inmate Jon Christopher Blaylock is charged with Gonzalez's murder, which occurs at the California Institution for Men at Chino, California. On June 10, 2005, warden Lori DiCarlo and two of her deputies are formally removed from their positions at the Chino prison based on findings by the state inspector general that they failed to monitor safety procedures at the prison.
- *January 27:* The California Department of Corrections orders an end to its long-standing policy of allowing male corrections officers to perform searches of female prisoners. The change in policy is the result of pressure brought by Dignity for Women Prisoners, a coalition of advocacy groups dedicated to reforming conditions of confinement for female prisoners in the United States.
- *February 23:* The U.S. Supreme Court rules in *Johnson v. California* (543 U.S. 499) that the policy of racial segregation at the California Department of Corrections inmate classification center is unconstitutional. The 5 to 3 decision overturns a lower court ruling that upheld the policy, which was defended by California prison officials as necessary to curb inmate violence, especially gang-related violence.
- *March 1:* The U.S. Supreme Court rules in *Roper v. Simmons* (543 U.S. 551) that imposing the death penalty on individuals whose crimes were committed before the age of 18 is a violation of the Eighth Amendment's ban against cruel and unusual punishment. The 5 to 4 decision spares the lives of some 72 individuals on death row in 12 states.

Chronology

- *April 15:* The British medical journal *Lancet* publishes a study on executions in the United States that reports that death by lethal injection may inflict unnecessary pain and suffering as the result of using an inadequate amount of anesthesia during the execution process. The report's findings, based on a study of 49 autopsies of individuals executed in the United States, concludes that in 43 of the executed inmates the concentration of anesthesia was less than that required to numb a surgical patient prior to making an incision.
- *September 3:* William Rehnquist, the 16th Chief Justice of the U.S. Supreme Court, dies at 80. Nominated as Associate Justice by President Richard Nixon and succeeding in 1986 to Chief Justice. In *Roper v. Simmons* (543 U.S. 551), one of his last rulings on the Supreme Court, he joins in the 5 to 4 dissent that the imposition of the death penalty on individuals whose crimes were committed prior to the age of 18 is a violation of the Eight Amendment's ban against cruel and unusual punishment.
- *September 22:* John Roberts becomes the 17th Chief Justice of the U.S. Supreme Court following his nomination to the Court by President George W. Bush and the death of former Chief Justice William Rehnquist. During the first year of Chief Justice Robert's tenure, the Court rules in *Hamdan v. Rumsfeld* (548 U.S. 557) that the Bush administration's use of military commissions to try suspected terrorists held at the Guantánamo Bay prison camp violated the Geneva Conventions and was unconstitutional because the practice was established without the authorization of the U.S. Congress. Chief Justice Roberts does not participate in the Court's 5 to 3 ruling because, as a federal appeals court judge, he previously ruled in favor of the Bush administration's use of the military commissions.

2006

- *January 31:* Samuel Alito becomes an Associate Justice of the U.S. Supreme Court following his nomination to the Court by President George W. Bush. Justice Alito replaces former Associate Justice Sandra Day O'Connor, who retired from the Court.
- *February 16:* A United Nations report recommends the closure of the Guantánamo Bay prison camp based on an investigation of conditions at the camp, including the alleged use of "enhanced interrogation techniques" on detainees. The report also recommends that detainees either be released or stand trial for alleged terrorist acts.
- *June 7:* The report "Confronting Confinement," sponsored by the Vera Institute of Justice, finds that, while some $60 billion per year is spent on corrections in the United States, funding is lacking for prison programs to reduce recidivism and assist inmates after their release from custody.

The report also finds an high level of violence and inadequate medical and mental health treatment in prisons nationwide.

- *June 12:* The U.S. Supreme Court rules unanimously in *Hill v. McDonough* (547 U.S. 573) that inmates in U.S. prisons have the right to challenge a state's choice of drugs used for lethal injection in the administration of the death penalty.
- *June 29:* The U.S. Supreme Court holds in *Hamdan v. Rumsfeld* (548 U.S. 557) that the use of military commissions to try suspected terrorists held at Guantánamo Bay prison camp was both a violation of the Geneva Conventions and unconstitutional because the practice was implemented without authorization by the U.S. Congress. The ruling is viewed as a rebuke to the administration of George W. Bush, which implemented and argued for the continuation of the practice.
- *September 6:* Former Illinois governor George Ryan is sentenced to six years in federal prison for crimes including racketeering and conspiracy. In 2003, Ryan had commuted the death sentences of 167 individuals on death row in Illinois, sentencing most of them to life without possibility of parole. Ryan, a Republican, explains that he issued the commutations because of his belief that the death penalty as administered in Illinois was unfair, resulting in some defendants, especially African Americans, receiving death for the same crime committed by other defendants who were sentenced to life in prison.
- *December 21:* California governor Arnold Schwarzenegger announces a plan to overhaul the state's overcrowded prison system. The plan includes spending $10 billion on building and expanding prison facilities, allowing more inmates to serve prison sentences in county jails, and the creation of a commission to recommend changes in the state's sentencing laws to divert certain offenders into rehabilitation or community corrections programs.

2007

- *February 14:* A report by the Pew Charitable Trusts projects that the number of inmates in U.S. prisons will likely increase by 13 percent over the next five years at an estimated cost of $27.5 billion to states nationwide. The report attributes the projected increase in imprisonment to mandatory minimum sentencing laws, declining rates of parole, and high rates of recidivism.
- *March 26:* The Australian David Hicks, the first terrorist suspect detained at the Guantánamo Bay prison camp, pleads guilty to assisting al-Qaeda and is convicted by a military commission.
- *April 24:* Inmates at the New Castle Correctional Facility in Indiana riot due to overcrowding after some 600 prisoners from Arizona are transferred to the Indiana prison to ease overcrowding at the Arizona

facility. Two staff members and seven inmates receive minor injuries. In the aftermath of the uprising Indiana officials decide not to accept any additional inmates from out of state at the facility.

- *July 20:* The *New York Times* reports that a study conducted by psychologists at the Federal Bureau of Prisons finds that as much as 85 percent of individuals convicted of consuming child pornography admitted that they sexually molested children. The study is the first in-depth survey of online sex offenders.

- *August 24:* The number of detainees incarcerated by U.S.-led coalition forces in Iraq reaches 24,500 including some 800 juveniles, having risen some 50 percent in the preceding six months, according to statistics reported by the *New York Times.*

- *November 19:* A report by the JFA Institute authored by eight criminologists from major U.S. universities finds that an eightfold increase in the number of individuals incarcerated in U.S. prisons since 1970 has had little effect on crime rates. The report recommends reforming sentencing laws, including the implementation of alternative community-based sentences, and decriminalizing certain drug offenses.

- *December 11:* The U.S. Sentencing Commission unanimously votes to lower sentences for crimes involving the possession and sale of crack cocaine in order to more closely align them with sentences for crimes involving powder cocaine. The Commission acts, in part, because of the disproportionate imposition of longer sentences on African Americans for the use of crack cocaine.

2008

- *January 22:* Jose Padilla is sentenced to 17 years and 4 months in prison for conspiracy to commit terrorism. Padilla is initially arrested in Chicago in 2002 for plotting to explode a dirty bomb inside the United States and detained as an enemy combatant until 2006, when his case was transferred to the federal court system.

- *February 28:* The Pew Center on the States releases the report *One in 100: Behind Bars in America 2008.* Findings include that, for the first time in U.S. history, more than one in every 100 adults in the U.S. population is confined in an American prison or jail. The report concludes that three decades of rising incarceration rates in the United States is "saddling cash-strapped states with costs they can ill afford and failing to have a clear impact either on recidivism or overall crime rates."

- *March 9:* The Corrections Corporation of America announces plans to spend $205 million to construct a private prison in Eloy, Arizona, that will house some 3,000 inmates.

Prisons

- *April 17:* In *Baze v. Rees* (553 U.S. 35), the U.S. Supreme Court sustains Kentucky's method of lethal injection for the administration of the death penalty, a commonly used sequence of three drugs. In so doing, the Court rejects the claim that the method poses a sufficient risk of inducing pain and suffering to constitute a violation of the Eighth Amendment's ban against cruel and unusual punishment.
- *May 6:* *Forbes* magazine reports several recently released international studies on the rising rate of incarceration in the United States. Reported causes for the increase in U.S. incarceration rates include tougher sentencing laws and high recidivism due to felony disenfranchisement and a lack of post-release programs to reintegrate former inmates in society.
- *June 12:* In *Boumediene v. Bush* (553 U.S. 723) the U.S. Supreme Court rules 5 to 4 that enemy combatant detainees at Guantánamo Bay prison camp have the constitutional right of habeas corpus and therefore may challenge in federal district court the circumstances of their detention. The Court holds as unconstitutional the limited judicial review provided to the detainees under the Military Commissions Act.
- *June 12:* In *Munaf v. Geren* (200 U.S. 321) the U.S. Supreme Court unanimously rules that U.S. citizens who are arrested and detained abroad by the U.S. military may seek relief in federal court from unlawful imprisonment under habeas corpus. The Court rejects the U.S. government's argument that that federal courts lack jurisdiction over such detainees because the U.S. forces that had captured the detainees were acting as part of a multinational military force.
- *June 25:* In *Kennedy v. Louisiana* (28 S. Ct. 2641), the U.S. Supreme Court rules 5 to 4 that the Eighth Amendment's ban of cruel and unusual punishment prevents a state from imposing the death penalty for the crime of child rape. More broadly, the ruling restricts the power of the state to impose the death penalty to crimes that result in the death of the victim, with the exception of crimes against the state such as treason and espionage.
- *July 27:* In an effort to ease overcrowding in California state prisons, officials at the West Tennessee Detention Facility announce plans to show a video of their facility to California inmates to entice them to request transfers to the Tennessee facility.
- *August 4:* A *USA Today*/Gallup poll finds that a majority of Americans believe that racism against African Americans is widespread in the United States and accounts for many of the problems in the African-American community, including a high incarceration rate among African-American males.
- *September 25:* The U.S. Bureau of Justice Statistics reports that, in the United States, some 1.7 million children have a parent in prison.

Chronology

- *October 25:* A study by researchers at the UCLA School of Medicine finds that up to 31 percent of inmates in U.S. prisons and jails are infected with chronic hepatitis C and recommends a cost-effective standard treatment to reduce the number of new infections and curb future medical expenses for treatment of advanced liver disease.
- *November 6:* The Pew Center on the States reports that states spend some $49 billion annually to feed, house, clothe, supervise, and provide medical treatment to state prisoners nationwide.
- *December 11:* The Bureau of Justice Statistics reports that one out of every 31 adults in the United States is in prison, in jail, or on probation. The figure represents the highest rate of incarceration of any country in the world.

2009

- *January 13:* The National Institute on Drug Abuse releases the results study on drug treatment in U.S. prisons. According to its findings, approximately half of all inmates in state and federal prisons report having a substance abuse problem but less than 20 percent received substance abuse treatment in prison.
- *January 22:* President Barack Obama signs executive orders for the closing of all secret prisons and detention camps under U.S. jurisdiction, including the Guantánamo Bay prison camp. The executive orders also ban the use of coercive interrogation of detainees.
- *March 18:* New Mexico governor Bill Richardson signs legislation abolishing the state's death penalty and mandating the imposition of life without the possibility of parole instead. Richardson notes that, since 1999, some 130 death row inmates have been exonerated, including four in New Mexico.
- *April 30:* Associate Justice David Souter announces his retirement from the U.S. Supreme Court. Souter is considered a moderate on the Court.
- *May 4:* The U.S. Supreme Court agrees to review two cases from Florida brought by juvenile offenders who claim their sentences of life in prison without possibility of parole constitute a violation of the Eighth Amendment's ban of cruel and unusual punishment. The cases of *Joe Harris Sullivan v. Florida* and *Terrance Jamar Graham v. Florida* are scheduled to be heard during the Court's 2009–2010 term. (See May 17, 2010.)
- *June 25:* The U.S. Supreme Court rules in *District Attorney's Office v. Osborne* (129 S. Ct. 2308) that inmates do not have a right to DNA testing to determine their guilt or innocence of a crime under the Fifth Amendment's due process clause, even if the DNA testing could exonerate the inmate. In the 5 to 4 decision, the Court defers to the states to

determine if inmates should have access to DNA testing and refuses to establish a constitutional principle on the issue.

- *June 25:* The National Prison Rape Elimination Commission releases a report, as mandated by the Prison Rape Elimination Act of 2003. The report's nine findings include that 4.5 percent of U.S. inmates report being victimized by sexual violence and that the rate of sexual abuse was as high as 15 percent at some facilities.
- *July 16:* The Federal Bureau of Prisons announces the closing of 14 prison factories operated by Federal Prison Industries, also known as UNICOR. The closings are attributed to a loss of some $20 million in revenue from the factories since January 2009.
- *August 4:* A panel of three federal judges orders the State of California to reduce its inmate population because of prison overcrowding. If fully implemented, some 43,000 prisoners are to be released over a two-year period in order to reduce the inmate population in California prisons to 137.5 percent of design capacity.
- *August 6:* The U.S. Senate approves by a vote of 68 to 31 President Obama's nomination of Judge Sonia Sotomayor to become the 111th Associate Justice of the U.S. Supreme Court. Justice Sotomayor of the U.S. Court of Appeals in New York becomes the first Hispanic and the third woman in U.S. history to serve on the Court.
- *August 8:* Rioting at the California Institute for Men state prison in Chino, California, is blamed on severe overcrowding and the attempted racial desegregation of the facility, as mandated in 2005 by the U.S. Supreme Court in *Johnson v. California* (543 U.S. 499). Some 250 inmates are injured in the rioting and 700 inmates are relocated to other prisons in the state due to the damage caused by the rioting.
- *September 10:* The U.S. Justice Department announces that reports of sexual misconduct by prison staff members with federal inmates doubled since 2001, and that incidents of staff-on-inmate sexual misconduct were reported at all but one of the 93 federal prisons in the United States.
- *October 19:* The U.S. Justice Department issues a directive that the federal government will not longer prosecute individuals who use or sell marijuana for medical purposes if they are complying with state law. At the time 14 states permit the use of marijuana for the treatment of certain medical conditions.
- *November 12:* U.S. Attorney General Eric Holder announces that five detainees held at the Guantánamo Bay prison camp for their alleged involvement in the terrorist attacks on the United States on September 11, 2001, will stand trial in federal court in New York City rather than before a military tribunal.
- *November 13:* Ohio becomes the first state to adopt a single-drug protocol for lethal injection in the administration of the death penalty.

Under the new protocol an overdose of a single anesthetic will be used to induce death; the previous protocol had required the injection of multiple drugs that, if not administered correctly, had the potential to cause severe pain.

■ *December 15:* The administration of President Barack Obama announces the transfer of a limited number of detainees held at the Guantánamo Bay prison camp to the Thomson Correctional Center in rural Illinois. The Thomson facility, built in 2001 as a state prison for maximum-security inmates but never fully operational due to a lack of funding, is slated to be purchased by the U.S. government, upgraded with enhanced security features, and operated as a federal maximum security prison.

2010

■ *May 17:* The U.S. Supreme Court rules that, under the Eighth Amendment's Cruel and Unusual Punishment Clause, juvenile offenders cannot be sentenced to life in prison without parole for crimes other than homicide. The Court's ruling arises from two cases—*Graham v. Florida*, in which Terrance Jamar Graham was sentenced to life without parole in 2004 for his participation in an armed home invasion when he was 17 years of age, and *Sullivan v. Florida*, in which Joe Harris Sullivan was convicted of raping an elderly woman in 1989 when he was 13 years old.

CHAPTER 4

BIOGRAPHICAL LISTING

John Augustus, shoemaker in Boston, Massachusetts, who in 1841 began the practice of bailing out convicted criminal offenders from court and assisting them in finding, among other things, housing and employment. Augustus later reported on each offender's progress to the court, and the judge customarily fined each offender court costs plus one cent instead of sentencing the offender to prison. The system devised by Augustus was the basis for the practice of probation.

Sanford Bates, the first director of the federal Bureau of Prisons, from 1930 to 1937. During his tenure, Bates implemented a classification system unique in U.S. penology that identified federal prisoners according to factors including age, sex, and type of offense, with the goal of developing individualized programs for rehabilitation. Bates established five regional training centers for correctional staff, and by 1937, all federal correctional personnel were under the jurisdiction of the Civil Service Commission. In addition, under Bates, federal parole was reorganized, and the supervision of parolees was transferred from the U.S. Marshall's Office to the probation offices of the federal courts in order to develop an after-care system that was more treatment-oriented and less punitive in its approach to ex-convicts.

Cesare Beccaria, Italian philosopher and author on issues of crime and punishment who in 1764 published his most widely known work, *An Essay on Crimes and Punishment*. Among the ideas advanced by Beccaria were that punishment should be humane and serve the purpose of deterring crime, not exacting social revenge. For the most serious crimes, Beccaria advocated life imprisonment over the death penalty, which he cautioned was impossible to correct if mistakes were later discovered in the criminal justice process.

James V. Bennett, director of the federal Bureau of Prisons (BOP) from 1937 to 1964 who succeeded Sanford Bates, the first director of the BOP. Under Bennett, rules against the mistreatment of federal prisoners were strictly enforced, and the BOP expanded programs for psychiatric counseling and medical care for inmates. Bennett's commitment to the rehabilitation of prisoners fell out of favor with later directors of the BOP, resulting in the demise of many programs developed and expanded by Bennett during his tenure.

Jeremy Bentham, social philosopher born in London, England, in 1748 who was influenced by the writings of Cesare Beccaria. Bentham designed a prison that he called the *panopticon,* which was shaped like a half-sphere with tiers of cells around a central area, where one guard could conceivably keep all prisoners under surveillance. Although Bentham's panopticon prison was never built, it served as a model for the Eastern State Penitentiary in Philadelphia, Pennsylvania, which was built in 1835 around a central hub from which rows of cell blocks extended like the spokes of a wheel.

George Beto, commissioner of the Texas Department of Corrections from 1962 to 1972. Known as a strict disciplinarian, Beto advocated the use of hard labor and literacy training for all prisoners. Under Beto, some of the most violent and brutal prisoners were enlisted to run cellblocks and maintain order with an iron hand. This practice, known as the tender system, was harshly criticized in the U.S. Supreme Court's 1980 ruling in *Ruiz v. Estelle,* a class action suit brought by Texas inmates in which the Court held that conditions of confinement at Texas prisons were unconstitutional.

John Billington, a passenger on the *Mayflower* who landed at Plymouth Rock in 1620 to help establish the American colonies. In 1630, Billington killed one of his neighbors, John Newcomen, and was quickly tried and put to death, thereby becoming the first person to be executed in colonial America.

Zebulon Brockway, the first superintendent of the reformatory at Elmira, New York, which in 1876 was the first reformatory built in the United States. Originally designed to house adult felons, Brockway used the reformatory for first-time male offenders between the ages of 16 and 30, in the hope that they were more amenable to rehabilitation than hardened criminals. The programs implemented by Brockway at Elmira included educational and vocational training and a system of indeterminate sentencing, including a grading system that allowed inmates to earn points for early release through good conduct and hard work. Many of Brockway's reforms reflected the principles advanced in 1870 by the National Prison Association. By 1913, reformatories modeled after Elmira were built in 17 U.S. states.

Charles Brooks, convicted murderer who, on December 6, 1982, in Texas, was the first person in the United States executed by lethal injection, which became the primary mode of execution in both the federal and state correctional systems.

Clement XI, Roman Catholic pope, under whose papacy the Hospice of San Michele was built in Rome in 1704. The Hospice of San Michele was one of the first correctional institutions designed for juvenile offenders. The design of separate cells for sleeping quarters and a large central hall for working was modeled after monasteries and became a model for U.S. penal institutions built during the 19th century under the Auburn system.

Donald Clemmer, author of *The Prison Community* (Holt, Rinehart, and Winston, 1958), in which he drew national attention to the social codes and subculture of prisoners. Clemmer's book presented a detailed sociological study of life in a maximum security prison and included interviews with inmates and essays written by inmates. Among Clemmer's findings was the tendency of prisoners to form groups according to their offense history, political beliefs, and sexual preferences. Clemmer documented how heterosexual male prisoners sometimes engage in homosexual relationships in order to help alleviate the loneliness of prison life. Clemmer also identified the process of prisonization, which is the assimilation into a prison culture with its own code of behavior.

Rhoda M. Coffin, a Quaker and prison reformer who in 1870 helped to persuade the National Congress on Penitentiary and Reformatory Discipline to include among its principles the use of separate prisons for women. In 1873, Coffin helped to found the Indiana Reformatory Institution for Women and Girls in Indianapolis, Indiana, after investigations of the Indiana state prison revealed that women prisoners were sometimes whipped by male guards and forced to have sexual contact with male prisoners. The Indiana Reformatory Institution for Women and Girls was the first independent women's prison in the United States and was run entirely by female staff.

Sir Walter Frederick Crofton, Irish reformer who in 1850 developed a system of indeterminate sentencing that became know as the Irish system. Crofton reasoned that if penitentiaries were designed as places of repentance and personal reform, then there must be a mechanism in place for prisoners to benefit when they demonstrate their reform.

Katharine Bement Davis, social worker and superintendent of the State Reformatory for Women in Bedford Hills, New York, from 1901 to 1913. Davis pioneered the use of research studies on the characteristics of inmates and was one of the first penologists to segregate mentally impaired inmates from the general population. After her tenure at the Bedford Hills reformatory, Davis was appointed as New York City's first female commissioner of corrections and later as the chairperson of the New York City Board of Parole.

Dorothea Lynde Dix, teacher and prison reformer who in 1841 visited the House of Corrections in East Cambridge, Massachusetts, to teach Sunday school and witnessed deplorable conditions, including the confinement of female inmates in subzero temperatures without blankets or appropriate clothing. Dix began a personal crusade against inhumane conditions of confinement and toured correctional facilities throughout Massachusetts and the United States, pressing courts and legislators to institute reforms.

Draco, ruler of ancient Greece, who in 621 B.C. implemented a harsh set of laws under which any citizen could prosecute an offender in the name of the injured party for the protection of society, thus shifting the goal of punishment from personal vengeance to maintenance of social order.

Clinton T. Duffy, prison warden and advocate for the rehabilitation of prisoners who in 1949 was appointed as warden of San Quentin state prison in California. Duffy, the son of a corrections officer, ended the practice of corporal punishment for prisoners at San Quentin and implemented a disciplinary system that awarded privileges for good conduct and revoked privileges for violations of prison rules. Duffy also established a night school for inmates and permitted inmates to operate a prison radio station. After his 12-year tenure as warden, Duffy continued to advocate for prison reform and was credited with the abolition of hanging as a mode of execution in California.

Louis Dwight, ordained minister and director, from 1825 to 1854, of the Prison Discipline Society of Boston, Massachusetts. Dwight distributed Bibles to prisoners, and was an advocate of the Auburn system, which allowed prisoners to congregate during the day for work and meals.

Eliza Farnham, chief matron at the prison for women at Mount Pleasant, New York, from 1844 to 1847. Farnham's attempt to rehabilitate inmates through medical treatment was a precursor to the medical model later advanced by Sanford Bates, the director of the Bureau of Prisons from 1930 to 1937. Farnham broke from the tradition of requiring absolute silence from prisoners and allowed inmates to have 30 minutes of quiet conversation each day. Farnham's reforms were harshly criticized by officials at Sing Sing prison, which was located next door to the Mount Pleasant prison, and Farnham was ultimately pressured to resign.

Lois Fraley, corrections officer who, on January 18, 2004, was taken hostage along with officer Jason Auch and held by two prisoners in an observation tower at the Lewis state prison in Buckeye, Arizona. Auch was held until January 24, 2004. Fraley, however, was not released until February 1, 2004, ending the 15-day standoff.

Benjamin Franklin, inventor, social reformer, and signer of the U.S. Declaration of Independence who in 1790 was among prominent Quakers who received permission from the Pennsylvania legislature to open a wing of the Walnut Street jail in Philadelphia as a penitentiary for convicted felons. Franklin helped to develop a system of prison discipline at the jail that borrowed from the principles for the humane treatment of inmates advanced by Quaker William Penn and European reformers like Cesare Beccaria and John Howard. The system developed at the Walnut Street jail became known as the Pennsylvania system.

Erving Goffman, author of the classic work *Asylums*, published in 1961, in which prisons are described as *total institutions* in which similarly situated individuals are kept in social isolation, cut off from society, in regimented and dehumanizing conditions.

Gregory IX, Roman Catholic pope who began the Inquisition in 1233 to abolish heresy on matters of church teachings. As a result, prisons were built within monasteries to confine those accused of heresy against the church, and solitary confinement was sometimes utilized to create an atmosphere of atonement and penitence for prisoners.

Jean Struven Harris, educator who in 1981 was convicted of second-degree murder and sentenced to 15 years to life for the murder of Herman Tarnower, the author of *The Scarsdale Diet* (Rawson Wade, 1979). While incarcerated at the women's prison at Bedford Hills, New York, Harris taught parenting classes to inmate mothers and helped to establish the Children's Center in the prison, where children could visit with their inmate mothers. In 1993, Harris was released from prison and placed on parole.

John Haviland, British architect who in 1820 was commissioned to design the Eastern Penitentiary in Cherry Hill, Pennsylvania. Havilands design was based on the Pennsylvania system of individual cells for solitary confinement but included a walled yard that was adjacent to each cell for an hour of daily exercise. Under Haviland's design, rows of individual cells extended outward from a central hub, giving the appearance of a spoked wheel. Each cell had two opposing doors, one of solid steel and the other of metal lattice that was usually draped with a black curtain. Although somewhat popular in the United States, Haviland's prison design was widely copied abroad in Europe, Asia, and Africa.

Rutherford B. Hayes, 19th president of the United States who in 1870, as the governor of Ohio, became the first president of the National Prison Association, renamed the American Correctional Association in 1954. The principles advanced by the National Prison Association included establishing a three-stage system of punishment, reform, and probation in all prisons and using indeterminate sentencing as a way to reward inmates for good behavior and hard work. Other principles included educational and treatment programs for prisoners, minimizing the use of physical force against inmates, and segregating juveniles, females, and males in separate facilities.

Herbert Hoover, 31st president of the United States who in 1930 signed into law the legislation creating the Federal Bureau of Prisons (BOP) and appointed as its first director, Sanford Bates, then president of the National Prison Association.

Willie Horton, convicted murderer and rapist who, while serving a life sentence in a Massachusetts state prison, was released on a work furlough and never returned to prison. Horton was later arrested and convicted for raping a woman and assaulting her fiancé while Horton was at large in Maryland. The Horton case was used in political ads in the 1988 presidential election by Republican George Bush as an example of the ineffective policies of his Democratic opponent, Massachusetts governor Michael Dukakis. As a result of the publicity, work furlough programs were restricted in many states.

John Howard, English reformer and writer who in 1777 published *State of Prisons,* in which he described the best of the correctional facilities he had visited during his tours of correctional facilities throughout Europe. The book was aimed at reforming the deplorable conditions that Howard witnessed in prisons and jails. Among his recommendations were regular inspections of correctional facilities to ensure compliance with basic standards of sanitation and living conditions and the implementation of work and educational programs designed to deter criminals from reoffending.

John Irwin, author who, with Donald Cressey, identified the importation model, which views violent prison culture as a reflection of the criminal culture in the outside world and, as such, is not developed in prison or unique to prison. Irwin and Cressey divided the society of prison inmates into three subgroups: The thief subculture, which comprised professional criminals who kept to themselves; the convict subculture, which consisted of inmates concerned with obtaining power in prison and controlling others for their own needs; and the conventional subculture, which comprised inmates trying to retain some of the values of the outside world in their daily lives.

George Jackson, inmate at Soledad state prison in California in 1969 when three African-American prisoners were shot to death by a white correctional officer, who was later beaten to death. Jackson, who along with two other inmates was charged with killing the officer, was transferred to San Quentin state prison, where he was killed in 1971. Jackson's death attracted national attention because of the success of his book, *Soledad Brother: The Prison Letters of George Jackson* (Coward-McCann, 1970). In 1971, after Jackson's death, Jackson's two codefendants were acquitted of all charges in connection with the 1969 killing of the correctional officer at Soledad.

James B. Jacobs, sociologist and author of *New Perspectives on Prisons and Imprisonment* (Cornell University Press, 1983), in which he concluded that the development of the Black Power movement in the 1960s significantly influenced prison life. As a result of the movement, African-American and

Latino inmates became more cohesively organized than their white inmate counterparts, giving rise to the formation of inmate groups, such as the Black Muslims, and some street and prison gangs, including La Familia, the Blackstone Rangers, and the Crips in California.

Robert Johnson, author and critic of prisons, especially maximum security facilities, for their dehumanizing and stressful conditions of confinement. Johnson's works included *Culture and Crisis in Confinement* (Lexington Books, 1976) and *Hard Time: Understanding and Reforming the Prison* (Brooks Cole, 1987).

James A. Johnston, prison administrator who in 1934 was appointed the first warden at the maximum security federal prison at Alcatraz Island in San Francisco Bay in California. Previously, Johnson had served as warden at the Folsom and San Quentin state prisons in California, where he established a reputation as a reformer. At Alcatraz, however, Johnson imposed some of the most restrictive regulations in the federal prison system, including an enforced rule of silence for the first four years of his administration. In 1948, Johnson retired as the warden of Alcatraz.

Gee Jon, convicted murderer who, on February 8, 1924, in Carson City, Nevada, became the first U.S. prisoner to be put to death in the gas chamber.

Justinian I, Byzantine emperor, under whose rule the legal code *Corpus Juris Civilis* was compiled from 529 to 535 B.C. The concept of proportionality, that the punishment should fit the crime, was established under the Justinian code, and the scales of justice were first depicted in art from the Justinian period.

William Kemmler, convicted murderer who, on August 6, 1890, at the Auburn penitentiary in New York became the first prisoner executed in the electric chair.

Lewis Edward Lawes, prison administrator who began his career in 1905 as a corrections officer, like his father. In 1915, at the age of 32, Lawes became the superintendent of the New York City reformatory and was later appointed by New York governor Alfred E. Smith as the warden of Sing Sing prison. At Sing Sing, Lawes established a unique system of inmate self-governance that did not allow any inmate to have control over other inmates, unlike the tender system in Texas. Lawes also allowed inmates to leave the prison to attend family funerals or visit dying relatives. As warden at Sing Sing, Lawes presided over executions, although he was an outspoken critic of capital punishment and even toured the country in a campaign to abolish the death penalty.

Ralph Lobaugh, ex-convict who in 1977 was released from an Indiana state prison after serving 30 years. Two months after his release, Lobaugh returned to the prison and requested a cell where he could reside. Lobaugh is cited as a classic case of release-from-prison trauma, which is an inability of an ex-convict to adjust to life in society after years of incarceration.

Cesare Lombroso, 19th century Italian criminologist who classified criminals as atavistic, or throwbacks, to an earlier stage of human evolution. Lombroso cataloged what he believed were the physical traits that were unique to criminals, including an asymmetrical face, receding forehead, darker skin, and long hair. In the United States, Lombroso's theories made an impact in the emerging field of criminology, and studies were conducted in California's San Quentin state prison and other U.S. prisons documenting and cataloging the physical characteristics of prisoners.

Josephine Shaw Lowell, prison reformer who in 1876 was appointed as the first female commissioner of the New York State Board of Charities. In that capacity, Lowell observed the often dangerous conditions to which women inmates were subjected while with male inmates. As a result, Lowell founded several institutions for women, including the State Reformatory for Women at Bedford Hills, New York.

Elam Lynds, former army captain who in 1816 was appointed as the chief warden of the state prison at Auburn, New York. Under Lynds, prisoners were known only by their inmate number and were required to wear black-and-white striped uniforms to discourage individuality. Lynds did not believe in rewarding inmates for good behavior, and he used flogging to punish violations of prison rules. In 1825, Lynds was commissioned to build the new state prison at Ossining, New York, which became known as Sing Sing. Lynds served as the warden at Sing Sing until 1830, when he resigned after an investigation criticized his management methods.

Alexander Maconochie, British officer who in 1840 was placed in charge of a British penal colony on Norfolk Island that housed some of the United Kingdom's worst offenders. Maconochie implemented a series of reforms, including a system of early release earned by good conduct and hard work. In 1870, the reform-minded principles advanced by the American Prison Congress were based in part on Maconochie's work.

Edna Mahan, prison reformer and administrator who in 1928 became the superintendent of the Reformatory for Women in Clinton Farms, New Jersey, a position that she held for over 40 years. Under her administration, Mahan implemented reforms that encouraged the humane treatment of inmates, including the use of low levels of security and the removal of iron bars on windows. As a result of Mahan's reforms, the Clinton Farms reformatory became known as one of the most progressive penal institutions in the United States. In 1967, Mahan opened Carpenter House, the first halfway house for women in New Jersey. After Mahan's death in 1968, the Clinton Farms reformatory was renamed the Edna Mahan Correctional Facility for Women in honor of Mahan's contributions to prison reform.

Robert Martinson, sociologist who in 1974 published the report "What Works? Questions and Answers about Prison Reform," in which Martinson concluded that none of the 231 correctional treatment programs he had studied between 1945 and 1967 was effective in rehabilitating inmates. Martinson's conclusions were embraced by conservatives, who wanted to abolish rehabilitative programs in favor of determinate sentencing, and by liberals, who contended that poor treatment programs hampered the chances for inmates to succeed after their release from prison, causing higher rates of recidivism.

Marc Mauer, author and assistant director of the Sentencing Project, a nonprofit organization dedicated to advocacy and reform on issues of incarceration and criminal justice policies in the United States. Mauer coauthored with Ryan S. King the 2004 report by the Sentencing Project, "Schools and Prisons: 50 Years after *Brown v. Board of Education*," which examined the rising trend of imprisonment of African Americans since the desegregation of education in the United States in 1954.

Timothy McVeigh, convicted murderer who, on June 11, 2001, became the first federal prisoner executed by lethal injection for his role in the deaths of 168 people in the 1995 bombing of the Alfred P. Murrah Federal Building in Oklahoma City, Oklahoma.

The Mecklenburg Six, death row prisoners who, on May 31, 1984, escaped from the correctional center at Mecklenburg, Virginia. Linwood Briley, the leader of the group, was joined by his brother, James B. Briley, Earl Clanton, Willie Leroy Jones, Derick Peterson, and Lem Tuggle. Their escape, which was planned for months and originally included 12 death row inmates, was carried out when the Mecklenburg Six surprised prison guards, put on the guards' uniforms, and forced one of the guards to supply a prison van for transportation. The inmates were eventually captured, although the Briley brothers remained at large the longest, for 19 days. All six prisoners were eventually executed by the state of Virginia.

Montesquieu, Charles-Louis de Secondat, baron de, 18th-century French historian and philosopher who advanced the idea that harsh punishment undermined social morality.

Thomas O. Murton, professor of criminal justice who in 1966 was appointed warden at Tucker Prison Farm, a 300-bed unit of the Arkansas state penitentiary. One year later in 1967, Murton became the warden at the Cummins Farm Unit, a 1,300-bed facility in the Arkansas state prison system. Murton was a strong advocate for prison reform, and he was forced to resign after only two years at Cummins Farm when his views embarrassed state prison officials. Based on his experiences at the Tucker and Cummins facilities, Murton published the book *Accomplices to the Crime: The Arkansas Prison Scandal* (Grove Press, 1970). Murton's efforts at reforming the Arkansas prison system were the basis of the 1980 movie *Brubaker*, starring Robert Redford.

George O. Osborne, prison reformer and warden at the state prison in Trenton, New Jersey, in the late 19th and early 20th centuries. As warden, Osborne instituted reforms that eliminated standard practices at most U.S. prisons, including striped uniforms for convicts, shaved heads, and requiring prisoners to be attached to a ball and chain. Osborne also established prison schools and implemented new parole procedures that facilitated the reintegration of inmates into society.

Thomas Mott Osborne, businessman turned prison reformer who in 1913 was appointed to the New York State Commission on Prison Reform. In 1914, Osborne became the warden at Sing Sing prison in New York, where he instituted a program that paid inmates for their work. After resigning as warden in 1917, Osborne wrote books based on his experiences at Sing Sing, including *Within Prison Walls*, *Society and Prisons*, and *Prisons and Common Sense*.

William Penn, a Quaker who in 1681 founded the Quaker settlement at Pennsylvania in colonial America. Penn advocated more humane treatment of lawbreakers, in accordance with the Quakers' Great Law, which called for hard labor in a house of correction as the punishment for most offenses. The Quakers' concept of confinement as a component of punishment, instead of a prelude to execution or corporal punishment, was unique in colonial America. Also, under the Quaker code, offenses were secular in nature and did not include religious offenses as the earlier English codes did.

Helen Prejean, Roman Catholic nun whose work as a spiritual adviser to death row inmates in Louisiana was the basis of her book *Dead Man Walking: An Eyewitness Account of the Death Penalty in the United States* (Vintage Books, 1994). In 1996, the book was adapted into the movie *Dead Man Walking*, starring Susan Sarandon as Prejean and Sean Penn as Patrick Sonnier, a death row inmate at the state penitentiary in Angola, Louisiana, who was counseled by Prejean.

Joseph E. Ragen, warden of the Statesville and Joliet state prisons in Illinois for 26 years who implemented paramilitary-like standards of discipline among both inmates and correctional officers. Based on his experience, Ragen cowrote the book, with Charles Finston, *Inside the World's Toughest Prisons* (Charles C. Thomas Publishers Limited, 1962).

Wilbert Rideau, prisoner serving a life sentence at the state penitentiary in Angola, Louisiana, for bank robbery and murder. Rideau confessed to his crimes. In 1975, Rideau became the editor of Angola prison's institutional journal the *Angolite*. Rideau also became a filmmaker in prison. In 1999, his movie, *The Farm*, about life at Angola prison, shared the Grand Prize Award at the Sundance Film Festival.

Prisons

Sir Samuel Romilly, attorney and reformer of British criminal law in the 18th and early 19th centuries. In 1816, Romilly helped to spearhead efforts to build the first modern English prison, at Millbank.

Benjamin Rush, member of the Continental Congress and signer of the Declaration of Independence who advocated for the humane treatment of prisoners and helped found the Walnut Street jail in Philadelphia, Pennsylvania, in 1790.

Richard Speck, mass murderer who was sentenced to death for killing eight student nurses in Chicago in 1966. Speck's death sentence was commuted after the 1972 decision by the U.S. Supreme Court in *Furman v. Georgia*. In 1991, Speck died of a heart attack in prison. Following his death, a videotape was released showing Speck taking drugs in prison and in various sex acts with another prisoner. On the tape, Speck claimed that he was having fun in prison.

Dennis J. Stevens, author of the study *Violence Begets Violence*, published in 1997, which correlated strict enforcement of disciplinary rules in prison with a higher incidence of disciplinary problems among inmates.

Robert Stroud, ornithologist and federal prisoner who was portrayed by Burt Lancaster in the 1962 film *Birdman of Alcatraz*. Stroud was convicted of murder at the age of 19 and spent the rest of his life as a federal prisoner after he was convicted of stabbing a guard to death in 1916. In 1920, President Woodrow Wilson commuted Stroud's death sentence, and Stroud was transferred to Alcatraz from the Leavenworth federal prison in Kansas. At Alcatraz, Stroud was not allowed to work with birds, and he spent his time writing about the prison system. In 1959, Stroud was transferred to the medical center for federal prisoners in Springfield, Missouri, where he died in 1963.

Gresham Sykes, sociologist who, building on the ideas of Donald Clemmer, explored the social roles of inmates in prison culture. Sykes identified a specific inmate social code that included rules against arguing or quarreling with other inmates, never taking the side of a member of the prison staff against another inmate, and being prepared to deal with conflict, including fighting, if necessary in order not to lose dignity.

The Texas Seven, prisoners who, on December 13, 2002, escaped from the Connally Unit Prison, a maximum security facility in Karnes City, Texas. Escapees George Rivas, Michael Anthony Rodriguez, Larry Harper, Joseph Garcia, Patrick Murphy, Jr., Donald Keith Newbury, and Randy Halprin remained at large for several weeks as they traveled from Texas to Colorado. On January 22, four of the seven were captured at a trailer park in Woodland Park, Colorado. A fifth convict, Larry Harper, committed suicide rather than surrender to police. On January 24, the remaining two, Donald Keith Newbury and Patrick Murphy, Jr., were apprehended by federal agents at a Holiday Inn near Colorado Springs,

Colorado. The six surviving members were charged with the murder of police officer Aubrey Hawkins during a robbery in Irving, Texas, on Christmas Eve. By 2004, George Rivas, Donald Newbury, Michael Rodriguez, and Joseph Garcia were convicted of the crime and sentenced to death.

Hans Toch, author who examined the coping strategies used by prison inmates to adjust to their conditions of confinement in his book *Living in Prison* (Free Press, 1977).

Miriam Van Waters, psychologist and superintendent of the Massachusetts State Reformatory for Women from 1932 to 1957. In 1925, Van Waters published the book *Youth in Conflict* (AMS Press), based on her experiences as superintendent of the Los Angeles County Juvenile Hall. In 1929, Van Waters began work on a juvenile delinquency project at Harvard Law School and was appointed by President Herbert Hoover to serve on the Wickersham Commission and report on the treatment of juveniles in the federal prison system. Van Waters was a proponent of prisoner rehabilitation.

Jean-Jacques Vilain, Belgian government official who in 1773 became the administrator of the Maison de Force, a newly built workhouse in Ghent, Belgium. Vilain segregated females and juveniles from serious offenders and utilized a system of individual cells to house inmates. Although Vilain required prisoners to work in silence, he opposed cruelty as a means of inmate control.

Voltaire (François-Marie Arouet), 18th-century French philosopher who objected to the legally sanctioned practice of torture in France and believed that shame was an effective deterrent to crime.

Earl Warren, Chief Justice of the U.S. Supreme Court from 1953 to 1969. In 1942, as governor of California, Warren ordered an investigation into the California state prison system, which led to its reorganization around the principle of inmate rehabilitation.

Enoch Cobb Wines, professor of classical languages who in 1862 became secretary of the New York Prison Association and devoted the rest of his life to prison reform. In 1867, Wines and reformer Theodore Dwight authored *Report on the Prisons and Reformatories of the United States and Canada,* in which they concluded that inmates were released from prison in worse psychological condition than when they entered. In 1870, Wines was among the prison reformers who founded the American Prison Association in Cincinnati, Ohio, and he helped to formulate many of the principles advanced by the organization.

Frederick Howard Wines, minister and prison reformer who opposed the classification of inmates according to their physical characteristics by adherents to the theories of Cesare Lombroso. Wines, who was the son of prison reformer Enoch Cobb Wines, also advocated for the segregation of mentally ill inmates. Wines's book *Punishment and Reformation* was published in 1919, seven years after his death in 1912.

Malcom C. Young, author and executive director of the Sentencing Project, a nonprofit organization dedicated to advocacy and reform on issues of incarceration and criminal justice policies in the United States. Young is coauthor, with Marc Mauer and Ryan S. King, of the report "The Meaning of Life: Long Prison Sentences in Context," released by the Sentencing Project in May 2004. The report examines the trend in sentencing to eliminate indeterminate life sentencing (such as "25 years to life") and to impose sentences without the possibility of parole.

Philip Zimbardo, Stanford University professor who set up a mock prison to investigate the psychological impact of incarceration. In the experiment, called the Stanford Prison Experiment, Zimbardo videotaped students playing prisoners and corrections officers. The student guards became cruel to the student inmates, who began to experience psychological deterioration, and the experiment was called off by Zimbardo after only six days.

CHAPTER 5

GLOSSARY

This chapter presents a glossary of terms relevant to issues of incarceration and correctional institutions, with emphasis on prisons in the United States.

abscond To leave the area of jurisdiction prescribed by prison rules or by conditions imposed under probation or parole.

administrative segregation Separation and isolation of an inmate from the prison's general population when the inmate's continued presence in the general population would pose a serious threat to the safety of the inmate, prison staff, or other prisoners. Administrative segregation may be imposed by correctional staff as punishment for an inmate's unacceptable behavior or as a means of protecting an inmate who is at risk of harm that is self-inflicted or inflicted by other inmates.

alternative facility A placement, such as a drug treatment center, that is used as an alternative to incarceration in a traditional correctional institution.

commitment An action by a court ordering an adjudicated juvenile or a sentenced adult to be admitted to a correctional institution.

community corrections A community-based alternative to incarceration in prison that provides for the management of offenders through programs that include community service, substance abuse treatment, and electronic monitoring.

community facility A correctional facility that allows residents unsupervised leave for prescribed periods of time to attend school, treatment or counseling programs, or to work.

community service A period of service to the community that is commonly imposed by courts as a condition of probation in lieu of incarceration.

conditional release The release of a defendant who agrees to meet specified conditions imposed by the court that may include steady employment, avoiding contact with the victim or associates in the alleged crime, participating in treatment, and avoiding certain behaviors, such as consuming alcoholic beverages.

confinement facility A correctional facility from which inmates may not depart without supervision.

convict An adult convicted of a criminal offense who is incarcerated in a correctional institution in order to serve the sentence imposed by the court.

conviction A judgment in court imposed by a jury or a judge, or on the basis of a guilty plea by the defendant, that the defendant is guilty of the criminal offense for which the defendant was charged.

correctional agency A federal, state, or local criminal justice agency under a single administrative authority with the principal function of intake screening, supervision, custody, confinement, or treatment of adjudicated juvenile offenders or convicted adult criminal offenders.

correctional facility A physical setting, such as a building, a part of a building, or a set of structures, operated and administered by a government or private agency for the custody or treatment of adjudicated juveniles and convicted or committed adults as the result of a juvenile or criminal justice proceeding.

correctional institution A confinement facility commonly referred to as a prison or penitentiary that is administered by a state or federal agency for the incarceration of adults for a period of confinement of one year or more. In addition, the term *correctional institution* is sometimes used to describe facilities for juvenile offenders committed to a period of confinement of one year or more.

corrections A term that includes all agencies, facilities, programs, procedures, personnel, and techniques concerned with the intake, custody, confinement, supervision, or treatment of convicted criminal offenders or adjudicated juvenile offenders.

crimes of violence The crimes of murder, voluntary manslaughter, forcible rape, robbery, and aggravated assault, according to the Uniform Crime Reports by the Federal Bureau of Investigation.

day reporting center A community-based facility where an offender or parolee is required to report on a regular basis to receive certain services, including counseling, substance abuse treatment, and employment training.

death row A specialized maximum-security unit within a prison system where inmates sentenced to the death penalty are housed while awaiting execution and where the death penalty is administered at the time of execution.

defendant A person against whom a legal action is pending in a court of law. A criminal defendant is someone facing criminal charges.

detention The legally authorized confinement of a person who is subject to criminal or juvenile court proceedings from the time of arrest until release or incarceration.

Glossary

detention center A government facility for juveniles that provides temporary care and restriction pending court disposition.

detention facility A general term used to describe facilities that hold adults or juveniles in confinement pending trial or adjudication or adults for a period of confinement of one year or less. Detention facilities include jails, county farms, honor farms, work camps, road camps, detention centers, and juvenile halls.

detention hearing In juvenile proceedings, a hearing by a judge or judicial officer to determine if a juvenile is to be detained or released while proceedings are pending in juvenile court.

diagnosis or classification center A unit within a correctional institution, or a separate facility, where individuals sentenced to incarceration are held and evaluated to determine their appropriate placement in permanent correctional institutions or programs. For example, a diagnosis or classification center may determine if an inmate requires incarceration at an institution with mental health services.

disposition A final judgment, settlement, or determination by a court to terminate proceedings in a case.

diversion The halting or suspension of formal criminal or juvenile justice proceedings against an alleged offender. Commonly, minor drug offenders are offered diversion in a treatment program as an alternative to incarceration. If, during the diversionary period, the individual successfully complies with all conditions imposed by the court, the criminal proceedings against the individual may be dismissed without any record of a conviction.

early release Release from a confinement facility before the sentence imposed by the court is completed. Early release can be achieved by parole, by time off for good behavior while incarcerated, or by a modification in the original sentence by the court.

felony A criminal offense punishable by death or by incarceration in a state or federal correctional facility for a period of time prescribed by law, usually one year or more.

felony disenfranchisement The practice of prohibiting individuals who have been convicted of a felony from voting. Felony disenfranchisement laws exist in many states.

fugitive An individual attempting to avoid prosecution or confinement by fleeing from a jurisdiction or attempting concealment from authorities in some other way.

good time Days subtracted from a inmate's sentence for good behavior while in custody, thereby reducing the total amount of time in custody.

habeas corpus A writ (court order) that is usually used to bring an inmate before the court to determine the legality of his or her imprisonment.

Prisons

halfway house In general, a residential facility for adjudicated juveniles or convicted adults that is an alternative to incarceration in a traditional correctional facility or is used in an after-care setting to house individuals released from prison who are on parole or require certain services for reintegration into the community.

hearing A proceeding in which arguments, evidence, or witnesses are heard by a judicial officer or an administrative body. For example, in a probable-cause hearing, arguments, evidence, and witnesses are presented to a court to determine if an individual accused of a crime should be prosecuted or released.

indeterminate sentence A type of sentence to imprisonment in which the exact length of imprisonment and parole supervision is later determined by a parole authority, generally based on the criminal offender's conduct while in confinement and the degree to which the offender demonstrates rehabilitation.

indictment A formal written accusation by a grand jury and filed in criminal court alleging that certain crimes were committed by certain individuals.

information A formal written accusation filed in criminal court by a prosecutor that alleges that a certain person committed a specific offense.

infraction An offense punishable by a fine or other penalty, such as community service, but not by incarceration.

inmate A person in custody who is confined in a jail, prison, or other correctional institution.

institutional capacity The maximum number of inmates or residents that a correctional facility is designed to house.

intake unit A government agency or branch of an agency that receives juvenile referrals from police or other agencies and screens them for possible referral to the juvenile court or to a social service agency.

jail A confinement facility intended for adults and administered by a local law enforcement agency, or by a city or county, that holds individuals pending trial or sentencing in criminal cases or persons convicted of crimes and sentenced to a brief period of incarceration, generally for one year or less.

judicial officer Any person exercising judicial powers in a court of law. Judges are judicial officers, but they are not the only type of judicial officer. Court commissioners or administrators, for example, may also serve as judicial officers, depending upon the laws of a particular jurisdiction.

jurisdiction A territory, subject matter, or person over which lawful authority may be exercised. For example, under Title 42 of the U.S. Code, section 1983, federal courts were given jurisdiction over state prisoners alleging violations of their civil rights under the U.S. Constitution.

jury A statutorily defined number of persons selected according to law and sworn to determine matters of fact in criminal or civil matters and to render a verdict of guilty or not guilty. A grand jury is a body of persons who are selected and sworn to investigate criminal activity and the conduct of public officials and to hear evidence against those accused in order to determine if there is sufficient cause to file an indictment in criminal court.

lethal injection   A means of execution by which a lethal dose of drugs is administered by injection. The type and dosage of drugs used for lethal injected is determined by state or federal laws.

LWOP   A commonly used abbreviation for a prison sentence of life without possibility of parole.

mandatory sentence   A statutory requirement of certain fixed penalties for certain criminal offenses.

misdemeanor   An offense punishable by incarceration in a local jail or confinement facility, usually for a period of one year or less.

monitored release   The release of a criminal defendant facing pending charges under conditions of supervision that may require the individual to be electronically monitored or confined to a residence except when going to and from court.

pardon   An act of executive clemency that absolves someone in part or in full from the legal consequences of a crime and conviction.

parole   The conditional release of a criminal offender from a correctional facility before the expiration of the offender's full sentence. A paroled offender is placed under the supervision of a parole agency, which is commonly administered by a department of corrections.

parole authority   A person or correctional agency with the authority to release on parole adults or juveniles committed to confinement facilities, to revoke parole, and to discharge from parole.

parolee   A person who is conditionally released from a correctional institution before the expiration of his or her sentence and who is placed under the supervision of a parole agency and required to comply with all conditions imposed by that parole agency.

parole violation   An act by an individual who is on parole that does not conform with the conditions of parole imposed upon that individual. Parole violations include violations of the law and technical violations of conditions of parole, such as reporting to a parole agent on a regular basis. Although technical violations of parole do not rise to the level of a criminal offense, they can nonetheless result in the reincarceration of the parole violator.

partial confinement   An alternative to a traditional jail sentence, such as a weekend sentence that permits a criminal offender to work during the week and live at home and to report to jail on weekends. Furlough programs that allow offenders to leave jail or prison for limited periods of time to work or visit family members are another example of partial confinement.

petition   In juvenile court, a document alleging that a juvenile has violated the law or a status offense and asking the court to assume jurisdiction over the juvenile pending adjudication of the allegations.

prison   A confinement facility with custodial authority over adults sentenced to incarceration of one year or more for criminal offenses.

prisoner   A person in custody in a confinement facility or in the personal custody of a criminal justice official while being transported between confinement facilities.

prison industries   Businesses operated inside prisons, often by private companies, that employ inmates at low wages to manufacture goods or produce services that are sold for profit.

probable cause   A set of facts and circumstances that would cause a reasonably intelligent person to believe that a person has committed a crime of which he or she stands accused.

probation   The conditional freedom granted by a judge or other judicial official to an adult or juvenile offender on the condition that the offender complies with certain conditions imposed by the court. Probation may be imposed in lieu of incarceration or in addition to a limited period of incarceration, usually in a county jail.

probation officer   An employee of a probation agency whose primary duties include enforcing the functions of a probation agency.

probation violation   An act, or failure to act, by a person on probation that does not conform to the conditions of probation imposed by the court. Probation violations include violations of the law as well as violations of conditions of probation that do not rise to the level of a criminal offense.

reception center   A unit within a prison or a stand-alone facility where inmates who are entering prison undergo classification, an assessment process that determines their appropriate housing assignment within the prison system.

recidivism   The repetition of criminal behavior by a previously incarcerated individual that commonly results in a new period of incarceration. Recidivism is measured by criminal acts that result in a conviction by a court, when committed by individuals who are under correctional supervision or who have been released from correctional supervision within the past three years. Recidivism is also measured by technical violations of probation or parole that result in an adverse change to the offender's legal status, such as conviction or incarceration.

release from prison   Any lawful exit from a federal or state confinement facility for adults who are generally serving sentences of one year or more. Releases may be discretionary, as determined by a parole authority, or they may be mandatory, as determined by statute. Release may also be accomplished by a transfer of the individual to another jurisdiction.

Glossary

residential treatment center   A facility for juvenile offenders who do not require confinement in a secure facility. Residential treatment centers allow offenders to have greater contact with the community, thereby enhancing the prospects for reintegration into society.

restitution   Usually a cash payment by a criminal offender to the victim in an amount deemed appropriate, usually by a court or by statute, to offset the loss sustained by the victim. Restitution payments are commonly made in monthly installments that fit the offender's earning capacity.

revocation   An administrative act performed by a parole authority or by a court that removes an individual from parole or probation as a result of a violation of parole or probation by that individual.

revocation hearing   An administrative or judicial hearing on the question of whether to revoke an individual's probation or parole status as the result of an alleged violation of the conditions of parole or probation.

sentence   The penalty imposed by a court on a convicted person, which may include capital punishment, incarceration, payment of fines, or the imposition of a term of probation for a period of time.

stay   The act of stopping a judicial proceeding by court order. The term is commonly used in the context of "stay of execution," when an imminent execution is halted by a court based upon a review of a legal appeal brought by the inmate who is about to be executed or by the inmate's representative.

supermax   The term for a super maximum security prison that is either a stand-alone facility or a unit within a larger facility where violent or seriously disruptive inmates are segregated under the highest level of security controls, including single-person cells, severely restricted movement, and limited access to prison staff.

supervised release   A type of release requiring regular monitoring and contact with designated correctional officials.

suspended sentence   The decision by a court to postpone the setting of a penalty for a criminal offense, often by imposing probation for the period of the sentence in lieu of incarcerating the offender in prison or jail.

third-party release   The release of a criminal offender or defendant to another person who assumes responsibility for the offender or defendant.

time served   The total time spent in confinement by a convicted adult before and after sentencing.

warden   A corrections administrator who is in charge of a prison.

work release   A prison program in which an inmate who is deemed to be a low-level security risk is allowed to work at a place of employment outside the prison. Work release programs commonly require the inmate to return to the prison immediately after completing a work shift and to remain at the prison until the next work shift.

PART II

GUIDE TO FURTHER RESEARCH

CHAPTER 6

How to Research Prisons and Correctional Issues

The subject of prisons is a broad area of study within the field of corrections. Major areas of interest to the researcher include the history of punishment, the legal rights of prisoners, the prison population, and the administration of state, federal, and private correctional systems. Related topics include rates of incarceration, sentencing laws, parole, community corrections, the death penalty, corrections professionals, the treatment and rehabilitation of prisoners, inmate labor and vocational programs, and the demographics of those sentenced to prison in the United States. Fortunately, there are many resources available for both the general researcher and the specialist.

PRINT RESOURCES

BOOKS

The following books on prisons and corrections in the United States provide an overview of the topic and are a good starting point for the general researcher and an efficient way to identify specific areas of interest for further inquiry.

American Corrections, 8th Edition (Thomson Wadsworth, 2009) by Todd R. Clear, George F. Cole, and Michael Dean Reisig explores issues in corrections from the perspectives of corrections officials and inmates. Descriptions of high-profile cases and real-life incidents in correctional settings are used to provide context to correctional issues, which are divided into three parts. Part One describes historical issues in corrections, including the early history of correctional theory and practices, with emphasis on U.S. corrections. Also discussed is the impact of correctional law and societal forces associated with crime and the criminal offender. Part Two examines the current practice of corrections in the United States, including juvenile corrections, incarceration of women, treatment programs in correctional settings, and prison industries. Part Three presents U.S. trends in corrections, including incarceration rates and an examination of the death penalty.

Briefs of Leading Cases in Corrections, 5th Edition (Anderson Publishing, 2008) by Rolando V. del Carmen, Susan E. Ritter, and Betsy A. Witt provides a comprehensive overview of legal issues relating to inmates and incarceration. Briefs of cases from the U.S. Supreme Court and some cases from lower federal courts are arranged in six chapters: Prisons and Jails, Probation, Parole, Death Penalty, Juvenile Justice, and Sexual Assault Offender Laws. Each case brief includes a useful capsule that states the legal significance of the case in one or two sentences. In addition, case briefs include the facts of the case, legal issues, the holding of the court, the court's reasoning, and an explanation of the case's legal significance.

Corrections in America: An Introduction, 12th Edition (Prentice Hall, 2009), by Harry E. Allen, Edward J. Latessa, and Bruce S. Ponder, provides a comprehensive overview of the prison system in the United States. Included are chapters on the history of punishment, state and federal correctional systems, correctional ideologies, prisoners' rights, prisoner populations, and parole and community corrections. Earlier editions of the textbook, written by Allen and Clifford E. Simonsen, are also useful. Although statistical information may be dated, and recent court decisions and legislation may not be included, earlier editions of the textbook remain largely unchanged on topics including prison history, the development and organization of state and federal correctional agencies, and landmark court cases on prisoners' rights.

Essentials of Corrections, 4th Edition (Wadsworth Publishing, 2008) by G. Larry Mays and L. Thomas Winfree, Jr., offers an overview of corrections in the United States. Topics include the history of corrections; issues of race, ethnicity, and gender in correctional settings; parole; and community corrections and alternatives to incarceration.

The Oxford History of the Prison: The Practice of Punishment in Western Society (Oxford University Press, 1995), edited by Norval Morris and David J. Rothman, traces the development of prisons and the idea of incarceration as a form of punishment from biblical times. In addition to essays on prison history, there are chapters on such topics as female prisoners, juvenile detention, and political prisoners, as well as an overview of correctional facilities in the United States and Europe.

Prisons in America (LFB Scholarly Publishing, 2008) by Marilyn D. McShane provides a concise and comprehensive presentation of issues in corrections in the United States. The book is divided by topic into 12 chapters, including punishment and rehabilitation; a history of corrections in the United States; prison industries; prison management; classification; prison violence; legal issues in corrections; the medical care of inmates; prison overcrowding; and the privatization of prisons.

PERIODICALS

The following periodicals are devoted to various topics of interest in corrections. They provide information that is generally more current than that found in books. Their availability at local or school libraries may vary. Some of the publications offer full-text articles or abstracts, which are brief summaries of articles, that are available for download from the publication's web site.

The Angolite, a monthly magazine published by inmates at the Louisiana state prison at Angola, presents articles on current issues in corrections and aspects of daily life in prison. Subscription information is available by writing to *The Angolite*, Louisiana State Penitentiary, Angola, LA 70712 or online at URL: http://www.corrections.state.la.us/LSP/programs.php.

Corrections Compendium is a research journal published six times a year by the American Correctional Association (ACA). Issues are commonly organized around a central topic, including health care, family visitation and reunification, and corrections staff training and education. Each issue also includes commentary and reviews of books on corrections-related areas of interest. Subscription information is available from the ACA, 206 N. Washington Street, Suite 200, Alexandria, VA 22314 or online at URL: http://www.aca.org/images/form_ccsubscription.pdf.

Corrections Today, also published by the ACA, is a magazine that covers topics of general interest in corrections. Articles from current and archived issues are available for download free of charge at URL: http://www.aca.org/publications/ctmagazine.asp.

Journal of Correctional Health Care is a quarterly research journal published by the National Commission on Correctional Health Care (NCCHC) that addresses issues of medicine, law, and medical ethics in correctional settings. Abstracts of articles from current and past issues are available free of charge online at URL: http://www.ncchc.org/pubs/journal.html. Subscriptions are available online or by writing to Sage Publications, 2455 Teller Road, Thousand Oaks, CA 91320.

Journal of Offender Rehabilitation is a professional journal that focuses on methods of treatment and rehabilitation of criminal offenders. Contributing writers are experts in various fields of study, including psychology, social work, penology, and administration of justice. A free sample issue, abstracts of articles from current and past issues, and subscription information is available online at URL: http://www.informaworld.com/smpp/title~content=t792306909~db=all, or by calling 800-354-1420.

National Prison Project Journal, a quarterly newsletter published by the American Civil Liberties Union (ACLU), provides information on issues related to prisoners' rights, including recent court decisions and updates on ongoing litigation. Subscriptions are available by writing to the ACLU National Prison Project, 915 15th Street, NW, 7th Floor, Washington, DC 20005.

The Prisoner Express is a newsletter circulated to inmates in prisons nationwide that features artwork, essays, poetry, fiction, and commentary by prisoners. Subscriptions and free issues are available online at URL: http://www.prisonerexpress.org/?mode=newsletter, or by writing to Prisoner Express, 127 Anabel Taylor Hall, Cornell University, Ithaca, NY 14853.

The Prison Journal is the official publication of the Pennsylvania Prison Society, which was founded in 1787 and is the oldest prison reform organization in the United States. The journal, published quarterly, explores various issues in corrections and has special issues on current topics of interest, which have included women prisoners, inmates with substance abuse problems, and education in correctional settings. Subscription information is available online at URL: http://tpj.sagepub.com, or by writing to *The Prison Journal*, Sage Publications, Inc., 2455 Teller Road, Thousand Oaks, CA 91320.

LIBRARY RESOURCES

Library catalogs allow the researcher to identify books, audiovisual materials, and other sources of information on prisons. The success of locating information depends on good searching techniques. For example, the Library of Congress, with the largest library catalog in the world (URL: http://catalog.loc.gov) allows the researcher to conduct a basic search by title, author, subject, call number, keywords, and by LCCN, ISSN, or ISBN publishing numbers. A more advanced guided search is also possible, and its search parameters are explained on the web page. Searches may be streamlined through manipulation of the search phrase. Local libraries as well as university and law libraries offer similar electronic catalogs that can be efficiently searched by using the same techniques.

PERIODICAL INDEXES

Most libraries subscribe to online periodical indexes, which are searchable databases of articles from newspapers and magazines. Although libraries pay to subscribe to periodical indexes, registered library patrons are often given free access to the databases. One of the more popular periodical indexes is

Info Trac, which provides coverage for about 1,000 general interest magazines. Depending on the publication, InfoTrac allows the researcher to view abstracts or to view and download full-text articles. In addition, helpful tips are provided on how to efficiently search the InfoTrac database.

The Internet Public Library (IPL), an online library service sponsored by the University of Michigan's School of Information and freely available to the general public (URL: http://www.ipl.org), provides a directory of periodical indexes. From the web site's main page, click on *Ready Reference* and follow the link *Periodical Directories* to a listing of periodical directories.

FindArticles.com (URL: http://www.findarticles.com) is a useful archive of some 300 magazine and journal articles from 1998 to the present. Access to FindArticles.com is free, and some full-text articles may be downloaded and printed at no cost.

BOOKSELLER CATALOGS

Online booksellers like Amazon and Barnes and Noble provide a valuable bibliographic source that allows the researcher to easily identify other titles on corrections-related topics and issues. Conducting a simple keyword search of the bookseller's web site is one approach to finding books of interest. Another useful feature of many online booksellers, however, is their ability to identify books that are similar in theme or subject matter to a known book title. For example, on amazon.com, by selecting *Books* from the pull-down menu and entering the partial book title *Corrections in America*, a list was generated of other corrections-related books, including *Exploring Corrections in America*, Second Edition (LexisNexis/Matthew Bender, 2008), by John T. Whitehead, Mark Jones, and Michael C. Braswell; *It's About Time: America's Imprisonment Binge* (Wadsworth Publishing Company, 2010) by James Austin and John Irwin; and *Prime Time Prisons on U.S. TV: Representation of Incarceration* (Peter Lang Publishing, 2009) by Bill Yousman.

Another benefit of online booksellers is their ability to connect the researcher with a nationwide network of reputable used booksellers. Used copies of current or previous editions of books of interest are often available for purchase at substantially discounted prices. This is especially helpful to the researcher with limited library resources.

INTERNET RESEARCH

Searching the Internet through the World Wide Web is an excellent way to conduct research on prisons. However, due to the vast amount of online information that is available on prisons and corrections in the United States, the large number of results generated by using a simple search engine may be overwhelming. Some commonly used Internet search engines available to the researcher include:

- Alta vista (www.altavista.com)
- AOL (www.AOL.com)
- Ask (www.ask.com)
- Google (www.google.com)
- Lycos (www.lycos.com)
- Yahoo! (www.yahoo.com)

Also useful are meta search engines, which generate results for a search term by simultaneously utilizing several standard search engines. Some commonly used meta search engines are:

- all+ (www.allplus.com)
- Clusty (www.clusty.com)
- Dogpile (www.dogpile.com)
- Excite (www.excite.com)
- WebCrawler (www.webcrawler.com)

Like periodical indexes and library catalogs, Internet search engines and metasearch engines are used most effectively by developing a focused search phrase. For example, using the Clusty meta search engine, the search term *prisons* generated 2.6 million results. Clusty displayed the top 153 results and also provided a listing of "clusters," which are links to subtopics under the general search term *prisons*, including *inmates, Federal, sentence,* and *crime*. However, by narrowing the general search term to *U.S. prisons for women* the search generated about 444,000 results and displayed the top 93 results. Also, the links displayed in "clusters" were more focused, including *Abuse, sexual; mentally ill;* and *statistics on women.*

WEB DIRECTORIES

Web directories, or indexes, are another way of using search engines such as Yahoo! or Google. Web directories provide a structured listing of topics and issues within a given subject area. When researching a broad subject, such as prisons, web directories are especially helpful in narrowing a search and identifying useful search phrases for further research.

For example, clicking on yahoo.com from the main web page under *Yahoo! Web Directory*, following the links *Society and culture* to *Crime* to *Corrections and Rehabilitation* generated a listing of links to subcategories, including *Inmates, Prison History, Prisoner Rape, Women,* and *Supermax Prisons.* Also, by entering *prisons* in the search window on the yahoo.com main page and selecting the *in Directory* button—some 1,315 results were generated, including *Federal Bureau of Prisons, Prisons and Prisoners's Rights,* and *Private Prisons.*

Another helpful web directory is Prentice Hall's Cybrary: The World's Criminal Justice Directory (URL: http://www.talkjustice.com/cybrary.asp). Category links include *Community Corrections, Corrections, Prisons, Probation and Parole,* and *Sentencing.* Following the link *Prisons* generated an extensive listing of annotated web links to organizations and agencies with corrections-related information, including *Behind Bars: Substance Abuse and America's Prison Population, Control Unit Prisons, Correctional News Online, Corrections Connection, Family and Corrections Network, Federal Bureau of Prisons,* and the *National Institute of Corrections.*

The Librarians Index to the Internet (URL: http://www.lii.org) is also a useful resource for the researcher that generates annotated links to subjects of interest.

NEWS ON PRISON ISSUES

Many popular Internet search engines, including Google and Yahoo!, allow the researcher to investigate current news and feature articles on prison-related issues. For example, on Google.com, following the link *News* generated more than 9,000 links to news stories on subtopics including detainees at Guantánamo Bay prison camp, a prison escape in Texas, and the need for more educational programs in U.S. prisons. Links on the left side of the Web page allow the results to be sorted by date or within the past hour, day, week, or month. Also useful are links to news stories on prisons archived over previous decades, dating back to 1930.

LIBRARY OF CONGRESS ONLINE RESEARCH TOOLS

For the serious researcher, the Library of Congress provides an extensive listing of online research tools on its Databases and E-Research Web page (URL: http://www.loc.gov/rr/ElectronicResources/dbs.php). The main page provides a search box to begin an immediate search. Located above the search box are links to three major subsections of the database: *Getting Started, Web Search Tools,* and *General Databases.* The *Getting Started* section offers an accessible overview of the electronic resources that are available and includes links to general topics. The *Web Search Tools* section provides an extensive listing of links to search engines, including many specialized by topic. Especially useful are the brief descriptions provided for the specialized search engines. The *General Databases* section provides an extensive listing of educational and commercial databases of periodicals, articles, and abstracts, many of which are available to the general public.

ONLINE RESOURCES FOR LAW AND LEGISLATION

The Legal Information Institute (LII) is an online research service by Cornell Law School that is available free of charge to the Internet user at URL: http://www.law.cornell.edu. Information available from the LII web site includes:

- U.S. Supreme Court decisions since 1990 and selected historic decisions by the Supreme Court
- The United States Constitution, with linked court decisions of significance
- Decisions of the U.S. Courts of Appeal
- The U.S. Code, which is a compilation of all federal legislation enacted into law

As discussed in Chapter 2, there are a significant number of U.S. Supreme Court decisions on issues relating to imprisonment. LII makes it relatively easy for the researcher to identify significant court decisions on constitutional issues. For example, entering *due process* in the search window on the LII main web page and following the link *Law About . . . Prisons and Prisoners* generated a page that contained an overview of prisoners' rights on the issue of due process as guaranteed by the Fourteenth Amendment to the U.S. Constitution. Clicking the "Resources" tab displays a menu of sources, including links to the *Eighth Amendment* of the U.S. Constitution, which forbids cruel and unusual punishment, *U.S. Supreme Court Historic Decisions Dealing with Prisoners*, and *Recent Prison Decisions*. Other links included state *Appellate Decisions* on prisoners' rights, *Commentary, Human Rights Treaties*, and other online sources for information on prisons and the law. Selecting *U.S. Supreme Court Historic Decisions Dealing with Prisoners* generated a page with the search options *All decisions, Only decisions since 1991, Only summaries of decisions*, and *Only historic decisions*. Entering *prisoners & "due process"* in the search window generated links to landmark Supreme Court rulings, including *Estelle v. Gamble* (1976), *Hudson v. Palmer* (1984), *Sandin v. Connor* (1995), and *Lewis v. Casey* (1996).

It is also possible to find U.S. Supreme Court cases by case name on the LII Web site. For example, entering *"Estelle v. Gamble"* on the search page for the U.S. Supreme Court (URL: http://supct.law.cornell.edu/supct/search) generated links to a syllabus of the Supreme Court's decision and the Court's full opinion.

STATISTICS ON PRISONS AND PRISONERS

The Bureau of Justice Statistics (BJS) provides comprehensive statistical information on the criminal justice system in the United States. The BJS is a division of the Office of Justice Programs in the U.S. Department of Justice. The BJS web page (URL: http://www.ojp.usdoj.gov/bjs) contains links to corrections-related publications and statistical surveys. For example, following the link *Corrections* from the main web page generated links to statistical reports on a range of topics, including *capital punishment, prisons*, and *probation and parole*. Following the link *Corrections facts at a glance* generated links to graphical representations of statistics on the number of adults in the correctional population, increases in the prison population over time, and the number of prisoners under sentence of death.

The BJS publishes a number of annual reports on corrections-related areas of interest, including *Prison and Jail Inmates at Midyear, State Prison Expenditures, Census of State and Federal Correctional Facilities*, and *Prisoners*—all available by download. Links are also provided to current statistical information on the criminal justice system in the United States. Topics include criminal offenders, courts and sentencing, and special topics including prisoner reentry trends and drugs and crime.

OTHER USEFUL WEB SITES

The following selected web sites provide information on myriad corrections-related issues and valuable links for further research.

American Correctional Association (ACA) (URL: http://www. aca. org.), founded in 1870 as the National Prison Association, is the oldest professional association in the field of corrections, with a membership that includes researchers, policymakers, and correctional agency staff in federal, state, and local corrections. The ACA publishes the monthly magazine *Corrections Today*, which is linked from the main web page and is helpful in identifying current issues of interest in the field of corrections. The *Corrections Today* web page offers links to downloadable articles from the current issue and two years of archived issues. Each issue is devoted to a corrections-related topic. Archived issues covered topics including probation and parole, juvenile corrections, military corrections, correctional health care, the correctional workforce, and inmate reentry and reintegration.

American Federation of State, County and Municipal Employees (AFSCME) is the largest labor union of public service employees in the United States. The AFSCME provides a comprehensive listing of corrections-related links on their AFSCME Corrections United (ACU) web page at URL: http://www.afscme.org/acu/workers/67.cfm. Especially helpful are the links to issues related to U.S. corrections officers, including a feature that allows the researcher to conduct a state-by-state search on the salaries and employment trends for state corrections officers.

American Probation and Parole Association (APPA) (URL: http://www.appa-net.org.) is a professional association with membership throughout the United States and Canada. The APPA Web site provides a "Resources" link with a helpful link to *Free Publications*, which offers annotated links to articles and research reports on issues relating to parole and offender reentry. For example, there were downloadable reports on topics including community corrections and new programs in probation and parole.

The **Association of State Correctional Administrators** (ASCA) (URL: www.asca.net) is a professional association established in 1970 to promote training, education, and the exchange of information on prison administration and management. The ASCA web site offers a helpful link to *Publications*, where articles and reports on issues of prison administration are available by download. Although sometimes technical in nature, the publications offer insight into the challenges of managing correctional facilities. For example, there are links to articles on assessing the performance of correctional institutions, financing prisons and correctional programs, and the outsourcing of prison services, such as food service and health care.

The **Center for Community Corrections** (URL: http://www.centerforcommunitycorrections.org) was established in 1987 to conduct research and disseminate information to corrections professionals, researchers, and academics. The center's Web site offers a number of helpful resources to researchers.

The **Centers for Disease Control and Prevention Correctional Health** (URL: http://www.cdc.gov/correctionalhealth) was created by the Centers for Disease Control and Prevention (CDC) to encourage collaboration between public health organizations and the correctional agencies. The CDC Correctional Health web page provides links to information and publications on correctional health that are useful to both beginning and advanced researchers. Among the Web site's offerings are links to a primer on correctional health care, government agencies in correctional health care, and special health issues, including health-care issues for females and juveniles in correctional institutions, chronic and infectious diseases, health-care delivery in correctional settings, and mental health.

How to Research Prisons and Correctional Issues

The **Corrections Connection** (URL: http://www.corrections.com) was established in 1996 to create a forum for the exchange of information and ideas by corrections professionals. The Corrections Connection web page offers an extensive database on corrections-related news, information, and downloadable publications available to the general public. The Web site's main page provides a link to "Today's Headlines" for news about prisons and corrections from newspapers and periodicals nationwide. There are also links to corrections-related topics including education, health care, juvenile detention, and legal issues.

Criminal Justice Links (URL: http://www.criminology.fsu.edu/), sponsored by the Florida State University School of Criminology and Criminal Justice, provides links to online information in all areas of the U.S. criminal justice system. The Web site's main page offers a portal Research, Publications and Resources, which provides links to published research, publications, and resources.

Criminal Justice Resources: Periodicals Available on the Web (URL: http://www.lib.msu.edu/harris23/crimjust/per.htm) offers an extensive listing of annotated web links to periodicals in all areas of criminal justice, including corrections, some of which offer full text articles online. Sponsored by Michigan State University, the web page also offers links to electronic journals in criminal justice and the law, with links to descriptions of the periodicals listed and links to each periodical's web page.

The **Federal Bureau of Prisons** (BOP) (URL: http://www.bop.gov) is a federal agency within the U.S. Department of Justice created in 1930 to administer the federal prison system in the United States. The BOP Web site provides an extensive database of information on the federal prison system, including a federal inmate locator and links to current facts and statistics on inmate populations at BOP facilities nationwide. Among downloadable publications are the *State of the Bureau*, which provides an annual summary of statistical data on all phases of the BOP.

USA.gov (URL: http://www.usa.gov) is the U.S. government's clearinghouse for information from the executive, legislative, and judicial branches of the federal government and from state, local, and tribal governments. From the main web page, the link *Public Safety and Law* provides a gateway to online information in all areas of the U.S. criminal justice system, including prisons, correctional agencies, inmates, and parole.

The **National Archive of Criminal Justice Data** (NACJD) (URL: http://www.icpsr.umich.edu/NACJD), established in 1978 as an interuniversity consortium for political and social research, provides an extensive online database of publications from federal and state agencies in criminal justice, including corrections. The NACJD Web site offers a user-friendly search engine to access downloadable publications in specific areas of interest.

Search results are displayed with links to a description of the publication and links to related literature in that field of study.

The **National Criminal Justice Reference Service** (NCJRS) (URL: http://www.ncjrs.gov) is a federally sponsored database of publications in all areas of criminal justice. The NCJRS Web site's main page offers a link to *Corrections*, where linked subcategories are listed that allow the researcher to easily narrow a search. In addition, the *Corrections* page lists corrections-related publications available by download that can be sorted by title, date, or document number. Also linked is a searchable database of library abstracts and full-text articles from hundreds of periodicals. A helpful online research tutorial includes a *thesaurus term search* feature that helps the researcher narrow a search by generating a list of subcategories for a general search term. For example, the general search term *corrections* generated over 50 links to subcategories, including *assaults on corrections officers, correctional agencies, correctional reform, corrections research,* and *juvenile corrections.* The NCJRS *thesaurus term search* (URL: http://abstractsdb.ncjrs.org/content/Thesaurus/Thesaurus_Search.asp) can be accessed from the main page by clicking on the *Help* link, then clicking on the *How do I search the NCJRS web site* link, then clicking on *What is the Advanced Thesaurus Search?*

The **National Institute of Corrections** (NIC) (URL: http://www.nicic.org) is an agency within the Federal Bureau of Prisons, U.S. Department of Justice, that provides training and correctional program development assistance and funding to federal, state, and local corrections agencies. The NIC Web site offers an extensive collection of information and downloadable publications on corrections-related topics available through the *Library*, which is linked from the Web site's main page. The database provides a search engine that allows the researcher to narrow the search, by the type of publication and the search phrase. The correction *Library* offers links to recent publications and a search tool that provides a topic index and permits searches by search terms.

The **Prison Policy Initiative** (PPI) (URL: http://www.prisonpolicy.org) is a prisoners' rights advocacy organization. The PPI Web site provides numerous links to news articles, reports, and other publications on a range of corrections-related social issues including conditions of confinement, racial disparity in incarceration rates, and felony disenfranchisement laws. Among the links available from the main web page is *Research*, which provides links to research and reports, prison factsheets, graphs and charts, and legal resources for prisoners.

The **World Criminal Justice Library Network** (WCJLN) (URL: http://andromeda.rutgers.edu/~wcjlen/WCJ) was established at a meeting of librarians and criminal justice information specialists in 1991 at the Rutgers University School of Criminal Justice with the mission of sharing criminal justice information worldwide. As such, the WCJLN provides a clearinghouse for information on criminal justice systems in the United States and some 70 other countries. The WCJLN web page offers links to statistical resources, general reference sources, and online periodicals, some of which are corrections-related.

The **United States Parole Commission** (USPC) (URL: http://www. justice.gov/uspc) is an agency within the U.S. Department of Justice with jurisdiction over the parole of federal prisoners, military prisoners, and state parolees in the federal Witness Protection Program. The USPC Web site provides links to the rules and procedures of federal parole, statutes governing parole, and statistics on the federal parole system.

CHAPTER 7

ANNOTATED BIBLIOGRAPHY

The following annotated bibliography focuses on prisons and corrections-related issues in the United States. Entries are grouped in the following three categories:

Correctional Systems, Facilities, and Staff
Classification, Treatment, and Parole
Prisoners, Inmates' Rights, and Sentencing

Each category is subdivided into three sections: *Books, Articles and Papers,* and *Web Documents.*

CORRECTIONAL SYSTEMS, FACILITIES, AND STAFF

BOOKS

Allen, Harry E., et al. *Corrections in America: An Introduction, 12th Edition.* Upper Saddle River, N.J.: Prentice Hall, 2009. Presents a comprehensive overview of the prison system in the United States. Included are chapters on the history of punishment and prison development, state and federal correctional systems, correctional philosophies, prisoner's rights, inmate populations, parole, and community corrections.

American Correctional Association. *2009–2010 National Jail and Adult Detention Directory, 11th Edition.* Lanham, Md.: American Correctional Association, 2009. Offers comprehensive informational listings on local, state, and federal correctional institutions for adult offenders in the United States.

Ayers, E. L. *Vengeance and Justice: Crime and Punishment in the 19th Century in the American South.* New York: Oxford University Press, 1984. Presents a historical overview of crime and punishment in the South, with emphasis on the period between the Civil War and 1900. Includes a discussion of the plantation model for leasing prisoners for their labor that was widely adopted in southern prisons.

Baker, J. E. *The Right to Participate: Inmate Involvement in Prison Administration.* Metuchen, N.J.: Scarecrow Press, 1974. Presents a historical overview of inmate participatory management in U.S. prisons from 1793 to 1973.

Barnes, Harry Elmer. *The Evolution of Penology in Pennsylvania: A Study in American Social History.* Indianapolis, Ind.: Bobbs-Merrill, 1927. Presents a historical overview of the development of the Pennsylvania system, including an analysis of the system and its impact on the development of correctional institutions in the United States.

Bates, Sanford. *Prisons and Beyond.* New York: Macmillan, 1971. An analysis of the structure and administration of the federal prison system by the first director of the Federal Bureau of Prisons. Originally published in 1936, the book includes a discussion of the medical model of inmate classification and rehabilitation.

Bayse, Daniel J. *Working in Jails and Prisons: Becoming Part of the Team.* Lanham, Md.: American Correctional Association, 1995. Basic primer presents models for effective interaction between prison staff and inmates. Includes a brief history of corrections, discusses the differences between jail and prison, and provides a reference list and a glossary of terms of prison-related issues.

Beaumont, Gustave de, and Alexis de Tocqueville. *On the Penitentiary System in the United States and Its Application in France.* Carbondale: Southern Illinois University Press. Reprint, originally published in 1833. Presents an assessment of the prison system in the United States in the early 19th century, based upon visits to American prisons by the authors. Includes a proposal to establish a model prison in France based upon the Pennsylvania system.

Bennett, James V. *I Chose Prison.* New York: Alfred A. Knopf, 1970. A history of corrections in the United States by the former director of the Federal Bureau of Prisons from 1937 to 1964.

Berritas, Gregory N., ed. *Controlling Federal Prison Costs.* Hauppauge, N.Y.: Nova Science, 2009. Provides a short collection of viewpoints on strategies to curtail costs in the U.S. federal prison system.

Bosworth, Mary. *Explaining U.S. Imprisonment.* Thousand Oaks, Calif.: Sage Publications, Inc., 2009. Provides a comprehensive overview of the history and culture of corrections in the United States. Includes statistical information on incarceration rates and inmate demographics in U.S. prisons and the conflict between managing the costs of incarceration and the increasing reliance on detention in the modern era.

Braswell, Michael, et al. *Prison Violence in America.* Cincinnati: Anderson, 1994. Presents an overview of the types and causes of violence in U.S.

prisons and discusses strategies for minimizing violence and its effects on inmates and correctional staff.

Brown, Jim. *Folsom Prison*. Charleston, S.C.: Arcadia, 2008. Account by a former corrections officer of the history of the California State Prison at Folsom. Includes descriptions of the interior of the prison and describes various types of inmates formerly incarcerated at the prison.

Carlson, Peter M., and Judith S. Garrett. *Prison and Jail Administration: Practice and Theory, Second Edition*. Sudbury, Mass.: Jones and Bartlett, 2008. Examines in detail the organizational structure and management of correctional facilities, including food service, personnel issues, and the impact of technology on correctional institutions.

Clear, Todd R., and George F. Cole. *American Corrections*. Belmont, Calif.: Wadsworth, 1994. Textbook that presents a comprehensive overview of corrections in the United States, including the evolution of prisons in America.

Clemmer, Donald. *The Prison Community*. New York: Holt, Rhinehart, and Winston, 1940. Presents findings of a classic sociological study of imprisonment that examined prison subculture, language, and norms in U.S. state prisons with inmate populations of 2,300 or more.

Colvin, Mark. *Penitentiary in Crisis: From Accommodation to Riot in New Mexico*. New York: State University of New York Press, 1992. Presents a historical overview of inmate control strategies used at the New Mexico penitentiary.

Cox, Stephen D. *The Big House: Image and Reality of the American Prison*. New Haven, Conn.: Yale University Press, 2009. Examines and compares the popular images of U.S. prisons and the realities of incarceration, including issues of inmate control and discipline and efforts to reform the correctional system in the United States.

Currie, Elliott. *Crime and Punishment in America*. New York: Henry Holt, 1998. Examines the growth of prisons in the United States, including supermax prisons, and presents alternatives to incarceration, including social programs for individuals at high risk for criminal conduct.

Delucia, Robert C., and Thomas J. Doyle. *Career Planning in Criminal Justice*. Cincinnati: Anderson Publishing Company, 1990. Examines a range of employment opportunities in the field of criminal justice, including the requisite qualifications and job descriptions for careers in corrections.

Edge, Laura Bufano. *Locked Up: A History of the U.S. Prison System*. Minneapolis: Twenty-first Century Books, 2009. Reviews the historical development of American prisons, beginning in colonial New England. Includes discussions correlating rising incarceration rates with the growth of the U.S. population, the work of prison reformers, and the evolution of modern practices in corrections.

Annotated Bibliography

Ellis, Alan, and J. Michael Henderson. *Federal Prison Guidebook*. Costa Mesa, Calif.: James Publishing, 2008. A directory of federal prisons in the United States with detailed information on programs offered at each facility, health and counseling services, visiting hours, and mail regulations.

Forer, Lois G. *Rage to Punish: The Unintended Consequences of Mandatory Sentencing*. New York: W. W. Norton, 1994. A former judge advocates for the abolition of capital punishment, sentencing guidelines, and mandatory sentencing rules because of their alleged failure to reduce the rate of crime in the United States and their cost to taxpayers by increasing the rate of incarceration nationwide.

Fortunate Eagle, Adam. *Alcatraz! Alcatraz! The Indian Occupation of 1969–1971*. New York: Heyday Books, 1992. Personal account of the Native American occupation of Alcatraz Island after the closing of the prison there in 1963 by the Bureau of Prisons. Includes a historical overview of Alcatraz when it was a maximum security prison.

Foster, Burk, et al., eds. *The Wall Is Strong: Corrections in Louisiana*. Lafayette: Center for Criminal Justice Research, University of Southwestern Louisiana, 1989. Includes chapters by various authors, with the focus on the history of the Louisiana state prison at Angola, including the administration of the facility and prison life there. Other state correctional facilities in Louisiana are also examined.

Fox, Vernon B., and Jeanne B. Stinchcomb. *Introduction to Corrections, Fifth Edition*. Englewood Cliffs, N.J.: Prentice Hall, 1999. Textbook presents an overview of corrections in the United States, including trends in correctional administration.

Friedman, Laurie S. *Prisons*. Detroit: Greenhaven Press, 2008. Collection of essays on various issues in U.S. corrections, including faith-based prison programs, inmate labor, medical and mental health care in prison, the functions of military prisons, and the costs and effectiveness of incarceration for society.

Friedman, Lawrence. *Crime and Punishment in American History*. New York: Basic Books, 1993. Discusses the development of the U.S. criminal justice system beginning in the colonial era in three major areas: law enforcement, the courts, and prisons.

Geltner, Guy. *The Medieval Prison: A Social History*. Princeton, N.J.: Princeton University Press, 2008. Reconstructs life inside prisons in medieval Europe, comparing their administration and classification of inmates to those of modern prisons and presenting differences between medieval prisons and their modern counterparts. The book challenges the commonly held view that modern prisons are an outgrowth of the Enlightenment's philosophy of man's ability to reform his soul and traces modern correctional practices to the century.

203

Gildemeister, Glen A. *Prison Labor and Convict Competition with Free Workers in Industrialized America, 1840–1890.* New York: Garland Press, 1987. Historical analysis of the prison labor movement in the United States, including discussions of how prison-made goods competed with goods manufactured in the private sector.

Gottfredson, Don, et al. *Guidelines for Parole and Sentencing.* Lexington, Mass.: Lexington Books, 1978. Includes a comprehensive overview of the evolution of parole and sentencing in the United States.

Gourevitch, Philip, and Errol Morris. *The Ballad of Abu Ghraib.* New York: Penguin Books, 2009. Profiles U.S. soldiers who took and appeared in widely publicized photographs taken at Abu Ghraib prison in Iraq and presents a discussion of the perspectives of guards and inmates at the prison.

Griset, Pamela L. *Determinate Sentencing: The Promise and the Reality of Retributive Justice.* Albany: State University of New York Press, 1991. Discusses determinate sentencing and the impact of determinate sentencing laws that remove or reduce the authority of sentencing decision makers, such as judges.

Hall, Basil. *Travels in North America in the Years 1827 and 1828, Volumes I and II.* Reprint, New York: Arno Press, 1974. Includes a firsthand report on a tour of New York's Sing Sing prison and a discussion of the Auburn system.

Hall, Henry. *The History of Auburn.* Auburn, N.Y.: Dennis Brothers and Company, 1869. A history of the town of Auburn, New York, including a discussion of the Auburn prison system and its development.

Hawkins, Richard, and Geoffrey P. Alpert. *American Prison Systems: Punishment and Justice.* Englewood Cliffs, N.J.: Prentice Hall, 1989. Presents a historical overview of the origins and objectives of imprisonment in the United States.

Hirsch, Adam Jay. *The Rise of the Penitentiary: Prisons and Punishment in Early America.* New Haven, Conn.: Yale University Press, 1992. Historical analysis of the development of penitentiaries in the United States and the use of corporal punishment for inmate control.

Hurley, Dennis James. *Alcatraz Island Memories.* Petaluma, Calif.: Barlow Printing, 1987. Account of the son of a former federal corrections officer of his life on Alcatraz Island from the age of seven to 18, including a historical overview with emphasis on the period when Alcatraz was a federal prison from 1934 to 1963.

———. *Alcatraz Island Maximum Security.* Petaluma, Calif.: Barlow Printing, 1989. Presents biographical sketches of the most famous inmates housed at Alcatraz federal prison and includes a discussion of the attempted escapes from the maximum security facility from its opening in 1934 to its closure in 1963.

Irwin, John. *Prisons in Turmoil*. Boston: Little, Brown, 1980. Presents a historical overview of violence in U.S. prisons, including violence arising from racial tensions among inmate groups.

Irwin, John, and James Austin. *It's about Time: America's Imprisonment Binge*. Belmont, Calif.: Wadsworth Corporation, 1994. A discussion of sentencing and imprisonment in the United States and possible alternatives.

James, Adrian A., et al. *Privatizing Prisons: Rhetoric and Reality*. Thousand Oaks, Calif.: Sage Publications, 1997. Examines practical and ethical issues related to the privatization of correctional facilities and compares U.S. private prisons to privatized correctional institutions in Europe and Australia.

Jing, Yijia. *Prison Privatization: A Study of the Causes and Magnitude*. Hauppauge, N.Y.: Nova Science, 2009. Presents research on prison privatization in the United States with a focus on state prison privatization. The book compares governmental and private-sector management of correctional facilities and includes a detailed analysis of data on the impact of prison privatization on inmates and society.

Johnston, Norman. *A Brief History of Prison Architecture*. New York: Walker and Company, 1973. Presents a historical analysis of the architecture of U.S. prisons, beginning with the design of the Walnut Street jail in Philadelphia, Pennsylvania.

Kahan, Paul. *Eastern State Penitentiary: A History*. Charleston, S.C.: History Press, 2008. Presents the history of the Philadelphia prison from its inception as a model of the Pennsylvania system of incarceration in 1829 and examines the tensions created an atmosphere of violence at the prison throughout its history.

Keve, Paul W. *The History of Corrections in Virginia*. Charlottesville: University Press of Virginia, 1986. Historical analysis of corrections in Virginia from the colonial period to the modern era, including a discussion of the political and social forces that shaped the style of management in Virginia prisons.

———. *Prisons and the American Conscience: A History of U.S. Federal Corrections*. Carbondale: Southern Illinois University Press, 1991. Historical analysis of federal imprisonment from the colonial era to 1987, including a discussion of the contributions to American corrections made by James Bennett during his tenure from 1937 to 1964 as director of the Federal Bureau of Prisons.

LaFave, Wayne R. *Search and Seizure: A Treatise on the Fourth Amendment*. St. Paul, Minn.: West Publishing, 1987. Presents a comprehensive discussion of the protection against unreasonable search and seizure guaranteed by the Fourth Amendment, including the legal precedents for search and seizure without consent in correctional settings.

LaMaster, Kenneth M. *U.S. Penitentiary Leavenworth*. Charleston, S.C.: Arcadia, 2008. A history of the federal prison at Leavenworth, Kansas, from the planning stage beginning in 1895, for a prison to house the most serious offenders. Describes the construction of the prison by federal inmates and profiles some of the individuals housed at the prison, including George "Machine Gun" Kelly, Frank "the Enforcer" Nitti, and George "Buggs" Moran.

Lamott, Kenneth. *Chronicles of San Quentin: The Biography of a Prison.* New York: David McKay Company, 1961. Presents a historical overview of the state prison at San Quentin, California.

Latessa, Edward J., et al. *Correctional Contexts: Contemporary and Classical Readings, Second Edition.* Los Angeles: Roxbury Publishing Company, 2001. Previously published articles and papers by authors in various disciplines, including penology, psychology, and sociology, are organized into seven parts: History of Punishment and Origins of Imprisonment, Living in Prison, Working in Prison, Prison Litigation and Inmate's Rights, Institutional Programming and Treatment, Release from Prison and Parole, and New Directions.

Lewis, W. David. *From Newgate to Dannemora: The Rise of the Penitentiary in New York, 1796–1848.* Ithaca, N.Y.: Cornell University Press, 1965. An analysis of the historical development of the prison system in New York State, including a discussion of correctional practices and the trend of the increasingly repressive management of inmates.

Lockwood, Daniel. *Prison Sexual Violence.* New York: Elsevier North/Holland, 1980. Discusses the causes and effects of sexual violence among prisoners and the role of correctional staff in responding to reports of incidents of sexual violence.

Logan, Charles H. *Private Prisons: Cons and Pros.* New York: Oxford University Press, 1990. Discusses the advantages and disadvantages of privately operated correctional facilities and compares private and public prisons in terms of operating costs, accountability, corruption, and security.

Lombardo, Lucien X. *Guards Imprisoned: Correctional Officers at Work.* New York: Elsevier North-Holland, 1981. Presents findings of a research study based on extensive interviews of correctional officers at the Auburn correctional facility in New York.

Marshall, H. E. *Dorothea Lynde Dix: Forgotten Samaritan.* Chapel Hill, N.C.: University of North Carolina Press, 1937. Biography of Dorothea Dix that focuses on her contributions to the field of corrections and the prison reforms that resulted from her work.

Martin, Steve J., and Sheldon Ekland-Olson. *Texas Prisons: The Walls Came Tumbling Down.* Austin: Texas Monthly Press, 1987. Analysis of the Texas state prison system from 1967 to 1987, including the use of the tender system, in which stronger and sometimes more violent inmates were given authority over other prisoners. Includes a discussion of the impact of *Ruiz v. Estelle* (1980) 503 F. Supp. 1265, which found in favor of a Texas state inmate who alleged that unsafe and overcrowded conditions in Texas prisons were unconstitutional.

Mays, G. Larry, and L. Thomas Winfree. *Essentials of Corrections, 4th Edition.* Belmont, Calif.: Wadsworth Publishing, 2008. Provides an overview of corrections in the United States. Topics include the history of corrections; issues of race, gender, and ethnicity in correctional settings; parole; community corrections; and alternatives to incarceration.

McGee, Richard A. *Prisons and Politics.* Lexington, Mass.: Lexington Books, 1981. Presents a historical analysis of the influence of political objectives on the management of the California state prison system.

McKelvey, Blake. *American Prisons: A History of Good Intentions.* 1936. Reprint, Montclair, N.J.: Patterson-Smith, 1977. Historical primer on the state and federal prison systems in the United States from 1835 to 1977 that addresses such issues as changing standards of correctional administration, prison reform, criminological theories, and the impact of state and federal legislation on prison industries.

McShane, Marilyn D. *Prisons in America.* New York: LFB Scholarly Publishing, 2008. Explores the development of corrections systems in America and examines political, economic, and philosophical issues related to incarceration. Includes reviews of legislation, legal cases, and social trends in corrections.

McShane, Marilyn D., and Franklin P. Williams. *Encyclopedia of American Prisons.* New York: Garland Press, 1996. Presents a collection of some 160 corrections-related essays arranged alphabetically by topics, including prison history and administration, prisoners' rights, mental illness among the prison populations, and prison overcrowding.

Melossi, Dario D., and Massimo Pavarina. *The Prison and the Factory: Origins of the Penitentiary System.* London: Macmillan, 1981. Historical analysis correlating the rise of capitalism and the expansion of prison systems throughout Europe and the United States.

Morris, Norval, and David J. Rothman, eds. *The Oxford History of the Prison: The Practice of Punishment in Western Society.* New York: Oxford University Press, 1995. Traces the development of prisons and the idea of incarceration as a form of punishment from biblical times. In addition to essays on prison history, there are chapters on such topics as female prisoners, juvenile detention, political prisoners, and an overview of correctional facilities in the United States and Europe.

Morris, Roger. *The Devil's Butcher Shop: The New Mexico Prison Uprising.* New York: Franklin Watts, 1983. Chronicles the inmate riot in 1980 at the New Mexico state penitentiary at Sante Fe using eyewitness statements and reports by the New Mexico attorney general and the prison intelligence office.

Murton, Thomas O. *The Dilemma of Prison Reform*. New York: Holt, Rinehart and Winston, 1976. Examines the failure of prison reform movements in the United States, including the author's own experiences with reform as a warden with the Arkansas Department of Corrections.

Murton, Thomas O., and Joe Hyams. *Accomplices to the Crime: The Arkansas Prison Scandal*. New York: Grove Press, 1969. Examines styles of management, including the use of corporal punishment, throughout the state prison system in Arkansas. Coauthor Murton was the former superintendent at the Arkansas Prison Farm.

Nagel, William G. *The New Red Barn: A Critical Look at the Modern American Prison*. New York: Walker, 1973. Presents an overview of the design of modern U.S. prisons and the impact of prison design on the security and treatment of prisoners.

Nelson, William Ray, et al. *New Generation Jails*. Boulder, Colo.: Library Information Specialists, 1983. Discusses the design and management of modern jails, as well as the potential effectiveness of these if implemented in U.S. prisons.

New York State Special Commission on Attica. *Attica: The Official Report of the New York State Special Commission on Attica*. New York: Bantam Books, 1972. Examines the prison uprising at Attica that began on September 9, 1971, including an overview of the New York state prison system at the time of the rioting and a summary of prison conditions and events that led to the siege. Includes a description of the riot and its aftermath and presents recommendations for the reform of the New York state prison system.

Osborne, Thomas Mott. *Society and Prisons*. New Haven, Conn.: Yale University Press, 1916. A classic analysis of inmate participatory management by the former warden of Sing Sing prison in New York and a discussion of the improvement in overall inmate behavior when prisoners participated in the management of the prison.

Oswald, Russell G. *My Story*. Garden City, N.Y.: Doubleday, 1972. Personal account of the inmate uprising at the New York state prison at Attica in 1971 by the then commissioner of the New York state prison system.

Parenti, Christian. *Lockdown America, Revised Edition*. London: Verso, 2008. Explores political and economic historical trends and their impact on mass incarceration. Documents daily life in U.S. prisons and includes a discussion of issues arising from the U.S. detention of so-called enemy combatants.

Perkinson, Robert. *Texas Tough: The Rise of America's Prison Empire*. New York: Metropolitan Books, 2009. Historical analysis of the development of the prison system in the United States emphasizing the contributions of correctional practices in the South.

Raphael, Steven, and Michael A. Stoll, eds. *Do Prisons Make Us Safer?: The Benefits and Costs of the Prison Boom*. New York: Russell Sage Foundation,

2009. Presents essays on various corrections-related issues, including increasing rates of incarceration in the United States, the impact of incarceration on the crime rate, criminal psychology, and the effects on children.

Ross, Jeffrey Ian. *Special Problems in Corrections.* Upper Saddle River, N.J.: Pearson/Prentice Hall, 2007. Identifies major issues in U.S. correctional systems and organizes them into two categories: those impacting inmates and correctional facilities and those impacting correctional staff and administration. Presents empirical research and examines topics including inmate classification and assessment, rehabilitation, and overcrowding.

Scott, David. *Penology.* Los Angeles: Sage, 2008. Provides a comprehensive introduction to the academic study of penology, including a detailed glossary of academic terms in the study of corrections.

Shoham, S. Giora, et al., eds. *International Handbook of Penology and Criminal Justice.* Boca Raton, Fla.: CRC Press, 2008. Provides a comprehensive overview from an international perspective. Includes chapters on prisons and jails, community corrections, victim restitution, comparative roles of the prosecution and defense in Western trial systems, sentencing, and white collar and corporate crime.

Sifakis, Carl. *The Encyclopedia of American Prisons.* New York: Facts On File, 2003. Entries are arranged alphabetically and include listings for significant individuals in the history of corrections and notorious prisoners. There are also expanded listings on certain topics, including execution methods and jails and prisons.

Simon, Rita J., and de Waal, Christiaan. *Prisons the World Over.* Lanham, Md.: Lexington Books, 2009. Examines and compares the practices of confining criminal offenders from an international perspective. Includes a bibliography for further research.

Sullivan, Larry E. *The Prison Reform Movement: Forlorn Hope.* Boston: Twayne Publishers, 1990. Presents a historical overview of the prison reform movement, beginning with reform efforts in the 19th century. Includes a discussion of the decline of treatment programs in the modern era, combined with rising inmate violence and a repressive management model in many U.S. correctional facilities.

Sykes, Gresham M. *Society of Captives: A Study of a Maximum Security Prison.* Princeton, N.J.: Princeton University Press, 1958. Presents findings of a classic sociological study of maximum security prisons, including organizational dysfunction in prison administration and the norms and language of prison subculture.

Teeters, Negley K. *The Cradle of the Penitentiary: The Walnut Street Jail at Philadelphia, 1773–1835.* Philadelphia: Pennsylvania Prison Society, 1955. Presents a historical overview of the Walnut Street jail in Philadelphia,

Pennsylvania, and the influence of Quakers in the development and operation of the facility.

Tewksbury, Richard A., and Dean A. Dabney, eds. *Prisons and Jails: A Reader.* New York: McGraw-Hill, 2009. A collection of contemporary readings written by scholars and experts on a variety of issues in modern corrections in the United States.

Useem, Bert, and Anne Morrison Piehl. *Prison State: The Challenge of Mass Incarceration.* Cambridge: Cambridge University Press, 2008. Examines the causes and consequences of increasing rates of incarceration in the United States and the growth of the corrections industry.

Unseem, Bert, et al. *Resolution of Prison Riots: Strategies and Policies.* New York: Oxford University Press, 1996. Examines the causes of inmate uprisings in U.S. prisons nationwide and discusses managerial policies aimed at reducing the tensions that lead to prison riots.

Ward, David A., and Gene G. Kassebaum. *Alcatraz: The Gangster Years.* Berkeley, Calif.: University of California Press, 2009. Presents accounts of the lives of inmates, including Al Capone and Alvin Carpis, who were incarcerated from 1934 to 1948 at the California State Prison at Alcatraz, which was designed as America's first super maximum security prison, or supermax.

Welch, Michael. *Corrections: A Critical Approach.* New York: McGraw-Hill, 1995. Presents an overview of corrections in the United States, including a social history of punishment and incarceration and a discussion of prison violence, the death penalty, and alternatives to imprisonment.

Wellman, G. L. *A History of Alcatraz Island 1853–2008.* Charleston, S.C.: Arcadia, 2008. Presents the history of the California State prison at Alcatraz, from the facility's use as strategic military outpost through its 1934 conversion into a federal penitentiary, with the purpose of housing America's most violent offenders, to the closure of the prison in 1963, when it became part of the Golden Gate National Recreation Area.

Wicker, Tom. *Time to Die.* New York: Times Books, 1975. Eyewitness account by reporter and writer Tom Wicker of the riot at the state prison at Attica, New York, including a discussion of the negotiations between inmates and prison officials during the siege.

Williamson, Harold E. *The Corrections Profession.* Newbury Park, Calif.: Sage Publications, 1990. Presents an overview of the professional roles in corrections and discusses career preparation, the tasks of various corrections professionals, and the working environment in correctional settings.

Yackle, Larry W. *Reform and Regret: The Story of Federal Judicial Involvement in the Alabama Prison System.* New York: Oxford University Press, 1989. Discusses prison reform in the Alabama state prison system as the result of the intervention of state and federal courts.

Yousman, Bill. *Prime Time Prisons on U.S. TV: Representation of Incarceration.* New York: Peter Lang, 2009. Examines media coverage of U.S. prisons, including news reporting on correctional issues as well as fictional and nonfictional programming portraying conditions of confinement and daily life inside American prisons.

ARTICLES AND PAPERS

Hill, Cece. "Gangs/Security Threat Groups." *Corrections Compendium* 34 (Spring 2009): 23. Presents data on prison gangs and security-threat groups reported by 45 correctional systems in the United States and two Canadian provincial correctional systems.

Johnston, Norman. "Evolving Function: Early Use of Imprisonment as Punishment." *The Prison Journal* 89 (March 2009): 10S. Provides a historical review of the uses of imprisonment from some 3,000 years ago to recent times. Includes a discussion of the evolution of prisons in the United States, including the Pennsylvania and Auburn systems and the expansion of the corrections industry in modern times.

Kozlowski, Jonathan. "Behind the Bars." *Law Enforcement Technology* 36 (March 2009): 32. Examines the problem of cell phones as contraband in prisons, including the use of cell phones by inmates to engage in criminal activity inside and outside of the prison, to threaten to victims and prosecutors, and to coordinate escapes.

Lahm, Karen F. "Inmate Assaults on Prison Staff: A Multilevel Examination of an Overlooked Form of Prison Violence." *Prison Journal* 89 (June 2009): 131. Presents findings of a study of inmates in 30 state prisons in Kentucky, Ohio, and Tennessee on assaults by inmates on prison staff that suggest that such assaults are commonly personal in nature and that refined inmate classification procedures that identify psychological issues may help to predict the likelihood of inmates to assault staff members. Additional findings include a higher incidence of inmate on staff violence among juvenile offenders in both adult and juvenile facilities.

Marsh, Shawn C., and William P. Evans. "Youth Perspectives on Their Relationships With Staff in Juvenile Correction Settings and Perceived Likelihood of Success on Release." *Youth Violence and Juvenile Justice* 7 (January 2009): 46. Presents findings of a study examining the perspectives of detained juvenile offenders on their relationships with staff in juvenile correctional settings as well as their perceived likelihood of success after their release. Study data were collected in June and July 2006 through surveys of some 543 youths in juvenile correctional facilities in Alaska, Idaho, Nevada, and Oregon.

Moore, Solomon. "States Export Their Inmates as Prisons Fill." *New York Times*, July 31, 2007, p. A1. Reports on efforts by corrections officials in eight states to ease prison overcrowding by moving inmates to less crowded facilities in other states.

Moster, Aviva N., and Elizabeth L. Jeglic. "Prison Warden Attitudes Toward Prison Rape and Sexual Assault: Findings Since the Prison Rape Elimination Act (PREA)." *The Prison Journal* 89 (March 2009): 65. Presents findings of a study on the attitudes and beliefs of some 60 state prison wardens toward prison rape since the Enactment in 2003 of the Federal Prison Rape Elimination Act (PREA), which mandated a zero-tolerance policy for sexual assaults in prisons and the collection of national data on prison rape and sexual assault.

Peak, Kenneth J., et al. "Hostage Situations in Detention Settings: Planning and Tactical Considerations." *FBI Law Enforcement Bulletin* 77 (October 2008): 1. Examines the history of rioting and hostage-taking in U.S. prisons and jails and discusses emergency planning, warning signs of impending violence, and tactical measures in the event of an incident, including the use of force and the process of negotiation.

Petersilia, Joan. "Influencing Public Policy: An Embedded Criminologist Reflects on California Prison Reform." *Journal of Experimental Criminology* 4 (December 2008): 335. Discusses a wide range of issues in corrections in the context of the study of criminology, including the relationship between research on best practices in corrections and development of public policy, with emphasis on efforts to reform the California state prison system.

Ross, Michael W., et al. "Measurement of Prison Social Climate: A Comparison of an Inmate Measure in England and the USA." *Punishment & Society* (October 2008): 447. Examines findings of a study of federal prisons in the United States and Great Britain comparing prison social climate, which refers to the social, organizational, and physical characteristics of correctional institutions as perceived by inmates and prison staff.

Saunders, Mark H. "Security in the Round." *Corrections Today Magazine* 70 (October 2008): 44. Examines the issue of securing a modern correctional facility, including technological advances such as tracking bracelets for inmates and retina scanning for accurate identification. Discusses non-technological aspects of prison security, including the proper training of correctional staff on techniques of observation and visual assessment of inmate behavior.

Souryal, Sam S. "Deterring Corruption by Prison Personnel: A Principle-Based Perspective." *The Prison Journal* 89 (March 2009): 21. Discusses corruption by prison personnel in U.S. prisons and proposes the implementation of anti-corruption measures, including an emphasis on ethics during the training of correctional personnel.

Steiner, Benjamin, and John Wooldredge. "Rethinking the Link Between Institutional Crowding and Inmate Misconduct." *Prison Journal* 89 (June

2009): 205. Reviewing previous research since 1990 on the relationship between prison overcrowding and inmate misconduct, the article presents findings of a study designed for corrections policymakers. The study examine underlying explanations for the effects of overcrowding on inmate misconduct.

Steinhauer, Jennifer. "To Cut Costs, States Relax Prison Policies." *New York Times*, March 24, 2009, p. A1. Reports on cost-saving measures by states to reduce corrections expenditures, including the closures of prisons in Colorado and Kansas, the use of community programs in lieu of prison for parole offenders in New Jersey and Michigan, and the repeal of the death penalty in New Mexico, in part because its implementation was too costly.

Trulson, Chad R., et al. "Racial Desegregation in Prisons." *The Prison Journal* 88 (June 2008): 270. Examines racial desegregation in U.S. prisons resulting from the U.S. Supreme Court ruling in *Johnson v. California* (2005). According to this ruling, prisons are bound by the same laws as society on issues of race and the racial segregation of inmates is unlawful except under extraordinary circumstances to ensure the safety and security of inmates, staff, and institutions.

Wethal, Tabatha. "Under Constant Watch." *Law Enforcement Technology* 36 (March 2009): 22. Examines TSI Prism technology, introduced in 2001, and its effectiveness in tracking the real-time locations of inmates in large correctional facilities, including a jail in Washington, D.C., housing some 2,500 inmates.

WEB DOCUMENTS

Bulman, Philip. "Using Technology to Make Prisons and Jails Safer." Washington, D.C.: National Institute of Justice, March 2009. Available online. URL: http://www.ncjrs.gov/pdffiles1/nij/225764.pdf. Examines technologies utilized to enhance safety in U.S. prisons and jails, including portable scanners for detecting improvised weapons and transponders to track inmate movements and identify areas within the prison or jail with increased incidence of violence.

California Legislative Analyst's Office. "Corrections Spending and Impact of Possible Inmate Population Reduction." Sacramento, Calif.: California Legislative Analyst's Office, February 24, 2009. Available online. URL: http://www.lao.ca.gov/handouts/crimjust/2009/02_24_09_corrections_spending_population_reduction.pdf. Provides a detailed analysis of budgetary and legal factors for consideration in efforts to lower corrections costs by releasing certain offenders from California state prisons.

Duff, Marc C. "Corrections Privatization Generates Savings and Better Service." *Wisconsin Interest* 12 (Winter 2003): 12. Available online. URL:

http://www.wpri.org/wiinterest/vol12no1/duff12.1.pdf. Discusses the economic impact of the 254 percent increase in the number of Wisconsin state prisoners from 1992 to 2000 and corrections privatization as a possible way to ease the state's costs of incarceration.

Lawrence, Sarah, and Jeremy Travis. "The New Landscape of Imprisonment: Mapping America's Prison Expansion." Research Report, Urban Institute Justice Policy Center, April 2004. Available online. URL: http://www.urban.org/Uploaded PDF/410994_mapping_prisons.pdf. Presents an overview of the overall growth in the number of prisons between 1979 and 2000, including statistics on the state-by-state rate of growth in the number of new correctional facilities, and assesses the impact of newly built correctional facilities on local communities.

McDonald, Douglas, and Carl Patten. "Governments' Management of Private Prisons." Report, National Institute of Justice, January 2004. Available online. URL: http://www.ncjrs.org/pdffiles1/nij/grants/203968.pdf. Examines the management of private prisons by state and federal governments in the United States and by private firms under contract to state and federal correctional agencies. Topics include the prevalence of contracting of private prisons, payment structures, performance standards, state and federal monitoring, and case studies of prison privatization in Florida, Oklahoma, and Texas.

108th U.S. Congress. "Prison Rape Elimination Act of 2003." Available online. URL: http://frwebgate.access.gpo.gov/cgi-bin/getdoc.cgi?dbname=108_cong_public_laws&docid=f:publ079.108.pdf. Presents the Prison Rape Elimination Act of 2003, as passed by the 108th U.S. Congress. The act, which provides for the analysis of the incidence and effects of prison rape in federal, state, and local correctional institutions and mandates federal funding to protect prisoners from the threat of rape, was signed into law on September 4, 2003, by President George W. Bush.

Petteruti, Amanda. "Pruning Prisons: How Cutting Corrections Can Save Money and Protect Public Safety." Washington, D.C.: Justice Policy Institute, May 2009. Available online. URL: http://www.justicepolicy.org/images/upload/09_05_REP_PruningPrisons_AC_PS.pdf. Examines the lack of cost-effectiveness in the management of U.S. prisons and jails and explores corrections-related and social issues including public safety, the impact of incarceration on individuals and families, and the impact of prisons on local communities. Includes statistical graphics illustrating the scope of cost-effectiveness problems both nationally and at the state level.

Shaley, Sharon. *Sourcebook on Solitary Confinement.* London: Mannheim Centre for Criminology, London School of Economics and Political Science, 2008. Available online. URL: http://www.solitaryconfinement.org/uploads/sourcebook_web.pdf. Examines the practice and effects of solitary confinement in correctional settings, emphasizing the impact of prolonged solitary confinement and the ethical and professional issues on the use of solitary confinement for purposes of punishment, segregation, and institutional safety. This 98-page online book includes background information on documented physical and psychological effects of solitary confinement, and presents standards, safeguards and recommendations for the protection of inmates who are placed in solitary confinement.

U.S. Bureau of Prisons. "Prison Rape: A Selected Bibliography." Central Office Library, April 2004. Available online. URL: http://www.nicic.org/pubs/2004/019587.pdf. Lists of videos, web sites, books, reports, and articles dealing with the issue of prisoner rape and sexual assault.

U.S. Department of the Interior. "Neither Safe Nor Secure: An Assessment of Indian Detention Facilities." Report, Office of the Inspector General, September 2004. Available online. URL: http://www.oig.doi.gov/main.php?menuid=0&approve=Y. Reports on conditions in Indian jails and detention facilities in the United States, which in 2002 held some 2,080 inmates. Among myriad problems discussed in the report was the failure to segregate juveniles and adults in some detention centers.

Young, Malcom C. "Controlling Corrections Costs in Illinois: Lessons from the Coasts." Report, Bluhm Legal Clinic of the Northwestern School of Law, June 3, 2009. Available online. URL: http://www.law.northwestern.edu/legalclinic/docs/CorrectionsReportFinal.pdf. Compares and contrasts sentencing practices an outcomes in New York and California. More lenient incarceration and sentencing practices New York state resulted in decreases in crime and the state's prison population, while California achieved the opposite results with harsher sentencing laws, including the so-called Three Strikes law. This law allows for the imposition of a life sentence upon any offender convicted of a third felony offense, even a nonviolent third offense.

CLASSIFICATION, TREATMENT, AND PAROLE

BOOKS

Brown, Michelle. *The Culture of Punishment: Prison, Society, and Spectacle.* New York: New York University Press, 2009. Examines the issue of imprisonment as an infliction of punishment upon an individual by a society in which, according to the author, those who are the most unaware of the human toll and racial inequities of incarceration are more likely to favor harsher punishments for offenders.

Cavender, Gary. *Parole: A Critical Analysis.* Port Washington, N.Y.: Kennikat Press, 1982. Presents a historical overview of the development of parole in U.S. correctional systems, with emphasis on the modern use of parole as a rehabilitative tool.

Champion, Dean J. *Probation, Parole, and Community Corrections, Sixth Edition*. Upper Saddle River, N.J.: Prentice Hall, 2007. Presents the roles of probation and parole in the U.S. criminal justice system and describes probation and parole agency personnel and operations in the adult and juvenile justice systems. Chapters address such topics as a description of the components of the U.S. criminal justice system, the role of community corrections, the distinction between probation and parole, the philosophy and functions of parole, the nature of parolees, prerelease programs, and parole revocation.

Cohen, Fred. *The Mentally Disordered Inmate and the Law*. Kingston, N.J.: Civic Research Institute, 2008. Provides an overview of legal issues surrounding prison inmates with mental illness or mental retardation, including the right to treatment, disciplinary proceedings for mentally disordered offenders, and the impact of the Americans with Disabilities Act. Includes discussions of laws regarding mentally disordered juvenile offenders and sexually violent predators.

Cusac, Anne-Marie. *Cruel and Unusual: The Culture of Punishment in America*. New Haven, Conn.: Yale University Press, 2009. Surveys the practices of confinement and imprisonment throughout U.S. history, from the colonial era to modern supermax prisons, with emphasis on shifting trends of rehabilitation versus punishment of offenders.

Delgado, Melvin, and Denise Humm-Delgado. *Health and Health Care in the Nation's Prisons: Issues, Challenges, and Policies*. Lanham, Md.: Rowman & Littlefield, 2009. Presents a comprehensive overview of deficiencies in the health care system in state and federal prisons and proposes recommendations for resolving problems in health care delivery in U.S. correctional systems. Includes assessments of the health care needs of various subgroups in prison populations, including women, older adults, and inmates of different races and ethnic backgrounds.

Earley, Kevin E., ed. *Drug Treatment Behind Bars: Prison-Based Strategies of Change*. Westport, Conn.: Praeger, 1996. Presents essays by mental health practitioners in drug treatment and therapy programs in correctional settings and includes a discussion of the impact of substance abuse on recidivism.

Flanagan, Timothy J., et al., eds. *Incarcerating Criminals: Prisons and Jails in Social and Organizational Context*. New York: Oxford University Press, 1998. Presents essays on the environments within U.S. correctional facilities, including staffing and programming, classification, treatment, and social control.

Fleury-Steiner, Benjamin, and Carla Crowder. *Dying Inside: The HIV/AIDS Ward at Limestone Prison*. Ann Arbor, Mich.: University of Michigan

Press, 2008. Between 1999 and 2003, 43 HIV-positive inmates died at Limestone Prison in Alabama. This book provides an in-depth examination of the deaths of these inmates, focusing on possible contributing factors to the deaths, including rationing of health care due to decreased funding and an overriding emphasis on security at the expense of medical care.

Gelsthorpe, Loraine, and Nicola Padfield, eds. *Exercising Discretion: Decisionmaking in the Criminal Justice System and Beyond.* Portland, Ore.: Willan Publishing, 2003. Presents essays on the exercise of discretion in the administration of the criminal justice system in the United States, including judicial discretion in sentencing, the use of discretion by corrections staff, and the discretionary release of certain types of inmates, including violent offenders and the mentally ill.

Glaser, Daniel. *Preparing Convicts for Law-Abiding Lives: The Pioneering Penology of Richard A. McGee.* Albany: State University of New York Press, 1995. Discusses the work of Richard McGee, former director of the California Department of Corrections who promoted the rehabilitation of inmates. During his tenure, McGee provided drug treatment services in correctional settings and instituted conjugal visits at California state prisons.

Harden, Judy, and Marcia Hills, eds. *Breaking the Rules: Women in Prison and Feminist Therapy.* Binghamton, N.Y.: Haworth Press, 1998. Presents essays by authors in the fields of psychology, criminology, sociology, and women's studies on services and treatment programs in correction settings for female inmates. Includes a discussion of the experiences of women prisoners, including childhood sexual abuse, and issues relating to motherhood during their incarceration.

Kratcoski, Peter C., ed. *Correctional Counseling and Treatment.* Prospect Heights, Ill.: Waveland Press, 1994. Various contributors discuss treatment programs available in U.S. prisons and factors that contribute to the success of treatment, including the role of inmate classification in properly identifying the needs of inmates and the role of the prison environment and correctional officers' characteristics in facilitating effective treatment in correctional settings.

Kupers, Terry A. *Prison Madness: The Mental Health Crisis Behind Bars and What We Must Do about It.* San Francisco: Jossey-Bass Publishers, 1999. Analysis of the treatment of mentally ill inmates in which the author, a physician, argues that prisons are warehousing and mistreating large numbers of mentally ill inmates and that prison management policies are traumatizing formerly normal prisoners and making them angry, violent, and vulnerable to severe emotional problems.

Kusha, H. R. *Islam in American Prisons: Black Muslims' Challenge to American Penology.* Farnham, England: Ashgate, 2009. Examines correctional and societal issues arising from the increasing rates of religious conversion to Islam among African-American inmates in U.S. prisons.

Lester, David, et al. *Correctional Counseling.* Cincinnati: Anderson Publishing Company, 1992. Presents an overview of counseling in a correctional setting, including discussions of inmate classification systems, individual and group treatment methods, and the effectiveness of treatment in prison.

Leukefeld, Carl G., and Frank M. Tims, eds. *Drug Abuse Treatment in Prisons and Jails.* Rockville, Md.: National Institute on Drug Abuse, 1992. Presents an overview of drug abuse treatment programs in correctional settings, including evaluations on the efficacy of certain types of substance abuse treatment and recommendations for new approaches to drug abuse treatment in U.S. prisons and jails.

McShane, Marilyn D. *Community Corrections.* New York: Macmillan, 1993. Presents an overview of community corrections in the United States and discusses interstate compact agreements for criminal offenders who commit crimes outside of their state of origin.

Pisciotta, Alexander W. *Benevolent Repression: Social Control and the American Reformatory-Prison Movement.* New York: New York University Press, 1994. Presents a historical analysis of the adult reformatory movement in the United States, with the focus on the reform efforts of Zebulon Brockway, the chief administrator at the Elmira reformatory in New York from 1876 to 1920.

Pollack, Joycelyn M. *Counseling Women in Prison.* Thousand Oaks, Calif.: Sage Publications, 1998. Discusses treatment and counseling in correctional settings for female inmates and the importance of addressing factors in the female inmate's background, including drug abuse and cultural issues.

Rafter, Nicole Hahn. *Creating Born Criminals.* Urbana: University of Illinois Press, 1997. Discusses the history of biological theories of crime and their impact on the U.S. prison system in terms of the classification and treatment of inmates. Includes a discussion of eugenics, a popular 19th-century theory that blamed criminal behavior on bad breeding and the commonly held belief in the mid-19th century that the mentally retarded were inherently prone to criminal behavior.

Rhine, Edward E., et al. *The Practice of Parole Boards.* Lexington, Ky.: Association of Paroling Authorities International, 1994. Presents findings of a study of the function of parole boards in prisons nationwide, including the role of the victim in the parole process and issues concerning adequate parole supervision.

Simon, Jonathan. *Poor Discipline: Parole and the Social Control of the Underclass, 1890–1990.* Chicago: University of Chicago Press, 1993. Presents a historical overview of the parole system in the United States and discusses the disciplinary, clinical, and managerial models for parole.

Swanson, Cheryl G. *Restorative Justice in a Prison Community; Or Everything I Didn't Learn in Kindergarten I Learned in Prison.* Lanham, Md.: Lexington Books, 2009. Provides a first-person account of the development of an "Honor Dorm" at Holman Prison in rural Alabama. Discusses policy decisions that enabled the creation of the dorm and issues confronted by inmates housed in the dorm.

Toch, Hans, and Kenneth Adams. *The Disturbed Violent Offender.* New Haven, Conn.: Yale University Press, 1989. Discusses the connection between mental illness and criminal violence among inmates in the New York state prison system in 1985.

Travis, Jeremy, and Michelle Waul, eds. *Prisoners Once Removed: The Impact of Incarceration and Reentry on Children, Families, and Communities.* Washington, D.C.: Urban Institute Press, 2003. Each chapter addresses an issue related to the impact of imprisonment on families and communities, including the impact of imprisonment on larger social networks linked to families of prisoners, parenting while incarcerated, and the special problems of the adolescent children of prison inmates.

Wood, Jane, and Theresa Gannon, eds. *Public Opinion and Criminal Justice.* Devon, England: Willan Publishing, 2009. Examines the formation and function of public opinion about criminal justice issues, including mentally ill offenders and victims of crime, and what the data show about public opinion regarding victims and offenders, both in general and with regard to specific types of offenses. Includes chapters written by experts in various fields of study, including psychology, criminology, and criminal justice.

ARTICLES AND PAPERS

Baumer, Eric P., et al. "Porous Prison: A Note on the Rehabilitative Potential of Visits Home." *The Prison Journal* 89 (March 2009): 119. Presents results of a study of prisoners in Ireland who were allowed to leave prison for brief periods of time for visits with family, friends, and potential employers. The study found that inmates allowed to leave prison periodically were less likely to reoffend than other inmates.

Campbell, Mary Ann, et al. "Prediction of Violence in Adult Offenders: A Meta-Analytic Comparison of Instruments and Methods of Assessment." *Criminal Justice and Behavior* 36 (June 2009): 567. Reviews some 88 studies conducted between 1980 and 2006 for risk factors and psychological measurements utilized to predict violent behavior in male criminal offenders, including violence while incarcerated in prison.

Carlson, Joseph R., Jr. "Prison Nurseries: A Pathway to Crime-Free Futures." *Corrections Compendium* 34 (Spring 2009): 17. Reviews the recent history of infant nurseries in U.S. prisons, focusing on the success of former inmates who participated in the infant nursery program in the Nebraska prison system. Also examines infant nursery programs in state prison systems in New York, Washington, Massachusetts, Ohio, California, Illinois, Indiana, West Virginia, and South Dakota.

Craig, Susan C. "Historical Review of Mother and Child Programs for Incarcerated Women." *The Prison Journal* 89 (March 2009): 35S. Reviews the historical evolution of prison programs for incarcerated mothers and their children, including the emergence of a mother-child program in England in the 19th century and the practice of allowing children to stay with their mothers in federal prisons in the United States from 1930 to 1960.

Ferszt, Ginette G., et al. "Houses of Healing: A Group Intervention for Grieving Women in Prison." *The Prison Journal* 89 (March 2009): 46. Presents findings of a study on the impact on participants of facilitator-led therapy groups to deal with emotional losses sustained by female inmates while in prison, including the death of a close family member or significant other and separation from children due to imprisonment. Includes references and graphical statistics.

Fisher-Giorlando, Marianne. "The History of Prisons and Punishment." *The Prison Journal* 89 (March 2009): 1S. Presents the evolution of the use of imprisonment as punishment for criminal offenses and examines the use of prison programs, including child reunification for incarcerated women and convict-leasing.

Gaes, Gerald G., and Scott D. Camp. "Unintended Consequences: Experiment Evidence for the Criminogenic Effect of Prison Security Level Placement on Post-Release Recidivism." *Journal of Experimental Criminology* 5 (June 2009): 139. Examines the claim that assignment to higher security levels of inmates with the same classification scores increases the likelihood of recidivism. The article presents findings from a study of misconduct reports and recidivism among inmates who were randomly assigned to prison security levels. Includes graphical statistics and references.

Gerkin, Patrick M. "Participation in Victim-Offender Mediation: Lessons Learned from Observations." *Criminal Justice Review* 34 (June 2009): 226. Reviews 14 victim-offender mediations and presents findings that offenders provided a high level of participation in approximately half of all mediations. Suggests that both victims and offenders lacked knowledge of the restorative justice principles underlying the use of victim-offender, especially the offender's need to accept responsibility for the harm done to the victim.

Gideon, Lior. "What Shall I Do Now?: Released Offenders' Expectations for Supervision Upon Release." *International Journal of Offender Therapy and Comparative Criminology* 53 (February 2009): 43. Presents findings of a study examining the continuum of treatment and supervision after release. It suggests ways to improve post-release supervision, including counseling inmates, prior to their release, on treatment programs and the requirements of supervision after their release from prison.

Gover, Angela R., et al. "Gender Differences in Factors Contributing to Institutional Misconduct." *Prison Journal* 88 (September 2008): 378. Examines findings of a study to determine if theoretical predictors of inmate misconduct were similar for male and female inmates. It finds a higher incidence of misconduct among previously incarcerated male prisoners and a lower incidence of misconduct among female inmates with prior prison time.

Grady, Melissa D. "Sex Offenders Part I and II: Theories and Models of Etiology, Assessment, and Intervention." *Social Work in Mental Health* 7 (January 2009): 353, 372. Part I presents the clinical issues of sex offenders from the perspective of social workers. It reviews research on treatment of sex offenders, including a national study on the demographic characteristics of some 60,000 sex offenders nationwide and a study of juvenile sex offenders that found most were sexually abused prior to offending. Part II focuses on forensic clinical approaches to sex offenders, including the justice model and the community protection model, and examines the civil commitment of convicted sex offenders after completion of their prison sentences.

Harawa, Nina T. "Using Arrest Charge to Screen for Undiagnosed HIV Infection Among New Arrestees: A Study in Los Angeles County." *Journal of Correctional Health Care* 15 (April 2009): 105. Presents data from a cross-sectional study of newly incarcerated inmates in two jail facilities in Los Angeles County to determine if specific types of arrest charges were associated with undiagnosed HIV infection. Presents findings that male and female parole violators, males arrested for sex or theft charges, and females arrested for drug or violent crimes were more likely to have undiagnosed HIV infections than males and females arrested for other types of offenses.

Heaps, Melody M., et al. "Recovery-Oriented Care for Drug-Abusing Offenders." *Addiction Science Clinical Practice* 5 (April 2009): 31. Profiles the Treatment Alternatives for Safe Communities (TASC) program in Illinois. Through a multiagency approach to drug treatment of offenders, TASC designed a system to address the problem of drug offending at various stages of the criminal justice system, including preadjudication, probation, incarceration, and parole.

Herzberg, Philipp Yorck, and Jurgen Hoyer. "Personality Prototypes in Adult Offenders." *Criminal Justice and Behavior* 36 (March 2009): 259. Presents findings of an evaluation of two samples of prison inmates on their personality prototypes as measured by five factors: neuroticism, extroversion, openness to experience, agreeableness, and conscientiousness.

Hill, Cece. "Survey Summary: Inmate Mental Health Care." *Corrections Compendium* 33 (September/October 2008): 12. Presents findings of a survey of U.S. prisons and jails on the mental health problems of inmates and the treatment available to them. Findings include that female inmates had higher rates of metal health problems than male inmates and that about one-third of all state prisoners had received mental health treatment since incarceration.

Jackson, Arrick L., et al. "Externalization and Victim-Blaming Among a Sample of Incarcerated Females." *Journal of Offender Rehabilitation* 248 (April 2009): 228. Findings of a study examining the effectiveness of a one-week program, Impact of Crime on Victims Class (ICVC), on female inmates in Missouri. Its goal was to decrease an offender's propensity to externalize blame and to increase the likelihood of the offender accepting responsibility for her offense. Results included an increased tendency among violent offenders to blame the victim and society for the actions that resulted in their incarceration.

Jones, Richard S., et al. "First Dime: A Decade of Convict Criminology." *Prison Journal* 89 (June 2009): 151. Examines the development of convict criminology, an area of study and research that focuses on teaching and mentoring in prison settings. Its goal is to present real-life accounts of prison conditions and experiences in the criminal justice system in order to develop a better understanding of issues in crime and criminal justice and to identify areas for improvement.

Kennon, Suzanne S., et al. "Parenting Education for Incarcerated Mothers." *Journal of Correctional Education* 60 (March 2009): 10. Findings of a study on parent education programs implemented in prison to reinforce emotional bonds between mothers and their children.

Kerley, Kent R., and Heith Copes. "Keepin' My Mind Right: Identity Maintenance and Religious Social Support in the Prison Context." *International Journal of Offender Therapy and Comparative Criminology* 53 (April 2009): 228. A study of 63 inmates who experienced a religious conversion in prison examining how their perception of religious life in prison contributed to their expectation of a higher likelihood of success after release.

Knollenberg, Laura, and Valerie A. Martin. "Community Reentry Following Prison: A Process Evaluation of the Accelerated Community Entry Program." *Federal Probation* 72 (September 2008): 54. A study of the efficacy of the Accelerated Community Entry (ACE) Program in the Federal Western District of Michigan. Entry, or reentry, courts utilize the model of drug courts to facilitate reintegration of offenders into the community upon their release from prison by providing community services including counseling and supervision in an effort to decrease the incidence of reoffending.

Kuanliang, Attapol, et al. "Juvenile Inmates in an Adult Prison System: Rates of Disciplinary Misconduct and Violence." *Criminal Justice and Behavior: An International Journal Volume* 35 (September 2008): 1186. A study examining violent misconduct among juveniles incarcerated in adult facilities in the Florida Department of Corrections. It found a higher incidence of violent misconduct among juveniles in adult facilities compared with both juveniles of the same age in juvenile facilities and adults in general population correctional settings.

Lalonde, Robert J., and Rosa M. Cho. "Impact of Incarceration in State Prison on the Employment Prospects of Women." *Journal of Quantitative Criminology* 24 (September 2008): 243. Findings based on a study of administrative records on employment rates of former female inmates in Illinois state prisons. It reports that postprison employment rates among former female inmates was slightly higher than the employment rates among the same group prior to incarceration.

Lanes, Eric. "Identification of Risk Factors for Self-Injurious Behavior in Male Prisoners." *Journal of Forensic Sciences* 54 (May 2009): 692. Examines identified risk factors for self-injurious behavior among a sample of male prisoners with histories of engaging in such behavior. It finds that factors related to self-injurious behavior include abuse or neglect in childhood, impairment of the central nervous system, and lack of formal education.

Listwan, Shelley Johnson. "Reentry for Serious and Violent Offenders: An Analysis of Program Attrition." *Criminal Justice Policy Review* 20 (June 2009): 154. The results of a study examining the success of prisoner reentry for inmates who participated in the Serious and Violent offender Reentry Initiative (SVORI), a 2003 federal program designed to develop and improve reentry services for inmates being released on parole. Findings include a higher incidence of failure among parolees who were unemployed and not residing with a family member after release.

Lurigio, Arthur J., et al. "Predicting Rearrests Among Felony Probationers: The Effects of Setting, Analyses and Probation Status." *Corrections Compendium* 34 (Spring 2009): 1. Results of a study meant to identify predictive factors for rearrests of adult probationers in Illinois. It identified four major variables that contribute to rearrest: initial classification level, discharge classification level, educational level, and age of the probationer.

Moore, Solomon. "Mentally Ill Offenders Strain Juvenile System." *New York Times*, August 10, 2009, p. A1. A newspaper report on the increasing trend of states to cut mental health programs for juveniles in communities and schools and to rely on the juvenile corrections system to manage juveniles with psychiatric disorders.

Perelman, Abigayl M., and Carl B. Clements. "Beliefs About What Works in Juvenile Rehabilitation: The Influence of Attitudes on Support for 'Get Tough' and Evidence-Based Interventions." *Criminal Justice and*

Behavior: An International Journal 36 (February 2009): 184. A study examining the opinions of some 130 college students enrolled in introductory psychology courses about the effectiveness of various types of treatment of juvenile offenders.

Phillips, Laura L., et al. "Care Alternatives in Prison Systems: Factors Influencing End-of-Life Treatment Selection." *Criminal Justice and Behavior* 36 (June 2009): 620. Findings of a study examining the impact of age, physical and emotional health, attitudes toward death, and religious beliefs on end-of-life treatment preferences for inmates whose sentence would end after 75 years of age compared to inmates scheduled for release prior to 75 years of age.

Prendergast, Michael L., et al. "Reducing Substance Use in Prison: The California Department of Corrections Drug Reduction Strategy Project." *Prison Journal* 84 (June 2004): 265. Reports on the management and efficacy of the California Department of Corrections' Drug Reduction Strategy Project, which included random urine testing and drug interdiction programs in California state prisons.

Proctor, Janice. "Impact Imprisonment Has on Women's Health and Health Care from the Perspective of Female Inmates in Kansas." *Women and Criminal Justice* 19 (January/March 2009): 1. Findings of a study of women incarcerated at the Topeka Correctional Facility on factors that influence the health status of female inmates before and during their incarceration. Includes predictive indicators of the quality of health of female prisoners in prison and after release from prison.

Robbers, Monica L. P. "Lifers on the Outside: Sex Offenders and Disintegrative Shaming." *International Journal of Offender Therapy and Comparative Criminology* 53 (February 2009): 5. A study of the incidence and effects of so-called disintegrative shaming, self-reported by 153 registered sex offenders residing in four counties in Virginia. "Disintegrative shaming" involves being labeled as a social outcast, harassment by neighbors, job losses as the result sex-offender status, separation from family and other social support networks, and erroneous arrests.

Salisbury, Emily J., and Patricia Van Voorhis. Gendered Pathways: A Quantitative Investigation of Women Probationers' Path to Incarceration." *Criminal Justice and Behavior* 36 (June 2009): 541. The results of a study of some 300 female probationers in Missouri on factors that increase the risk of reoffending, including childhood victimization, mental illness, substance abuse, and dysfunctional intimate relationships.

Schlager, Melinda D., and Kelly Robbins. "Does Parole Work?—Revisited: Reframing the Discussion of the Impact of Postprison Supervision on Offender Outcome." *The Prison Journal* 88 (June 2008): 234. Examines and compares demographic characteristics of offenders released on parole and those released from prison without community supervision. The article presents evidence suggesting that parolees provided with community-based supervision and services were less likely to reoffend and return to prison.

Severance, Theresa A. "Concerns and Coping Strategies of Women Inmates Concerning Release: It's Going to Take Somebody in My Corner." *Journal of Offender Rehabilitation* 38 (2004): 73. Presents findings of a study of 40 adult female inmates in the Ohio Reformatory for Women on their concerns and plans after release from prison. Among the findings: Inmates were primarily concerned about their basic survival needs after release, including sources of income, employment, and housing. Other concerns were relapse and recidivism, relationships with children, and community acceptance.

Shinkfield, Alison J. and Graffam, Joseph. "Community Reintegration of Ex-Prisoners: Type and Degree of Change in Variables Influencing Successful Reintegration." *International Journal of Offender Therapy and Comparative Criminology* 53 (February 2009): 29. Presents findings of a study of variables that contribute to successful community reentry by recently releases prisoners, including the negative impact of substance abuse on the potential for reoffending.

Specht, Matthew W., et al. "Schemas and Borderline Personality Disorder Symptoms in Incarcerated Women." *Journal of Behavior Therapy and Experimental Psychiatry* 40 (June 2009): 256. Presents results of a study on factors contributing to borderline personality disorder among female inmates and examines the relationship between childhood maltreatment and borderline personality disorder.

U.S. Departments of Justice and Labor. "Report of the Reentry Policy Council: Charting the Safe and Successful Return of Prisoners to the Community." Report, National Institute of Justice, 2004. Describes the goals of the Reentry Policy Council (RPC), established by the Council of State Governments to develop programs that assist reentering prisoners with housing and employment opportunities while promoting public safety.

Ward, Allison and Roe-Sepowitz, Dominique. "Assessing the Effectiveness of a Trauma-Oriented Approach to Treating Prostituted Women in a Prison and a Community Exiting Program." *Journal of Aggression, Maltreatment & Trauma* 18 (April/May 2009): 293. Evaluates the effectiveness group trauma and abuse intervention therapy for females convicted of prostitution who were in prison or community corrections settings.

Willis, Gwenda M., and Randolph C. Grace. "Assessment of Community Reintegration Planning for Sex Offenders: Poor Planning Predicts Recidivism." *Criminal Justice and Behavior* 36 (May 2009): 494–512. The findings of a research study investigating whether, poor planning for community reintegration corresponds to an increase in recidivism for sex offenders and measuring the quality of reintegration planning for groups of recidivist and nonrecidivist sex offenders.

Wilper, Andrew P., et al. "The Health and Health Care of U.S. Prisoners: Results of a Nationwide Survey." *American Journal of Public Health* 99 (April 2009): 666. Presents findings of the first nationwide study on standards of health care for prison inmates. It focuses on the prevalence of chronic illnesses, including mental illness, among inmates and access to health care services in correctional settings.

Zimring, Franklin E. "California's Prison Healthcare Mess." *Los Angeles Times*, October 25, 2008, p. A10. Discusses the strains on the health care system in California state prisons as the result of rapidly rising incarceration rates and budget shortfalls.

WEB DOCUMENTS

Abt Associates, Inc. "Adam II 2008 Annual Report: Arrestee Drug Abuse Monitoring Program II." Washington, D.C.: United States Office of National Drug Control Policy, April 2009. Available online. URL: http://www.whitehousedrugpolicy.gov/publications/pdf/adam2008.pdf. Provides an overview and analyzes statistical data from 2008 of drug use and drug market activity for arrestees in the United States. Includes statistical graphics, a discussion of methodology, and a fact sheet.

Crowe, Ann H., et al. "Community Corrections Response to Domestic Violence: Guidelines for Practice." Lexington, Ky.: American Probation and Parole Association, May 2009. Available online. URL: http://www.appa-net.org/eweb/docs/APPA/pubs/CCRDV.pdf. Reviews practical approaches for developing or improving proactive community supervision programs for domestic-violence cases throughout each phase of the criminal justice process.

Davis, Lois M., et al. *Understanding the Public Health Implications of Prisoner Reentry in California*. Report, The Rand Corporation, 2009. Available online. URL: http://www.rand.org/pubs/technical_reports/2009/RAND_TR687.pdf. Book-length report examines public health issues surrounding prisoner reentry in California, the types of health care needs of ex-offenders, and the impact on communities and local health care systems.

Duwe, Grant. "Residency Restrictions and Sex Offender Recidivism: Implications for Public Safety." *Geography & Public Safety* 2 (May 2009): 6–8. Washington, D.C.: Office of Community Oriented Policing Services (COPS), U.S. Department of Justice, 2009. Available online. URL: http://www.cops.usdoj.gov/files/RIC/Publications/e050919205-gps.pdf. Reports on studies in Minnesota and other states examining residency restrictions for sex offenders and the incidence of reoffending. Findings suggest that residency restrictions have little impact on the risk of reoffending.

MacGowan, Robin J. "HIV Testing Implementation Guidance for Correctional Settings." Atlanta, Ga.: Centers for Disease Control and Prevention, January 2009. Available online. URL: http://www.cdc.gov/hiv/topics/ testing/resources/guidelines/correctional-settings/pdf/Correctional_ Settings_Guidelines.pdf. Provides statistics on HIV/AIDS in correctional facilities and examines issues relating to inmate privacy and confidentiality. Topics include HIV screening and testing procedures in correctional medical clinics, HIV/AIDS case reporting and related legal issues in jails, juvenile facilities, and state and federal prisons.

Maruschak, Laura M. "HIV in Prisons, 2007–08." Bulletin, Bureau of Justice Statistics, U.S. Department of Justice, December 2009. Available online. URL: http://www.ojp.usdoj.gov/content/pub/pdf/hivp08.pdf. Provides a detailed statistical overview of the rate of HIV/AIDS infection in state and federal prisons nationwide, including the incidence of death from HIV/AIDS infection among prisoners.

Wartell, Julie. "Residency Restrictions: What's Geography Got to Do with It?" *Geography & Public Safety* 2 (May 2009): 1–2. Washington, D.C.: Office of Community Oriented Policing Services (COPS), U.S. Department of Justice, 2009. Available online. URL: http://www.cops.usdoj.gov/files/RIC/ Publications/e050919205-gps.pdf. The 2006 passage of California's Proposition 83, known as Jessica's Law, which banned sex offenders going within 2,000 feet of schools, parks and other designated gathering places for children. This document presents the impact of sex offender registry restriction as analyzed by the district attorney's office of San Diego County.

Watson, Jamie, et al. "Portrait of Prisoner Reentry in Texas." Report, The Urban Institute, March 2004. Available online. URL: http://www. urban. org/uploadedpdf/410972_tx_reentry.pdf. Discusses the process of prisoner reentry in Texas and presents the characteristics and demographic distribution of the inmates released from Texas state prisons in 2001, their preparation for release, post-release supervision, and the social and economic environments in the neighborhoods of returning prisoners.

PRISONERS, INMATES' RIGHTS, AND SENTENCING

BOOKS

Abbott, Jack. *In the Belly of the Beast: Letters from Prison.* New York: Vintage Books/Random House, 1991. Chronicles the author's life in prison as culled from letters written by the author to writer Norman Mailer. The letters to Mailer include an account of Abbott's childhood, his experiences in juvenile correctional facilities from the age of 12, and the impact of imprisonment as an adult on Abbott.

American Correctional Association. *The Female Offender: What Does the Future Hold?* Washington, D.C.: St. Mary's Press, 1990. Presents findings of the Task Force Study of Female Offenders by the American Correctional Association to determine the correctional needs for the rising number of female prisoners nationwide.

Andrews, D. A., and James Bonta. *The Psychology of Criminal Conduct.* Cincinnati: Anderson Publishing Company, 1994. Presents a general theory of the psychological underpinnings of criminal conduct.

Baunach, Phyllis Jo. *Mothers in Prison.* New Brunswick, N.J.: Transaction Press, 1985. Examines correctional programs that allow inmate mothers to maintain contact with their children during incarceration. Includes a discussion of the effects of the separation on incarcerated mothers and their children.

Bedau, Hugo Adam. *The Death Penalty in America.* New York: Oxford University Press, 1982. Presents historical, sociological, psychological, legal, and political analysis of capital punishment in the United States, including a discussion of landmark rulings on the death penalty by the U.S. Supreme Court.

Bloom, Barbara E., and David Steinhart. *Why Punish the Children? A Reappraisal of the Children of Incarcerated Mothers in America.* San Francisco: National Council on Crime and Delinquency, 1993. Presents findings of research on the increasing trend of female incarceration and its impact on inmate mothers and their children.

Bowker, Lee H. *Prison Victimization.* New York: Elsevier North-Holland, 1980. Presents an overview of the victimization of inmates in prison, including the physical and psychological damage experienced by both inmates and staff as the result of such victimization.

Byrne, James M., et al. *The Culture of Prison Violence.* Boston: Pearson/Allyn and Bacon, 2007. Provides a comprehensive examination of the causes, prevention, and management of prison violence, including discussions of new research on programs to reduce prison violence and the culture of violence in U.S. prisons.

Carlen, Pat, and Anne Worrall. *Analysing Women's Imprisonment.* Portland, Ore.: Willan Publishing, 2004. Introductory text for students analyzes key issues associated with increases in the number of women in prison in the United Kingdom and throughout the world, with the intent of exploring prison issues in general and the historical and contemporary politics of gender and penal justice.

del Carmen, Rolando V., et al. *Briefs of Leading Cases in Corrections, 5th Edition.* Cincinnati: Anderson Publishing, 2008. Provides a comprehensive overview of legal issues relating to inmates and incarceration. Briefs of cases from the U.S. Supreme Court and some cases from lower federal courts are arranged in six chapters: "Prisons and Jails," "Probation," "Parole," "Death Penalty," "Juvenile Justice," and "Sexual Assault Offender Laws." Each case brief includes a useful capsule that states the legal significance of the case in one or two sentences. In addition, case briefs include the facts of the case, legal issues, the holding of the court, the court's reasoning, and an explanation of the case's legal significance.

Champion, Dean J., and G. Larry Mays. *Transferring Juveniles to Criminal Courts: Trends and Implications for Criminal Justice.* New York: Praeger, 1991. Presents a comprehensive overview of the legal mechanism by which juveniles are transferred to criminal court and tried as adults. Describes various types of transfers.

Cucullu, Gordon. *Inside Gitmo: The True Story Behind the Myths of Guantánamo Bay.* New York: Collins, 2009. Presents interviews conducted by a former U.S. Army colonel of various personnel assigned to the military detention center at Guantánamo Bay, Cuba. Describes daily life for detainees and guards, levels of detention, and details of the treatment of detainees, including the use of interrogation techniques and medical care.

Cummins, Eric. *The Rise and Fall of California's Radical Prison Movement.* Stanford, Calif.: Stanford University Press, 1994. Presents a history of the so-called radical prison movement in California and discusses the influences of groups, including the Black Panther Party and the Symbionese Liberation Army, and state inmates who were active in the movement, including Caryl Chessman, Eldridge Cleaver, and George Jackson.

DeRosia, Victoria R. *Living Inside Prison Walls: Adjustment Behavior.* Westport, Conn.: Praeger, 1998. Presents findings of a study of New York state prisoners comparing the adjustment of inmates with low social status prior to incarceration to that of inmates who earned college degrees and were successfully employed prior to their imprisonment.

Eisenberg, James R. *Law, Psychology, and Death Penalty Litigation.* Sarasota, Fla.: Professional Research Press, 2004. Examines the role of forensic psychology in death penalty trials. Includes a discussion on the historical and legal issues related to capital punishment in the United States.

Elias, Stephen, and Susan Levinkind. *Legal Research: How to Find and Understand the Law.* 4th ed. Berkeley, Calif.: Nolo Press, 1995. A study guide for the legal novice on how to conduct legal research. Includes photographs of legal texts to assist in locating them in a law library.

Fleisher, Mark S. *Beggars and Thieves: Lives of Urban Street Criminals.* Madison: University of Wisconsin Press, 1995. Examines the lives of criminal offenders before and after imprisonment. Includes a bibliography and a glossary of slang terms.

Fletcher, Beverly R., et al. *Women Prisoners: A Forgotten Population.* Westport, Conn.: Praeger, 1993. Presents findings of a longitudinal study of recidivism of female inmates at two correctional facilities in Oklahoma.

Prisons

Fletcher, Laurel E., et al. *The Guantánamo Effect: Exposing the Consequences of U.S. Detention and Interrogation Practices.* Berkeley, Calif.: University of California Press, 2009. Reports on the results of a two-year study of former prisoners at the Guantánamo Bay Detention Facility based on interviews of some 60 former detainees as well as former guards, interrogators, and attorneys for detainees.

Fleury-Steiner, Benjamin. *Jurors' Stories of Death: How America's Death Penalty Invests in Inequality.* Ann Arbor: University of Michigan Press, 2004. Presents the views of jurors who served in death-penalty trials on the effect of race on the sentencing process. Among the author's findings are that jurors who view themselves as more moral than the defendant often have difficulty examining complex mitigating evidence for the defense.

Freedman, Estelle B. *Their Sisters' Keepers: Women's Prison Reform in America: 1830–1930.* Ann Arbor: University of Michigan Press, 1981. Presents findings of a study of female prisoners in the 19th century, including an analysis of the first state prisons designed exclusively for women.

Gabel, Katherine, and Denise Johnston. *Children of Incarcerated Parents.* New York: Free Press, 1997. Discusses the impact of incarceration on the children of prisoners, including children who are born in prison and separated from their mothers or provided with long-term care in prison nurseries.

Giallombardo, Rose. *Society of Women: A Study of Women's Prison.* New York: John Wiley and Sons, 1966. Discusses correctional institutions for women from a sociological perspective, including the effects of prisonization on female inmates.

Girshick, Lori B. *Soledad Women: Wives of Prisoners Speak Out.* Westport, Conn.: Praeger, 1996. Examines the impact of incarceration on the spouses of inmates based on interviews with the wives of some 25 prisoners incarcerated at the California state prison at Soledad.

Harris, Jean. *They Always Call Us Ladies: Stories from Prison.* New York: Scribner, 1988. Firsthand account of an inmate's experience at the Bedford Hills correctional facility in New York State, including a history of the prison.

Harris, Mary B. *I Knew Them in Prison.* New York: Viking Press, 1942. Autobiography that focuses on Harris's work in penology, including her tenure as warden at the Federal Industrial Institution for Women in Alderson, West Virginia.

Hassine, Victor. *Life Without Parole: Living in Prison Today.* Los Angeles: Roxbury Publishing Company, 1996. Describes adapting to prison life, prison subculture, living conditions, prison violence, and the underground prison economy. Written by an inmate at the state correctional institution at Graterford, Pennsylvania, who in 1981 was convicted of murder and sentenced to life in prison without the possibility of parole.

Head, Ian, and Rachel Meeropol. *The Jailhouse Lawyer's Handbook.* 4th ed. Center for Constitutional Rights and the National Lawyers' Guild, 2003.

Presents an overview of inmate rights in the form of a manual designed to assist prisoners in the filing of court actions. Includes guidelines on the drafting of legal documents.

Hemmens, Craig, et al. *Criminal Justice Case Briefs: Significant Cases in Corrections.* Los Angeles: Roxbury Publishing Company, 2004. Presents briefings on important Supreme Court cases on issues including sentencing, the death penalty, access to courts, conditions of confinement, inmate medical care, due process, parole, and the Prison Litigation Reform Act. A section on case holdings offers a short synopsis of one or two sentences for each case that is briefed in the book. Each chapter is devoted to a single issue, such as sentencing or due process, and includes a brief introduction that provides an overview of that issue.

Hersokowitz, Suzan. *Legal Research Made Easy.* Clearwater, Fla.: Sphinx Publications, 1995. Straightforward and streamlined guide for the legal novice on how to conduct legal research and identify legal issues.

Irwin, John. *Lifers: Seeking Redemption in Prison.* New York: Routledge, 2009. Presents profiles of inmates on death row, focusing on California death-row inmates. Includes discussions of the crimes that result in their death sentences and the personal efforts of some death row inmates to atone for their offenses.

Jackson, George. *Soledad Brother.* New York: Coward McCann, 1979. A collection of letters written by inmate George Jackson while incarcerated in California state prisons. Initially sentenced to serve one year to life for stealing $70 from a gas station, Jackson was convicted of killing a correctional officer while in prison. In 1971 Jackson was killed at San Quentin state prison in what was considered to be an act of retaliation for the correctional officer's death.

Jewkes, Yvonne. *Prisons and Punishment.* London: Sage, 2008. Examines issues associated with incarceration and punishment from an international perspective and includes references for further research.

Johnson, Robert. *Condemned to Die: Life under Sentence of Death.* Prospect Heights, Ill.: Waveland Press, 1989. Describes life on death row, based on interviews of some 35 death row inmates in Alabama.

———. *Death Work.* Pacific Grove, Calif.: Brooks/Cole Publishing Company, 1990. Provides an overview of capital punishment in the United States and discusses the impact of stress on death row inmates and corrections personnel who work on death row units.

Kunzel, Regina. *Criminal Intimacy: Prison and the Uneven History of Modern American Sexuality.* Chicago: University of Chicago Press, 2008. Examines prison sexual culture, including the history of same-sex relationships between inmates and the varying explanations for prison homosexuality advanced by corrections officials, reformers, and prison activists.

Livingstone, Stephen, et. al. *Prison Law.* Oxford: Oxford University Press, 2008. Provides a comprehensive overview of international laws governing prisons and inmates and presents legal remedies available to prisoners, including civil claims, judicial review, and claims under the Human Rights Act. Also discusses aspects of prison life, including classification, living conditions, disciplinary procedures.

Loury, Glen C. *Race, Incarceration, and American Values.* Cambridge, Mass.: MIT Press, 2008. Examines trends in incarceration in the United States and the impact on American society. Explores issues including disenfranchisement of African Americans and economic class as a greater indicator than race of who is likely to be incarcerated.

Moyer, Imogene. *The Changing Roles of Women in the Criminal Justice System.* Prospect Heights, Ill.: Waveland Press, 1992. Examines characteristics of female prisoners based on race and other factors.

Muraskin, Roslyn, and Ted Alleman. *Women and Justice.* Englewood Cliffs, N.J.: Prentice Hall, 1993. Presents an overview of females in the criminal justice system and discusses factors including abortion, drug abuse, AIDS, and violence on the rising number of female prisoners.

O'Shea, Kathleen. *Women and the Death Penalty in the United States, 1900–1998.* Westport, Conn.: Praeger, 1998. Discusses the legal history of capital punishment in the United States and methods of execution; includes interviews of female death row inmates, some of whom were later executed.

Othmani, Ahmed, and Sophie Bessis. *Beyond Prison: The Fight to Reform Prison Systems Around the World.* New York: Berghahn Books, 2008. Account of former prisoner Othmani's advocacy for the rights of prisoners worldwide and his founding of Penal Reform International (PRI).

Pollock-Byrne, Joycelyn M. *Women, Prison and Crime.* Pacific Grove, Calif.: Brooks/Cole Publishing Company, 1990. A discussion of issues relating to female prisoners, including female criminality, a history of women's prisons in the United States, rehabilitative approaches to female inmates, and legal issues faced by female inmates.

Rideau, Wilbert, and Ron Wikberg. *Life Sentences: Rage and Survival Behind Bars.* New York: Times Books, 1992. A discussion of criminal sentencing, with emphasis on capital punishment and life without possibility of parole, based on a review of the literature and interviews with inmates. Written by two inmates at the Louisiana state prison at Angola.

Schwartz, Sunny, and David Boodell. *Dreams from the Monster Factory: A Tale of Prison, Redemption and One Woman's Fight to Restore Justice to All.* New York: Scribner, 2009. A presentation of factual stories of former prison inmates and their crime victims in the context of a central question: What do we do with those released from prisons and jails who return to society? Also includes a discussion of author Schwartz's work with Resolve to Stop the Violence Project (RSVP) in San Francisco, the goal of which is to create a prison environment that does not reinforce violence and that provides an opportunity for offenders to accept accountability for their offenses.

Seymour, Cynthia B., and Creasie Finney Hairston, eds. *Children with Parents in Prison: Child Welfare Policy, Program, and Practice Issues.* New Brunswick, N.J.: Transaction Publishers, 2001. Presents an overview and selected issues on the problems faced by the nearly two million children in the United States with an imprisoned mother or father.

Shelden, Randall G. *Controlling the Dangerous Classes: A History of Criminal Justice in America.* Boston: Pearson Allyn and Bacon, 2008. Presents a history of criminal justice from the standpoint of historical biases in the criminal justice system, as demonstrated in the making and application of laws that embody biases of class, gender, and race. The book traces the development of criminal law through the development of law enforcement agencies, the juvenile justice system, and the prison system.

Shook, Chadwick L., and Robert T. Sigler. *Constitutional Issues in Correctional Administration.* Durham, N.C.: Carolina Academic Press, 2000. Presents briefs of landmark Supreme Court cases on corrections-related issues and includes discussions of significant issues, including the evolution of prisoners' rights, the impact of the Prison Litigation Reform Act, constitutional issues related to private prisons, and the involuntary civil commitment of sex offenders.

Simon, Rita J., and Heather Heitfield. *Crimes Women Commit: The Punishments They Receive.* Lexington, Mass.: Lexington Books, 2004. Examines social, economic, and environmental factors in the lives of females who commit crimes, based on 25 years of demographic data on female prisoners nationwide.

Smith, Caleb. *The Prison and the American Imagination.* New Haven, Conn.: Yale University Press, 2009. Explores the dehumanizing effects of incarceration in the context of the law, politics, and literature and discusses conditions in federal and state prisons as well as detention facilities such as the facility for detainees at Guantánamo Bay, Cuba.

Trulson, Chad R., and James W. Marquart. *First Available Cell: Desegregation of the Texas Prison System.* Austin, Tx.: University of Texas Press, 2009. Traces the historical progression from the segregation of Texas prison inmates to their desegregation as an outgrowth of state legislation in 1975 that banned racial discrimination in Texas correctional facilities. Includes an examination of the pioneering work of former Texas prison director George J. Beto, who in 1965 defied contemporary southern norms by allowing inmates of different races to be housed at the same correctional facility.

Walens, Susann. *War Stories: An Oral History of Life Behind Bars.* Westport, Conn.: Praeger, 1997. Profiles 15 inmates confined in U.S. maximum security prisons.

Watterson, Kathryn. *Women in Prison: Inside the Concrete Womb.* Boston: Northeastern University Press, 1996. Discusses personal experiences of women in prison, including the trauma of separation from their children, the process of developing relationships in a prison setting, and the stress caused by the prospect of returning to society after release from prison.

Western, Bruce. *Punishment and Equality in America.* New York: Russell Sage Foundation, 2006. Examines the rising rate of incarceration in the United States, its impact on prisons nationwide, and its effects on poor and minority communities as a result of the disproportionately high percentage of young, urban, and poorly educated African-American male inmates.

Zehr, Howard. *Doing Life: Reflections on Men and Women Serving Life Sentences.* Intercourse, Pa.: Good Books, 1996. A discussion of the effectiveness of victim-offender reconciliation programs by the director of the Mennonite Central Committee's U.S. Office on Crime and Justice. Includes some 60 interviews of male and female inmates who discuss the impact of their criminal offenses on victims, the community, and the families of prisoners.

ARTICLES AND PAPERS

Alexander, Rudolph, Jr. "The United States Supreme Court and the Civil Commitment of Sex Offenders." *Prison Journal* 84 (September 2004): 361. Presents analyses of four significant court cases from 1940 to 2002 in which the U.S. Supreme Court ruled on the constitutionality of civil commitment for sex offenders to mental institutions. The four cases examined are *Pearson v. Probate Court of Ramsey County* (1940), *Kansas v. Hendricks* (1997), *Seling v. Young* (2001), and the 2002 case *Kansas v. Crane.*

Allender, David M., and Frank Marcell. "Career Criminals, Security Threat Groups, and Prison Gangs: An Interrelated Threat." *FBI Law Enforcement Bulletin* 72 (June 2003): 8. Examines the threats to correctional security posed by career criminals and prison gangs, including the failure to respect personal boundaries, disdain for authority, and the use of physical and psychological coercion to gain power.

Ammar, Nawal H., et al. "Muslims in Prison: A Case Study from Ohio State Prisons." *International Journal of Offender Therapy and Comparative Criminology* 48 (August 2004): 414. Presents findings of a study of Muslim male inmates in 30 Ohio state prisons between 1999 and 2000 to determine their characteristics, patterns of identification with Islam, religious behavior inside the prisons, and the relationship, if any, between their conversion to Islam and the crime for which they were sent to prison.

Beck, Allen J., et al. "Implementing the 2003 Prison Rape Elimination Act in Juvenile Residential Facilities." *Corrections Today* 66 (July 2004): 26. Reports on measures undertaken by the U.S. Justice Department's Bureau of Justice Statistics (BJS) to implement the provisions of the 2003 Prison Rape Elimination Act (PREA) in juvenile residential facilities. Under PREA, the BJS was mandated to institute a new national data collection system on the incidence and prevalence of rapes and sexual assault within all correctional facilities nationwide.

Belbot, Barbara. "Report on the Prison Litigation Reform Act: What Have the Courts Decided So Far?" *Prison Journal* 84 (September 2004): 290. Reviews significant court cases addressing the provisions of the Prison Litigation Reform Act (PLRA), which was enacted in 1996 by the U.S. Congress in response to concerns over the amount of prisoner litigation, and the involvement of the federal courts in the operations of state prison systems. The article is divided into two sections. Part one discusses court cases that have interpreted those parts of the PLRA aimed at reducing the amount of prisoner litigation, while part two reviews court cases that have interpreted the intent of the PLRA to curtail federal court intervention in state prisons.

Blackburn, Ashley G., et al. "Sexual Assault in Prison and Beyond: Toward an Understanding of Lifetime Sexual Assault Among Incarcerated Women." *Prison Journal* 88 (September 2008): 351. Presents findings of a study of demographic characteristics and predictors of sexual victimization in prison of 436 female inmates at southern state prisons.

Buell, Maureen. "Children of Inmates: An Issue for Criminal Justice." *Corrections Today* 66 (June 2004): 12. Discusses the Children of Prisoners initiative by the National Institute of Corrections to utilize private sector or nonprofit organizations to administer programs to assist the minor children of prisoners.

Bushfield, Suzanne. "Fathers in Prison: Impact of Parenting Education." *Journal of Correctional Education* 55 (June 2004): 104. Presents findings of a study on the short-term impact of parenting education on fathers in prison who were enrolled in a 30-day parenting class. Among the findings: While prisoners who attended parenting classes expressed that they were motivated to be good fathers to their children, most reported difficulty in maintaining contact with their children while in prison.

Eaton, Judy and Anna Theurer. "Apology and Remorse in the Last Statements of Death Row Prisoners." *Justice Quarterly* 26 (June 2009): 327. Reports on an analysis of the sentiments expressed by death row inmates in their last statements prior to execution. Findings included that some one third of offenders apologized to the victim's family, and that only a small percentage offered excuses for their actions or claimed that their crime was an accident.

Prisons

Fortune, Sandra H. "Prison Gang Leadership: Traits Identified by Prison Gangsters." *Journal of Gang Research* 11 (Summer 2004): 25. Discusses the traits characteristic of prison gang leaders, based on data from interviews with prison gang leaders in the Northeast Correctional Complex in Johnson County, Tennessee. According to the article, gang leaders serve as a role model of commitment to gang rules and gang life and use coercion and their status to impose their will on the gang's rank and file members.

Goodrum, Sarah, et al. "Urban and Rural Differences in the Relationship Between Substance Use and Violence." *International Journal of Offender Therapy and Comparative Criminology* 48 (October 2004): 613. Reports on findings of a study of 637 male inmates in Kentucky state prisons with a history of substance abuse and violence, grouped into two categories: those from rural Appalachian regions and those from non-rural localities with populations of 50,000 or more.

Johnson, Brian R. and Phillip B. Bridgmon. "Depriving Civil Rights: An Exploration of 18 U.S.C. 242 Criminal Prosecutions 2001–2006." *Criminal Justice Review* 34 (June 2009): 196. This review of federal prosecutions from 2001 to 2006 of criminal civil rights violations under U.S. Code 18 U.S.C. 242 reports that that most complaints under the statute were brought against local police officials and correctional officers. The majority of cases brought against corrections officers were for use of excessive force on inmates.

Johnson, Robert, and Sandra McGunigall-Smith. "Life Without Parole, America's Other Death Penalty: Notes on Life Under Sentence of Death by Incarceration." *The Prison Journal* 88 (June 2008): 328. Examines, based on interviews of inmates, the personal experiences of inmates who will spend the remainder of their lives in prison as the result of sentences of death or life in prison without possibility of parole.

Lahm, Karen F. "Physical and Property Victimization Behind Bars: A Multilevel Examination." *International Journal of Offender Therapy and Comparative Criminology* 53 (June 2009): 348. Findings of a study on the dynamics of victimization among inmates at state prisons in Kentucky, Tennessee, and Ohio. The article suggests strategies for reducing inmate victimization that include better classification criteria for identifying the victimization risk of individual prisoners.

Liptak, Adam. "On Death Row, a Battle over the Fatal Cocktail." *New York Times*, September 16, 2004, p. A16. Discusses efforts in Kentucky and other states to change the three-chemical combination used for executions by lethal injection because of claims by some medical experts that the drug combination causes death by suffocation, in violation of the Eighth Amendment's ban against cruel and unusual punishment.

Mageehon, Alexandria. "Caught Up in the System: How Women Who Have Been Incarcerated Negotiate Power." *The Prison Journal* 88 (December 2008): 473. Presents findings of a study of how female inmates use their sense of power, or lack thereof, to manage situations in prison. Examines patterns of power-brokering behavior prior to incarceration as a comparison to such behavior after incarceration.

McMurran, Mary, and Gary Christopher. "Social Problem Solving, Anxiety, and Depression in Adult Male Prisoners." *Legal and Criminological Psychology* 14 (February 2009): 101–107. Examines the relationship between social problem-solving, anxiety, and depression in adult male prisoners and presents research-based recommendations for intervention programs for some prisoners in order to better cope with feelings of anxiety, threat and fear in respect to problems.

Schneider, Rachel Zimmer, and Kathryn M. Feltey. "No Matter What Has Been Done Wrong Can Always Be Redone Right: Spirituality in the Lives of Imprisoned Battered Women." *Violence Against Women* 15 (April 2009): 443. Examines the life experiences and spirituality of battered women incarcerated for killing or attempting to kill intimate partners or fathers who were abusive to them. Based on in-depth interviews of 12 incarcerated battered women.

Serin, Ralph C., et al. "Evaluation of the Persistently Violent Offender Treatment Program." *International Journal of Offender Therapy and Comparative Criminology* 53 (February 2009): 57. Examines the comprehensive evaluation of the Persistently Violent Offender treatment program in Canada. The evaluation found no differences in postrelease outcomes of offenders who completed the program compared with inmates who did not participate in the program.

Spelman, William. "Crime, Cash, and Limited Options: Explaining the Prison Boom." *Criminology & Public Policy* 8 (February 2009): 29. Analyzing state prison populations from 1977 to 2005, Spelman concludes that the prison boom during that time period was due to persistently increasing crime rates, sentencing guidelines that resulted in the incarceration more offenders for longer periods of time, and significant increases in state funding of prison building and expansion.

Thombre, Avinash, et al. "If I Could Only Say It Myself: How to Communicate with Children of Incarcerated Parents." *Journal of Correctional Education* 60 (March 2009): 66. Presents findings of a study of perceptions of inmates in Arkansas on ways of effectively communicating with their children about reasons for incarceration, the function of the criminal justice system, and the importance of education in their children's lives.

Tobolowsky, Peggy M. "Capital Punishment and the Mentally Retarded Offender." *Prison Journal* 84 (September 2004): 340. Presents analyses of two significant U.S. Supreme Court cases on the constitutionality of the execution of mentally retarded criminal offenders. In *Penry v. Lynaugh* (1989), the U.S. Supreme Court held that the Eighth Amendment's ban on cruel and unusual punishment did not categorically bar the execution of mentally retarded offenders. In *Atkins v. Virginia* (2002), the Court revisited the issue and held that the execution of mentally retarded offenders is categorically barred by the Eighth Amendment.

Vollum, Scott, et al. "Should Jurors Be Informed about Parole Eligibility in Death Penalty Cases? An Analysis of *Kelly vs. South Carolina.*" *Prison Journal* 84 (September 2004): 395. Analyzes the implications of the U.S. Supreme Court decision in *Kelly v. South Carolina* (2002) entitling a defendant to a jury instruction regarding parole eligibility when the only alternative to a death sentence is life without parole. The article examines potential legal issues raised in *Kelly,* including the contention that the *Kelly* decisions did not go far enough by guaranteeing that all criminal defendants in death penalty cases be allowed a jury instruction that the only alternative to a death sentence is life without parole.

Wakeman, Sarah, et al. "Preventing Death among the Recently Incarcerated: An Argument for Naloxone Prescription Before Release." *Journal of Addictive Diseases* 28 (April–June 2009): 124. Examines the findings of a research study of overdose among recently released prisoners who were long-term opiate users. Presents statistical data that opiate users recently released from institutional settings, especially prison, have a greater risk of fatal overdose that nonincarcerated opiate users.

Wolff, Nancy, et al. "Racial and Ethnic Disparities in Types and Sources of Victimization Inside Prison." *The Prison Journal* 88 (December 2008): 451. Presents findings of a study comparing the racial and ethic backgrounds of male prisoners to the reporting of victimization. Findings included that African Americans and Hispanics were less likely to report victimization by other inmates but more likely to report victimization by prison staff, while the opposite pattern was found among white inmates.

Wolff, Nancy and Jing Shi. "Type, Source, and Patterns of Physical Victimization: A Comparison of Male and Female Inmates." *Prison Journal* 89 (June 2009): 172. Outlines a study comparing victimization of some 7,000 male inmates and 500 female prisoners housed in general population settings. Findings include a higher rate of victimization among male prisoners for both property and violent offenses.

Wright, Randall. "Care as the Heart of Prison Teaching." *Journal of Correctional Education* 55 (September 2004): 191. Presents findings of a study that attempted to correlate the extent of a correctional teacher's interest in inmate students with inmates' successful completion of educational programs.

Zhang, Yan, et al. "Impact of State Sentencing Policies on the U.S. Prison Population." *Journal of Criminal Justice* 37 (March/April 2009): 190. Presents findings of a study of changes in state prison populations as the result of sentencing reforms, including voluntary sentencing guidelines, three-strike laws, and the abolition of parole.

WEB DOCUMENTS

Amnesty International. "USA: The Promise of Real Change President Obama's Executive Orders on Detentions and Interrogations." London: Amnesty International, 2009. Available online. URL: http://www.amnesty. org/en/library/info/AMR51/015/2009/en. Posted January 30, 2009. Reviews three executive orders and one memorandum signed by President Barack Obama in January 2009 to reform U.S. policies of detaining so-called enemy combatants that were implemented in the aftermath of the terrorist attacks on September 11, 2001.

Bauldry, Shawn, et al. "Mentoring Formerly Incarcerated Adults." Philadelphia: Public/Private Ventures, January 2009. Available online. URL: http://www.ppv.org/ppv/publications/assets/265_publication.pdf. Report on the U.S. Labor Department's Ready4Work Program, which provides mentoring to former inmates in an effort to increase the likelihood of successful reentry into society. The program focuses on increased employment opportunities and job satisfaction for former inmates who received mentoring.

Chiara, Margaret M., et al. "National Prison Rape Elimination Commission Report," June 2009. Available online. URL: http://nprec.us/files/ pdfs/NPREC_FinalReport.PDF. Presents findings of a study, authorized by the Prison Rape Elimination Act of 2003, on the incidence of rape in U.S. prisons and recommends measures intended to address the issue and reduce acts of rape in prisons nationwide.

Cobbina, Jennifer E. "From Prison to Home: Women's Pathways In and Out of Crime." Washington, D.C.: National Institute of Justice, May 2009. Available online. URL: http://www.ncjrs.gov/pdffiles1/nij/ grants/226812.pdf. Presents findings of a study, based on survey interviews and official records, that examined the reentry experiences of white and African-American females in St. Louis, Missouri, after their release from state prison. Drug dependence was a major cause of reoffending among both groups of women.

Collins, William C. "Jails and the Constitution, Second Edition." Report, National Institute of Corrections, U.S. Department of Justice, September 2007. Available online. URL: http://www.nicic.org/Library/022570. Reviews the history of U.S. correctional law and analyzes the impact of major court decisions on issues related to jails and prisons in the United States. Discussion includes the use of the balancing test by courts to evaluate claims brought by inmates and overviews of the First, Fourth, Eighth and Fourteenth Amendments to the U.S. Constitution as applied to corrections.

Daskal, Jennifer, and Joanne Mariner. "Locked Up Alone: Detention Conditions and Mental Health at Guantánamo." New York: Human Rights Watch, June 2008. Available online. URL: http://www.hrw.org/reports/2008/us0608/us0608webwcover.pdf. Reports on the conditions for detainees at the Guantánamo Bay detention center, including the incidence of mental health deterioration of detainees, based on interviews of U.S. government officials and attorneys of detainees.

Durose, Matthew R., and Christopher J. Mumola. "Profile of Nonviolent Offenders Exiting State Prisons." Fact Sheet, Bureau of Justice Statistics, October 2004. Available online. URL: http://bis.ojp.usdoj.gov/content/pub/pdf/pnoesp.pdf. Provides a description of the general characteristics of individuals who served time for nonviolent crimes at the time of their release from state prisons. The report defined nonviolent crimes as property, drug, and public order offenses that do not involve a threat of harm or an attack upon a victim.

Egley, Arlen, Jr., and Christina E. O'Donnell. "Highlights of the 2007 National Youth Gang Survey." Fact sheet, office of Juvenile Justice and Delinquency Prevention, April 2009. Washington, D.C.: Juvenile Justice Clearinghouse, U.S. Department of Justice, April 2009. Available online. URL: http://www.ncjrs.gov/pdffiles1/ojjdp/225185.pdf. Fact sheet summarizing findings based on a nationally representative sample of youth gangs in some 3,550 jurisdictions. According to the fact sheet, an estimated 788,000 gang members and 27,000 gangs were active in the United States in 2007. Includes graphical statistics.

Fortune, Sandra H. "Inmate and Prison Gang Leadership." Dissertation, East Tennessee State University, December 2003. Available online. URL: http://etd-submit.etsu.edu/etd/theses/available/etd-1103103-220112/unrestricted/fortunes11250 3f.pdf. Presents findings of a study identifying the characteristics of gang and non-gang inmate leaders based on interviews with 20 inmates in the Northeast Correctional Complex in Mountain City, Tennessee.

Garcia, Michael John, et al. "Closing the Guantánamo Detention Center: Legal Issues." Washington, D.C.: Congressional Research Service, Library of Congress, January 22, 2009. Available online. URL: http://assets.opencrs.com/rpts/R40139_20090115.pdf. Provides an overview of major legal issues likely to arise as the result of executive or legislative action to close the Guantánamo Bay detention facility. Includes discussions of legal issues related to the transfer or release of detainees to a foreign country or into the United States, their continued detention in U.S. prisons, and constitutional issues that may arise in the criminal prosecution of detainees.

Glaze, Lauren E., and Laura M. Maruschak. "Parents in Prison and Their Minor Children." Washington, D.C.: Special Report, Bureau of Justice Statistics, U.S. Department of Justice, August 8, 2008. Available online.

URL: http://www.ojp.usdoj.gov/bjs/pub/pdf/pptmc.pdf. Statistics on state and federal prison inmates with minor children, including detailed analysis by gender, age, and race as well as background information, such as level of education, criminal history, employment prior to incarceration, homelessness, and substance abuse.

Griffin, Patrick. "Different from Adults: An Updated of Juvenile Transfer and Blended Sentencing Laws, with Recommendations for Reform." Report, National Center for Juvenile Justice, November 2008. Available online. URL: http://www.modelsforchange.net/publications/181. Presents a comprehensive review and examines the impact of state juvenile transfer laws, which permit juveniles accused of certain crimes to be transferred from the jurisdiction of the juvenile court and prosecuted as adults in criminal court.

Grotpeter, Jennifer, et al. "Sexual Violence: Longitudinal, Multigenerational Evidence from the National Youth Survey." Washington, D.C.: Report, National Criminal Justice Reference Service, May 22, 2008. Available online. URL: http://www.ncjrs.gov/pdffiles1/nij/grants/223284.pdf. With the objective of understanding the potential causes of sexual violence, this survey examines patterns of behavior based on self-reporting and interviews of respondents to the National Youth Survey Family Study who engaged in sexual assaults during adolescence and early adulthood.

Hamm, Mark S. "Prisoner Radicalization: Assessing the Threat in U.S. Correctional Institutions." *NIJ Journal* 261 (October 2008): 14. Available online. URL: http://www.ojp.usdoj.gov/nij/journals/261/prisoner-radicalization.htm. Examines trends in U.S. prisons on the so-called radicalization of inmates, who while in prison, adopt extremist views, such as condoning violent measures for political or religious purposes. Includes data culled from reports by gang intelligence officers in Florida and California state departments of correction of potential terrorist plots by inmates.

Hayes, Lindsay M. "Characteristics of Juvenile Suicide in Confinement." Juvenile Justice Bulletin, Office of Juvenile Justice and Delinquency Prevention, U.S. Department of Justice, February 2009. Available online. URL: http://www.ncjrs.gov/pdffiles1/ojjdp/214434.pdf. Data on the extent, characteristics, and distribution of suicides within juvenile detention facilities nationwide. Includes statistics on the demographic characteristics and social histories of juvenile offenders who committed suicide while incarcerated in a juvenile detention facility.

Mauer, Marc, and Ryan Scott King. "Schools and Prisons: Fifty Years after *Brown v. Board of Education.*" Report, The Sentencing Project, March 2004. Available online. URL: www.sentencingproject.org/doc/publication/rd_brownvboard.pdf. Reports on the disproportionate rates of imprisonment among African Americans in the United States during the 50 years following the U.S. Supreme Court decision in *Brown v. Board of Education* (1954), which resulted in the desegregation of public schools in the United States and is commonly perceived as the beginning of the civil rights movement in America. Includes a statistical overview of rates of incarceration among African Americans from 1954 to 2002 and offers causal factors for the rise in such rates, including crime rates, crack cocaine sentencing laws, and habitual offender mandatory sentencing statutes.

Mauer, Marc. "The Changing Racial Dynamics of the War on Drugs." Report, The Sentencing Project, April 2009. Available online. URL: http://www.sentencingproject.org/doc/dp_raceanddrugs.pdf. Statistical findings on incarceration for drug offenses in the United States. Findings include a significant decline in the incarceration of African Americans for drug offenses.

Nellis, Ashley, and Ryan S. King. "No Exit: The Expanding Use of Life Sentences in America." Report, The Sentencing Project, July 2009. Available online. URL: http://www.sentencingproject.org/doc/publications/inc_noexitseptember 2009.pdf. Presents statistical findings on incarceration rates in the United States, including 140,610 individuals serving life sentences in state and federal prisons, approximately one third of whom were serving life sentences without possibility of parole. Also includes statistics on the rate of incarceration of juveniles.

Ostrom, Brian J., et al. "Assessing Consistency and Fairness in Sentencing: A Comparative Study in Three States." Washington, D.C.: Report, National Criminal Justice Reference Service, August 2008. Available online. URL: http://www.ncjrs.gov/pdffiles1/nij/grants/223854.pdf. Presents the methodology and findings of a study examining the degree to which sentencing guidelines in Michigan, Minnesota, and Virginia achieved various objectives. Such objectives included, consistency of sentences among similar types of cases, proportionality of harsher sentences imposed on more serious offenders, and equality across age, gender, and race of offenders.

Schirmer, Sarah, et al. "Incarcerated Parents and Their Children, Trends 1991–2007." Report, The Sentencing Project, February 2009. Available online. URL: http://www.sentencingproject.org/doc/publications/publications/inc_ incarceratedparents.pdf. Reviews data from the Bureau of Justice Statistics on the incarceration of parents in the United States and assesses the impact on inmates, their children, and their families.

Sheffer, Susannah. "Double Tragedies, Victims Speak Out against the Death Penalty for People with Severe Mental Illness." Report, The National Alliance on Mental Illness, 2009. Available online. URL: http://www.nami.org/Template.cfm?Section=Issue_Spotlights&template=/ContentManagement/ContentDisplay.cfm&ContentID=81845. Based on interviews of 21 families of murder victims in 10 states whose relative was murdered by a mentally ill offender who received the death penalty, the report examines the need for reform in sentencing violent offenders convicted of serious crimes.

U.S. Department of Health and Human Services. "Prisoner Reentry, Religion and Research." Report, 2004. Available online. URL: http://peerta. acf.hhs.gov/pdf/prisoner_reentry.pdf. Discusses faith-based prisoner reentry programs, focusing on the Kairos Prison Ministry's residential rehabilitation program for prisoners and their families.

U.S. Department of Justice. "The Federal Bureau of Prisons' Witness Security Program." Washington, D.C.: U.S. Department of Justice, Office of the Inspector General, Audit Division, October 2008. Available online. URL: http://www.usdoj.gov/oig/reports/BOP/a0901/final.pdf. Provides a comprehensive overview of the program, in which some 500 inmates are provided with protective custody in exchange for their testimony against serious offenders, including drug traffickers and members of organized crime organizations.

U.S. Sentencing Commission. "Report on Federal Escape Offenses in Fiscal Years 2006 and 2007." Washington, D.C.: United States Sentencing Commission, November 2008. Available online. URL: http://www.ussc. gov/general/escape_FY0607_final.pdf. Provides an analysis of federal escape cases and offers comparisons of various types of escape with respect to the potential for risk or injury to others.

Warren, Jenifer. "One in 100: Behind Bars in America 2008." Washington, D.C.: The Pew Center on the States, February 2008. Available online. URL: http://www.pewcenteronthestates.org/uploadedFiles/8015PCTS_ Prison08_FINAL_2-1-1_FORWEB.pdf. Presents a detailed statistical overview of incarceration rates in the United States among the general population and among minority groups, including graphical data. Discusses the impact of rising incarceration rates on society and imprisoned individuals, and examines policies driving the increase in incarceration rates.

Zweig, Janine M., and John Blackmore. "Strategies to Prevent Prison Rape by Changing the Correctional Culture." Washington, D.C.: National Institute of Justice, U.S. Department of Justice, October 2008. Available online. URL: http://www.ncjrs.gov/pdffiles1/nij/222843.pdf. Reports on measures to reduce sexual violence in state prisons based on interviews with prison officials nationwide, focusing on four basic recommendations: the development of comprehensive programs to coordinate victim services; investigation, documentation, and prosecution of incidents of sexual violence; cultivation of a cooperative effort among inmates and prison staff to identify and report such incidents; development of training for staff on methods of dealing with allegations of prison rape; and utilization of inmate education programs to explain prison policies, inmates' rights, and techniques to avoid sexual assault in prison.

CHAPTER 8

ORGANIZATIONS AND AGENCIES

A wide variety of information is available from the following organizations, including statistical data on prisons and inmates, reports on prison conditions, and links to prison-related issues, such as prisoners' rights and the death penalty. Also provided is a listing of state correctional agencies, whose web sites offer state-specific information on prison facilities, inmate populations, treatment programs, and correctional administration. Many state corrections agency web sites also provide links to local, state, and national organizations in the field of corrections.

360 Degrees: Perspectives on the U.S. Criminal Justice System
URL: http://www.360degrees.org
176 Grand Street
3rd Floor
New York, NY 10013
Phone: (212) 226-3099
A joint venture by National Public Radio (NPR) and Picture Projects, a producer of online documentaries, to examine the criminal justice system in the United States. Included in the 360 Degrees web site are links to online audio diaries by prisoners and corrections officers and online documentaries on issues related to corrections and prisoners' rights.

American Bar Association (ABA)
URL: http://www.abanet.org
321 North Clark Street
Chicago, IL 60654
Phone: (312) 988-5000
Professional association of attorneys and legal professionals that sponsors research and training on a wide range of law-related issues, including the criminal justice system. The ABA's *Criminal Justice* magazine, accessible via the Web site's Publications link, offers article on topics including female criminal offenders, sentencing issues, and juvenile detention.

American Civil Liberties Union (ACLU)
URL: http://www.aclu.org
E-mail: webform
125 Broad Street
18th Floor
New York, NY 10004
Phone: (212) 607-3300

Organizations and Agencies

Founded in 1920 and privately funded, the ACLU offers legal support in defense of the constitutional rights of federal and state prisoners through its National Prison Project. The ACLU's web site offers links to in-depth coverage of issues relating to prisoners' rights, including conditions of confinement, medical care, and the right to privacy.

American Correctional Association (ACA)
URL: http://www.aca.org
206 North Washington Street
Suite 200
Alexandria, VA 22314
Phone: (800) 222-5646
Founded in 1870 as the National Prison Association, the ACA is the oldest professional association in the field of corrections, with a membership that includes researchers, policymakers, and correctional agency staff. The ACA publishes *Corrections Today* magazine and the research journal *Corrections Compendium*, as well as books, articles, and manuals on correctional standards, many of which are linked on their Web site and available to the general public.

American Friends Service Committee
URL: http://www.afsc.org
E-mail: afscinfo@afsc.org
1501 Cherry Street
Philadelphia, PA 19102
Phone: (215) 241-7000
A Quaker organization with members of various religious faiths working for social reform in a variety of areas, including prisoners'

rights and the death penalty. The committee's Web site includes links to numerous reports and articles on prison-related issues.

Association for the Treatment of Sexual Abusers (ATSA)
URL: http://www.atsa.com
E-mail: atsa@atsa.com
4900 S.W. Griffith Drive
Suite 274
Beaverton, OR 97005
Phone: (503) 643-1023
Nonprofit organization established in 1984 to sponsor research on the treatment of sexual abusers. Publishers of the *ATSA Journal*, which features scholarly articles on topics including the treatment of sexual abusers in correctional settings and aftercare for sexual abusers after release from prison.

Association of State Correctional Administrators (ASCA)
URL: http://www.asca.net
E-mail: web form
213 Court Street
6th Floor
Middletown, CT 06457
Phone: (860) 704-6410
Established in 1970 with the goal of improving services and standards in state correctional facilities, the ASCA funds research and disseminates information on prisons and prison administration.

Bureau of Justice Statistics (BJS)
URL: http://bjs.ojp.usdoj.gov/bjs
E-mail: askbjs@usdoj.gov
U.S. Department of Justice

245

810 7th Street, NW
Washington, DC 20531
Phone: (203) 307-0765
Advances research and disseminates information on a wide variety of criminal justice issues, including corrections. BJS publications on issues related to prisons include special reports and annual surveys of inmates and correctional facilities nationwide, all available to the general public free of charge by mail or by downloading from the BJS Web site. The BJS also conducts and disseminates data from the National Victim Crime Survey, an annual survey that measures the incidence of violent and property offenses based on reports by victims.

California Prison Focus
URL: http://www.prisons.org
E-mail: contact@prisons.org
1904 Franklin Street
Suite 507
Oakland, CA 94612
Phone: (510) 836-7222
An advocate for prisoners' rights, California Prison Focus disseminates information on a range of prison-related issues, including the use of special housing units to isolate inmates and medical care for prisoners with serious illnesses. Although the focus is on California state prisons, many issues have a broader application to prisons nationwide.

Center for Community
  Alternatives (CCA)
URL: http://www.community
  alternatives.org

39 West 19th Street
10th Floor
New York, NY 10011
Phone: (212) 691-1911
Private, nonprofit agency founded in 1981 with the goal of advancing the use of community-based alternatives to incarceration in New York State, the CCA offers publications on a range of topics in the field of community corrections, including issues related to female and juvenile offenders and the restoration of rights for former inmates.

Center for the Children of
  Incarcerated Parents
URL: http://www.e-ccip.org
E-mail: cciponline@yahoo.com
P.O. Box 41-286
Eagle Rock, CA 90041
Phone: (626) 449-2470
Founded in 1989 with the goal of advancing the development of model services for the children and families of incarcerated parents in the areas of education, family reunification, therapeutic services, and the dissemination of information to the general public.

Centurion Ministries
URL: http://www.centurion
  ministries.org
221 Witherspoon Street
Princeton, NJ 08542
Phone: (609) 921-0334
Nonprofit organization that works with a national network of attorneys and forensic experts to advocate for wrongly convicted prisoners in the United States and Canada and to assist with the social reintegration

of exonerated inmates after their release from prison.

Citizens United for Rehabilitation of Errants (CURE)
URL: http://www.curenational.org
E-mail: cure@curenational.org
P.O. Box 2310
National Capital Station
Washington, DC 20013-2310
Phone: (202) 789-2126
National organization established in 1972 that promotes reform in the U.S. criminal justice system. Among the main issues supported by CURE are prison labor and educational reform, prison rape prevention, private prison accountability, and alternatives to incarceration, including community corrections programs and post-release rehabilitation and vocational placement services.

Correctional Education Association (CEA)
URL: http://www.ceanational.org
E-mail: office@ceanational.org
8182 Lark Brown Road
Suite 202
Elkridge, MD 21075
Phone: (800) 783-1232
An affiliate of the American Correctional Association, the CEA is a nonprofit professional association for educators and educational administrators in correctional settings that conducts research and publishes papers on issues related to education in prisons. Publications are available on the CEA Web site, as are links to other organizations in the field of corrections.

The Corrections Connection
URL: http://www.corrections.com
159 Burgin Parkway
Quincy, MA 02169
Phone: (617) 471-4445
An association for professionals in corrections that provides information and publications on all facets of corrections, including juvenile corrections and prison privatization. The Corrections Connection Web site provides links to a wide range of national and state organizations with information on prisons and prison management.

The Edna McConnell Clark Foundation
URL: http://www.emcf.org
E-mail: info@emcf.org
415 Madison Avenue
10th Floor
New York, NY 10177
Phone: (212) 551-9100
Sponsor of the Program for Justice, which sponsors research on reforming the U.S. criminal justice system, with focus on issues of sentencing reform, prison overcrowding, conditions of confinement, and prisoners' rights. The foundation's Web site offers links to publications and news articles on issues of interest.

Families Against Mandatory Minimums (FAMM)
URL: http://www.famm.org
E-mail: web form
1612 K Street, NW
Suite 700
Washington, DC 20006
Phone: (202) 822-6700

247

National nonprofit organization founded in 1991 to challenge mandatory sentencing laws and to promote more equitable sentencing polices at the state and federal levels. The FAMM Web site offers links to news articles and publications available by download on issues relating to sentencing and corrections.

Family & Corrections Network (FCN)
URL: http://fcnetwork.org
E-mail: fcn@fcnetwork.org
93 Old York Road
Suite 1 # 510
Jenkintown, PA 19046
Phone: (215) 526-1110
Established in 1983 as a resource for families of prisoners, the FCN facilitates communication between families of prisoners on their Web site, which offers links to publications available by download on the issues of incarcerated parents and family members.

Federal Bureau of Prisons (BOP)
URL: http://www.bop.gov
E-mail: info@bop.gov
320 First Street, NW
Washington, DC 20534
Phone: (202) 307-3198
Federal agency within the U.S. Department of Justice that was created in 1930 to administer federal prisons in the United States. In addition to the central office in Washington, D.C., the BOP maintains six regional offices in Atlanta; Dallas; Philadelphia; Burlingame, California; Annapolis, Maryland;

and Kansas City, Kansas. The BOP provides a wide range of publications on corrections-related issues. Among the services offered by the BOP is the federal inmate locator (URL: http://inmateloc.bop.gov/locator/FindInmateHttpServlet), with a database that is updated daily on all federal prisoners who are incarcerated and those who have been released since 1982.

Federal Prison Industries, Inc. (UNICOR)
URL: http://www.unicor.gov
400 First Street, NW
Washington, DC 20534
Phone: (800) 827-3168
Government corporation established by Congress in 1934 with the mandate to provide vocational training to federal inmates. Commonly referred to by its trade name, UNICOR, Federal Prison Industries is a self-sustaining organization funded by the profits from goods manufactured by federal prisoners.

Human Rights Watch
URL: http://www.hrw.org
E-mail: hrwnyc@hrw.org
350 Fifth Avenue
34th Floor
New York, NY 10118
Phone: (212) 290-4700
Private, nonprofit group advocating for human rights worldwide that offers in-depth reports on prison-related issues, including prison rape, and offers links to information on prisoners' rights and conditions of confinement in correctional facilities nationwide.

Organizations and Agencies

Innocence Project
URL: http://www.innocence
  project.org
E-mail: info@innocenceproject.
  org
100 Fifth Avenue
3rd Floor
New York, NY 10011
Phone: (212) 364-5340
Nonprofit legal clinic founded in 1992 by attorneys Barry Scheck and Peter Neufeld to provide legal assistance in cases where post-conviction DNA testing of evidence may result in proof of innocence.

Just Detention International
URL: http://www.justdetention.
  org/
E-mail: info@justdetention.org
3325 Wilshire Boulevard
Suite 340
Los Angeles, CA 90010
Phone: (213) 384-1400
Nonprofit group that seeks to end sexual violence against incarcerated individuals by advocating for legislation and disseminating information on the issue of sexual violence in prison. JDI offers resources for survivors of sexual assault in prisons.

Legal Services for Prisoners
  with Children
URL: http://www.prisonerswith
  children.org
E-mail: info@prisonerswith
  children.org
1540 Market Street
Suite 490
San Francisco, CA 94102
Phone: (415) 255-7036
Advocacy group founded in 1978 to provide legal assistance to incarcerated parents and to promote reform on legal and policy issues related to sentencing and imprisonment. The organization's Web site offers links to articles, self-help manuals, and other publications on issues of interest.

National Commission on
  Correctional Health Care
  (NCCHC)
URL: http://www.ncchc.org
E-mail: info@ncchc.org
1145 West Diversey Parkway
Chicago, IL 60614
Phone: (773) 880-1460
Established in 1981 by the American Medical Association to promote reform in correctional health care, the NCCHC collaborates with other national organizations in the field of corrections to improve the quality of medical care in prisons, jails, and juvenile detention facilities. The NCCHC publishes the annual report *Standards for Health Services in Prisons*.

National Correctional Industries
  Association (NCIA)
URL: http://www.nationalcia.org
E-mail: info@nationalcia.org
1202 North Charles Street
Baltimore, MD 21201
Phone: (410) 230-3972
Nonprofit association of state and federal correctional industries professionals, founded in 1941 as the Penal Industries Association. The NCIA Web site provides links to information on correctional indus-

tries in prisons nationwide and products manufactured in state and federal correctional industry programs.

National Criminal Justice Reference Service (NCJRS)
URL: http://www.ncjrs.org
E-mail: web form
P.O. Box 6000
Rockville, MD 20849-6000
Phone: (800) 851-3420
Clearinghouse for publications produced by the U.S. government on a wide range of criminal justice issues, including corrections. The NCJRS web site provides a corrections page (URL: http://virlib.ncjrs.org/Corrections.asp) with links to topics including inmate characteristics, mentally ill offenders, sex offenders, parole, recidivism, community-based corrections, corrections technology, correctional personnel, and death row. The NCJRS Web site also provides links to articles and abstracts on criminal justice issues culled from some 600 publications.

National GAINS Center for People with Co-Occurring Disorders in the Justice System
URL: http://www.gainscenter.
samhsa.gov/html
E-mail: web form
Policy Research Associates, Inc.
345 Delaware Avenue
Delmar, NY 12054
Phone: (800) 311-4246
Established in 1995 as a national center for the collection and dissemination of information on the treatment of individuals with co-occurring mental health and substance abuse issues in the criminal justice system. Offers an online clearinghouse which includes publications on issues of mental health and substance abuse treatment in correctional settings.

National Institute of Corrections (NIC)
URL: http://www.nicic.org
E-mail: web form
320 First Street, NW
Washington, DC 20534
Phone: (800) 995-6423 or
(202) 307-3106
Government agency within the Federal Bureau of Prisons that provides training, technical assistance, and information to federal, state, and local corrections agencies. The NIC Web site provides links to NIC publications and to corrections-related web sites with information on a range of prison-related issues.

The National Lawyers Guild
URL: http://www.nlg.org
132 Nassau Street, #922
New York, NY 10038
Phone: (212) 679-5100
Professional association of attorneys, law students, and other legal professionals that promotes reform in corrections and other social issues. Publishes *The Jailhouse Lawyer Handbook*, a primer on prisoners' rights and a reference guide for inmates seeking legal remedy for violations of their civil rights while in prison or jail.

Office of National Drug Control Policy (ONDCP)
URL: http://www.whitehouse drugpolicy.gov
E-mail: web form
Drug Policy Information Clearinghouse
P.O. Box 6000
Rockville, MD 20849-6000
Phone: (800) 666-3332
Established by the Anti-Abuse Drug Act of 1988, the legislative mandate of the ONDCP is to implement a national drug policy program and disseminate information on drug abuse and its impact on society, including the criminal justice system. The Web site of the ONDCP provides a link to federal drug data sources (URL: http://www.whitehousedrugpolicy. gov/drugfact/sources.html), which references publications available by download on the interface between drug abuse and corrections.

Prison Activist Resource Center (PARC)
URL: http://www.prisonactivist. org
E-mail: web form
P.O. Box 70447
Oakland, CA 94612
Phone: (510) 893-4648
Provides information on prisoners' rights and other issues related to the mistreatment of prisoners in U.S. prisons.

Prison Law Office
URL: http://www.prisonlaw.com
Prison Law Office
General Delivery
San Quentin, CA 94964
Phone: (415) 457-9144
Provides free legal services to California state prisoners and parolees seeking legal recourse on issues relating to conditions of confinement in prison. The Prison Law Office Web site offers links to publications on corrections-related topics.

Prison Policy Initiative
URL: http://www.prisonpolicy. org
E-mail: web form
P.O. Box 127
Northampton, MA 01061
Phone: (413) 586-4985
Prisoners' rights advocacy organization that conducts research and provides information on a range of corrections-related social issues including conditions of confinement, racial disparity in incarceration rates, and felony disenfranchisement laws.

The Sentencing Project
URL: http://www.sentencing project.org
E-mail: staff@sentencing projecft.org
514 Tenth Street, NW
Suite 1000
Washington, DC 20004
Phone: (202) 628-0871
Established in 1986 to develop alternative sentencing programs and conduct research on criminal justice policy in the United States. The Sentencing Project Web site offers links to publications on issues including the U.S. rate of incarceration, racial disparities among

the prison population, and felony disenfranchisement.

U.S. Sentencing Commission
URL: http://www.ussc.gov
E-mail: pubaffairs@ussc.gov
One Columbus Circle, NE
Washington, DC 20002
Phone: (202) 502-4500
Independent agency within the judicial branch of the federal government that establishes sentencing policies for the federal courts and monitors their implementation. The commission's Web site offers links to articles and publications on the issues of federal sentencing, including significant court decisions on issues related to sentencing.

Volunteers of America
URL: http://www.voa.org
E-mail: communications@voa.org
1660 Duke Street
Alexandria, VA 22314
Phone: (800) 899-0089
National nonprofit organization that advocates for the humane treatment of prisoners and programs aimed at the successful reintegration of former inmates into society. Sponsors the Guiding Responsive Action in Corrections at End-of-Life Project (GRACE), a collaboration of organizations dedicated to the development of hospice and palliative care programs for prison and jail inmates.

STATE DEPARTMENTS OF CORRECTIONS

The following state departments of corrections provide state-specific information on prison facilities, inmate populations, treatment program, and correctional administration. In many cases, the information is Web-based and can be downloaded from the department of corrections' web site. Many state correctional agency Web sites also provide links to local, state, and national organizations in the field of corrections.

Alabama Department of Corrections
URL: http://www.doc.state.al.us
301 South Ripley Street
Montgomery, AL 36104
Phone: (334) 353-3883

Alaska Department of Corrections
URL: http://www.correct.state.ak.us
802 3rd Street
Douglas, AK 99824
Phone: (907) 465-4640

Arizona Department of Corrections
URL: http://www.adc.state.az.gov
Phoenix, AZ 85003
Phone: (602) 542-1212

Arkansas Department of
Corrections
URL: http://www.adc.arkansas.
gov
P.O. Box 8707
Pine Bluff, AR 71611-8707
Phone: (870) 267-6999

California Department
of Corrections and
Rehabilitation
URL: http://www.cdcr.ca.gov
P.O. Box 942883
Sacramento, CA 94283-0001
Phone: (888) 562-5874
or (916) 445-7682

Colorado Department of
Corrections
URL: http://www.doc.state.co.us
2862 South Circle Drive
Colorado Springs, CO 80906-
4195
Phone: (719) 579-9580

Connecticut Department of
Correction
URL: http://www.ct.gov/doc
24 Wolcott Hill Road
Wethersfield, CT 06109
Phone: (860) 692-7780

Delaware Department of
Corrections
URL: http://doc.delaware.gov
245 McKee Road
Dover, DE 19904
Phone: (302) 739-5601

Florida Department of
Corrections
URL: http://www.dc.state.fl.us

1126 East Park Ave
Tallahassee, FL 32301
Phone: (850) 222-4761

Georgia Department of
Corrections
URL: http://www.dcor.state.ga.us
2 Martin Luther King, Jr. Drive
NE
Atlanta, GA 30334
Phone: (404) 656-9772

Hawaii Department of Public
Safety
URL: http://www.hawaii.gov/psd
Department of Public Safety
919 Ala Moana Boulevard
Honolulu, HI 96814
Phone: (808) 587-1340

Idaho Department of
Correction
URL: http://www.corr.state.id.us
1299 North Orchard Street
Suite 110
Boise, ID 83706
Phone: (208) 658-2000

Illinois Department of
Corrections
URL: http://www.idoc.state.il.us
1301 Concordia Court
P.O. Box 19277
Springfield, IL 62794-9277
Phone: (217) 558-2200

Indiana Department of
Correction
URL: http://www.in.gov/idoc
302 West Washington Street
Indianapolis, IN 46222
Phone: (317) 232-5715

Iowa Department of
 Corrections
URL: http://www.doc.state.ia.us
510 East 12th Street
Des Moines, IA 50319
Phone: (515) 725-5701

Kansas Department of
 Corrections
URL: http://www.dc.state.ks.us
Landon State Office Building
900 SW Jackson
4th Floor
Topeka, KS 66612-1284
Phone: (888) 317-8204
or (785) 296-3317

Kentucky Department of
 Corrections
URL: http://www.corrections.
 ky.gov
Health Services Building
275 East Main Street
P.O. Box 2400
Frankfort, KY 40602-2400
Phone: (502) 564-4726

Louisiana Department of Public
 Safety and Corrections
URL: http://www.doc.louisiana.
 gov
P.O. Box 94304
Baton Rouge, LA 70804-9304
Phone: (225) 342-9711

Maine Department of
 Corrections
URL: http://www.state.me.us/
 corrections
25 Tyson Drive
3rd Floor
Augusta, ME 04333
Phone: (207) 287-2711

Maryland Department of Public
 Safety and Correctional
 Services
URL: http://www.dpscs.state.
 md.us/
300 East Joppa Road
Suite 1000
Towson, MD 21286-3020
Phone: (410) 339-5081 or (877)
 379-8636

Massachusetts Department of
 Correction
URL: http://www.mass.gov/doc
50 Maple Street
Suite 3
Milford, MA 01757
Phone: (508) 422-3300

Michigan Department
 of Corrections
URL: http://www.michigan.gov/
 corrections
Grandview Plaza
206 East Michigan Avenue
P.O. Box 30003
Lansing, MI 48909
Phone: (517) 335-1426

Minnesota Department of
 Corrections
URL: http://www.corr.state.
 mn.us
1450 Energy Park Drive
Suite 200
St. Paul, MN 55108-5219
Phone: (651) 361-7200

Mississippi Department of
 Corrections
URL: http://www.mdoc.state.
 ms.us
723 North President Street

Jackson, MS 39202
Phone: (601) 359-5600

Missouri Department of
  Corrections
URL: http://www.doc.mo.gov
2729 Plaza Drive
Jefferson City, MO 65109
Phone: (573) 751-2389

Montana Department of
  Corrections
URL: http://www.cor.mt.gov
1539 11th Avenue
Helena, MT 59620-1301
Phone: (406) 444-3930

Nebraska Department of
  Correctional Services
URL: http://www.corrections.
  state.ne.us
P.O. Box 94661
Lincoln, NE 68509-4661
Phone: (402) 471-2654

Nevada Department of
  Corrections
URL: http://www.doc.nv.gov
P.O. Box 7011
Carson City, NV 89702
Phone: (775) 887-3285

New Hampshire Department of
  Corrections
URL: http://www.nh.gov/nhdoc
P.O. Box 1806
Concord, NH 03302-1806
Phone: (603) 271-5600

New Jersey Department of
  Corrections
URL: http://www.state.nj.us/
  corrections

Whittlesey Road
P.O. Box 863
Trenton, NJ 08625
Phone: (609) 292-4036

New Mexico Corrections
  Department
URL: http://corrections.state.
  nm.us
P.O. Box 27116
Santa Fe, NM 87502
Phone: (505) 827-8660

New York State Department of
  Correctional Services
URL: http://www.docs.state.
  ny.us
1220 Washington Avenue
Building 2
Albany, NY 12226-2050
Phone: (518) 457-8126

North Carolina Department of
  Correction
URL: http://www.doc.state.nc.us
4202 Mail Service Center
Raleigh, NC 27699-4202
Phone: (919) 716-3700

North Dakota Department
  of Corrections and
  Rehabilitation
URL: http://www.nd.gov/docr
3100 Railroad Avenue
Bismarck, ND 58501
Phone: (701) 328-6362

Ohio Department of
  Rehabilitation and Correction
URL: http://www.drc.ohio.gov
770 West Broad Street
Columbus, OH 43222
Phone: (614) 752-1159

Oklahoma Department of
Corrections
URL: http://www.doc.state.ok.us
3400 North Martin Luther King
Avenue
Oklahoma City, OK 73111
Phone: (405) 425-2500

Oregon Department of
Corrections
URL: http://www.oregon.gov/
DOC
2575 Center Street, NE
Salem, OR 97301-4667
Phone: (503) 945-9090

Pennsylvania Department of
Corrections
URL: http://www.cor.state.pa.us
2520 Lisburn Road
P.O. Box 598
Camp Hill, PA 17001-0598
Phone: (717) 975-4859

Rhode Island Department of
Corrections
URL: http://www.doc.state.ri.us
40 Howard Avenue
Cranston, RI 02920
Phone: (401) 462-1000

South Carolina Department of
Corrections
URL: http://www.doc.sc.gov
4444 Broad River Road
P.O. Box 21787
Columbia, SC 29210
Phone: (803) 896-8578

South Dakota Department of
Corrections
URL: http://doc.sd.gov
3200 East Highway 34

c/o 500 East Capitol Avenue
Pierre, SD 57501
Phone: (605) 773-3478

Tennessee Department of
Correction
URL: http://www.state.tn.us/
correction
Rachel Jackson Building
320 6th Avenue North
6th Floor
Nashville, TN 37243-0465
Phone: (615) 741-1000

Texas Department of Criminal
Justice
URL: http://www.tdcj.state.
tx.us
Capitol Station
P.O. Box 13084
Austin, TX 78711-3084
Phone: (512) 475-3250

Utah Department of
Corrections
URL: http://www.cr.ex.state.
ut.us
14717 South Minuteman Drive
Draper, UT 84020
Phone: (801) 545-5500

Vermont Department of
Corrections
URL: http://www.doc.state.vt.us
103 South Main Street
Waterbury, VT 05671-1101
Phone: (802) 241-2276

Virginia Department of
Corrections
URL: http://www.vadoc.state.
va.us
P.O. Box 26963

Richmond, VA 23261-6963
Phone: (804) 674-3000

Washington State Department
of Corrections
URL: http://www.doc.wa.gov/
P.O. Box 41100
Olympia, WA 98504-1100
Phone: (360) 753-8213

West Virginia Division of
Corrections
URL: http://www.wvdoc.com/
wvdoc
1409 Greenbrier Street
Charleston, WV 25311
Phone: (304) 558-2036

Wisconsin Department of
Corrections
URL: http://www.wi-doc.com
3099 East Washington Avenue
P.O. Box 7925
Madison, WI 53707-7925
Phone: (608) 240-5000

Wyoming Department of
Corrections
URL: http://doc.state.wy.us/doc/
index.html
1934 Wycott Drive
Suite 100
Cheyenne, WY 82002
Phone: (307) 777-7208

PART III

APPENDICES

APPENDIX A

STATISTICS ON STATE AND FEDERAL PRISONERS

	STATE AND FEDERAL PRISONERS, 2000 TO 2008			
Year	Total Jail and Prison Inmates	Federal Inmates	State Inmates	Incarceration Rate per 100,000 U.S. Population
2000	1,391,261	145,416	1,245,845	684
2001	1,404,032	156,993	1,247,039	685
2002	1,440,144	163,528	1,276,616	701
2003	1,468,601	173,059	1,295,542	712
2004	1,497,100	180,328	1,316,772	723
2005	1,527,929	187,618	1,340,311	737
2006	1,569,945	193,046	1,376,899	751
2007	1,598,245	199,618	1,398,627	756
2008	1,610,446	201,280	1,409,166	754
Average annual change, 2000–2007	2.0%	4.6%	1.7%	1.4
Percent change, 2007–2008	0.8	0.8	0.8	-0.2

Source: William J. Sabol et al. "Prisoners in 2008." *Bulletin,* Bureau of Justice Statistics, U.S. Department of Justice, December 2009, p. 16.

Prisons

MALE INMATES IN STATE AND FEDERAL PRISONS

Year	Total	Federal	State	Percent of all sentenced prisoners
2000	1,246,234	116,647	1,129,587	93.6%
2001	1,260,033	127,519	1,132,514	93.7
2002	1,291,450	133,732	1,157,718	93.5
2003	1,315,790	142,149	1,173,641	93.4
2004	1,337,730	148,930	1,188,800	93.3
2005	1,364,178	155,678	1,208,500	93.3
2006	1,401,317	162,417	1,238,900	93.1
2007	1,427,064	167,676	1,259,388	93.1
2008	1,434,784	170,755	1,264,029	93.2
Average annual change, 2000–2007	2.0%	5.3%	1.6%	:
Percent change, 2007–2008	0.5	1.8	0.4	:

Source: William J. Sabol et al. "Prisoners in 2008." *Bulletin,* Bureau of Justice Statistics, U.S. Department of Justice, December 2009, p. 26.

FEMALE INMATES IN STATE AND FEDERAL PRISONS

Year	Total	Federal	State	Percent of all sentenced prisoners
2000	85,044	8,397	76,647	6.4%
2001	85,184	8,990	76,194	6.3
2002	89,066	9,308	79,758	6.5
2003	92,571	9,770	82,801	6.6
2004	95,998	10,207	85,791	6.7
2005	98,688	10,495	88,193	6.7
2006	103,343	11,116	92,227	6.9
2007	105,786	11,528	94,258	6.9
2008	105,252	11,578	93,674	6.8
Average annual change, 2000–2007	3.2%	4.6%	3.0%	:
Percent change, 2007–2008	-0.5	0.4	-0.6	:

Source: William J. Sabol et al. "Prisoners in 2008." *Bulletin,* Bureau of Justice Statistics, Office of Justice Programs, U.S. Department of Justice, December 2009, pp. 16–27.

Appendix A

GROWTH IN THE RATE OF IMPRISONMENT IN THE UNITED STATES

In 1980, some 139 out of every 100,000 Americans in the U.S. population were sentenced inmates incarcerated in state and federal prisons in the United States. By 2008, the rate of imprisonment had more than tripled to just over 500 out of every 100,000 Americans in the U.S. population.

IMPRISONMENT RATE, 1980–2008

Source: Bureau of Justice Statisics "Corrections: Key Facts at a Glance." Available online. URL: http://bjs.ojp.usdoj.gov/content/glance/incrt.cfm. Last updated December 8, 2009

© Infobase Learning

APPENDIX B

NATIONAL PRISON RAPE
ELIMINATION COMMISSION
REPORT (2009)

*In 2003 the Prison Rape Elimination Act (PREA) became federal law and estab-
lished a zero-tolerance policy for prison rape in state and federal prisons. The PREA
established the National Prison Rape Elimination Commission and mandated the
commission to issue a report on the incidence of sexual abuse in U.S. prisons. In
June 2009 the commission released its report, which included the following Executive Summary of the report's findings.*

EXECUTIVE SUMMARY

Rape is violent, destructive, and a crime—no less so when the victim is incarcerated. Until recently, however, the public viewed sexual abuse as an
inevitable feature of confinement. Even as courts and human rights standards increasingly confirmed that prisoners have the same fundamental
rights to safety, dignity, and justice as individuals living at liberty in the
community, vulnerable men, women, and children continued to be sexually
victimized by other prisoners and corrections staff. Tolerance of sexual
abuse of prisoners in the government's custody is totally incompatible with
American values.

Congress affirmed the duty to protect incarcerated individuals from
sexual abuse by unanimously enacting the Prison Rape Elimination Act of
2003. The Act called for the creation of a national Commission to study the
causes and consequences of sexual abuse in confinement and to develop
standards for correctional facilities nationwide that would set in motion a
process once considered impossible: the elimination of prison rape.

This executive summary briefly discusses the Commission's nine findings
on the problems of sexual abuse in confinement and select policies and

practices that must be mandatory everywhere to remedy these problems. It also covers recommendations about what leaders in government outside the corrections profession can do to support solutions. The findings are discussed in detail and thoroughly cited in the body of the report, where readers will also find information about all of the Commission's standards. Full text of the standards is included as an appendix to the report.

In the years leading up to the passage of PREA and since then, corrections leaders and their staff have developed and implemented policies and practices to begin to prevent sexual abuse and also to better respond to victims and hold perpetrators accountable when prevention fails. They have been aided by a range of robust Federal initiatives, support from professional corrections associations, and advocates who have vocally condemned sexual abuse in confinement. The landscape is changing. Training curricula for corrections staff across the country now include information about sexual abuse in confinement and how to prevent it.

Some agencies and facilities have formed sexual assault response teams to revolutionize their responses to sexual abuse. Despite these and other achievements, much remains to be done, especially in correctional environments in which efforts to address the problem of sexual abuse have been slow to start or have stalled. Protection from sexual abuse should not depend on where someone is incarcerated or supervised; it should be the baseline everywhere.

More than 7.3 million Americans are confined in U.S. correctional facilities or supervised in the community, at a cost of more than $68 billion annually. Given our country's enormous investment in corrections, we should ensure that these environments are as safe and productive as they can be. Sexual abuse undermines those goals. It makes correctional environments more dangerous for staff as well as prisoners, consumes scarce resources, and undermines rehabilitation. It also carries the potential to devastate the lives of victims. The many interrelated consequences of sexual abuse for individuals and society are difficult to pinpoint and nearly impossible to quantify, but they are powerfully captured in individual accounts of abuse and its impact.

Former prisoner Necole Brown told the Commission, "I continue to contend with flashbacks of what this correctional officer did to me and the guilt, shame, and rage that comes with having been sexually violated for so many years. I felt lost for a very long time struggling with this. . . . I still struggle with the memories of this ordeal and take it out on friends and family who are trying to be there for me now."

Air Force veteran Tom Cahill, who was arrested and detained for just a single night in a San Antonio jail, recalled the lasting effects of being gang-raped and beaten by other inmates. "I've been hospitalized more times than I can count and I didn't pay for those hospitalizations, the tax payers paid.

My career as a journalist and photographer was completely derailed. . . . For the past two decades, I've received a non-service connected security pension from the Veteran's Administration at the cost of about $200,000 in connection with the only major trauma I've ever suffered, the rape."

Since forming, the Commission has convened public hearings and expert committees, conducted a needs assessment that involved site visits to 11 diverse correctional facilities, and thoroughly reviewed the relevant literature. Throughout the process, corrections leaders, survivors of sexual abuse, health care providers, researchers, legal experts, advocates, and academics shared their knowledge, experiences, and insights about why sexual abuse occurs, under what circumstances, and how to protect people.

The Commission used what it learned about the nature and causes of sexual abuse in correctional settings and its impact to develop mandatory standards to prevent, detect, and punish sexual abuse. Two 60-day periods of public comment were critical junctures in the creation of the standards. The Commission tailored the standards to reflect the full range of correctional environments across the country: adult prisons and jails; lockups and other short-term holding centers; facilities for juveniles; immigration detention sites; and probation, parole and other forms of community corrections. Many of the Commission's standards reflect what corrections professionals acknowledge to be good practices—and are already operational in some places—or are requirements under existing laws. If correctional agencies incur new costs to comply with the Commission's standards, those costs are not substantial compared to what these agencies currently spend and are necessary to fulfill the requirements of PREA.

The Eighth Amendment of the U.S. Constitution forbids cruel and unusual punishment—a ban that requires corrections staff to take reasonable steps to protect individuals in their custody from sexual abuse whenever the threat is known or should have been apparent. In *Farmer v. Brennan*, the Supreme Court ruled unanimously that deliberate indifference to the substantial risk of sexual abuse violates an incarcerated individual's rights under the Eighth Amendment. As the Court so aptly stated, sexual abuse is "not part of the penalty that criminal offenders pay for their offenses against society."

FINDING 1

Protecting prisoners from sexual abuse remains a challenge in correctional facilities across the country. Too often, in what should be secure environments, men, women, and children are raped or abused by other incarcerated individuals and corrections staff.

Appendix B

Although the sexual abuse of prisoners is as old as prisons themselves, efforts to understand the scale and scope of the problem are relatively new. The first study specifically of prevalence—examining abuse in the Philadelphia jail system—was published in 1968. The most rigorous research produced since then—mainly of sexual abuse among incarcerated men—has yielded prevalence rates in the mid-to-high teens, but none of these are national studies.

With an explicit mandate from Congress under PREA, the Bureau of Justice Statistics (BJS) launched a groundbreaking effort to produce national incidence rates of sexual abuse by directly surveying prisoners. The survey results may not capture the full extent of the problem, but they confirm the urgent need for reform. The Commission recommends that BJS continue this important work and that Congress provide the necessary funding.

BJS conducted the first wave of surveys in 2007 in a random sample of 146 State and Federal prisons and 282 local jails. A total of 63,817 incarcerated individuals completed surveys, providing the most comprehensive snapshot of sexual abuse in prisons and jails to date. Four-and-a-half percent of prisoners surveyed reported experiencing sexual abuse one or more times during the 12 months preceding the survey or over their term of incarceration if they had been confined in that facility for less than 12 months. Extrapolated to the national prison population, an estimated 60,500 State and Federal prisoners were sexually abused during that 12-month period.

Although sexual abuse of prisoners is widespread, rates vary across facilities. For example, 10 facilities had comparatively high rates, between 9.3 and 15.7 percent, whereas in six of the facilities no one reported abuse during that time period. More prisoners reported abuse by staff than abuse by other prisoners: 2.9 percent of respondents compared with about 2 percent. (Some prisoners reported abuse by other inmates and staff.)

The rate of sexual abuse in jails appears to be slightly lower: 3.2 percent of inmates surveyed reported that they had been sexually abused at least once during the prior 6 months or since they had been confined in that facility. Again, reports of abuse by staff were more common than reports of abuse by other incarcerated persons: 2 percent of respondents compared with 1.6 percent. BJS has not surveyed individuals in halfway houses, treatment facilities, and other community-based correctional settings or individuals on probation or parole.

As the Commission's report goes to press, BJS is conducting the first nationally representative survey of sexual abuse among adjudicated youth in residential juvenile facilities. In a preparatory pilot study, BJS interviewed 645 youth in nine facilities—sites that volunteered to participate in the pilot and were selected based on convenience. Nearly one out of every five youth surveyed (19.7 percent) reported at least one nonconsensual sexual contact during the preceding 12 months or since they had arrived at the facility. Youth were just as likely to report abuse by staff as they were to report nonconsensual sexual encounters with their peers in the facility. These preliminary results are not necessarily an indicator of rates nationally because more than a quarter of the youth interviewed had been adjudicated for perpetrating a sexual assault, compared to less than 10 percent of youth in residential placement nationally.

In conducting this research, BJS has taken advantage of evolving survey technology, using laptop computers with touch screens and an accompanying recorded narration to guide respondents—especially helpful for individuals with limited reading abilities. This method increases the likelihood of capturing experiences of sexual abuse among individuals who would be afraid or ashamed to identify as a victim in face-to-face interviews. Prisoners still must believe strangers' assurances of confidentiality, however—a huge barrier for some—so the likelihood of underreporting still exists. Researchers also recognize that prevalence levels can be artificially elevated by false allegations. BJS designs its surveys to ask questions of prisoners in several different ways and also uses analytic tools to assess data for false reports.

FINDING 2

Sexual abuse is not an inevitable feature of incarceration. Leadership matters because corrections administrators can create a culture within facilities that promotes safety instead of one that tolerates abuse.

In 2006, the Urban Institute surveyed 45 State departments of corrections about their policies and practices on preventing sexual abuse and conducted in-depth case studies in several States. Not surprisingly, the surveys and case studies identified strong leadership as essential to creating the kind of institutional culture necessary to eliminate sexual abuse in correctional settings. The Commission has defined clear standards that corrections administrators can and must champion to prevent sexual abuse and make facilities safer for everyone—reforms in the underlying culture, hiring and promotion, and training and supervision that vanguard members of the profession are already implementing.

To begin with, every correctional agency must have a written policy mandating zero tolerance for all forms of sexual abuse in all settings, whether it is operated by the government or by a private company working under contract with the government. Although not mandated under the standards, collective bargaining agreements should feature an explicit commitment from unions and their members to support a zero-tolerance approach to sexual abuse. Without it, there is little common ground upon which to build when negotiating the many specific policies and procedures to prevent and respond to sexual abuse.

Ultimately, the culture of an institution is shaped by people not by policies. Leaders need the right staff to create a genuine culture of zero tolerance. In particular, administrators must thoroughly screen all new job applicants and make promotions contingent on a similarly careful review of each staff member's behavior on the job to prevent hiring, retaining, or promoting anyone who has engaged in sexual abuse. Conducting criminal background checks, making efforts to obtain relevant information from past employers to the extent permissible under law, and questioning applicants about past misconduct must be mandatory. Rigorous vetting is not enough, however. Correctional agencies urgently need support in developing competitive compensation and benefits packages so that they can recruit and retain appropriate staff. Equally important, administrators should support and promote staff that demonstrate a commitment to preventing sexual abuse.

Even qualified individuals need training on sexual abuse to fulfill their job responsibilities. Only through training can staff understand the dynamics of sexual abuse in a correctional environment, be well informed about the agency's policies, and acquire the knowledge and skills necessary to protect prisoners from abuse and respond appropriately when abuse does occur. The Commission recognizes the corrections profession's investment to date in training staff and the fruits of those efforts. The Commission designed its standards to ensure that no facility is left behind and that training everywhere meets certain basic criteria. Additionally, the Commission recommends that the National Institute of Corrections continue the training and technical assistance it has provided in the years leading up to PREA and since then and that Congress provide funding for this purpose.

The corollary to staff training is a strong educational program for prisoners about their right to be safe and the facility's commitment to holding all perpetrators of sexual abuse—staff and inmates—accountable. Facilities must convey at least basic information during intake in languages and other formats accessible to all prisoners. Armed with this information, prisoners are better able to protect themselves and seek help from staff before abuse occurs.

Supervision is the core practice of any correctional agency, and it must be carried out in ways that protect individuals from sexual abuse. The Commission believes it is possible to meet this standard in any facility, regardless of design, through appropriate deployment of staff. Direct supervision, which features interaction between staff and prisoners, should be used wherever possible because it is the most effective mode of supervision for preventing sexual abuse and other types of violence and disorder. In addition, correctional facilities must assess, at least annually, the need for and feasibility of incorporating additional monitoring equipment. Technologies are not replacements for skilled and committed security officers, but they can greatly improve what good officers are able to accomplish. The Commission recommends that the National Institute of Corrections help correctional agencies advance their use of monitoring technologies and that Congress fund this assistance.

Cross-gender supervision is an area in which the Commission has set clear standards. Some of the widespread abuse that occurred in women's prisons across Michigan in the 1990s was facilitated by rules that required officers, including men, to meet a daily quota of pat-down searches for weapons, drugs, or other contraband. Physical searches are necessary security procedures. The potential for abuse is heightened, however, when staff of the opposite gender conduct them. In the Commission's view, the risks are present whether the officers are female or male. Historically, few women worked in corrections, but this is rapidly changing.

The Commission understands that cross-gender supervision can have benefits for incarcerated persons and staff. The Commission's standard on this issue is not intended to discourage the practice generally or to reduce employment opportunities for men or women. However, strict limits on cross-gender searches and the viewing of prisoners of the opposite gender who are nude or performing bodily functions are necessary because of the inherently personal nature of such encounters. Court decisions have recognized that both male and female prisoners retain some rights to privacy, especially in searches of their bodies and in being observed in states of undress by staff of the opposite gender.

With proper leadership practices and clear policies, corrections administrators can foster a culture that promotes safety. The Commission's standards are intended to support these efforts. In addition, the Commission recommends that the Bureau of Justice Assistance continue to provide grants to diverse correctional agencies to support the development of innovative practices and programs and that Congress fund this important work as well as continued research by the National Institute of Justice on the nature of sexual abuse in correctional facilities.

FINDING 3

Certain individuals are more at risk of sexual abuse than others. Corrections administrators must routinely do more to identify those who are vulnerable and protect them in ways that do not leave them isolated and without access to rehabilitative programming.

Preventing sexual abuse depends in part on risk assessment. Unfortunately, knowledge in this area is still limited. Research to date has focused on vulnerability to abuse by other prisoners, rather than by staff, and on the risks for men and boys rather than for women and girls. This caveat aside, some risk factors do stand out.

Youth, small stature, and lack of experience in correctional facilities appear to increase the risk of sexual abuse by other prisoners. So does having a mental disability or serious mental illness. Research on sexual abuse in correctional facilities consistently documents the vulnerability of men and women with non-heterosexual orientations and transgender individuals. A 1982 study in a medium-security men's facility in California, for example, found the rate of abuse was much higher among gay prisoners (41 percent) than heterosexual prisoners (9 percent). A history of sexual victimization, either in the community or in the facility in which the person is incarcerated, tends to make people more vulnerable to subsequent sexual abuse.

Unless facility managers and administrators take decisive steps to protect these individuals, they may be forced to live in close proximity or even in the same cell with potential assailants. When Alexis Giraldo was sentenced to serve time in the California correctional system, her male-to-female transgender identity and appearance as a woman triggered a recommendation to place her in a facility with higher concentrations of transgender prisoners, where she might be safer. Yet officials ignored the recommendation and sent her to Folsom Prison in 2006, where she was raped and beaten by two different cellmates.

Some correctional agencies, including the Federal Bureau of Prisons and the California Department of Corrections and Rehabilitation, now use written instruments to screen all incoming prisoners specifically for risk of sexual assault. Evidence-based screening must become routine nationwide, replacing the subjective assessments that many facilities still rely on and filling a vacuum in facilities where no targeted risk assessments are conducted. The Commission's standards in this area accelerate progress toward this goal by setting baseline requirements for when and how to screen prisoners for risk of being a victim or perpetrator of sexual abuse. To be effective, the results of these screenings must drive decisions about housing and programming. Courts have commented specifically on the obligation of correctional agencies to gather and use screening information to protect prisoners from abuse.

The Commission is concerned that correctional facilities may rely on protective custody and other forms of segregation (isolation or solitary confinement) as a default form of protection. And the Commission learned that desperate prisoners sometimes seek out segregation to escape attackers. Serving time under these conditions is exceptionally difficult and takes a toll on mental health, particularly if the victim has a prior history of mental illness. Segregation must be a last resort and interim measure only. The Commission also discourages the creation of specialized units for vulnerable groups and specifically prohibits housing prisoners based solely on their sexual orientation or gender identity because it can lead to demoralizing and dangerous labeling.

The Commission is also concerned about the effect of crowding on efforts to protect vulnerable prisoners from sexual abuse. Crowded facilities are harder to supervise, and crowding system wide makes it difficult to carve out safe spaces for vulnerable prisoners that are less restrictive than segregation. When Timothy Taylor was incarcerated in a Michigan prison, internal assessments suggested that he was likely to be a target of sexual abuse because of his small size—he was five feet tall and 120 pounds—and diminished mental abilities, yet he was placed in a prison dormitory to save bed space for new arrivals. Shortly thereafter, he was sexually assaulted by another prisoner.

According to the Bureau of Justice Statistics, 19 States and the Federal system were operating at more than 100 percent of their highest capacity in 2007. An equal number of States operated at somewhere between 90 and 99 percent of capacity. When facilities operate at or beyond capacity, prisoners also have fewer or no opportunities to participate in education, job training, and other programming. Idleness and the stress of living in crowded conditions often lead to conflict. Meaningful activities will not end sexual abuse, but they are part of the solution. It is critical that lawmakers tackle the problem of overcrowding. If facilities and entire systems are forced to operate beyond capacity and supervision is a pale shadow of what it must be, our best efforts to identify and protect vulnerable individuals will be stymied.

Classification has evolved from little more than ad hoc decisions to an increasingly objective, evidence-based process. Although knowledge about the risk factors associated with sexual abuse is far from complete, corrections administrators can identify and protect many vulnerable individuals from abuse.

FINDING 4

Few correctional facilities are subject to the kind of rigorous internal monitoring and external oversight that would reveal why abuse occurs and how to prevent it. Dramatic reductions in sexual abuse depend on both.

The most effective prevention efforts are targeted interventions that reflect where, when, and under what conditions sexual abuse occurs. Sexual abuse incident reviews, as required under the Commission's standards, produce the kind of information administrators need to deploy staff wisely, safely manage high-risk areas, and develop more effective policies and procedures. A number of State departments of corrections already conduct some type of review.

Correctional agencies also must collect uniform data on these incidents, including at least the data necessary to answer all questions on the most recent version of the Bureau of Justice Statistics Survey on Sexual Violence. In aggregate form, the data can reveal important patterns and trends and must form the basis for corrective action plans that, along with the aggregated data, are released to the public. Transparency is essential.

Even the most rigorous internal monitoring, however, is no substitute for opening up correctional facilities to outside review. The Commission requires detailed, robust audits of its standards by independent auditors at least every 3 years. The auditor must be pre-qualified through the U.S. Department of Justice to perform audits competently and without bias. The Commission recommends that the National Institute of Corrections design and develop a national training program for auditors and that Congress provide funding specifically for this purpose.

The Commission also supports external oversight beyond the mandatory audits. In particular, the Commission endorses the American Bar Association's 2006 resolution urging Federal, State, and territorial governments to establish independent public entities to regularly monitor and report on the conditions in correctional facilities operating within their jurisdiction. Oversight by inspectors general, ombudsmen, legislative committees, or other bodies would work hand-in-hand with regular audits of the Commission's standards.

Courts provide a crucial role, especially when other modes of oversight fail. Civil court cases can spark reforms reaching far beyond the individual plaintiffs to protect other prisoners. The Commission is convinced that the Prison Litigation Reform Act (PLRA) that Congress enacted in 1996 has compromised the regulatory role of the courts and the ability of incarcerated victims of sexual abuse to seek justice in court. Under the PLRA, prisoners' claims in court will be dismissed unless they have exhausted all "administrative remedies" available to them within the facility.

In testimony to a House Judiciary Subcommittee, Garrett Cunningham recalled, "At first, I didn't dare tell anyone about the rape. . . . I would have had to file a first prison grievance within 15 days [to begin the process of exhausting the facility's administrative remedies]. . . . Even if I had known, during those first 15 days, my only thoughts were about suicide and . . . how to get myself into a safe place . . . so I would not be raped again." The Commission recommends that Congress amend two aspects of the PLRA for victims of sexual abuse: the requirement that prisoners exhaust all internal administrative remedies before their claims can proceed in court and the requirement to prove physical injury to receive compensatory damages, which fails to take into account the very real emotional and psychological injuries that often follow sexual assault. In the meantime, correctional agencies must deem that victims of sexual abuse have exhausted their administrative remedies within 90 days after the abuse is reported—or within 48 hours in emergency situations—regardless of who reports the incident and when it allegedly occurred.

Corrections administrators need robust mechanisms and systems to monitor their facilities, identify problems, and implement reforms. They must apply that discipline internally and accept it from outside. The very nature of correctional environments demands that the government and the public have multiple ways to watch over correctional settings and intervene when individuals are at risk.

FINDING 5

Many victims cannot safely and easily report sexual abuse, and those who speak out often do so to no avail. Reporting procedures must be improved to instill confidence and protect individuals from retaliation without relying on isolation. Investigations must be thorough and competent. Perpetrators must be held accountable through administrative sanctions and criminal prosecution.

Even when prisoners are willing to report abuse, their accounts are not necessarily taken seriously and communicated to appropriate officials within the facility. "When I told one of the guards I trusted how tired I was of putting up with abuse [by other youth in a Hawaii facility], he told me to just ignore it," Cyryna Pasion told the Commission. According to a 2007 survey of youth in custody by the Texas State Auditor's Office, 65 percent of juveniles surveyed thought the grievance system did not work.

Changing that dynamic begins by providing easy ways for individuals to report sexual abuse they have experienced or know about, backed up by clear policies requiring staff and administrators to act on every allegation. Although some correctional systems and individual facilities have made great strides in this area in recent years, the Commission's standards guarantee that all prisoners can easily report abuse, that staff are required to report abuse, and that reports are taken seriously in every facility across the country. A serious response to every report of sexual abuse is also the best way to handle any false allegations.

Victims and witnesses often are bullied into silence and harmed if they speak out. In a letter to the advocacy organization Just Detention International, one prisoner conveyed a chilling threat she received from the male officer who was abusing her: "Remember if you tell anyone anything, you'll have to look over your shoulder for the rest of your life." Efforts to promote reporting must be accompanied by policies and protocols to protect victims and witnesses from retaliation. And because some incarcerated individuals will never be comfortable reporting abuse internally, facilities must give prisoners the option of speaking confidentially with a crisis center or other outside agency.

Facilities have a duty to thoroughly investigate every allegation of sexual abuse without delay and to completion, regardless of whether or not the alleged victim cooperates with investigators. Six years after the passage of PREA, many statewide correctional systems and individual facilities now have policies, protocols, and trained staff in place to investigate allegations of sexual abuse. Yet there are still facilities—particularly those that confine juveniles, those under the umbrella of community corrections, and smaller jails—that lag behind in this crucial area. The Commission's standard establishing the duty to investigate is followed by a detailed standard to ensure the quality of investigations. Unless investigations produce compelling evidence, corrections administrators cannot impose discipline, prosecutors will not indict, and juries will not convict abusers.

In particular, when the sexual abuse has occurred recently and the allegation is rape, facilities must offer female and male victims a forensic exam by a specially trained professional. An evaluation of sexual assault nurse examiner (SANE) programs published in 2003 by the National Institute of Justice found that they improve the quality of forensic evidence and increase the ability of law enforcement to collect information, file charges, and prosecute and convict perpetrators while also providing better emergency health care. Correctional facilities must also implement a protocol that dictates how to collect, maintain, and analyze physical evidence and that stipulates the responsibilities of the forensic examiner and other responders—drawing on "A National Protocol for Sexual Assault Medical Forensic Examinations, Adults/Adolescents" created by the Department of Justice in 2004 to improve investigations of sexual abuse in the community. To facilitate the implementation of this standard, the Commission recommends that the Department of Justice adapt the protocol specifically for use in correctional facilities nationwide.

The work of investigating sexual abuse in a correctional environment is complex, requiring skill and sensitivity. According to a report published in 2007 by the National Institute of Corrections, many sexual abuse investigators are so unfamiliar with the dynamics inside a correctional facility that they cannot operate effectively. Because the deficits in some jurisdictions are so great, the Commission's standard in this area requires facilities to ensure that investigators are trained in up-to-date approaches and specifies certain minimum training requirements. And whenever correctional agencies outsource investigations to local law enforcement agencies, they must attempt to forge a memorandum of understanding with the agency specifying its role and responsibilities. Investigators do not work alone; any report of sexual abuse in a correctional facility must also trigger an immediate response from security staff; forensic, medical, and mental health care practitioners; and the head of the facility. To meet the needs of victims while conducting a thorough investigation, these professionals must coordinate their efforts.

No national data have been collected on how often correctional facilities investigate reported abuses, and there is no body of research describing the quality of those investigations. But correctional facilities substantiate allegations of sexual abuse at very low rates. According to the Bureau of Justice Statistics, facilities substantiated just 17 percent of all allegations of sexual violence, misconduct, and harassment investigated in 2006. In 29 percent of the alleged incidents, investigators concluded that sexual abuse did not occur. But in the majority of allegations (55 percent) investigators could not determine whether or not the abuse occurred. Substantiation rates in some states are considerably lower than the rate nationally. Standards that mandate investigations and improve their quality should increase the proportion of allegations in which the finding is definitive and perpetrators can be held accountable.

Despite that fact that most incidents of sexual abuse constitute a crime in all 50 States and under Federal law, very few perpetrators of sexual abuse in correctional settings are prosecuted. Only a fraction of cases are referred to prosecutors, and the Commission repeatedly heard testimony that prosecutors decline most of these cases. Undoubtedly, some investigations do not produce evidence capable of supporting a successful prosecution. But other dynamics may be at play: Some prosecutors may not view incarcerated individuals as members of the community and as deserving of their services as any other victim of crime.

Allegations of sexual abuse must also trigger an internal administrative investigation, and when the allegations are substantiated, the perpetrator must be disciplined. Until more cases are successfully prosecuted, many inmate and staff perpetrators of serious sexual abuse will be subject only to administrative discipline, making sanctions especially important. Individuals conducting administrative investigations must base their conclusions on what the "preponderance of the evidence" shows—a standard less stringent than that required to convict someone of a crime but adequate to protect individuals from being labeled as perpetrators and sanctioned internally without cause.

Sanctions must be fair, consistent, and sufficiently tough to deter abuse. It is crucial that labor and management reach agreements that allow reassigning officers during an investigation when safety is at issue and appropriate sanctions for staff perpetrators. Prisoners should never be punished for sexual contact with staff, even if the encounter was allegedly consensual. The power imbalance between staff and prisoners vitiates the possibility of meaningful consent, and the threat of punishment would deter prisoners from reporting sexual misconduct by staff.

Everyone who engages in sexual abuse in a correctional setting must be held accountable for their actions. There has been too little accountability for too long. The Commission's standards in these areas encourage incarcerated individuals and staff to report abuse and require correctional facilities to protect those who speak out, conduct effective investigations, and ensure appropriate punishment.

FINDING 6

Victims are unlikely to receive the treatment and support known to minimize the trauma of abuse. Correctional facilities need to ensure immediate and ongoing access to medical and mental health care and supportive services.

As corrections administrators work to create a protective environment in the facilities they manage, they also have a legal duty to ensure that when systems fail and abuse occurs, victims have access to appropriate medical and mental health services. Healing from sexual abuse is difficult; without adequate treatment, recovery may never occur.

Although sexual abuse typically leaves few visible scars, most victims report persistent, if not lifelong, mental and physical repercussions. After Sunday Daskalea was abused on multiple occasions by staff and other inmates in the District of Columbia jail, she became crippled by fear and anxiety. She slept only during the day, afraid of what might happen to her at night. Even after being released, Daskalea suffered from insomnia, struggled with eating disorders, and spent months emotionally debilitated, withdrawn and depressed. At age 18, Chance Martin was sexually abused while incarcerated in the Lake County Jail in Crown Point, Indiana. "I've abused drugs and alcohol and tried to kill myself on the installment plan," Martin told the Commission.

The psychological aftereffects of sexual abuse are well documented. They include posttraumatic stress disorder, anxiety disorders, fear of loud noises or sudden movements, panic attacks, and intense flashbacks to the traumatic event. Each of these consequences alone has the ability to re-traumatize victims for years. The trauma can also lead to serious medical conditions, including cardiovascular disease, ulcers, and a weakened immune system. Studies indicate that sexual abuse victims have poorer physical functioning in general and more physical ailments than non-abused individuals, even after controlling for emotional disturbances such as depression. In addition, many victims are physically injured during the course of a sexual assault. A study of incarcerated men showed that more than half of all sexual assaults resulted in physical injury. Moreover, the study found that internal injuries and being knocked unconscious were more common outcomes of sexual abuse than of other violent encounters in prison.

Exposure to HIV and other sexually transmitted infections are other potential consequences of sexual abuse. Michael Blucker tested negative for HIV when he was admitted to the Menard Correctional Center in Illinois, but approximately 1 year later, after being raped multiple times by other prisoners, he tested positive. According to testimony before the Commission, the Centers for Disease Control and Prevention (CDC) lacks data to assess the extent to which sex in correctional facilities, whether rape or consensual, contributes to the high prevalence of HIV in prisons and jails. One CDC study did find that individuals in confinement may contract HIV in a variety of ways, including sexual contact.

Because of the disproportionate representation of minority men and women in correctional settings, it is likely that the spread of these diseases in confinement would have an even greater impact in minority communities. As such, the Commission recommends that Congress provide funding to appropriate entities for research into whether consensual and/or nonconsensual sexual activity in the correctional system plays a role in infecting populations outside of corrections with HIV/AIDS and other sexually transmitted infections.

It has been more than three decades since the Supreme Court established in *Estelle v. Gamble* that deliberate indifference to the health of prisoners is a form of cruel and unusual punishment. Since then, correctional agencies have struggled, and sometimes failed with tragic results, to meet the medical and mental health care needs of a large and often ill prisoner population. Correctional health care is under-funded nearly everywhere, and most facilities are in dire need of additional skilled and compassionate health care practitioners. Recently, independent researchers analyzed the Bureau of Justice Statistics' 2002 survey of jail inmates and 2004 survey of State and Federal prisoners and found that many prisoners with persistent problems had never been examined by a health care professional in the facility where they were incarcerated. The failing was much worse in jails than in prisons: 68 percent of jail inmates with medical problems reported never being examined, compared with 14 percent of Federal prisoners and 20 percent of State prisoners.

Given the potentially severe and long-lasting medical and mental health consequences of sexual abuse, facilities must ensure that victims have unimpeded access to emergency treatment and crisis intervention and to ongoing health care for as long as necessary—care that matches what is generally acceptable to medical and mental health care professionals. Because some victims feel pressure to conceal abuse, all health care practitioners must have the training to know when a prisoner's mental or physical health problems might indicate that abuse has occurred.

Health care practitioners working in correctional facilities, like all staff, have a duty to report any indications of sexual abuse and must alert prisoners about their duty before providing treatment. Confidential treatment is not in the best interest of the victim or the safety of the facility. At the same time, they must provide care regardless of whether the victim names the perpetrator. Without such a policy, sexual abuse victims may decide that the risk of retaliation is too great and choose not to seek treatment.

Because some victims will never feel comfortable or safe disclosing their experience of sexual abuse to a corrections employee, agencies must give prisoners information about how to contact victim advocates and other support services in the community—underscoring that their communications will be private and confidential to the extent permitted by law. Collaborations with community-based service providers can also increase the likelihood that victims of sexual abuse are supported as they transition from a correctional facility back to their home communities.

For some victims of sexual abuse, cost may be a barrier to treatment. In the majority of States, legislatures have passed laws authorizing correctional agencies to charge prisoners for medical care—fees as little as $5 that are beyond the means of many prisoners. Under the Commission's standards, agencies must provide emergency care to victims of sexual abuse free of charge. Additionally, the Commission encourages correctional systems to define common and persistent aftereffects of sexual abuse as chronic conditions and to exempt them from fees.

Financial barriers to treatment come in other forms, as well. Guidelines for distributing funds provided under the Victims of Crime Act (VOCA) prohibit serving any incarcerated persons, including victims of sexual abuse. Similarly, grants administered under the Violence Against Women Act (VAWA) cannot be used to assist anyone convicted of domestic or dating violence, sexual assault, or stalking. All survivors of sexual abuse need and deserve treatment and support services. The Commission recommends that the VOCA grant guidelines be changed and that Congress amend VAWA.

Unimpeded access to treatment by qualified medical and mental health care practitioners and collaboration with outside providers are critical to ensuring that victims of sexual abuse can begin to heal.

FINDING 7

Juveniles in confinement are much more likely than incarcerated adults to be sexually abused, and they are particularly at risk when confined with adults. To be effective, sexual abuse prevention, inves-

279

tigation, and treatment must be tailored to the developmental capacities and needs of youth.

A daily snapshot of juveniles in custody in 2006 showed that approximately 93,000 youth were confined in juvenile residential facilities in the United States and more than half of them were 16 years or younger. Preventing, detecting, and responding to sexual abuse in these facilities demands age-appropriate interventions. The Commission's set of standards for juvenile facilities parallels those for adult prisons and jails, with modifications to reflect the developmental capacities and needs of youth.

When the State exercises custodial authority over children, "its responsibility to act in the place of parents (in loco parentis) obliges it to take special care." Youth may pass through the justice system once or twice, never to return. Yet if they are sexually abused, they may live with lifelong consequences that can include persistent mental illness and tendencies toward substance abuse and criminality. Juvenile justice agencies thus have a responsibility and a challenge: prevent sexual abuse now, or risk long-term consequences for victims.

Rates of sexual abuse appear to be much higher for confined youth than they are for adult prisoners. According to the Bureau of Justice Statistics (BJS), the rate of sexual abuse in adult facilities, based only on substantiated allegations captured in facility records, was 2.91 per 1,000 incarcerated prisoners in 2006. The parallel rate in juvenile facilities was more than five times greater: 16.8 per 1,000. The actual extent of sexual abuse in residential facilities is still unknown. BJS is currently conducting the first nationally representative survey of confined youth.

Juveniles are ill-equipped to respond to sexual advances by older, more experienced youth or adult caretakers. Based on reports of rampant physical violence and sexual abuse in a juvenile correctional facility in Plainfield, Indiana, the U.S. Department of Justice began investigating conditions of confinement in 2004. Investigators were shocked by the age and size disparity between many of the youth involved. Youth as old as 18 were assaulting or coercing children as young as 12; children weighing as little as 70 pounds were sexually abused by youths outweighing them by 100 pounds.

Simply being female is a risk factor. Girls are disproportionately represented among sexual abuse victims. According to data collected by BJS in 2005–2006, 36 percent of all victims in substantiated incidents of sexual violence were female, even though girls represented only 15 percent of confined youth in 2006. And they are much more at risk of abuse by staff than by their peers. Pervasive misconduct at a residential facility for girls in Chalkville, Alabama, beginning in 1994 and continuing through 2001, led 49 girls to bring charges that male staff had fondled, raped, and sexually harassed them. Abusive behavior is not limited to male staff. In 2005, the Department of Justice found that numerous female staff in an Oklahoma juvenile facility for boys had sexual relations with the youth under their care.

Youth are also vulnerable to sexual victimization while under juvenile justice supervision in the community. Nearly half (48 percent) of the more than 1.1 million youth who received some juvenile court sanction in 2005 were placed under the supervision of State, local, or county probation officers or counselors. A 50-year-old man who had served as a youth probation officer for 11 years with the Oregon Youth Authority was convicted of sexually abusing boys in his care, including a 14-year-old mentally disabled boy with attention deficit/hyperactivity disorder. Victims and their families had complained for years about this officer, but officials took no action.

Staff training and supervision are crucial. Staff need to understand the distinctive nature of sexual abuse involving children and teens and its potential consequences. Their responsibilities—including a duty to report any information about abuse—must be clear, and they must be informed that they will be held accountable for their actions and omissions. Administrators must uphold these policies and ensure that every report of abuse is promptly investigated.

Although research has yet to pinpoint the characteristics of youth who are at greatest risk of being victimized or perpetrating sexual abuse in juvenile facilities, many of the factors associated with vulnerability to sexual abuse among adults also appear to place juveniles at risk. In addition to screening all youth, facilities can take a simple step to protect youth from sexual abuse: encourage all residents during intake to tell staff if they fear being abused. This message, combined with affirmative statements about the facility's commitment to safety and zero tolerance of sexual abuse, makes it more likely that vulnerable youth will seek protection when they need it—before an assault occurs. Youth may be segregated only as a last resort and for short periods of time when less restrictive measures are inadequate to keep them safe.

Reducing sexual abuse also requires creating conditions that encourage youth to report abuse. Internal reporting procedures must be simple and secure; victims and witnesses must have unimpeded access to their families, attorneys, or other legal representatives; and facilities must provide parents and lawyers with information about the rights of residents and internal grievance procedures. Because many youth fail to recognize certain coercive and harmful behaviors as "abuse," juvenile facilities must improve sexual education programs and sexual abuse prevention curricula.

Youth who perpetrate sexual violence in juvenile facilities present a challenge for facility administrators who must apply developmentally appropriate interventions. They may need treatment as much as, or more than, punishment. Studies have shown that youth who commit sexual offenses typically have a history of severe family problems. Correctional medical and mental health practitioners must be trained to recognize the signs of sexual abuse and to provide age-appropriate treatment. And because young victims may lack the confidence to seek help from corrections staff, they must have access to victim advocates in the community to ensure that they are not left without support and treatment.

More than any other group of incarcerated persons, youth incarcerated with adults are probably at the highest risk for sexual abuse. According to BJS, 7.7 percent of all victims in substantiated incidents of violence perpetrated by prisoners in adult facilities in 2005 were under the age of 18. Data collected by BJS in 2006 show that on any given day, almost 8,500 youth under the age of 18 are confined with adults in prisons and jails. Civil rights attorney Deborah LaBelle told the Commission that 80 percent of the 420 boys sentenced to life without parole in Michigan, Illinois, and Missouri reported that, within the first year of their sentence, they had been sexually assaulted by at least one adult male prisoner. Because of the extreme risk of sexual victimization for youth in adult facilities, the Commission urges that individuals under the age of 18 be held separately from the general population.

The Commission's inquiry into the sexual abuse of youth in juvenile justice and adult corrections has revealed disturbing information about its prevalence, gravity, and consequences. Hope lies in the fact that necessary precautions and remedies are clear and rehabilitation remains a guiding principle in the field of juvenile justice.

FINDING 8

Individuals under correctional supervision in the community, who outnumber prisoners by more than two to one, are at risk of sexual abuse. The nature and consequences of the abuse are no less severe, and it jeopardizes the likelihood of their successful reentry.

By the end of 2007, there were more than 5.1 million adults under correctional supervision in the community, either on probation or parole, and the numbers are growing. They too are at risk of sexual abuse. As both Federal and State governments attempt to reduce incarceration costs in the face of looming deficits, the number of individuals under some form of community supervision—before, after, or in lieu of confinement—is likely to rise. Despite the number of individuals under supervision in the community, there is a lack of research on this population, and responses to PREA have been slow to take root in this area of corrections. The Commission has developed a full set of standards governing community corrections.

Community corrections encompasses a diverse array of agencies, facilities, and supervision structures on the Federal, State, and local levels. Supervision can occur in halfway houses, prerelease centers, treatment facilities, and other residential settings. Nonresidential supervision can include probation, parole, pretrial supervision, court-mandated substance abuse treatment, court diversionary programs, day-reporting centers, community service programs, probation before judgment, furloughs, electronic monitoring, and home detention.

As in other correctional settings, courts have found that sexual abuse in community corrections violates the Eighth Amendment of the U.S. Constitution prohibiting cruel and unusual punishment. As a result, community corrections agencies, like prisons and jails, have a special responsibility to protect the people they supervise. Courts also have determined that the authority staff have over the individuals they monitor makes a truly consensual sexual relationship impossible. Community corrections agencies are accountable for sexual abuse incidents, regardless of whether the circumstances in which the abuse occurred were under the direct control of the agency or a separate organization working under contract with the agency. Anyone in a supervisory position can be held liable for abuse. For example, in *Smith v. Cochran*, Pamela Smith was in jail but participating in a work release program. Her supervisor on the job sexually assaulted her, and the court ruled that important "penological responsibilities" had been delegated to him.

Although individuals under correctional supervision in the community may experience sexual abuse at the hands of other supervisees, the dynamics of supervision make them particularly vulnerable to abuse by staff. Coercion and threats carry great weight because individuals under supervision are typically desperate to avoid being incarcerated. Staff also have virtually unlimited access to the individuals they supervise, sometimes in private and intimate settings. In Ramsey County, Minnesota, for example, a male community corrections officer visiting a former prisoner's apartment to discuss her failure in a drug treatment program instead requested and had sex with her.

The diverse roles and obligations of staff present risks. They operate as enforcement officers in the interest of public safety and also function as counselors and social workers. Drawing and maintaining boundaries is a challenge even for staff with the best intentions. Moreover, because community corrections staff operate with significantly less direct supervision than their counterparts in secure facilities, it is easier for them to conceal sexual misconduct. Clear policies rooted in an ethic of zero tolerance for sexual abuse coupled with good training can mitigate these dangers by giving staff the direction, knowledge, and skills they need to maintain appropriate relationships with the individuals they supervise. Of course, preventing sexual abuse begins with hiring the right staff.

Although community corrections agencies face significant challenges in preventing abuse, they may have advantages in responding to victims. By definition, community corrections agencies tend to have access to skilled professionals and other resources that are beyond the reach of many secure correctional facilities, especially prisons sited in remote locations. For example, coordinated sexual assault response teams, widely recognized as an optimal way to respond to incidents of sexual abuse, exist in many communities and may be available to partner with local correctional agencies. Partnerships with victim advocates and counselors in the community also ensure that people under correctional supervision are able to disclose abuse and receive treatment confidentially, if they so choose. Some individuals under supervision will disclose abuse that occurred while they were incarcerated. Agencies must report past abuse to the facilities where the abuse occurred. This is necessary to trigger an investigation and also to improve the accuracy of facility records and provide insights on reasons incarcerated victims of sexual abuse remain silent.

The mission of community corrections is centered on helping offenders establish productive and law-abiding lives. Protecting them from sexual abuse and helping victims recover from past abuses is an essential part of that mission.

FINDING 9

A large and growing number of detained immigrants are at risk of sexual abuse. Their heightened vulnerability and unusual circumstances require special interventions.

Preventing, detecting, and responding to sexual abuse of immigrants in custody require special measures not included in the Commission's standards for correctional facilities. These measures are contained in a set of supplemental standards that apply to any facility that houses individuals detained solely because their right to remain in the United States is in question. The Commission's work in this area advances efforts by U.S. Immigration and Customs Enforcement (ICE) to protect detainees from sexual abuse.

In the 15 years from 1994 to 2009, the number of immigrants held in detention pending a judicial decision about their legal right to remain in the United States increased nearly 400 percent. For the 2009 fiscal year, ICE has budgeted enough money to detain 33,400 people on any given night and more than 400,000 people over the course of the year. The population of immigration detainees includes adults, thousands of "unaccompanied" children, and whole families confined together.

The prevalence of sexual abuse among immigration detainees is unknown and has yet to receive the attention and research it merits, but accounts of abuse by other detainees and staff have been coming to light for more than 20 years. Many factors—personal and circumstantial, alone or in combination—make immigration detainees especially vulnerable to sexual abuse. One of the most pervasive factors is social isolation. Individuals are often confined far from family or friends and may not speak the language of other detainees or staff. Those who have already suffered terrifying experiences in their home countries or in the United States can be almost defenseless by the time they are detained and may even expect to be abused.

Preventing abuse requires precautions beyond those mandated for other prisoners. In particular, when immigration detainees are confined in ordinary prisons, jails, and lockups—a common practice—they must be housed apart from the general population, but they should not be placed in segregation. Depending on the conditions in protective custody cells and units, the experience can enhance the feeling of aloneness already common among immigration detainees and lead to depression and other problems.

Families who are in ICE custody are currently detained in several facilities in the United States. Stays are not always brief: women with children, including babies and toddlers, may be detained for days, weeks, or even months. In testimony before a congressional subcommittee on immigration, Texas Representative Sheila Jackson noted that families in these facilities often are "deprived of the right to live as a family unit, denied adequate medical and mental health care, and face overly harsh disciplinary tactics." Facilities face the challenge of protecting residents of all ages from sexual abuse while also preserving family unity. One specific challenge is ensuring that both adults and children can report sexual abuse in a confidential manner, which is especially important for situations in which children are at risk of abuse within the family unit.

Because immigration detainees are confined by the agency with the power to deport them, officers have an astounding degree of leverage—especially when detainees are not well informed of their rights and lack access to legal counsel. The Commission learned that officers have propositioned women whose cases they control, telling them that if they want to be released they need to comply with their sexual demands. The fear of deportation cannot be overstated and also functions to silence many individuals who are sexually abused. Those brave enough to speak out may face retaliation. After women detainees at the Krome immigration detention facility in Miami reported sexual abuse by staff, several of them wrote, "We are afraid . . . each time one of us is interviewed by investigating officers. . . . [S]ome of the women who have given statements have either been transferred or deported to their countries." Transfers can completely derail the complaint process, which has lasting consequences for victims who may be eligible for a special visa to remain in the United States. When staff cannot protect victims and witnesses in the facility where the abuse occurred,

ICE must consider releasing and monitoring them in the community during the course of the investigation.

There also are institutional barriers that block or discourage victims and witnesses from reporting abuse. Grievance procedures can seem impossibly complex, especially for detainees who speak languages other than English or Spanish. A 2006 audit by the U.S. Department of Homeland Security's Office of the Inspector General revealed that detainees often do not receive information on reporting abuse and other grievances in a language they can understand.

Although detainees have periodic contact with immigration judges, those judges have no jurisdiction over the conditions of their detention. Even advocacy groups in the local community may lack the language skills and cultural competency to assist them. Detainees need access to outside entities able and authorized to receive and respond to reports of sexual abuse. Specifically, facilities must provide immigration detainees with access to telephones with free, preprogrammed numbers to ICE's Office for Civil Rights and Civil Liberties and to the Department of Homeland Security's Office of the Inspector General. They also must have access to telephones to contact diplomatic or consular personnel from their countries of citizenship, along with a list of those phone numbers.

Detainees who are victims of sexual abuse also need a lifeline to outside organizations with experience counseling immigrant victims of crime and assurances that their communications with outside advocates are confidential to the extent permitted by law. At the same time, facilities must still ensure that their own staff have the training to respond in culturally appropriate ways to sexual abuse.

Protection for all immigration detainees and services for victims of sexual abuse are not what they should be. And little is known about this fast-growing area of confinement, one in which preventing, detecting, and responding to sexual abuse is especially challenging.

The Commission sunsets 60 days following the submission of its report and standards to Congress, the President, the Attorney General, and other Federal and State officials. The real work of implementation begins then, particularly on the part of the Attorney General and his staff. Within a year of receiving the Commission's report and standards, the Attorney General is required to promulgate national standards for the detection, prevention, reduction, and punishment of detention facility sexual abuse.

The Commission recommends that the Attorney General establish a PREA Advisory Committee pursuant to the Federal Advisory Committee Act of 1972. The purpose of the Advisory Committee is to assist the Attorney General with the promulgation of the PREA standards and thereafter assess their implementation and propose amendments as needed to increase their efficacy. The Commission also recommends that the Attorney General create a full-time Special Assistant for PREA within the Office of the Deputy Attorney General. The Special Assistant would have primary responsibility for ensuring the implementation of the standards as central to the national effort of eliminating prison rape.

PREA represents a sea change in public consciousness and in national commitment to protecting individuals under correctional supervision from sexual abuse. Already, the Commission has seen ideas transformed into actions that by all accounts have the potential to improve safety. This is just the beginning. When the Attorney General issues mandatory standards, they will accelerate the pace of reform and ensure that the same fundamental protections are available in every correctional and detention setting. Our obligations, both moral and legal, require nothing less.

Source: Walton, Reggie B., chairperson, et al. "The National Prison Rape Elimination Commission Report," June 2009. Available online. URL: http://www.ncjrs.gov/pdffiles1/226680.pdf.

APPENDIX C

ENEMY COMBATANT DETAINEES: HABEAS CORPUS CHALLENGES IN FEDERAL COURT (2009)

In the aftermath of the terrorist attacks on the United States on September 11, 2001, individuals suspected of possible involvement in terrorist activities against the United States were taken prisoner and held in the custody of U.S. military forces abroad, primarily in theaters of war in Iraq and Afghanistan. Beginning in 2004 the U.S. Supreme Court issued a series of rulings on the legal rights of such prisoners, who were sometimes referred to as "detainees" or "enemy combatants," many of whom were held at the U.S. Naval base at Guantánamo Bay, Cuba. The following excerpts are from a report issued by the Congressional Research Service in 2009 on the evolution of U.S. Supreme Court rulings on the rights of such prisoners.

INTRODUCTION

Following the terrorist attacks of 9/11, Congress passed the Authorization to Use Military Force (AUMF), which granted the President the authority "to use all necessary and appropriate force against those . . . [who] planned, authorized, committed, or aided the terrorist attacks" against the United States. Soon thereafter, President Bush issued a military order formulating guidelines for the detention and treatment of foreign belligerents captured in the "war on terror" and establishing military commissions to try some detainees for violations of the law of war. Beginning in early 2002, the United States began transferring foreign belligerents captured in the "war on terror" to the U.S. Naval Station in Guantánamo Bay, Cuba, for preventative detention and potential prosecution for any war crimes they may have committed.

Appendix C

In 2004, the Supreme Court issued two key rulings concerning the Executive's authority to detain persons in the "war on terror." In *Hamdi v. Rumsfeld*, a majority of the Court found that the 2001 AUMF permitted the preventative detention of enemy combatants captured during hostilities in Afghanistan, including those who were U.S. citizens. A divided Court found that persons deemed "enemy combatants" have the right to challenge their detention before a judge or other "neutral decision-maker." The *Hamdi* case concerned the rights of a U.S. citizen detained as an enemy combatant, and the Court did not decide the extent to which this right also applied to non-citizens held at Guantanamo and elsewhere. However, on the same day that *Hamdi* was decided, the Court issued an opinion in the case of *Rasul v. Bush*, holding that the federal *Habeas Corpus* statute, 28 U.S.C. § 2241, provided federal courts with jurisdiction to consider *Habeas Corpus* petitions by or on behalf of persons detained at Guantanamo.

The Court's rulings in *Hamdi* and *Rasul* had two immediate consequences. First, the Department of Defense (DOD) established Combatant Status Review Tribunals (CSRTs), an administrative process to determine whether a detainee at Guantanamo was an "enemy combatant." Secondly, lawyers filed dozens of petitions on behalf of the detainees in the U.S. District Court for the District of Columbia, where judges reached conflicting conclusions as to whether the detainees have any enforceable rights to challenge their treatment and detention.

After the Supreme Court granted certiorari to hear a challenge by one of the detainees to his trial by military tribunal, Congress passed the Detainee Treatment Act of 2005 (DTA). The DTA requires uniform standards for interrogation of persons in the custody of the DOD, and expressly bans cruel, inhuman, or degrading treatment of detainees in the custody of any U.S. agency. At the same time, however, it divested the courts of jurisdiction to hear challenges by those detained at Guantánamo Bay based on their treatment or living conditions. The DTA also eliminated the federal courts' statutory jurisdiction over *Habeas* claims by aliens challenging their detention at Guantanamo Bay, but provided for limited appeals of status determinations made pursuant to the DOD procedures for CSRTs, along with final decisions by military commissions.

However, in the 2006 case of *Hamdan v. Rumsfeld*, the Supreme Court interpreted these provisions as being inapplicable to *Habeas* cases that were pending at the time the DTA was enacted, and it reviewed the validity of military commissions established pursuant to President Bush's 2001 military order. The Court held that the military tribunals established by the President did not comply with the Uniform Code of Military Justice or the law of war which the Code incorporates, including the 1949 Geneva Conventions. In response to the *Hamdan* ruling, Congress enacted the Military Commissions Act of 2006 (MCA). The act authorized the President to convene military commissions to try "unlawful alien combatants" for war crimes, and also established procedural requirements for the commissions. As was the case under the DTA, final decisions of military commissions are appealable to the D.C. Circuit. However, the MCA provided that appeals of military commission judgments shall first be routed through the newly-created Court of Military Commission Review. Of more immediate legal significance, the MCA also expressly eliminated court jurisdiction over all pending and future causes of action, other than pursuant to the limited review permitted under the DTA.

The complete elimination of *Habeas Corpus* review by Congress compelled the courts to directly address an issue they had avoided reaching in earlier cases: Does the constitutional writ of *Habeas* corpus extend to non-citizens held at Guantanamo? The Constitution's Suspension Clause prohibits the suspension of *Habeas Corpus* except when public safety requires it in the case of invasion or surrender. The MCA did not purport to be a suspension of *Habeas*, and the government did not make such a claim to the courts. Instead, the government argued that non-citizens detained at Guantanamo receive no constitutional protections. Therefore, denying these persons access to *Habeas* review would not run afoul of the Suspension Clause. In the 2008 case of *Boumediene v. Bush*, the Court rejected this argument in a 5-4 opinion, and ruled that the constitutional privilege of *Habeas* extends to Guantanamo detainees. As a result of the *Boumediene* decision, detainees currently held at Guantanamo may petition for *Habeas* review of their designation as enemy combatants. Several legal issues remain unsettled, including the scope of *Habeas* review available to detainees, the remedy available for those persons found to be unlawfully held by the United States, and the extent to which other constitutional provisions extend to non-citizens held at Guantanamo and elsewhere. The continuing availability of the judicial process established by the DTA is also uncertain given the D.C. Circuit's ruling in January 2009 that the *Boumediene* decision effectively nullified this review process.

In the meantime, the U.S. Court of Appeals for the Fourth Circuit addressed whether it retained jurisdiction under the MCA to hear a *Habeas* petition on behalf of Ali Saleh Kahlah al-Marri, an alien arrested in the United States and detained as an enemy combatant. In 2007, the appellate court initially granted relief to al-Marri, who had been arrested in Illinois on criminal charges but then transferred to South Carolina and detained in military custody as an "enemy combatant." While one judge on the panel dissented with respect to the holding that the detention was not authorized by Congress, all three judges on the panel agreed that the MCA did not divest it of jurisdiction to hear the petition, notwithstanding the MCA's lack of geographical limits. The government asked for, and was granted, a rehearing en banc. In 2008, the en banc court agreed that the jurisdictional issue had been resolved by the Supreme Court's decision in *Boumediene*, but found little agreement as to the scope of activity making a person an "enemy combatant." The petitioner subsequently sought to appeal the ruling to the Supreme Court, and the Court granted certiorari to review the appellate court's decision in December, 2008. In January 2009, President Barack Obama issued a memorandum instructing the Attorney General, Secretary of Defense, and other designated officials to review the factual and legal basis for al-Marri's continued detention as an enemy combatant, and "identify and thoroughly evaluate alternative dispositions." Subsequently, Al-Marri was indicted by a federal grand jury for providing material support to al-Qaeda and conspiring with others to provide such support. The government immediately requested that the Supreme Court dismiss al-Marri's pending case and authorize his transfer from military to civilian custody for criminal trial. On March 6, 2009, the Supreme Court granted the government's application concerning the transfer of al-Marri, vacated the Fourth Circuit's judgment, and remanded the case back to the appellate court with instructions to dismiss the case as moot. As a result, a definitive pronouncement by the Supreme Court regarding the President's authority to detain suspected terrorists captured inside the United States has been avoided, at least temporarily.

On January 22, 2009, President Obama issued an Executive Order requiring that the Guantanamo detention facility be closed as soon as practicable, and no later than a year from the date of the Order. The Order further requires specified officials to review all Guantanamo detentions to assess whether the detainee should continue to be held by the United States, transferred or released to a third country, or be prosecuted by the United States for criminal offenses. During this review process, the Secretary of Defense is required to take steps to ensure that all proceedings before military commissions and the United States Court of Military Commission Review are halted. The closure of the Guantanamo detention facility and its resulting effects seem likely to have implications for legal challenges raised by detainees, particularly if detainees are brought to the United States, where they would arguably receive additional constitutional protections.

In March 2009, the Obama Administration announced a new definitional standard for the government's authority to detain terrorist suspects, which does not use the phrase "enemy combatant" to refer to persons who may be properly detained. Under this new definition, the Administration claims that:

> *"The President has the authority to detain persons that the President determines planned, authorized, committed, or aided the terrorist attacks that occurred on September 11, 2001, and persons who harbored those*

responsible for those attacks. The President also has the authority to detain persons who were part of, or substantially supported, Taliban or al-Qaida forces or associated forces that are engaged in hostilities against the United States or its coalition partners, including any person who has committed a belligerent act, or has directly supported hostilities, in aid of such enemy armed forces."

This definitional standard is largely similar to that used by the Bush Administration to detain terrorist suspects as "enemy combatants." Like the previous Administration, the Obama administration claims the power to militarily detain members of the Taliban or Al Qaeda, regardless whether such persons were captured away from the battlefield in Afghanistan. However, there are a few differences in the standard used by the Bush and Obama Administrations. Most notably, whereas the Bush Administration claimed the authority to detain persons who supported Al Qaeda, the Taliban, or associated forces, the standard announced by the Obama Administration expressly requires such support to be "substantial." While the Obama Administration claims that activities constituting "substantial support" will be developed in application to individual cases, it has stated that it would not cover "unwitting or insignificant" support.

The Obama Administration has stated that this definitional standard is based upon the authority provided by the AUMF, as informed by the laws of war. The Obama Administration has also claimed that this standard does "not rely on the President's authority as Commander-in-Chief independent of Congress's specific authorization." The Bush Administration had previously argued that, separate from the authority provided by the AUMF, the President has the independent authority as Commander-in-Chief to order the detention of terrorist suspects. While the Obama Administration has not expressly rejected this claim, it appears that the Administration will not rely upon the notion of inherent constitutional authority to serve as a legal basis for the detention of terrorist suspects.

The full implications of this change in language and intent remain to be seen. One issue that is likely to be subject to debate is the Executive's authority under the AUMF and traditional law-of war principles to detain members of Al Qaeda or the Taliban who did not directly participate in battlefield hostilities. The nature of activities constituting "substantial support" for the groups may also merit significant judicial attention. It should also be noted that the new definitional standard refers only to detainees held by the United States at Guantanamo, and not those persons detained at other facilities (e.g., the Bagram Air Base in Afghanistan). It is not clear whether the Administration will rely upon a different standard to justify the detention of terrorist suspects at locations other than Guantanamo.

Appendix C

THE GENEVA CONVENTIONS AND THE LAW OF WAR

The *Habeas Corpus* statute permits those detained under U.S. authority to challenge their detention on the basis that it violates any statute, the Constitution, or a treaty. The D.C. Circuit nevertheless held that the Geneva Conventions are never enforceable in federal courts. The Supreme Court disagreed, finding the Conventions were applicable as incorporated by UCMJ Article 21, because "compliance with the law of war is the condition upon which the authority set forth in Article 21 is granted." In response to the alternative holding by the court below that *Hamdan*, as a putative member of Al Qaeda, was not entitled to any of the protections accorded by the Geneva Conventions, the Court concluded that Common Article 3 of the Geneva Conventions applies even to members of Al Qaeda, according to them a minimum baseline of protections, including protection from the "passing of sentences and the carrying out of executions without previous judgment pronounced by a regularly constituted court, affording all the judicial guarantees which are recognized as indispensable by civilized peoples."

While recognizing that Common Article 3 "obviously tolerates a great degree of flexibility in trying individuals captured during armed conflict," and that "its requirements are general ones, crafted to accommodate a wide variety of legal systems," the Court found that the military commissions under M.C.O. No. 1 did not meet these criteria. In particular, the military commissions did not qualify as "regularly constituted" because they deviated too far, in the Court's view, from the rules that apply to courts-martial, without a satisfactory explanation of the need for such deviation. Justice Alito, joined by Justices Scalia and Thomas, dissented, arguing that the Court is bound to defer to the President's plausible interpretation of the treaty language.

PROVISIONS REGARDING THE GENEVA CONVENTIONS

A continuing source of dispute in the detention and treatment of detainees is the application of the Geneva Conventions. As noted previously, the *Habeas Corpus* statute has traditionally provided for, among other things, challenges to allegedly unlawful detentions based on rights found in treaties. Thus, for instance, Common Article 3 of the 1949 Geneva Conventions, which prohibits the "passing of sentences and the carrying out of executions without previous judgment pronounced by a regularly constituted court,

293

affording all the judicial guarantees which are recognized as indispensable by civilized peoples," has been used as a basis for challenging the confinement of detainees.

Section 5 of the MCA, however, specifically precludes the application of the Geneva Conventions to *Habeas* or other civil proceedings. Further, the MCA provides that the Geneva Conventions may not be claimed as a source of rights by an alien who is subject to military commission proceedings. Rather, Congress deems that the military commission structure established by the act complies with the requirement under Common Article 3 of the Geneva Convention that trials be by a regularly constituted court.

In addition, the act provides that the President shall have the authority to interpret the meaning of the Geneva Conventions. The intended effect of this provision is unclear. While the President generally has a role in the negotiation, implementation, and domestic enforcement of treaty obligations, this power does not generally extend to "interpreting" treaty obligations, a role more traditionally associated with courts. In general, Congress is prohibited from exercising powers allocated to another branch of government. In *United States v. Klein*, the Congress passed a law designed to frustrate a finding of the Supreme Court as to the effect of a presidential pardon. Similarly, a law that was specifically intended to grant the authority of the President to adjudicate or remedy treaty violations could violate the doctrine of separation of powers, as providing relief from acts in violation of treaties is a judicial branch function. Instead, what appears to be the main thrust of this language is to establish the authority of the President within the Executive Branch to issue interpretative regulations by Executive Order. However, the context in which this additional authority would be needed is unclear.

One possible intent of this provision is that the President is being given the authority to "interpret" the Geneva Convention for diplomatic purposes (e.g., to define treaty obligations and encourage other countries to conform to such definitions). This interpretation seems unlikely, as the President's power in this regard is already firmly established. Another possible meaning is that the President is being given the authority to apply the Geneva Conventions to particular fact situations, such as specifying what type of interrogation techniques may be lawfully applied to a particular individual suspected of being an enemy combatant. This interpretation is possible, but it is not clear how the power to "interpret" would be significant in that situation, as the MCA precludes application of the Geneva Conventions in those contexts in which such interrogations would be challenged—military commissions, *Habeas Corpus*, or any other civil proceeding.

The more likely intent of this language would be to give the President the authority to promulgate regulations prescribing standards of behavior of employees and agents of federal agencies. For instance, this language might be seen as authorizing the President to issue regulations to implement how agency personnel should comply with the Geneva Conventions, policies which might otherwise be addressed at the agency level. Thus, for instance, if the CIA had established internal procedures regarding how to perform interrogation consistent with the Geneva Conventions, then this language would explicitly authorize the President to amend such procedures by Executive Order. Whether the President already had such power absent this language is beyond the scope of this report.

CONSTITUTIONAL RIGHT TO *HABEAS*

The petitioners in *Boumediene* argued that they possess a constitutional right to *Habeas*, and that the MCA deprived them of this right in contravention of the Suspension Clause, which prohibits the suspension of the writ of *Habeas* except "when in Cases of Rebellion or Invasion the public Safety may require it." The MCA did not expressly purport to be a formal suspension of the writ of habeas, and the government did not make such a claim to the Court. Instead, the government argued that aliens designated as enemy combatants and detained outside the de jure territory of the United States have no constitutional rights, including the constitutional privilege to *Habeas*, and that therefore stripping the courts of jurisdiction to hear petitioners' *Habeas* claims did not violate the Suspension Clause.

The Court began its analysis by surveying the history and origins of the writ of *Habeas Corpus*, emphasizing the importance placed on the writ for the Framers, while also characterizing its prior jurisprudence as having been "careful not to foreclose the possibility that the protections of the Suspension Clause have expanded along with post-1789 developments that define the present scope of the writ." The Court characterized the Suspension Clause as not only a "vital instrument" for protecting individual liberty, but also a means to ensure that the judiciary branch would have, except in cases of formal suspension, "a time-tested device, the writ, to maintain the delicate balance of governance" between the branches and prevent "cyclical abuses" of the writ by the executive and legislative branches. The Court stated that the separation-of-powers doctrine and the history shaping the design of the Suspension Clause informed its interpretation of the reach and purpose of the clause and the constitutional writ of *Habeas*.

The Court found the historical record to be inconclusive for resolving whether the Framers would have understood the constitutional writ of *Habeas* as extending to suspected enemy aliens held in foreign territory over which the United States exercised plenary, but not de jure control. Nonetheless, the Court interpreted the Suspension Clause as having full effect at Guantanamo. While the Court did not question the government's position that Cuba maintains legal sovereignty over Guantanamo under the terms of the 1903 lease giving the U.S. plenary control over the territory, it disagreed with the government's position that "at least when applied to noncitizens, the Constitution necessarily stops where de jure sovereignty ends."

Instead, the Court characterized its prior jurisprudence as recognizing that the Constitution's extraterritorial application turns on "objective factors and practical concerns." Here, the Court emphasized the functional approach taken in the Insular Cases, where it had assessed the availability of constitutional rights in incorporated and unincorporated territories under the control of United States. The Court deemed at least three factors to be relevant in assessing the extraterritorial scope of the Suspension Clause: (1) the citizenship and status of the detainee and the adequacy of the status determination process; (2) the nature of the site where the person is seized and detained; and (3) practical obstacles inherent in resolving the prisoner's entitlement to the writ.

While acknowledging that it had never before held that non-citizens detained in another country's territory have any rights under the U.S. Constitution, the Court concluded that the case before it "lack[ed] any precise historical parallel." In particular, the Court noted that the Guantanamo detainees have been held for the duration of a conflict that is already one of the longest in U.S. history, in territory that, while not technically part of the United States, is subject to complete U.S. control. Based on these factors, the Court concluded that the Suspension Clause has full effect at Guantanamo.

Source: Elsea, Jennifer K., et al. "Enemy Combatant Detainees: Habeas Corpus Challenges in Federal Court," Congressional Research Service, September 15, 2009. Available online. at URL: http://www.fas.org/sgp/crs/natsec/RL33180.pdf.

INDEX

Locators in **boldface** indicate major treatment of topics. Locators followed by *c* indicate chronology entries. Locators followed by *b* indicate biographical entries. Locators followed by *g* indicate glossary entries.

Index

Index

Index

Index

Index

309

Index